Telemodernities

Console-ing Passions Television and Cultural Power
A SERIES EDITED BY LYNN SPIGEL

Telemodernities Television and Transforming
Lives in Asia TANIA LEWIS, FRAN MARTIN, AND WANNING SUN

Duke University Press / Durham and London / 2016

© 2016 Duke University Press. All rights reserved

Designed by Courtney Leigh Baker
Typeset in Minion Pro by Graphic Composition, Inc., Bogart, Georgia

Library of Congress Cataloging-in-Publication Data

Names: Lewis, Tania, author. | Martin, Fran, [date] author. | Sun, Wanning, [date] author.
  Title: Telemodernities : television and transforming lives in Asia / Tania Lewis, Fran Martin, and Wanning Sun. Other titles: Console-ing passions. Description: Durham : Duke University Press, 2016. | Series: Console-ing passions : television and cultural power | Includes bibliographical references and index.
Identifiers: LCCN 2016007859 (print)
LCCN 2016009285 (ebook)
ISBN 9780822361886 (hardcover)
ISBN 9780822362043 (pbk.)
ISBN 9780822373902 (e-book)
Subjects: LCSH: Reality television programs—China. | Reality television programs—India. | Reality television programs—Taiwan.
Classification: LCC PN1992.8.R43 L49 2016 (print)
LCC PN1992.8.R43 (ebook)
DDC 791.45/655—dc23
LC record available at http://lccn.loc.gov/2016007859

COVER ART:
Cover: Photograph by Kiran Mulenahalli

CONTENTS

Acknowledgments / vii   Introduction: Telemodernities / 1

ONE. **Lifestyle Television in Context** Media Industries, Cultural Economies, and Genre Flows / 25

TWO. **Local versus Metropolitan Television in China** Stratification of Needs, Taste, and Spatial Imagination / 52

THREE. **Here, There, and Everywhere** Mediascapes, Geographic Imaginaries, and Indian Television / 82

FOUR. **Imagining Global Mobility** TLC Taiwan / 106

FIVE. **Gurus, Babas, and Daren** Popular Experts on Indian and Chinese Advice TV / 126

SIX. **Magical Modernities** Spiritual Advice TV in India and Taiwan / 157

SEVEN. **Risky Romance** Navigating Late Modern Identities and Relationships on Indian and Chinese Lifestyle TV / 196

EIGHT. **A Self to Believe In** Negotiating Femininities in Sinophone Lifestyle Advice TV / 222

Conclusion: Negotiating Modernities through Lifestyle Television / 254

Notes / 273   Works Cited / 281   Index / 305

ACKNOWLEDGMENTS

The large-scale, transnational nature of the multiyear project on which this book is based is not only the result of the labors of its three authors but also owes much to a number of other individuals' valued contributions. First we would like to thank the many audience members and householders who participated in this project and the numerous industry representatives who gave their time and energy to be interviewed for the study.

We also want to express our deep appreciation for the many onsite and Australia-based research assistants who supported us during this project, including John Alexander, Tripta Chandola, Gin Chee Tong, Yajie Chu, Isabelle de Solier, Jacinthe Flore, Phyllis Yu-ting Huang, Vikrant Kishore, Amber Lim, Peihua Lu, Wokar Rigumi, Claire Tsai, Min Wang, Zhonghua Wu, and Juliet W. Zhou. Tania Lewis would like to particularly thank Delhi-based colleague Kiran Mullenhalli for his humor and enthusiasm, and his terrific fieldwork and translation skills, and Wokar Rigumi and Tripta Chandola for their critical feedback on the Indian material in this book. Thanks also to H. J. Padmaraju and Hirehalli Devraj for helping recruit interviewees in Tovinkere village in Southern India and P. Nandagopala for recruiting interviewees in Bengaluru (Bangalore).

We are also indebted to the generosity and support of a number of academic colleagues, including Professor John Sinclair, who was a key early collaborator on this research, Professor Graeme Turner, Professor Koichi Iwabuchi, Professor Lu Ye, Dr. Kelly Hu, and Dr. Ti Wei.

General thanks also to Dr. Bao Xiaoqun, CEO of Channel Young, SMG; Mr. Han Song, CEO of Bengbu TV; Christine Che, CTS Taiwan; Harry Hu, CTS executive vice president, Taiwan; Mimi Wang, former assistant director of programming at TVBS Taiwan; Yvonne Wu, Da Ai TV Taiwan; Lin Shanshan, PTS Taiwan; and Sophie Yang.

We are especially grateful to Lynn Spigel for considering our book for her Console-ing Passions series and to the team at Duke University Press, in particular, Editorial Director Ken Wissoker for his enthusiasm in and support for our project, and Elizabeth Ault for her supreme professionalism.

Finally, we thank the Australian Research Council for funding the project DP1094355, "The role of lifestyle television in transforming culture, citizenship and selfhood: China, Taiwan, Singapore and India" (2010–13), which enabled the research on which this book is based.

INTRODUCTION. Telemodernities

On Location

In 2010 the South Indian TV channel Suvarna aired a fish-out-of-water-style TV program titled *Halli Haida Pyateg Bandha* (Village boys go to the city), which follows the adventures of eight lunghi-wearing "tribal youths" extracted from their villages and introduced to the bright lights of city life while being partnered with eight urbane and attractive city girls. Offered an instant consumption-oriented lifestyle makeover, the hapless and somewhat shell-shocked contestants are taken to their first malls to learn how to shop, taught handy life skills like how to walk on a cat walk, and coached to perform on stage in front of an audience. Although in some ways this show is a standard rags-to-riches reality format—premised on the desirability of learning to exude an air of cosmopolitan and entrepreneurial individualism—at the same time, the program also plays on a certain anxiety about a perceived loss of connection with the authenticity of village life. Indeed, the program followed the success of an earlier Suvarna show, *Pyate Hudgir Halli Life* (City girls, village life), where the story was reversed: eight young female contestants accustomed to living the urban high life were transported to a hitherto little known South Indian village to test their capacity to live traditionally for three months.

On the surface, these formats mimic numerous lifestyle swap shows familiar to Western audiences, from reality shows featuring ordinary urbanites struggling with the deprivations of the everyday lives of their forebears (*Colonial House*; *Frontier House*) to morally charged formats where rampant consumers are transported off to live frugally in developing regions like Africa (*Worlds Apart*). But what distinguishes these South Indian shows from their

Euro-American counterparts is their portrayal of a meeting of traditional and modern cultures and lifestyles *within* the single nation of India in the present day. Scenes where contestants learn to be savvy consumers or to dress for success are played out against the backdrop of competing cultural and religious identities, urban/rural and socioeconomic divides, and nostalgic yearnings for traditionalism at a time of rapid sociocultural transformation.

This book is about lifestyle television in Asia and its role in teaching people how to live. As our discussion of the South Indian examples above suggests, in *Telemodernities* we are concerned precisely with this type of programming's role in the social and cultural negotiation of modernization and modernities. For the above examples are far from isolated cases: in recent years, TV screens across Asia have become host to an explosion of programs aimed at providing modern lifestyle guidance to viewers, particularly the consumer middle classes. In this book, through a focus on three key countries—the People's Republic of China (PRC or mainland China), India, and Taiwan—we take up lifestyle-oriented popular factual television as a critical lens through which to examine shifting and emergent social and cultural formations. The wide range of life guidance shows we discuss takes in everything from magazine-style travel programs, to glossy reality shows helping contestants negotiate the complexities of modern love and dating, to home renovation formats aimed at aspirational urbanites, and religious lifestyle shows promoting a blend of spiritualism, entrepreneurialism, and self-help. From enterprising yogic spiritualism to cosmopolitan romance scripts negotiated through the family, we explore these shows' variegated engagements with cultural modernity across South and East Asia. Lifestyle television as a recognizable genre is unevenly distributed across South and East Asia and is not by any means the most popular or prevalent mode of programming on the small screen. Nevertheless, the characteristic directness of lifestyle television's instruction in correct ways of being—its blatant pedagogies of good taste, appropriate consumption, and desirable identity—make it a uniquely rich object of study when we seek to understand dominant and emergent templates for selfhood and constructions of the good life in a given society.

Another factor in lifestyle television's significance is the way in which it articulates to a series of ongoing social and economic changes in Asia today. Across South and East Asia, the past three decades have seen hyperaccelerated social, cultural, and economic transformation. Consumer culture increasingly shapes everyday life as market economies are fostered by (post)socialist states like China and India, and a dizzying diversity of media and consumer goods continues to proliferate in those nations where capitalism has been longer entrenched, like the four Asian "tiger economies" (Taiwan, Hong Kong, Singapore, and South Korea). Governments in Asia, as elsewhere in the world, increasingly address their citizens as individualized, sovereign consumers with reflexive choices about their lifestyles and identities.

It is against this backdrop that South and East Asia have seen a proliferation not only of lifestyle television but of a wide range of media aimed at instructing the middle classes in matters of consumption, taste, and "the good life." However, we argue that television plays a particularly central role in Asia, both as a broadcast and increasingly also as a digital and narrowcast medium. While Eurocentric media studies narratives now routinely depict television as a heritage form, in South and East Asia television is far from in decline; on the contrary, in many Asian countries it represents the most powerful and ubiquitous media form, with large and growing investment from the commercial and, in some cases, state sector.

These questions of social, political, and economic context and geocultural location are key to our analysis of lifestyle television. As Ana Cristina Pertierra and Graeme Turner note in *Locating Television*, much recent Western scholarship on television in the postbroadcast era has been not only Eurocentric but also decidedly *dis*located in its approach, preoccupied in a fairly abstract way with the affordances of technical convergence and new media developments and platforms in a multichannel environment. As a result, they argue, "what television *does*—how it is imbricated into the practices of everyday life, what kinds of social and cultural function it can perform, and how it participates in the construction of communities—has been much less explored" in the Western-centric mainstream of global television studies (2013, 10). As these remarks underline, while on the one hand television content is highly mobile, "ordinary television" (Bonner 2005) is also profoundly connected to the everyday, the domestic, and the personal, and to intensely localized modes of address. This is certainly true of lifestyle advice television, which offers a prime site for critical comparative analyses of specific, situated formations of lifestyle, modernity, and television cultures. What, for example, is the social and cultural significance of the appearance of a licensed version of the BBC's *MasterChef* in India, a country battling with ongoing issues of food security and malnutrition? How should we understand the popularity of a thinly disguised copy of *Changing Rooms* in China, where the emergence of individualized, consumption-based models of identity are shaped by persistent forms of collectivist cultural citizenship and a sense of social and familial duty? In addressing questions like these, the socially and culturally embedded, multiperspectival analysis offered in this book responds to Pertierra and Turner's contention that "to be understood in its complexity, television has to be studied from a range of research approaches and in a diversity of regional and historical contexts" (2013, 11).[1]

Moving beyond a geoculturally exceptionalist approach, however, we suggest that Asian popular factual programming as an object of inquiry also offers insights into the evolving sociocultural role of television more broadly. While media scholars often ask about the impact of global TV formats on local cultures outside the West, this book poses this question rather differently. With China and India now becoming major players in global television (and broader entertainment) industries, how might the experiences of these and other Asian sites impact on our thinking about *global* media processes? How does the evolution of lifestyle TV in a variety of national spaces—which need not be limited to Western European and Anglophone contexts—speak to changing relationships between popular media, audiences, and social, moral, and political engagement? What kinds of mediated civic spaces are emerging in postcolonial, postsocialist, and established Asian capitalist nation-states grappling with the potentials and challenges of globalizing commercial media and culture?

Framing Lifestyle: Late Modern Transformations in Identity and Social Life

A central focus of this book is television's relationship to projects of modernity—or projects of *modernities*, to be more precise. As we elaborate in detail below, we do not understand television as simply a global distributor of universal (read Euro-American) models of modernity, as in earlier theories of cultural imperialism where globalization was often equated with cultural homogenization. Instead, the "multiple modernities" paradigm that we adopt as a central framework is underpinned by the idea that modernity is not and never has been the sole preserve of the West. Studying lifestyle television in Asia demands that we balance an appreciation of the *plurality and specificity* of modern cultures beyond the West, with attentiveness to how the global mobility of lifestyle formats may bespeak certain *shared* experiences in the (late) modern world, particularly concerning the transformation of social identity (Bignell 2005; Kraidy and Sender 2011).

In relation to the latter issue, many scholars writing from Euro-American perspectives have argued that the rise of lifestyle TV reflects the increasing dominance of an individualist, consumerist approach to everyday life, in which selfhood is seen as endlessly malleable—a project to be worked on and invested in (Wood and Skeggs 2004; Lewis 2007; Redden 2007). Within

Euro-American contexts, the rise of this pliable conception of the self has been understood as a shift away from the predictability and structural certainties of traditional societies, marked by collective identities and communal norms and values, toward what Anthony Giddens (1991) has called a "post-traditional society." The mainstreaming of lifestyle television and lifestyle expertise over the past decade or so in Western Europe and the developed Anglophone world has been interpreted as offering new codes for living in an uncertain, post-traditional social landscape (Lewis 2008). As Giddens argues (1991, 5), as "reflexively organised life-planning . . . becomes a central feature of the structuring of self-identity," people increasingly turn to abstract, rationalized systems of expertise for guidance, much of which is provided today through the consumer marketplace (Lury 1996; Rose 1996; Petersen 1997).

Relatedly, Foucauldian-influenced scholarship on governmentality, particularly Nikolas Rose's work (1989), has proposed that the emergence of the lifestyle consumer is linked to new technologies of governing the self in late-modern Western societies. Rose contends that the rise of neoliberal governments in many nations in the 1980s (in particular in the United Kingdom and United States) has seen the figure of the self-governing citizen—an individual who is constructed as enterprising and self-directed—become a cultural dominant. On television, so the argument goes, such trends are reflected in the personal, health, and relationship advice offered on moralistic lifestyle-reality shows like the weight-loss show *The Biggest Loser*. Here, lifestyle gurus fill the gap left by the neoliberal state as it passes responsibility for once public concerns like obesity onto self-managing consumer citizens (Lewis 2008; Lewis 2011a; Ouellette and Hay 2008).

The proliferation of lifestyle programming in Western Europe, the United States, and Australasia can thus be seen as the product of a very particular historical-ideological moment. But to what extent does the emergence of lifestyle media in South and East Asia reflect similar sociopolitical developments? While we argue that lifestyle media in these contexts undoubtedly do speak to certain transnational trends associated with the consolidation of consumer culture and individualizing identities, as outlined above, we are also convinced that lifestyle media in China, Taiwan, and India need to be understood in the context of specific sociopolitical and cultural circumstances marked by distinct and variegated modernities. To develop that line of thought, in the following section, we offer a brief summary of the multiple modernities paradigm, followed by a discussion of the reasons behind our choice to focus on India, China, and Taiwan. We then offer introductory discussions of the distinctive modernizing processes that have shaped the public and media cultures of these three countries over recent decades. The final section of this chapter explains how we undertook our research on lifestyle television in these sites.

The Modernities Paradigm

While for Western viewers, competitive dating formats from China, such as *If You Are the One,* or Indian wedding makeover shows may, on the surface, appear to bear many familiar markers of competitive individualism and consumerism, a key argument in this book is that such shows also involve complex negotiations of social, political, economic, and cultural structures that are embedded in the specific, geolocated histories of modernity in their countries of production. A major limitation of the "post-traditional" arguments forwarded by social theorists like Giddens, discussed above, is that they assume a globally homogeneous experience of modernity. Sociological definitions of modernity in the Euro-American scholarship conventionally depict it as a fixed constellation of institutional developments, from the industrialization of production and the rise of capitalist market economies and wage labor to the emergence of bureaucratically administered states, democratization, the rule of law, and the emergence of mass media (Wittrock 2000; Gaonkar 2001). Oft-cited modern cultural transformations include secularization and the rise of scientific thinking, the doctrine of progress and self-improvement, the imagination of the nation as a community, and the detraditionalization of gender roles (Lefebvre [1971] 2002; Berman 1982; Anderson 1983; Bauman 2000; Eisenstadt 2000; Beck and Beck-Gernsheim 2002; Schmidt 2006).

While aspects of these processes are indeed undoubtedly shared—albeit unevenly, differentially, and unpredictably—across many societies in the world today, numerous critics agree that classic modernization theory is intrinsically limited by its tendency to posit Euro-American historical processes as normative. For example, arguing for "a non-Eurocentric interpretation of the history of the world-system," Enrique Dussel (2002, 224) contends that a narrow two-hundred-year focus on European modernity effaces the role of early modern formations elsewhere, such as China and India, in shaping modern processes. This observation foregrounds the complex, long-standing worlds of these civilizations not simply as varieties of a singular modernity but as *alternative* articulations of cultural modernization. Such arguments suggest the need to conceptualize moderni*ties* in the plural, despite the recent hegemony of Euro-American modernity (J. Abu-Lughod 1989; Ong and Nonini 1997; L. Lee 1999; Rofel 1999; Eisenstadt 2000; Wittrock 2000; S. Shih 2001; Knauft 2002; Chakrabarty 2007; Kraidy 2008; Shome 2012).

This recognition of the plural and variegated nature of modernities provides a key conceptual framework for our book. Indeed, we are primarily interested in engaging with the various modalities of Asian lifestyle programming discussed in this book as entry points into understanding the complexity of Asian modernities. As we illustrate in the chapters that follow, the local, national, and regional particularities of lifestyle advice television across the range of Asian contexts that we examine reinforce our conviction that people and institutions engage, produce, and mediate modern ways of thinking and being in geoculturally specific ways. Such engagements are shaped both by nationally specific state, economic, and political drives and by more recent global-scale processes (Larkin 1997; Liechty 2003; Kang 2004; Keane 2004a; L. Abu-Lughod 2008; Gerow 2010; Sundaram 2010; Wen 2013). However, in Asian media contexts the rise of discourses of self-improvement, individualized identity, and reflexive selfhood often mark the parallel (and at times distinctly divergent) evolution of these late modern concepts rather than a simple diffusion from, or convergence toward, any putative Western center (Beck and Grande 2010; Martin and Lewis 2016).

Taking seriously the plural and variegated character of cultural modernities becomes particularly urgent when dealing with the complex cultural and political economies of Asian media. East Asia is widely recognized as a semiautonomous media region whose transborder flows of TV dramas, variety shows, manga, anime, pop music, and commercial cinema knit together a specific "East Asian cultural imagination" of modernity (Iwabuchi 2002, 2004; Keane, Fung, and Moran 2007; Chua 2012). The wide transnational reach of Bollywood cinema, music, celebrity culture, and aesthetics provides another obvious challenge to Eurocentric diffusionist models (Athique 2010). In this context, it is clearly not tenable to assume that, following the partial erosion of national broadcast television and the increase in transnational televisual flows of various kinds, television—conceived as a singular, global force—must necessarily be advancing the worldwide spread of Western-style cultures and identities. Instead, adopting a multiple modernities paradigm cues us to pay detailed attention to how television is actually produced and consumed in specific contexts, and to remain alert to variations from Euro-American models in the visions of modern selfhood and citizenship that television projects.

Our use of the term *telemodernities* for this book's title puns on the two associations of the *tele-* prefix: tele as in television, and tele from the Greek τῆλε, meaning "at a distance." On the one hand, this latter sense of telemodernities relates to our intention to continue the work of provincializing Anglophone television studies, and to demonstrate the importance of centering formations of televisual modernity located at a geocultural distance from Western Europe, North America, and Australasia (Murphy and Kraidy 2003; Chakrabarty 2007). On the other hand, the telemodernities concept also implies that internal to modernity itself is a certain sense of subjective distance: modernity as an ideal to which one aspires rather than a state that is straightforwardly embodied. Given lifestyle television's repeated narratives of personal transformation, self-empowerment, and nimble adaptation to changing social and economic conditions, the aspirational character of modern formations of identity is clearly central to many examples of the genre being produced today—to some extent regardless of their countries of origin (Weber 2009). However, the concrete manifestations of these modern dreams in particular media contexts—dreams of ideal selfhood, good taste, appropriate consumption, optimally functioning relationships, proper gender—are very location-specific.

Eric Ma, among others, has observed the distinctive sharpness of cultural modernity as an aspirational ideal in developing countries in particular (Ma 2012; see also Knauft 2002; Robbins 2002; Karlström 2004; Mazzarella 2012). Ma's example is of Hong Kong as an embodiment of the dream of modernization for audiences of Hong Kong media in southern China's cities in the 1970s and 1980s. The locational specificity of people's modern dreams is undeniable, and is indeed often connected to a sense of their homeland's relative positioning in a global hierarchy of economic development. This is what Bruce M. Knauft refers to as "the force of the modern as an ideology of aspiration and differential power" (2002, 33); Pertierra and Turner concur, noting the immense force generated by the desire for modernity as channeled through television but also emphasizing that such a desire "works differently depending on where you are" (2013, 112). We take the locational specificity of people's modern aspirations as axiomatic: it is these specificities that we explore in the chapters that follow.

South and East Asian Modernities: China, Taiwan, and India

In the following sections, we offer a brief snapshot of the recent histories of modernity in China, Taiwan, and India, the three sites chosen for this study. In particular, we outline the distinctive social, cultural, and economic backgrounds for the emergence of middle-class formations in these countries as a broad context for understanding their lifestyle television cultures. Given lifestyle television's recurrent preoccupations with consumption, middle-class identity, people's emotional and economic survival in times of rapid social change, and the individualization of social life and civic responsibility, this outline of the basic conditions attending Chinese, Taiwanese, and Indian modernities provides crucial context for the detailed analyses that follow in the book's chapters.

Our relatively narrow range of focus sites is obviously not intended to present a comprehensive—or indeed even a representative—picture of lifestyle television across Asia as a whole. Instead, we have chosen our sites based on the principle of including the region's two largest media markets and the nations that are currently experiencing the fastest growing middle classes and consumer cultures (China and India). Taiwan is included as a representative of the earlier tiger economy nations that experienced industrialization, urbanization, and economic growth several decades prior, whose economies have experienced slowing growth in more recent years (Chua 2016). In chapter 8, we also draw upon audience research conducted in another tiger economy nation—Singapore—as a way of exploring the wider transnational reach of Taiwanese media culture in Sinophone Asia.

In addition to its role as a representative of the group of longer-established (post)industrial economies and national middle classes in the Asian region, there are also two more reasons behind our decision to include Taiwan in our study. First, disproportionately to its relatively small size, Taiwan remains a major player in transnational Chinese-language media circuits in East Asia and worldwide, especially through its production of Mandarin pop music and television (Chua 2012). While China remains a net importer of popular media by a wide margin (Chua 2012), Taiwanese and Hong Kong commercial media, known colloquially as Gang-Tai (Hong Kong–and–Taiwan) media, are widely influential throughout the transnational Sinophone world as vectors of what Eric Ma has called "satellite" modernity; that is, hybrid imaginaries of modernity that are Western-inflected and aspirational but also regionally specific (Ma 2012, 11–31; see also Kraidy 2007). Second and relatedly, as we will see, Taiwan television culture has a strong influence on television culture in China in particular, through its export of commercial entertainment genres, the cross-strait outflow of TV talents, and the direct consumption of Taiwan-produced content by Chinese audiences, today largely via online media piracy. In this sense, our focus on Taiwan television genres and trends offers enriching information on developments also affecting television in mainland China.

Chinese Modernity: The Tensions and Contradictions of Postsocialist Culture

China is often held up by multiple modernities theorists as the ultimate exemplar of an alternative, non-European modernity: until the eighteenth century, Europeans and neighboring Asian powers alike recognized China as a major economic, political, and cultural power (Dussel 2002). Since the turn of the twentieth century and the relative economic, military, and cultural hegemony of European formations of modernity, China's leaders and elites have dreamed of building a strong and modern China and restoring its former glory (Schwarcz 1986). As a direct response to imperial subjugation by the West, this modernization dream was fueled by nationalism. When the Chinese Communist Party took power in 1949, it promoted a vision of a modernized and unified nation, consisting of the Han majority and fifty-five other "ethnic minorities," all of which were loyal to the notion of China as a sovereign entity (C. Shih 2003). The standardization of the national language (Putonghua) and the simplification of the classic Chinese script during this era were crucial dimensions of achieving national unity and modernization. In the decades of socialism, with its collectivist farming, Soviet-style central planning, and isolation from the world economy, Chinese society was egalitarian but poor and underdeveloped (Goodman 2013). Subjecting its population to one political movement after another, China emerged in the mid-1970s with the lowest per capita income in the world, and with living standards that had remained stagnant for several decades (Naughton 2006).

The three decades of economic reforms that started in the late 1970s brought about an effective end to the socialist vision of modernity. Adopting developmental strategies and embracing the logic of market liberalization, from 1979 China opened itself to the world, welcomed foreign investment, set up special economic zones, and in 2001 joined the World Trade Organization (WTO). Between 1978 and 2004, China's GDP grew at an average rate of 9.4 percent per annum, with its per capita GDP growing at 8 percent (Shirk 2007). The result is nothing short of staggering. China is now the world's second-largest economy, with a national GDP of over US$9 trillion in 2013, and a per capita GDP (PPP) of $10,011 (International Monetary Fund 2013). It has had the highest average annual growth rate in the world over the past two decades, and is the world's largest energy consumer. China also boasts of being the world's largest exporter, second-largest importer, third-largest trader in services, and second-largest trading nation (Shambaugh 2013, 156).

Rapid economic growth has considerably reduced overall poverty. A World Bank statistic indicates that in 1990, China still had 360 million people living below the poverty line, but in 2011, only 170 million people lived on less than $1.25 per day (Vairon 2013). At the same time, however, the gap between the rich and poor has widened. In fact, three decades of economic reforms have transformed China from one of the most equal societies in Asia and the world to one of the most unequal ones (C. Lee and Selden 2007). With a third of the nation's wealth held by 1 percent of its citizens, it is widely felt in China that economic inequality could be a serious trigger for social instability (Kaiman 2014).[2]

Both the spectacular economic achievement and the deepening of inequality are results of China having pursued a neoliberal-style economic development trajectory. However, this is quite distinct from American-style economic and political neoliberalism. On the one hand, anthropologists and observers of China's cultural industries have produced ample evidence pointing to myriad neoliberal aspects of governance and subject formation (Rofel 2007; Yan 2008; Zhang and Ong 2008, Zhao 2008b, Hoffman 2010; Hong 2010; Ren 2010, 2013; Sun 2014). But on the other hand, China attributes its status as the main engine of global economic growth to the "China Model," which represents a unique alternative to the Washington Consensus approach to politics and economics (Callahan 2013, 66). Indeed, China remains a country where the party-state holds a considerable portion of the country's fixed assets, and where liberal institutions, such as the rule of law, transparent markets, and democracy, are largely missing. As Ching Kwan Lee observes, engaging critically with Harvey's (2005) proposal that China offers an example of neoliberalism with "Chinese characteristics," China has never had the prehistory of embedded economic liberalism from which neoliberalism purportedly grows out (2014, 245).

Nevertheless, the state-led project of instituting a market economy has fundamentally reshaped social and cultural life in China since the end of the 1970s. A fundamental difference between socialist and capitalist visions of modernity lies in their legitimation of social identities. Whereas workers, peasants, and soldiers embodied the most legitimate social groups in China's socialist discourses under Maoism, in the reforms era, they have been replaced by entrepreneurs, professionals, and managers (Chen and Goodman 2013a, 1). In China's cities, the middle classes are clearly expanding. The East Asian Middle Class Project (EAMC), a transnational collaborative research project led by Hsin-huang Michael Hsiao, estimated that by 2006—leaving aside the vast, relatively impoverished rural hinterland—the new middle class (professionals, managers, and government officials) accounted for 18.8 percent of the population, the old middle class (employers and owner-operators with small staffs, and the self-employed) 19.6 percent, and the marginal middle class (low white-collar workers or routine workers) 25.4 percent (Li 2014). Although the definition and size of the middle class remain contested, the reappearance of such a class in the last decades of the twentieth century was seen as politically, socially, and economically useful to the party-state. Considered as a stabilizing force, the middle class is seen as more likely than the underclass to support the authoritarian regime, thus hindering political radicalization; it functions as a buffer between the upper class and the underclass, thus ensuring social stability; and it constitutes the most active consumer group, thus stimulating economic growth (Li 2013). It is precisely for this reason that the development of a middle class is considered as a "state project of managing risks in Chinese society" (Ren 2013, 9).

Due to its perceived importance, it is not surprising that sociological work inside mainland China has paid significant attention to the middle class. In fact, the sociological categorization of the middle class in much of the state-funded research (for example, from the China Academy of Social Sciences) has been crucial in turning China's middle class into a normative category (Greenhalgh 2005). Such processes of legitimation cannot be completed without also normalizing certain values and lifestyles as proper to the middle class in the realm of consumption and everyday practices. Correspondingly, the reforms era has seen the socialist logic of class identity as the privileged measure of personhood (peasant, worker, or soldier good; bourgeois bad) effectively inverted by a new discourse of "human quality" (*suzhi*) that valorizes education, cultivation, competition, and broadly middle-class cultural norms (Bakken 2000; Kipnis 2006). Børge Bakken (2000) observes that the now-pervasive discourse of suzhi marks the establishment of a new suite of "exemplary norms" to which individuals are held accountable, as the state attempts to impose social order through population management at both micro- and macroscales during the chaotic process of accelerating modernization. Anthropological work has shown that in contrast to the putatively suzhi-deficit rural populace, middle-class, urban, educated professionals are considered "sites of high levels of *suzhi*" (Hoffman 2010, 105; see also Anagnost 2004; Jacka 2006; Yan 2008; Sun 2009). An understanding of how suzhi discourse makes reforms-era China an "exemplary society," by idealizing a type of personhood associated with urban modernity (Fong 2007, 86), has obvious resonance in our investigation of the pedagogies of life advice television in the following chapters.

Taiwanese Modernity: Neoliberal Transition in a Postindustrial Tiger Economy

The Republic of China that today occupies Taiwan was originally founded in 1911 on the Chinese mainland. It moved to exile on Taiwan with the Kuomintang (KMT, or Chinese Nationalist Party) in the late 1940s, when the KMT army and leadership fled to the island following their defeat by Mao Zedong's Communist forces in the Chinese civil war. Over the Cold War decades that followed, Taiwan's totalitarian regime, headed by Generalissimo Chiang Kai-shek, was supported politically, militarily, and economically by the United States as part of its strategy of creating a right-wing, capitalist bulwark against the spread of Communism in the Pacific. In significant part, it was this U.S. economic support and military protection that enabled Taiwan to number among the Asian tiger economies—along with Singapore, South Korea, and Hong Kong—that underwent rapid economic growth through industrialization in this postwar period. In Taiwan's case, these developments took place within a decentralized industrial structure based on small- and medium-sized family-based enterprises (SMEs), overseen by the KMT developmental state (A. Lee 2004). Between the late 1940s and the mid-1980s, culture, media, and politics in Taiwan were strictly controlled by the state, based on the political principle of anti-Communism and the cultural principle of ensuring the dominance of the Mandarin-speaking northern Chinese culture of the KMT regime, in opposition to both the Japanese language and culture of the island's former colonizers (1895–1945) and the southern Chinese Minnan and Hakka languages and cultures of the majority of the island's inhabitants.

Since the mid-1980s, the old statist model has shifted toward what some characterize as a neoliberal transition (Tsai 2001), with economic liberalization, the privatization of public-sector enterprises, and the introduction of market-oriented labor reforms. From the mid-1990s, a new wave of economic restructuring saw Taiwan's economy shift away from industrial manufacturing—which migrated across the strait to mainland China—and toward the service sector, which today constitutes the center of gravity of Taiwan's economic structure (DGBAS 2010, 16). At the same time, economic growth slowed, due in large part to the massive capital outflows to China (Tsai, Fan, Hsiao, and Wang 2014, 33). In 2012, GDP growth sat at just 1.32 percent (Executive Yuan 2013). Transforming from an agrarian to postindustrial society in about four decades, Taiwan, like Korea, has been aptly described as an example of compressed modernity (Chang and Song 2010).

Politically, socially, and culturally, Taiwan saw immense transformations in the late twentieth century, following the revocation of martial law by Chiang

Kai-shek's more liberal son, Chiang Ching-kuo, in 1987. The new middle classes that emerged from the economic growth of the preceding decades tended to favor democratization; this helped fuel the far-reaching political changes of the post–martial law period (Hsiao 2014). These include the rise of a multiparty democracy with direct presidential election, which resulted in the first non-KMT president, Chen Shui-bian of the Democratic Progressive Party (DPP), being elected in 2000. In this same period, the political censorship of media was lifted and state regulation of culture virtually abandoned. A vibrant civil society emerged, along with a wide range of social movements from trade unionism to environmentalism to advocacy for the rights of the island's indigenous peoples, an antinuclear movement, feminism(s), and queer activism. Minnan and Hakka languages and cultures emerged strongly in revivalist movements after the long decades of suppression by the old KMT regime; these movements have had significant, lasting impacts on televisual and other media, especially in their new linguistic pluralism. The same period witnessed Taiwan's intensifying interlinkage into transnational cultural, commodity, labor, and media circuits, and the rapid expansion and diversification of its media cultures following commercialization and deregulation in the early 1990s (see chapter 1).

Notwithstanding what some see as evidence of global neoliberal trends in Taiwan's government's economic strategies in recent decades, it is important to note that, as with China, many commentators argue for the specificity of Taiwan's engagement with economic neoliberalism. It is seen as markedly different from neoliberalism as manifested in Euro-American contexts due to the persistent structural legacies of the developmental state: like several other comparable examples in the Asian region, it is argued, Taiwan's economy might therefore be better described as postdevelopmental or neodevelopmental (Kong 2005; Chen and Li 2012; Wang 2012). In the cultural sphere, however (again, as is the case in China), it is undeniable that ideologies broadly consonant with neoliberalism—self-responsibilization, a privatized conceptualization of the social, the evaluation of human value in commodity terms, and so on—have become increasingly influential, as our analyses in the following chapters explore (Chen and Chien 2009; Pazderic 2013; Thomas and Yang 2013; Yang 2016).

As a result of the economic and social histories sketched out above, today, Taiwanese society is dominated by its middle classes. In 2013, Taiwan's GDP sat at US$494.85 billion, with a per capita GDP (PPP) of $40,392 (International Monetary Fund 2013). In postindustrial Taiwan, social inequality is markedly lower than across the strait in developing China: in 2011 its GINI coefficient sat at 0.34, compared to China's 0.74 (CIA 2013; Kaiman 2014). In 2006 over 70 percent of Taiwan's working population fell within the middle classes. These comprised 27 percent in the new middle class (professionals, managers, and government officials), 20 percent in the old middle class (small employers, small owner-operators, and the self-employed), and 23.1 percent in the marginal middle class (low white-collar workers or routine workers) (Li 2013; Tsai, Fan, Hsiao, and Wang 2014). Taiwan's expansive and well-established middle classes of today have consolidated as a result of upward class mobility enabled by business opportunities flowing from Taiwan's state-led industrialization during the 1960s to 1990s, coupled with rising levels of education over this period (Hsiao 2010, 254). As the analyses in the chapters that follow demonstrate, media produced in Taiwan and for Taiwanese audiences is, unsurprisingly, dominated by broadly middle-class interests.

Indian Modernity: From Postcoloniality to the Contested Middle Class

The third country of focus in this book is India, a nation whose contemporary media industries and institutions have emerged against the backdrop of a complex and extended engagement with globalization and vernacular modernities. Like China, India has played an important role in the *longue durée* of world history (Dussel 2002). With its key position in the spice trade, one of the main trades in the early world economy, it has also long been the site of European colonization. The expansion of British power in much of India in the early nineteenth century saw it transition from military-commercial domination (under the rule of the East India company) to a system of colonial governance (Guha 1997), with the British carving out the dominion into a manageable territory with maps, trains, and the introduction of demographic surveys (Prakash 1999). Colonial governance saw the British educating a class of indigenous elites as civil servants to mediate colonial rule (Chatterjee 1993), though this elite also sought to reclaim ancient Indic knowledge in order to articulate new modernities of their own (Prakash 1999). These largely cultural endeavors at salvaging Indian self-identity preceded the rise of a more radical generation of politicized leaders, unleashing the mass movements that would lead to India's independence in 1947 (Chatterjee 1986).

The first prime minister, Jawaharlal Nehru, driven by the pragmatics of nation-building, saw the state as the engine of change that would haul the nation into industrial modernity (Corbridge and Harriss 2013). Propelled by Nehru's famous maxim, "dams [are] the temples of modern India," the postindependence decade saw the creation of large public-sector companies, heavy industries, and a range of major public works. The developmental state, however, was fraught with difficulties, arguably due in part to its failure to mobilize big business toward developmental goals along the lines of state-led industrialization in East Asia, such as the rapid industrialization and economic success of South Korea (Chibber 2003). As a result, the economy languished from the 1950s to the 1980s at the infamous 3.5 percent "Hindu rate of growth."

In 1980 Prime Minister Indira Gandhi launched pro-business reforms that were subsequently aggressively expanded by her successor Rajiv Gandhi, who promoted and embraced the growing strength of domestic capitalists (Kohli 2006). A balance of payments crisis in 1991 drove India to deregulatory, pro–free market reforms in the changed global context of a disintegrating Soviet Union and the imminent arrival of the WTO (Corbridge and Harriss 2013). With the dismantling of the planned economy, market liberalization saw growth rates pick up to 6 percent in the 1990s and 8 percent in the 2000s, though rates have dropped to around 5 percent in recent years.

The benefits of economic liberalization have been bitterly debated, with a broad consensus now emerging that most of the post-1991 growth is owed to the 1980s reforms (Rodrik and Subramanian 2004), which achieved poverty reduction and job creation unequalled in the post-1991 period (Chandrashekhar and Ghosh 2002). Contrary to the pattern observed in other late-industrializing countries, the post-1991 period only saw minor expansion in manufacturing in the large-scale skill-intensive industries (Kotwal, Bharat, and Wilima 2011). On the other hand, the service sector grew exponentially, with the information technology (IT) boom creating business services within the domestic economy and outsourcing jobs from developed nations on the back of India's cheap, educated labor pool (Kotwal, Bharat, and Wilima 2011). India's contemporary rhetoric of integration into global markets has to be seen within this landscape of lopsided growth that has privileged skilled labor and largely reinforced existing class disparities.

As in China, this pairing of economic growth with a deepening of social inequality is often seen as the result of the pursuit of neoliberal policies. Again, though, there has been much debate as to whether this fully accounts for the complexity and specificity of what has taken place in the Indian context. For example, Akhil Gupta and Aradhana Sharma (2006) discuss the limitations of applying the Foucauldian concept of neoliberal governmentality in a postcolonial state where the coexistence of poverty and a neoliberalized economy has seen the rise of both state welfare and postwelfare "empowerment" programs aimed at the rural poor. Meanwhile, Patrick Neveling (2014) has challenged conceptions of the Nehruvian state as the radical other of reformist post-1991 India, showing that it already included significant and powerful institutional arrangements that might be labeled neoliberal. Similarly, there is a wide range of opinion on the degree to which neoliberalism as an everyday cultural logic is shaping people's lives in India today. Nandini Gooptu introduces her edited collection, *Enterprise Culture in Neoliberal India*, by noting its pervasiveness in current public discourse: "In India … multiple agents and institutions (state and non-state) [seek] to create heightened aspirations and expectations, promoting the ideology of self-making, providing self-help and self-development tools, [and] purveying the evidence of success of self-propelled individuals as [a] motivational instrument" (2013, 8–9).

At the same time, Steve Derné's longitudinal research from the 1980s to the 2000s on young male film viewers in a midsize town in Northern India suggests that the impact and experience of global ideologies of neoliberalism and individualism are highly stratified (Derné 2008). He argues that while "cultural globalization" has seen the Indian elite embrace forms of transitional cosmopolitanism and entrepreneurialism, such late modern cultural transformations have not dramatically impacted what he calls the locally oriented "ordinary middle class"; that is, non-English-speaking professionals, students, and successfully self-employed people, as well as drivers and clerks, who arguably form the bulk of the Indian solidly middle and lower middle class.

Derné's observations regarding the need to recognize the very different experiences and lifestyles of cosmopolitan upper-middle-class urbanites versus more ordinary middle-class Indians points to the complexity of the term *middle class* in the Indian context, with class hierarchies continuing to be shaped by residual caste and colonial influences (Deshpande 2004). Estimated to be anywhere between seventy and four hundred million by differing benchmarks, using the yardstick of a per capita daily income of above US$8–40, the middle class has grown from 5.7 percent of the population in 2001 to 12.8 percent in 2010 (153 million) (Shukla 2010). In India, extremely uneven economic development has seen the poverty rate reduce much more slowly compared with China. The incidence of people subsisting on $1.25 a day declined from 55 percent in 1990 to around 40 percent in 2005, with this impoverished section of the population still being a long way from reaching anything near middle-class status (Chen and Ravallion 2004). Meanwhile, the middle classes themselves experience significant precarity. As Jan Nijman shows, data on the distribution of household incomes in Mumbai demonstrate that while the upper-middle-class incomes have grown relative to the total, lower-middle-class incomes have shrunk, while much of the growth in consumption in the urban middle classes is credit based (Nijman 2006).

Given this context, Leela Fernandes argues that the rise of an entrepreneurial, cosmopolitan middle class in India is perhaps best understood in discursive rather than purely economic terms, as the production of a distinctive social and political identity that represents and lays claims to the benefits of neoliberalization (Fernandes 2006). Post 1991, the urban middle classes and their associated consumer goods and increasingly globally connected lifestyles have become the symbol of a new liberalizing India, replacing state-led modernization, rural development, and uplifting images of rural workers as symbols of national pride and progress (Mazzarella 2003; Fernandes 2006; Brosius 2010). In contemporary India, then—as in China and Taiwan—the increasing naturalization of representations of consumerist, urban, middle-class lifestyles on television, while not necessarily widely matched by people's material experiences, may contribute significantly to shaping the social horizons and aspirations of many ordinary people. It is this possibility that we investigate in depth in the chapters that follow.

Researching Lifestyle Television:
Contexts of Production and Consumption

The project that this book came out of involved a three-pronged approach to studying lifestyle television, designed to enable us to compare, contrast, and trace possible links and flows between our sites across the areas of television content, production, and reception. We employ the term *lifestyle television* to embrace a range of programs airing on both daytime and evening television. This includes everything from magazine and variety shows incorporating life advice segments, to cooking, health, home renovation, and personal makeover programs. As we will see, adopting this generic term is not without its difficulties, in relation both to different televisual conventions and to the varied meanings of lifestyle across these sites. However, in this book we adopt the term as a starting point for comparison and critical reflection.

The first part of our three-pronged approach was a series of industry studies. Between 2008 and 2011, we conducted a total of forty-four in-depth, semi-structured interviews with television professionals (14 in China; 18 in India; 9 in Taiwan; 3 in Singapore). We conducted these interviews in Shanghai, Bengbu (in Anhui province in mideastern China), Delhi, Mumbai, Bangalore, Taipei, and Singapore, targeting a mixture of programming heads with their big-picture take on programming strategies, and on-the-ground producers and other professional staff, across a range of public, commercial, and cable channels as well as independent production houses. These industry studies aimed to flesh out the regional industry history of lifestyle programming, to access information about the production context of lifestyle TV, and to map the role played by television producers as cultural intermediaries who shape the values promoted by lifestyle shows. In India and China, it was impossible to capture a comprehensive picture of *all* lifestyle content produced and consumed across national, regional, and municipal levels. We therefore chose to focus our industry studies on one major metropolis and media center in each country (Shanghai and Mumbai), plus one smaller regional city (Bengbu in China and the southern city of Bangalore in India). This allowed us to capture some sense of the diversity of television cultures in these massive media markets and also, importantly, to offer a partial corrective to the general neglect of nonmetropolitan sites in extant English-language studies of television in these countries. Insights gleaned from these industry interviews into the production contexts of the lifestyle advice shows that we analyze in our chapters are woven into our discussions throughout the book, especially chapter 1.

Our second research method involved textual studies of a range of free-to-air, cable, and satellite lifestyle programs, including both daytime and primetime programming, from each of our main sites. Between 2009 and 2014, we purchased and recorded hundreds of hours of programming across a wide variety of genres, the critical contextual analysis of which forms a central component of the chapters that follow. Given the diffusion of lifestyle advice-related content across a wide range of genres in the countries on which we focus, and the relative lack of a clearly defined lifestyle genre in some of them, we had to cast a wide net in our recording strategy. Our principle was to sample any nonfictional, non-news programming that incorporated direct advice to the viewer on the proper execution of everyday life activities. Using a mix of satellite and online feeds, DVD purchases, and recordings made with the help of our in-country research assistants, we archived everything from magazine-format daytime television on cooking and housekeeping; to prime-time comic variety shows from Taiwan with life advice sections embedded among the games, quizzes, and other hijinks; to the far straighter moral pedagogies of CCTV's psychological advice and personal makeover formats in China; and to morning yoga shows in India hosted by religious gurus. We then drew on this massive archive to refine our sense of the dominant genres and patterns in each country, and selected examples for analysis based on both the centrality of particular genres and themes (for example, *yangsheng* [health] shows in China, variety formats in Taiwan, and religious lifestyle television in India), and the popularity of specific programs, in both urban and rural sites. Our key question regarding our selected examples is how the programs make imaginable particular configurations of identity and lifestyle.

The third component of our method consisted of audience studies. Between 2011 and 2013, we conducted in-depth, semistructured interviews with viewers of lifestyle advice programming in Shanghai (32 viewers), Bengbu (8 viewers), Mumbai (18 household interviews with 36 viewers), Tovinkere, southern India (16 household interviews with 34 viewers), Bangalore (2 viewers), Taipei (30 viewers), and Singapore (16 viewers).[3] Our strategies with the China and India audience studies mirrored those adopted in the industry and content studies, focusing again on both metropolitan and regional sites. In the audience interviews, we sought to understand how different viewers interpret and subjectively relate to the lifestyle programming that they habitually consume; how the cultural, linguistic, gendered, and socioeconomic specificity of viewers' existing social identities affects their interpretation of the programs; and whether, and if so how, the consumption of lifestyle programs relates to viewers' elaboration of social identities and lifestyle practices in each location. The audience studies provide some of the richest, most complex data generated by this project. Viewer interactions with the programs in question constitute the key moment in which lifestyle television as media form(s) intersect directly with identity, subjectivity, and everyday practices; since that intersection between media and identity is the ultimate focus of our project, discussion of the audience studies constitutes a central focus in several of the chapters that follow.

As is implicit in the discussion above, the multisite research project on which this book is based is centrally structured by a transnational orientation. We have approached television not (only) as a series of national industries and apparatuses but also as an inherently transnational form that is marked by flows of content, talent, genres, and ideas across the borders of nation-states. The chapters that follow show how cross-border flows are often of defining significance within local manifestations of lifestyle TV (Chinese copies of American lifestyle makeover formats like *Queer Eye for the Straight Guy*; the outflow of Taiwanese TV talents to China and concomitant cross-strait spread of Taiwanese TV genres and styles; Indian versions of global formats such as the *MasterChef* franchise and *The Biggest Loser*). Beyond the *content* of our research, though, our research *method* has also been marked—and challenged—by the transnationality of its operations. Funded by the Australian Research Council, our project had its institutional location in Australia, with the central investigators employed in Australian universities, from where we had to find ways of researching television overseas. And notwithstanding the intensification of its movements beyond national borders via satellite, international cable, and online delivery (Chadha and Kavoori 2012), we were quickly reminded that television remains a medium whose flows are strongly channeled and directed by geospatial technologies and geographically delimited markets.

The project faced major technical challenges in capturing domestic TV content from a distance. For instance, to capture Chinese content, we ultimately installed a 2.3-meter-wide pole-mounted mesh satellite dish on top of a building at the University of Melbourne. Tuned to the seven relevant locally accessible satellites and routed through a baroque techno-legal configuration involving meters of in-wall cabling, a set-top box, a television, a hard-drive recorder, a personal computer (PC), and a public liability insurance purchase lest the dish detach itself from the six-story roof and descend onto students below, the dish allowed us to record a high-quality feed from *some* channels in mainland China, and a couple in Taiwan (though during the life of the project, more and more of the Chinese programs became available via video archives on channel websites). At the time of our research, however, local Bengbu television was utterly inaccessible in Australia, so we relied on our in-country research assistants to make DVD recordings, which they then mailed to us. For India, we accessed lifestyle programming via a domestic satellite dish and through a commercial subscription service delivered via Internet, and also sourced key shows via the now extensive range of catch-up television offered online by commercial channels in India, as well as via recordings provided by in-country research assistants. For Taiwan, we followed the lead of Melbourne's diasporic Taiwanese community and used an informal, gray, Internet-based distribution system (Lobato 2012, 95–109), purchasing an annual subscription to a service that delivered a pixelated feed of Taiwanese domestic television (more than 150 channels) live to PC, via an unlocking program provided on a USB stick. Such complex exigencies of simply getting access to overseas television continually brought home to us the still-located nature of TV. We suspect that this very practical issue may be one reason why there have been so few in-depth multisited studies of television to date.

Structure of the Book

While the chapters in this book can be read as stand-alone essays, we have structured the book to be ideally engaged as a whole, with each chapter connecting to, building on, and responding to conceptual frames and questions introduced earlier. This introduction and chapter 1 introduce the key conceptual, theoretical, and empirical contexts underpinning the book. Following this introductory chapter, chapter 1 discusses the political economy of lifestyle programming in China, India, and Taiwan. Combining policy analysis with institutional and historical snapshots, interviews with industry staffers, and mapping of television schedules and ratings, we outline the political, economic, and cultural forces that have shaped the rise of lifestyle-oriented TV programming in our three focus sites.

Chapters 2, 3, and 4 pivot around the question of imaginative geographies. Drawing from our interviews with viewers of lifestyle advice TV in China, India, and Taiwan, this section of the book focuses on how people's engagements with lifestyle television involve imagining place at a range of scales, from the link between regional localities and national metropolises to the relation between identification with a national homeland versus the alluring vision of limitless global mobility. Chapter 2 examines the complex, multiscalar nature of Chinese television through a discussion of metropolitan and regional lifestyle television industries, with a focus on two channels: Shanghai TV and Bengbu TV. Studies of Chinese television often betray an urban, technological, and class bias, ignoring formations of local media cultures below the scale of the province (Sun and Chio 2012). This chapter addresses this analytical and methodological gap in conceptualizing Chinese mediascapes, discussing a range of geographic imaginaries, and in the process exploring the links between lifestyle formats, structures of taste and perceived needs, and place.

Chapter 3 examines another vast televisual landscape, that of India. This chapter maps the shifting and varied constructions of place, space, and sociotemporalities that have formed Indian TV, noting that questions of scale in India are strongly shaped by social and cultural distinction, with media markets split along linguistic and regional lines (Bollywood versus Sandalwood, the Kannada-language film industry in southwest India, for instance) as well as religious, class, and caste lines. In discussing place and scale in the Indian context we draw upon Ash Amin's nonterritorial way of conceptualizing place, where place and spatiality are understood as increasingly virtual, such that "the proximate and the remote [can coexist] at the same geographical level" (Amin 2002, 389).

In chapter 4, we extend our analysis of lifestyle television's role in shaping imaginative geographies through a study of the American cable Travel and Living Channel—available in many countries across Asia—in Taiwan. Our interviews with Taiwanese viewers suggest that one of the most notable impacts of this channel is the way it works to shore up the global orientation of young, urban, middle-class internationalist subjects, consolidating their consciousness of their own perceived potential for future mobility both outward, toward the global, and upward, toward upper-middle-class consumer lifestyles. In using TLC to think through new identities based on the capacity for social and geographic movement, we argue that these viewers are accumulating an immaterial form of movement capital; it is through shoring up the value of such movement capital that lifestyle programming on TLC Taiwan contributes to the transformation of identities.

Chapters 5 through 8 offer in-depth analyses of specific examples of life advice television across our three countries, providing insights into the ways in which transforming relationships between state- and market-led regulation of culture are played out in lifestyle TV's representations of identity, interpersonal relations, and everyday life practices. Chapter 5 examines the proliferation of life experts on Chinese and Indian TV, from transnationally recognizable figures such as makeover experts and celebrity chefs to more culturally distinctive forms of popular expertise. Discussing the rise of psychologized, individualized models of everyday expertise aimed at responsibilizing citizens, and the growing rationalization and informationalization of everyday life, the chapter examines how culturally inflected forms of expertise and expert practices speak to the specificity of engagements with emergent forms of sociality and first and second modernities in China and India.

This theme is developed further in chapter 6 on enchanted rather than modern-rational forms of expertise. Here, we turn to religious, spiritual, and supernatural life advice television in India and Taiwan to explore the distinctive counternarratives of modernity that emerge there from the confluence of religious, supernatural beliefs and late modern media cultures. While religious programming is banned by the state in China, in India and Taiwan, a variety of gods, sages, sacred texts, and rituals are presented to and interpreted for viewers to help them manage the challenges of escalating risk, transcendent meaning, and collective affiliation in times of rapid social change. This chapter considers what is historically and locally specific about the interpenetration of religious and supernatural belief systems and contemporary media cultures, as well as how spiritual elements shape both the genre(s) of lifestyle advice TV and the forms of identity it projects in these countries.

Chapter 7 moves into the territory of love and relationships. In recent years, TV audiences in both China and India have been exposed to a growing number of reality and lifestyle shows focused on dating, marriage, parenting, and love relationships. While, like spirituality, the affective and intangible space of love might seem to inhabit a realm beyond the logics of late modern struggles, we argue that the study of televisual treatments of love and marriage offers a privileged perspective from which one can gain an understanding of the cultural process of modernity. Drawing on a range of examples, from game show–based dating formats to reality shows dealing with love and romance to more advice-oriented formats, we examine how these shows navigate the contradictions between apparent forms of gender empowerment and marketized aspirations toward social and cultural fluidity, versus the realities of powerful gendered social and economic inequities, and the continued cultural potency of familial and communitarian notions of duty.

Continuing the exploration of reflexive individualization and gender from chapter 7, chapter 8 surveys a range of women's lifestyle advice shows from China and Taiwan, drawing on audience research on the reception of these shows across China, Taiwan, and also Singapore, in order to explore transforming models of feminine identity in the transnational Sinophone world. The Chinese example analyzed in this chapter foregrounds the normative definition—promulgated in this case by state media (CCTV)—of adult femininity as an identity focused on familial care work. In contrast, an alternative subcategory of women's lifestyle television, originating in Taiwan, centers on an emergent and idealized feminine identity in Sinophone East Asia, the "young-mature lady" (*qingshounü*): urban, unmarried, white-collar women who are seen as individualistic in attitude, with a high level of education and a penchant for beauty and fashion consumption. However, based on our audience research, we show that the idealization of this emergent form of feminine identity does not reflect the self-perceived situation of Taiwanese viewers but rather provides imaginative resources for contesting the locally dominant cultural hegemony of patriarchal familialism.

Finally, the conclusion summarizes some of the central themes of the book, addressing key questions raised by the case studies. How does the impact and evolution of lifestyle TV in these sites speak to changing relationships between popular media, audiences, and social, moral, and political engagement? What kinds of mediated civic spaces are emerging in postcolonial, postsocialist, and post–economic miracle Asian nation-states grappling with the potentials and challenges of commercial global media? Returning to our multiple modernities framework, this chapter asks how developments in these rapidly shifting and emerging media spaces—marked by very different speeds and experiences of modernity—might speak back to and transform conventional understandings of the mediated relations between social identities, politics, and citizenship.

ONE. **Lifestyle Television in Context** Media Industries, Cultural Economies, and Genre Flows

While in the introduction we outline the social, cultural, and economic background to the emergence of modern middle classes in China, Taiwan, and India as a broad context for understanding their contemporary lifestyle programming, here our focus turns to the political economy of lifestyle television in these focus countries. The rise of popular advice and infotainment programming, alongside popular factual television more broadly, can be linked to a range of pivotal developments within the TV industry both in the region and globally, with the late 1980s and beyond seeing a broad transnational shift to a deregulated, multichannel environment characterized by audience fragmentation and increased pressure for inexpensive programming that could potentially move across a range of markets (Moran 1998; Ellis 2000; Bonner 2003; Waisbord 2004). The 1990s in particular was a time of dramatic change in television industries across much of South and East Asia. While in many Asian nations, as in our three focus countries, television had hitherto been tied to and regulated by the nation-state, varied degrees of economic and state deregulation across the region saw the growth of commercialized forms of television linked to transnational flows of capital and programming. Pivotal here was the impact of commercial satellite television across the region—heralded by Star TV's groundbreaking trans-Asian broadcasts in 1991, a move that opened the way to a surge in advertising-supported television, the increased availability of foreign programming, and a rapid expansion of the number of channels in many Asian countries (Sinclair, Jacka, and Cunningham 1996; Richards and French 2000; Thomas 2005; White 2005).

Although this opening up of links between territories has seen the proliferation of transnational TV channels and the growing role of major global media players in the region (most often in partnership with domestic media companies), as we show in our discussion of China, Taiwan, and India, such shifts did not necessarily spell the end of state involvement in television. Indeed, in his book on the "television revolution in Asia," James D. White suggests that the opening of East Asian TV industries to global flows "may ultimately make [the institution of the state] stronger, albeit transformed" (2005, 10). Furthermore, across the region there are strong trends toward the localization of program content, associated with a rise in regional language and dialect channels, a growing number of domestic satellite players transmitting to diasporic communities, and the rise of local production houses producing content for a range of local, regional, and global markets (Thomas 2005; Keane, Fung and Moran 2007).

Such trends also mark a relative fragmentation and dispersal of once national audiences, albeit alongside the continued presence of strong state broadcasting in the case of China. The trend toward consumer-driven narrowcast modes of viewing has been further underscored by the emergence of new delivery platforms such as YouTube, China's Youku, and video-on-demand for downloading and streaming TV. New technologies for accessing and interacting with TV content have also changed the way people watch TV, with the regional investment in the 1990s in commercial communications infrastructure enabling the growth of Internet and mobile phone services in Asia (Thomas 2005; Turner and Tay 2009). As Graeme Turner and Jinna Tay (2009) note, the shift toward the consumption of TV content on screens other than television, for example, via mobile phones, suggests a growing challenge to conventional associations between television and family-based, domestic viewing practices (see also Neves 2015). However, of course, in parts of Asia such as China and rural India, domestic viewing is a relatively recent development, with audiences historically viewing TV in public or communal settings (Zhu and Berry 2009).

Drawing on examples from China, India, and Taiwan, this chapter discusses the political economy of lifestyle programming in Asia, as well as the cultural economy of genres and formats in these geopolitical locations. Highlighting the distinctive sociopolitical assemblages of our three focus countries, we offer institutional and historical snapshots of television in China, India, and Taiwan, and an overview of today's television landscape in each place, contextualizing contemporary lifestyle advice programming within this field. Drawing upon both original empirical and secondary data, we shed light on the array of intertwined political, economic, and cultural forces that have shaped the rise of lifestyle-oriented TV programming in our focus sites in Asia.

The Arrival of Television, Life Advice, and Consumer Identities in Reforms-Era China

Television first arrived in China in 1958. It was mainly used for the mobilization of the nation's citizens in the Chinese Communist Party's nation-building project and the promotion of desirable values for the construction of socialist modernity (Sun 2007). For that reason, news and current affairs—the "hard" stuff of television content—were the staple fare of Chinese television throughout the 1960s and 1970s. In the 1980s and 1990s, however, television became the main source of entertainment as well as news, with television pioneering the marketization of Chinese media. Today, television has penetrated almost all Chinese households. While in 1978, there was only one television set per more than one hundred people and just ten million people with access to TV, today, television's penetration rate is estimated at 98 percent, and there are consoles in more than four hundred million households (Zhu and Berry 2009, 3; Neves 2015, 51). Television has thus transformed from a public medium commanding communal viewing to an everyday form of cultural consumption in the private home and, for younger people, a media form accessible via ubiquitous digital mobile devices (Neves 2015). Although still owned and controlled by the government, Chinese television is "simultaneously subservient and defiant, nationalistic and cosmopolitan, moralistic and fun-loving, extravagant and mundane" (Bai and Song 2015, 1). The content of Chinese television is now highly diverse, ranging from news, current affairs, and documentaries to myriad entertainment genres such as television dramas, quizzes and games, talk shows, reality shows, and a vast range of lifestyle programs. The dynamic and complex nature of Chinese television has been documented from the perspectives of funding, ownership, censorship, regulation, and institutional restructuring (Lull 1992; Chang 2002; Zhao 1998, 2008a, 2008b; Zhao and Guo 2005). Similarly, format development is seen as an area of dynamic change and innovation (Zhu 2012; Keane 2015). The cultural economy of television drama, one of China's most popular television genres, has also been a popular topic for analysis (Zhu, Keane, and Bai 2008).

To those unfamiliar with the development of mainland Chinese media, the multi-tiered structure of China's broadcasting industry today may be perplexing, yet grasping the breadth and complexity of this structure is crucial if we are to understand the institutional context in which China's lifestyle television programs are produced and consumed.[1] First, the national broadcaster, CCTV, runs more than a dozen channels. Second, each of the thirty-odd provincial television stations, which are usually based in provincial capitals ("tier-two" cities), runs about half a dozen channels. One channel from each provincial station is available to national audiences via satellite, along with the satellite-transmitted programs produced by half a dozen metropolitan television stations such as Beijing, Shanghai, Tianjin, Shenzhen, and Chongqing. These latter stations, due to their location in tier-one autonomous metropolitan cities, fall directly under the administration of the central government and produce their own programs. Further down the geographic scale is county- and city-level television. While county-level television stations simply relay national and provincial content, city-level television produces a large number of lifestyle programs that enjoy a steady and loyal viewership due to a strong local relevance. These channels' programs are free to air and are transmitted terrestrially, available only to the viewers of the city and its adjacent counties. We argue that a full understanding of Chinese TV cannot be attained without taking seriously this so-called fourth tier of city-level television, which we discuss in detail in chapter 2.

The television industry in China is marked by intense competition for audiences. Since 1998, all provinces send their main television channels via satellite to a national audience, rendering obsolete the old scenario whereby provincial TV content was only seen by viewers in one province. The availability in urban cable-connected households of nearly thirty provincial satellite stations—some with more than one channel—plus a whole range of local channels has dramatically changed the Chinese television landscape, putting a decisive end to the monopoly of CCTV (Zhao 2008a, 96; Zhu and Berry 2009). Furthermore, Chinese viewers are now provided with a perplexing variety of programming packages, including free-to-air CCTV and provincial satellite channels, and additional digital channels delivered via set-top box. This means that both national and provincial channels have to develop distinctive brands in order to remain competitive. For instance, while Hunan TV held an uncontested position as China's top entertainment channel in the first decade of the new millennium, its monopoly has now been challenged by other entertainment channels such as Zhejiang TV, which has captured peak national ratings with its singing contest shows, including *Zhongguo Hao Shengyin* (The voice of China) and Jiangsu TV, which is well known for having pioneered dating shows such as *Fei Cheng Wu Rao* (If you are the one).

In general, scholars have noted the role of television or media more broadly in transforming the public culture of China from a socialist to a market economy (Zha 1995; Barmé 1999). However, Chinese television defies the standard dichotomy between state and private ownership. As an integral part of reforms aimed at commercializing China's media and cultural sectors, the Chinese party-state has adopted a strategy of maintaining state control over the media and cultural sectors while at the same time allowing investment by private capital, both domestic and foreign. While the production of news and informational content is deemed to be too important to be left to the private sector, and thus remains directly under the control of the state, non-news content, including entertainment and advertising content—usually considered to be politically less sensitive—is open to private-sector investment (Zhao 2008a, 202).

The fact that such non-news genres are open to private investment does not mean, however, that entertainment programs are quarantined from direct, and sometimes quite heavy-handed, regulation by state agencies. In recent years, the intention of the State Administration of Radio, Film and Television (SARFT—which changed its title to SAPPRFT in 2013 to include Press and Publishing) has become increasingly interventionist in its drive to secure control over entertainment content. In October 2011 SARFT issued a set of directives that shook up Chinese television in a number of profound ways. Among the changes stipulated in its "Further Recommendations on the Regulation of Provincial Satellite Television Programs" was an increase in the quantity of news, a reduction in the quantity of entertainment content, and an improvement of the quality of remaining entertainment programs. According to SARFT's official spokesperson, these recommendations were intended to address a worrisome tendency toward "excessive entertainization" (*yule guodu hua*). It is clear that "excessive entertainization" referred to both the quantity and quality of entertainment programs. A survey commissioned by SARFT in 2011 found that there were 126 entertainment programs on 34 provincial satellite television stations, mainly dating shows, talent contests, melodramas, games and quizzes, generalist variety shows, and talk shows featuring celebrity hosts. In addition, the "vulgar taste" of entertainment programs and the "widespread uniformity of entertainment formats" on Chinese television were charged with leading to a waste of resources on the one hand and a stifling of content innovation on the other (*Xinhuanet* 2011).

To map the most popular prime-time genres in light of the dual system of regulation by the state and the market, sketched above, in July and August 2011 we conducted a schedule-mapping exercise on six of the highest-rating nationwide channels: Hunan Satellite, CCTV-1, CCTV-2, Liaoning Satellite, Shanghai Oriental, and Jiangsu Satellite.[2] The exercise revealed that on these popular channels, the commonest genres in the evening slots are drama, news and "soft" news (the latter encompassing current affairs, life advice, and talk shows), and entertainment genres including reality, game shows, variety, talent quests, and other competitions.

The ambiguity surrounding the issue of "ownership" in a state-directed commercialized context means that television professionals need to negotiate the dual mandate of making profit and delivering "correct" political content. This has led to three distinct arenas of Chinese television, which are reflected in the popular prime-time genres listed above: a politically "correct" but commercially unviable news sector, a highly popular but potentially risky entertainment sector, and a wide swathe of lifestyle advice programs that cannot compete with pure entertainment genres in terms of ratings but are much less controversial from the point of view of content regulation by state agencies. These lifestyle advice-themed programs feature across CCTV, provincial channels, and city-level television. They are hybrid in nature, combining news, entertainment, education, and public-service elements—and hence do not fit neatly into either news or entertainment categories. Furthermore, although not the highest-rating shows, they generate considerable revenue through product placement, infomercials, and product-sponsorship as well as advertising sales.

Seeing the Chinese version of *Chaoji Jianfei Wang* (The biggest loser) on CCTV's Financial Channel, one could be forgiven for thinking that Western-style reality-lifestyle TV formats had arrived in China in earnest. And indeed, a glance at Chinese TV schedules today reveals that the Chinese television industry has enthusiastically taken up lifestyle (in Mandarin, *shenghuo*) topics. Some of the locally produced lifestyle-oriented shows—like CCTV-2's *The Biggest Loser*—are the product of a rising tide of transnational format trades in recent years with European and U.S. copyright holders including Endemol, FremantleMedia, and the BBC, which as Keane rightly observes are fundamentally reshaping China's television industry (Keane 2015; see also Keane 2002; Keane and Moran 2003; Oren and Shahaf 2012).[3] Other programs combine lifestyle advice with regionally popular genres and aesthetics—for example, the studio-based comic variety shows that hark back to Japanese and Taiwanese roots, as exemplified by Channel Young's *New Queen*, discussed in chapter 2. Increasingly, locally produced lifestyle programs on metropolitan and national channels feature a mix of reality television, dramatized reenactments, studio interaction between audience and host, Oprah-style confessions, makeovers, and competitions between contestants. In addition to these globally familiar format elements, a large number of life advice programs also have a more distinctive local flavor, particularly those on city-level channels, which are mostly set in studio settings reminiscent of classroom learning. Perhaps the most notable example of indigenizing lifestyle TV in China is the accommodation of life advice topics into talk-show formats. The entertainment-oriented Hunan TV's *Baike Quan Shuo* (Encyclopedia), combining wisecracks and banter between hosts and guests with everyday life advice, is one such example (Guo 2011). Despite this wide variety, a couple of dominant themes stand out when we look at the bigger picture of lifestyle advice television in China today. First, there is a high concentration of programs targeting retired viewers—one of Chinese television's biggest audience segments—via health and well-being topics (*yangsheng*). Second, we also see many channels and programs targeting young urban adults aspiring to a cosmopolitan, middle-class ideal. Both of these trends form the basis of detailed discussion in the chapters that follow (see especially chapter 2).

Yet despite all this, "lifestyle television" is not a widely recognized genre in China's television industry. Instead, the term *shenghuo* (literally meaning "life") is used to designate programs covering a wide range of topics connected with daily living. In one of the few scholarly Chinese books on this topic, "shenghuo television" is simply defined as "programs which relate to clothing, eating, dwelling and traveling [*yi shi zhu xing*]" (Leng and Xu 2003, 2). Thus, rather than indicating a surge in glossy reality-lifestyle and makeover shows like those found in prime-time schedules in Western Europe and the United States in recent decades, China's broad shenghuo category captures much material that is akin to infotainment and magazine-style advice programming found on daytime schedules in Anglo-American contexts. The most common categories on these rather more "ordinary" forms of life TV, borrowing from Frances Bonner's use of the term *ordinary television*, are food-related and cooking shows, health and well-being shows, and to a lesser extent travel shows (Bonner 2003). As we argue in the chapters that follow, typical programs in these categories—especially on local city-level channels—suggest that audiences are enticed not so much by promises of cosmopolitanism or a middle-class lifestyle as by the need to reorient oneself in a deregulated, privatized, and therefore disorienting material, moral, and ethical world. Furthermore, our discussions with TV professionals in China reveal that their initial decision to produce these "ordinary" types of life advice programs was generally not a conscious strategy to transplant or indigenize Western-style "lifestyle TV." Instead, it was often aimed more at providing "life information" (*shenghuo xinxi*)—practical information useful for everyday life. This can be linked with a stream of life advice programming that has been present historically in

Chinese television for several decades. For instance, in the late 1950s, Beijing TV ran a number of life advice and hobbyist programs such as *Shenghuo Zhishi* (Life knowledge), *Yixue Guwen* (Medical advice), and *Jiyou Aihaozhe* (The philately enthusiasts) (Peng and Hu 2009). But it is CCTV's *Wei Nin Fuwu* (At your service), launched in August 1979, that is widely credited with having ushered in life advice programs on Chinese television. A studio-based show providing useful information on all aspects of everyday living, *At Your Service* was the first TV show in China ever to feature a television host, and it spawned a plethora of life-themed copycat shows on provincial channels (Guo 2011).

Another distinctive feature of life advice TV in China is its dispersal both throughout the daily schedule and across channels. Although most stations—national, provincial, and local—run a designated shenghuo channel, nevertheless, generally speaking, the programming of life advice content on Chinese television is much more scattered than in Euro-American contexts. Lifestyle programs are found across a wide range of channels that may not initially seem to have much to do with lifestyle topics. For example, *Gou Shishang* (Pretty trendy, discussed in chapter 8), a weekly show with all of the key elements of lifestyle TV—consumption, competition, makeover, confession, reality—airs on CCTV's Financial Channel (CCTV-2), and lifestyle advice programs are also common on CCTV's Science and Education Channel (CCTV-10). Further, segments with lifestyle themes are often embedded in other genres such as news, current affairs, and talk shows. Many shows dispensing life advice can also be found in programs targeting age-specific groups. For instance, *Xiyang Hong* (Red sunset) is a highly popular program on CCTV's flagship channel (CCTV-1), with senior viewers as the target audience. It consists of talk segments, quiz segments, and features segments addressing a wide range of social, economic, cultural, and practical issues facing China's vast aging population. Indeed, for a range of reasons that will be discussed in detail in chapter 2, compared with India and Taiwan, there is an explicit and disproportionate amount of advice offered on mainland Chinese television on topics of health and well-being, targeting senior viewers.

Also distinctive is the fact that in China, most life advice shows—including glossier, high-end versions—air on free-to-air channels and rely directly on advertising for revenue. This means that program producers, driven by ratings, must cater to the broadest spectrum of taste rather than cultivate a niche audience. That is why, as we will discuss in detail in chapter 2, Channel Young, the lifestyle channel of Shanghai Media Group (SMG), has to adopt the dual strategy of pursuing both a specific audience (the channel's primary target audience is young, female, professional viewers) and a more general viewership. Mr. Bao Xiaoqun, CEO of Channel Young, believes that there is a key difference between China's lifestyle programs and their counterparts in English-speaking countries, where high-end lifestyle programs are often aired on pay channels.[4] Channel Young is owned by the Shanghai Media Group, a conglomerate formed in 2004 to monopolize Shanghai's broadcasting, film, and cultural sectors. Like all other channels under the Shanghai Media Group, Channel Young is an operational entity responsible for meeting revenue creation objectives set by the conglomerate, yet it must defer to the group on matters of financial and personnel management (Y. Zhao 2008a). Mr. Bao outlines some of the consequences:

> In the West, there is usually the distinction between pay TV and free-to-air TV. In China, there is very little pay TV and very few specialized channels. As free-to-air channels, you need to rely on advertising, which means that your content has to be generalist. I need to worry about advertising and ratings, so I can't speak exclusively to cultural elites. . . . Shanghai is more cosmopolitan and on average people have more consumption power than in the rest of China, but even so, most of our viewers are ordinary people [*ping min*]. When watching cooking shows or dining-out guides, Chinese viewers are looking for tips on how to save money and find good value; most of them are not interested in style and elegance. . . . The ratings system also determines that Chinese television prioritize entertainment value over information value. . . . So, to put it bluntly, advertising to a large extent determines the content of my programs.

As Mr. Bao's remarks suggest, the particularities of audience demographics for lifestyle advice shows in China shape the types of content produced. Television continues to be the main form of media consumption for particular social groups in China, including rural residents, married women, and the aging and retired population (Zhao 2008a). For this reason, these groups make up the staple demographic groups for China's lifestyle programs. However, while these groups constitute the biggest audience segments, other demographics still represent significant markets. The remarkable rate at which young, educated, urban people's lives have become mediatized means that increasingly, television content is accessed courtesy of Wi-Fi, smart phones, tablet devices, and personal computers. There are now half a billion people in China who can access video material online, with the growth rate of online video access at 32 percent, second only to the growth rate of Weibo use (the Chinese Twitter-like microblogging platform) (Huang 2013, 26). This dramatic change in viewing habits potentially has major implications for the future of lifestyle programs in China, highlighting the potential to cater for audiences not captured by more "ordinary" kinds of daytime life advice programming but who want access to certain kinds of "just-in-time" life advice. As a *New Weekly* journalist remarks, "recipes, parental tips, health and well-being, home renovation, and travel are topics that will never make the flagship shows of a TV station, but they have become gold mines for the online video industry" (Ding 2013, 68). These developments mean that it is increasingly difficult to be sure where, when, and how lifestyle programs are accessed. Given the growing number of people who access video online, it is safe to say that increasingly, it is consumers who are deciding on the specific time, location, and setting in which lifestyle material is watched.

As we have noted, while there is a certain core audience for more ordinary modes of daytime life advice programming, the diversity of lifestyle advice channels, programs, and content on Chinese television indexes the fragmentation of both audiences and television cultures in China today. For instance, Beijing TV's flagship lifestyle program *Yangsheng House*—an example of a more ordinary mode of shenghuo programming—which claims to be the highest-rating health and well-being show (Wang 2012), accounts for its own popularity in terms of its authoritativeness, relevance to ordinary people's lives, and wide appeal to audiences of all groups, especially aging viewers. In contrast, SMG's Channel Young—notwithstanding Mr. Bao's observations about the need to capture a mass audience—consistently targets a "wide niche" consisting of young, professional, female viewers through topics related to beauty, fashion, urban consumption practices, and celebrities and popular culture. Further down the geographic scale, city-level television stations are also enthusiastic producers of local lifestyle shows. Made on a shoestring budget, heavily subsidized by local businesses, and looking decidedly basic—some might say crude—in style, presentation, and content, programs made by these stations (like Anhui's Bengbu TV, discussed in detail in chapter 2) aim to provide to ordinary viewers practical assistance with concrete problems they face in the course of everyday life.

Based on the analysis above, we see that the current situation of "lifestyle television" in the People's Republic of China is marked by three key characteristics. First, the complexly multi-tiered structure of the television industry—where free-to-air channels compete for mass audiences across national, metropolitan, provincial, county, and city levels—produces an extremely diverse array of lifestyle advice content, some of which challenges Euro-American definitions of lifestyle television, while other modes of life programming, particularly those aimed at young professional audiences, share something in common with global, cosmopolitan lifestyle TV. Second, the specific calibrations of regulation by the dual forces of the state and the market position lifestyle content in a uniquely liminal position in China. Lifestyle programs sit between "hard" and "soft" genres and are therefore neither directly controlled by the state (as news is) nor subject to the same degree of interventionist regulation as genres that are perceived as "pure entertainment." Nonetheless, lifestyle TV production remains subject to the just-as-exacting demands of the market, as well as fierce competition for advertising revenue. Third, the fragmentation of audiences and media cultures in China means that multiple points of focus coexist in lifestyle-related programming. These include, on the one hand, a very strong concentration of content targeting retired and elderly audiences, especially on local-level TV and especially via topics connected with health and well-being. On the other hand, we also see programs building a brand by targeting young urban adults aspiring to a cosmopolitan, middle-class ideal; this is especially the case on metropolitan channels like Shanghai's Channel Young (one of our central case studies over the chapters that follow).

Commercialization, "Varietization," Fragmentation: Lifestyle Advice TV in Taiwan

Television was launched in Taiwan in 1962. In the initial decades of its operation, the only channels available were the three terrestrials: TTV, CTS, and CTV. These were owned and managed by various arms of the old Kuomintang (KMT) party-state-military complex. During the dictatorship of the Chiang family (1947–87), media culture was subject to an extreme level of political regulation, in line with the KMT's anti-Communist ideology. Broadcast media, while running as commercial operations, essentially acted as the mouthpiece for the KMT, comparable to the situation across the straits in mainland China, where CCTV acted as the "throat and tongue" of the Chinese Communist Party (Kuang 2011). This situation transformed dramatically in the 1980s, as political reform proceeded hand in hand with media liberalization. Along with the lifting of martial law in 1987, the late 1980s saw the legalization of the opposition Democratic Progressive Party (DPP) and the beginning of a broad cultural and political thaw. Press censorship was lifted, broadcast media were deregulated, and media markets were opened up to private capital investment, both domestic and foreign (Kuang 2011, 74, 75). Two new terrestrial channels were established in the late 1990s. In 1997 FTV, associated with the Democratic Progressive Party—the main opposition party—was established. In 1998 the

Public Television Service Foundation launched Taiwan's first public channel (PTS), and in 2007 it became an umbrella organization for a suite of publicly funded TV enterprises including PTS, Hakka TV, TITV (Taiwan Indigenous Television), plus a recently (semi)nationalized CTS (Chinese Television System). However, the commercial channels outrank this handful of public channels in market share by a very wide margin. In particular, since the early 1990s, the rise of commercial cable channels has fundamentally transformed Taiwan's television landscape.

While free-to-air networks play a dominant role in China's television markets, the television market in Taiwan today is dominated by satellite-to-cable television (to which we refer hereafter simply as cable). Indeed, Taiwan has one of the most highly developed commercial cable television systems in East Asia (Oba and Chan-Olmstead 2005). Servicing a population of just twenty-three million, at the time of writing, the National Communications Commission lists some 270 channels in operation—mostly local, and including both general entertainment channels (GECs) and specialist channels—delivered via satellite to fifty-nine cable television system operators (GIO 2013). Cable channels began operating illegally in the 1970s and after their legalization in 1993 rapidly proliferated (Chen 2002). Based on rating and share figures per channel, the terrestrials were historically the most popular channels, but this dominance has now decisively waned. For example, cable channel San Lih Taiwan has ranked second overall since 2007 (just 0.01 percent of audience share behind terrestrial FTV in 2012), while by 2012 the lowest-rating free-to-air, CTS, had sunk to eleventh place.[5] With low subscription prices and cable packages offering a comprehensive bundle of the available channels, cable TV, considered as a block, is the primary choice of a large majority of viewers (GIO 2009, 2013).

The TV audience in Taiwan, as in much of the region, is increasingly fragmented as a result of the proliferation of domestically available channels, in this case, commercial cable channels. For example, in 2012 the highest-rating channel, FTV, secured an average share of just 6.78 percent (Taipei Media Agencies Association 2013, 12–14). This market fragmentation leads, as it does in China, to extremely intense competition for advertising revenue: indeed, one media researcher proposes that Taiwan's commercial media market may even be the most competitive in the world (Kuang 2011, 78). Given the relatively small size of the domestic audience, specialization based on genre innovation is not a viable strategy here. Although there are dedicated channels across the major genres (news, movies, drama, cartoons, sport, shopping, Japanese, music, finance, religious), the largest group of cable channels are generalist GECs (*zonghe*).[6] Lifestyle TV has not emerged as a viable market niche for local content providers, although as we will see lifestyle advice finds its way into a range of other genres. In Taiwan, international networks dominate this genre, intense competition discourages format innovation, and locally specific histories of content classification tend to turn audiences off at any whiff of the "educational," so that life advice has to be packaged in highly entertaining ways when targeted at a mass audience. We return to each of these points in more detail in the analysis that follows.

Both the television industry and TV content in Taiwan today are governed almost wholly by commercial logic and market forces. Since the legalization of cable systems in the early 1990s, a rash of mergers and acquisitions saw the ownership of cable systems and channels become concentrated in the hands of a small number of commercial media conglomerates (Chen 2002). Following the deregulation of foreign media investment in 1999, cable systems and content providers have been financed by a mix of domestic capital and both direct and indirect international investment, with indirect foreign investment now legalized up to a cap of 60 percent. Foreign part-ownership, however, has had negligible impact on content, with overseas investors treating their Taiwanese television interests simply as investments rather than as opportunities to intervene in the on-the-ground workings of the island's media industries.[7] Effectively, then, media liberalization has seen the KMT party-state's national oligopoly on television channel ownership during the mid to late twentieth century replaced by a transnational commercial oligopoly in the new millennium (Chen 2002; Kuang 2011). In terms of regulation, in contrast to the strict political regulation of TV content both in PR China and in Taiwan's own relatively recent past, Taiwan today has the loosest media control of any Chinese society in Asia, and there remains no direct government censorship of political content (Kuang 2011, 84).[8] Television content, however, is nevertheless highly politicized. Despite a 2005 law prohibiting direct investment in mass media by political parties, the political affiliations of the major commercial stations (whether pro-KMT or pro-DPP) are extremely clear from the political orientation of news and the language, regional, and class politics of drama and other entertainment genres, with these affiliations relating closely to each channel's target audience demographic.

In mid-2011 our schedule-mapping exercise on six of Taiwan's top-rating channels (FTV, San Lih Taiwan, TTV, CTV, CTS, and TVBS News) revealed that drama remains the clearly dominant prime-time genre, followed by news and "Taiwanized" Japanese-style variety shows (discussed below). Cable news channels are the most popular group of channels by genre and offer a mix of hard and soft news content including talk shows, sensationalized current affairs, and celebrity gossip. Daytime TV provides a mix of cartoons, drama reruns, news, and magazine-style infotainment—for example, cooking, health, and travel shows, which, as in China, often incorporate either product placement or thinly veiled infomercials to help recoup profits for ratings-poor morning television. Evening scheduling is remarkably homogeneous across the major commercial GECs. The evening news slot begins at 6 p.m. and is often followed by a current-affairs chat show or variety-style "soft" news program. The prime-time hours—or "golden" slot, as it is called in Chinese—from 8 p.m. to 10 or 11 p.m. are filled with Chinese-language drama serials. On weekends, this slot is typically given over to variety shows, plus, at the time of writing, a rash of talent quests and a sprinkling of life advice programs (cooking and travel shows in particular). Several of the TV industry personnel we spoke with recognized 10 p.m. to 2 a.m. as a slot that could be effectively targeted at the younger generation of professional workers, who typically return late to the multigenerational family apartment after working long hours into the evening, and are only at this hour able to wrest the TV remote away from the elder generation and their beloved dramas. Hence, it is in this slot that, amid the talk shows and drama and variety reruns, we occasionally find programs such as overseas travelogues and design shows whose content (if not genre or format) may in some respects appear comparable with midrange to high-end Anglo-American lifestyle shows.

As the above discussion suggests, in Taiwan as in China the concept of lifestyle television is not much entrenched in the industry, despite the scattered use of the term *shenghuo* (life) to designate various forms of info-ed programming with an everyday life theme. Among ten television professionals we interviewed, not all recognized the concept of lifestyle television, and some—including one senior executive—initially misunderstood the genre to which we were referring, thinking we had in mind either community-service programs directly sponsored by government or old-style hobbyist television (traditional cooking or gardening shows). Searching for locally produced, nonfiction programming instructing its viewer in stylized consumption and related skills pertaining to living in a late capitalist, consumption-oriented society, as in PR China, we find such content scattered throughout a wide array of other genres. As the examples we explore in the following chapters show, these include reality, hobbyist, travel, fashion, design, religious, talk, investment guides, and guides to feng shui, fortune-telling, and other forms of traditional folk belief as well as cultural-educational and sponsored program-length spots advertising particular products or services.

Given this lack of a clearly demarcated lifestyle genre in locally produced content in Taiwan, "lifestyle TV" functions *as a genre* mainly on the specialized cable channels Discovery Taiwan, National Geographic, and the Discovery daughter channel, TLC (Travel and Living Channel), which also operate in many other territories in Asia, including India, Singapore, and Hong Kong. Unlike the GECs, which despite the increase in foreign ownership since 2000 air overwhelmingly local content, these channels air mainly (though not exclusively) imported content, often in English and not always subtitled in local languages. They function as niche channels, narrowcasting to a specific market segment (younger, highly educated, English-competent, professional city-dwellers). As these transnational cable networks have a much wider, international market for their product than local networks, they thrive on a far smaller domestic audience: in 2012, for example, TLC's market share in Taiwan was a mere 0.21 percent (compared with market leader FTV at 6.78 percent) (Taipei Media Agencies Association 2013, 12–14). As we explore in chapter 4, the programs on specialist "lifestyle" channels like TLC Taiwan assume a certain cosmopolitan orientation in their viewer, not just through the largely overseas focus of their programs and the dominance of English but also in other more complex ways.

Why exactly, then, does Taiwan largely lack locally produced lifestyle programming in a more global, generic style? Professed discontent with the homogeneity of commercial programming in Taiwan was ubiquitous among the television professionals we interviewed in researching this book. Those working in the commercial sector expressed the collective view that while they would like to experiment with new genres like lifestyle, with the massive number of cable channels now competing for limited advertising revenue, they are working in an extremely risk-averse environment, with executives unwilling to gamble on departing from the scheduling formula or the tried and true genres. In those scattered instances where local channels have attempted to create copies of overseas lifestyle programs, the programs have failed the ratings test and promptly been canceled. Our industry interviewees suggested this has been due to inadequate budgets and the consequent feebleness of the productions. To the notion of lifestyle programs airing at prime time on major generalist channels, as has happened in Britain, Australia, the United States, and Singapore, the collective response of interviewees was a firm assertion that this is unthinkable in Taiwan under present conditions.

Lifestyle TV in Anglo-American contexts is a genre in which instructional life-advice and entertaining narratives are seamlessly combined. However, in discussing the (non)appearance of "lifestyle" as a clearly defined genre in Taiwan, several industry professionals noted that there may be a specific problem in this context with the attempt to combine instructional and entertainment values. In Taiwan's generic TV taxonomies, they noted, the "educational" is marked off in specific ways. This is most clearly seen in dedicated channels like CTS Culture and Education, which airs programs teaching English, art and poetry appreciation, calligraphy, and so on. The clear demarcation of education from entertainment is in large part a product of the history of TV regulation in Taiwan. The Radio and Television Law, brought into force in 1976, classified television programs into four categories: news, educational-cultural, public information service, and entertainment. Educational-cultural programs were tasked with promulgating the KMT ideology of a mainland China–centric (but anti-Communist) vision of Chinese culture; instructing (female) viewers in practical everyday know-how, including on housework; and supporting the school curriculum. Both viewers and TV producers in Taiwan today have been conditioned by this history to see the educational and the entertaining as fundamentally separate categories. For example, Mr. Wang (pseudonym), a stylist at CTS Culture and Education, noted candidly about his employer:

> It has the educational aspect, but frankly it lacks any entertainment value. It's very informational: a teacher standing there, telling you this and that. . . . [We] just don't seem to be able to get it to the level of, say, the National Geographic channel or Discovery. Everything we do seems to lack that little something. . . . Here, the educational is separated very strictly from the entertaining. . . . But that makes the [educational] shows feel very dead. So *lifestyle* as a genre is divided up between programs—a bit of it here, a bit of it there. No single show qualifies as pure *lifestyle*.[9]

Other industry interviewees concurred that programming perceived as "educational" is a sure-fire audience turn-off. Given the economic unviability of producing local versions of Western-style lifestyle TV, then, life advice content in Taiwan often appears embedded in other, more locally established genres. Key among these is the extremely popular genre of variety television, which is worth now exploring in specific detail.

The ubiquity of the Taiwan-style variety show (*zongyi jiemu*) is a defining feature of Taiwan's television landscape. Furthermore, exports of Taiwan-style variety TV have had defining impacts on overseas TV markets. Historically, this has been the case in the Chinese communities of East and Southeast Asia; today, it is increasingly also the case in PR China, where the popularity of the variety genre continues to grow each year (Wang Lanzhu 2012, 124–40). The case of the variety genre thus illustrates Taiwan's function as a "transfer station" for popular, commercial TV cultures across China, Southeast Asia, and the worldwide Chinese diaspora. It imports genres from elsewhere—especially Japan, as in the case of the variety genre—and "Sinifies" them through adaptation, copying, and Chinese translation, before marketing these to Chinese-speaking audiences worldwide via international distribution and syndication.

In Taiwan, the locally produced variety programs in which much life advice content is embedded today were adapted from Japanese variety formats from the mid-1990s.[10] The Japanese genre was introduced through formal format trades as unlicensed "clones" (direct copies) and as adaptations (with significant elements altered) (Liu and Chen 2003, 56–57, 62–64). Variety shows (*baraeti bangumi*) have been a prominent genre in Japan for several decades, and, along with related genres like the multisegment, multitopic daytime "wide-show" (*waidosho*), make up part of the major (trans)genre of Japanese infotainment TV (Holden and Ergül 2006). Imported Japanese variety shows became popular in Taiwan during the 1990s as part of the general wave of popularity for Japanese media and pop culture occurring at that time.[11] In the mid-1990s, some Taiwanese producers embarked on coproductions with Japanese variety producers, but due to the expense associated with this method it soon gave way to the practice of unlicensed cloning, where variety programs were closely copied, segment by segment, to make local versions.

Despite this ignominious history of copying, today in Taiwan the Japanese-style variety show is so ubiquitous that for the viewers we interviewed its familiarity, along with strong elements of localization (the use of the Minnan language, the centering of Taiwan celebrity culture, a general thematic emphasis on the local and colloquial), lead to variety TV feeling extremely local. It is certainly a significant presence in the weekly TV schedule and a high-rating genre. Our mid-2011 prime-time schedule analysis, discussed above, reveals the stable presence of variety shows between 7:30 and 10 p.m. on weeknights and Sunday nights (though in numbers lower than dramas), with an explosion of variety occurring on Saturday evening when FTV, San Lih, CTV, TTV, and CTS all air at least one variety show between 6 p.m. and midnight, with a rash of them dominating the latter three channels' schedules starting at 8 p.m. Ratings figures indicate that the top-rating variety shows rate in the same ballpark as, but slightly below, the top dramas.[12]

Variety television in Taiwan takes a number of forms, with elements often hybridizing with other genres to create syncretic formats, resulting in a sort of "pan-varietization" of a wide range of TV genres: the variety talk show; the variety talent quest; the variety game show (Yang 2002). In this context, programs classified in TV schedules as belonging to the "variety" category prove to be a rich source of life advice content, as our discussion of variety travel-and-food shows (chapter 4), a variety feng shui program (chapter 6), and variety beauty-and-fashion formats (chapter 8) illustrates. Typical elements of variety shows and variety hybrids include a brightly colored studio set; comedian hosts; groups of four or five people concurrently on set, including celebrity guests who engage in comic banter with the host/s and may also perform songs or other live entertainment; a dominance of group midshots with very few individual close-ups; high-key lighting; and lavish use of postproduction effects including wacky sound effects and vividly colored animated screen text and graphics. As noted above, Taiwanese variety shows are frequently licensed offshore to other Asian markets, especially Malaysia, Singapore, Indonesia, and Hong Kong. In recent years, adapted versions of the genre are also increasingly being produced by the provincial and metropolitan satellite channels in mainland China, often with the direct participation of Taiwanese talents who are increasingly drawn to the opportunities presented by the expansion of mainland China's media industries (Channel Young's *New Queen*, discussed in chapter 2, is one such example; see chapter 8 for a detailed discussion of the Taiwanese original).[13]

Our discussion in this section reveals that the current situation of "lifestyle television" in Taiwan is marked by three key characteristics. First, as in China, there is not a cogent or widely recognized locally produced genre known as "lifestyle television." Instead, lifestyle content in Taiwan appears on Euro-American cable channels like TLC, and, as in China, is scattered throughout a wide variety of locally produced programs and genres. In Taiwan, the variety genre is particularly prominent among these. Second, unlike China, Taiwan is home to a highly deregulated television industry governed almost entirely by market forces, with extremely low levels of state regulation and zero political censorship. The wild proliferation of commercial cable channels keeps risk-averse producers sticking to the established high-rating formats, and hence inhibits the development of a locally produced lifestyle genre. Also tending to discourage the development of such a genre is the specific local history of "educational-cultural" TV—perceived by audiences as boring, and by producers as a sure route to ratings death. Third, as in China, the proliferation of nationally available channels—in this case, cable channels—leads to an extreme fragmentation of the audience and, concomitantly, a very wide array of different types of lifestyle advice programming targeting different audiences, from middle-class urban cosmopolitans and unmarried female office workers to struggling working-class housewives and elderly retired Buddhists. In the chapters that follow, we explore a range of examples from across this wide spectrum.

From Doordarshan to Deregulation: Locating India's Lifestyle TV Industry

While India's first telecast occurred in 1959, television didn't become a mass medium until the late 1970s, with the formation of the state broadcaster, Doordarshan, in 1976, and the coordinated construction of an extensive national broadcast network. From the late 1970s until the opening up of the TV market in the mid-1990s, Doordarshan was the sole TV provider. In its early years the state channel operated as a colonial-style enterprise with a developmentalist ethos, with the first experiments in satellite TV (tellingly titled Satellite Instructional Television Experiment) aimed at "modernizing" the lives of rural audiences through uplifting educational programming on health, education, and agriculture (Jeffrey 2002; Roy 2008; Mazzarella 2012).

In the 1980s, under Indira Ghandi, Doordarshan started to become commercialized, with the broadcaster experimenting in entertainment-oriented programming and, in particular, Hindi soap operas and religious serials, as a means of combining its concern with public pedagogy with a popular commercial agenda (Rajagopal 2001). Following the opening up of the industry to private foreign investment in the early 1990s, Indian television has transformed from a rather narrow and exclusionary model of "nationalized" state television to become, today, one of the largest and most diverse television markets in the world. Programming has become highly commercialized with entertainment channels, featuring a mix of soap operas, movies, talent shows, and reality TV, taking the lion's share of viewership.

Today India has a highly privatized television industry, which, like that of Taiwan, is dominated by cable and satellite channels. In the context of a large nation divided into twenty-nine states and seven union (or federal) territories and characterized by significant linguistic and cultural diversity, television's privatization and deregulation has made for a highly complex industry and audience structure. When we interviewed Niret Alva, the producer of the hugely popular Indian version of *Idol*, in 2010, he suggested that "India isn't one market; it's five or six different markets, simultaneously broadcast in different languages existing on a daily basis, changing every day."[14] Indeed, Alva's comment doesn't come near to capturing the complexity of television in India today. Like China, India's televisual industry functions across a number of (often overlapping) spatial scales or registers including urban, diasporic, regional, and localized TV production and audiences, with audiences engaging with programs sourced and produced across the country, alongside an array of international fare dubbed into local languages.

Where under Doordarshan's statist and developmentalist logics the market tended to be hierarchically split between a middle-class, Mumbai-centric Hindi audience and a poor rural audience, the sociogeography of the TV industry today is more diverse and fragmented (Roy 2008; Chadha and Kavoori 2012). While Mumbai, the home of Bollywood, still functions as a hegemonic entertainment media center, with most of the Indian population living in rural areas (Ghosh 2012), rural-regional television has become one of the key areas of growth in an otherwise crowded media market, while many regional channels offer programming via satellite to "diasporic" urban Indian and global audiences craving television produced in their home town or state (McMillin 2001; Moorti 2004; Chadha and Kavoori 2012; Sen and Roy 2014).

The complexity and fragmentation of the contemporary Indian TV landscape post-deregulation, along with the fact that it has one of the fastest growing television markets in the world, make it hard to capture reliable figures on TV penetration and audience viewing patterns, and there has been much criticism of the limitations and urban bias of the key ratings agency, TAM Media Research, which is being replaced by a new ratings agency (FICCI-KPMG 2014).[15] Ratings measurements are further complicated by the large number of people living in informal settlements, serviced by unregistered cable and satellite connections, and the fact that many rural households participate in communal forms of access and viewing (Jensen and Oster 2009).

These limitations aside, TAM's figures from January 2014 indicate there are 153 million TV-owning households in India (that is, 60 percent of the population), with the large majority (145 million) of those having access to cable or satellite TV (TAM India 2014). While the market is dominated by pay TV, it is estimated there are over three hundred free-to-air, advertiser-driven channels (including those of Doordarshan), which cater to the poorer parts of metropolitan areas as well as to small towns and villages (Kohli-Khandekar 2014). Doordarshan, which now boasts thirty-seven channels and offers free direct-to-home TV via set-top boxes, claims to be the most widely available network (with 1,415 transmitters and 92 percent coverage of the country), especially in rural areas, where a majority of the population lives and where television penetration has hitherto been relatively low.

Pay TV, however, dominates the market in India and by 2018, it is estimated that 90 percent of TV households will have some form of paid cable and satellite access (FICCI-KPMG 2014). Depending on their location in the country, audiences have access to a large range of national broadcasters as well as international, regional, and local satellite and cable offerings. While on the one hand most Indian households have only one TV set and may be dogged by a lack of reliable electricity, on the other hand they have potential access to a growing array of TV technologies, from broadcast, satellite, and cable to direct-to-home television (satellite provided direct to home via a small dish and set-top box), which has become a growing part of the market, particularly in rural areas not well served by network technology.

As in Taiwan, the television industry in India today has been strongly shaped by market forces. The opening up of a once highly regulated state-run industry in the early 1990s to private foreign satellite companies witnessed a radical transformation in Indian television, albeit a transformation that was already ideologically preempted by Doordarshan's embrace of a commercial programming ethos in the 1980s (Rajagopal 2001; Mazzarella 2012). The now well known story of the entry of Murdoch's Star TV into the Indian market in 1991 (and into Asia more broadly)—by no means an easy move for Star, which initially struggled in the complex Indian context before "Indianizing" its production and content—was a key early moment in opening up the market to a range of international and local players, including Sony in 1995. This period also saw the rise of major private domestic channels such as the Hindi channel Zee TV in 1992, and the South Indian Sun network, which today lays claim to being the largest Tamil-language network in the world (Ray and Jacka 1996; Moorti 2004; Chadha and Kavoori 2012).

Against a wider backdrop of deregulation and the opening up of a range of sectors to direct foreign investment, the state went even further in deregulating the TV industry, with the early 1990s seeing the flourishing of satellite dishes and cable infrastructures often provided by entrepreneurial "cablewallahs" (similar to the situation in Taiwan from the 1970s to the early 1990s), providing viewers with their first glimpses of foreign news via CNN and American movies and soap operas (Bajaj 2007). In more recent years the government has further shored up its strongly market-based approach to TV broadcasting through a series of measures including reducing the net-worth requirement of companies to run television channels. The latter measure has not only seen the proliferation of a range of commercial players but has also meant that by 2007 most major political parties, from the Congress Party to the Marxists of Kerala, owned their own TV channels (Chadha and Kavoori 2012).

The Indian government, like that of Taiwan, has largely had a hands-off approach to regulating the industry. However, recent concerns about concentration of ownership and the role of politicians owning media groups for propaganda purposes and for sometimes dubious financial gains has seen intensified public debate over the need for media regulation, with the state now making some attempt to intervene in market processes (Kaul 2013). While India outwardly has a highly pluralized industry in terms of the number of players, as in Taiwan, there is a growing trend toward market concentration and cross-media ownership, with a growing number of alliances between local media companies and major global companies such as Viacom, which co-owns the major Hindi entertainment channel Colours (Chadha and Kavoori 2012). Furthermore, major media companies such as Sun TV and Star India own multiple media platforms while having complicated, hidden ownership structures.[16] Amid growing unease over media concentration and political parties owning media outlets, especially news channels, India's Ministry of Information and Broadcasting has recently pushed for transparency of ownership structures (Kaul 2013).

Much of the concern over ownership has been focused on TV news, where foreign ownership in news channels and newspapers is in fact substantially limited by the state. By contrast, India has allowed 100 percent foreign investment in entertainment television channels, suggesting a laissez faire approach to entertainment genres (Bajaj 2007; Chadha and Kavoori 2012). Here too, however, government has more recently intervened in what was a highly unregulated space, introducing a cap on the amount of advertising permitted in both news and entertainment programming (FICCI-KPMG 2014). While India has content regulations that govern private entertainment channels, which were first introduced through the 1994 Cable Network Television Rules and prevent the industry from advertising alcohol and tobacco, for instance (*Economic Times* 2008), it has had a much more ad hoc approach to regulating content compared with China, largely leaving channels to police content themselves.

However, in a country negotiating rapidly shifting social mores alongside complex religious and cultural sensitivities, content issues are a highly sensitive matter, and while TV channels often heavily self-censor, the government's censorship board is not averse to putting banning orders on channels deemed to have overstepped the moral mark. For instance, in 2013 the lifestyle channel FTV (Fashion TV) had its transmission stopped for ten days for showing "obscene and women-denigrating content" on fashion shows featuring lingerie. Likewise, the lifestyle channel NDTV Good Times was given a warning in 2013 for its show *Life's a Beach*, which features a female anchor dressed in swimwear exploring beaches around the world (*India Today* 2014). Thus, while entertainment genres in India have opened up to international capital and content flows, such interventions by the state alongside regular public controversy over morally dubious programming (as in China, where reality shows often find themselves under significant public scrutiny) mark significant social anxieties about the social and cultural values associated with global programming and formats.

Such controversies aside, the entertainment television sector takes up nearly half of the viewership pie in India, with Hindi general entertainment channels representing the dominant networks, while news channels (including Regional News) accounted for 7 percent of viewership in 2013 (TAM India 2014). As in China and Taiwan, over the period of July–August 2011 we conducted a schedule-mapping exercise of evening viewing (6 p.m. to 11 p.m.), in this case focusing on the six highest-rating Hindi general entertainment channels, which were then Star Plus, Colours, Zee TV, Sony Entertainment Television (SET), SAB (primarily a comedy channel), and Imagine TV.

While these entertainment channels featured a mixture of genres, by far the most commonly aired genre (excluding SAB) was drama, with *saas-bahu* (mother-in-law–daughter-in-law) soap operas featuring prominently in this category. The most common genres after drama were talent shows (singing and dancing competitions), reality shows (such as *Your Court*, a reality-justice show in the mold of *Judge Judy*), reality game shows (such as *Fear Factor India*), and movies, which constitute nearly twenty percent of programming schedules (Chadha and Kavoori 2012). The remaining genres include a smattering of talk shows, business news, and entertainment news. We note here that viewers' "hard" news needs are primarily catered for in India by the large number of cable and satellite news networks available across the country (Mehta 2008).

Given the highly globalized nature of Indian TV programming, lifestyle or infotainment is, not surprisingly, a well-known genre in the industry. As in Taiwan, high-quality international-style lifestyle shows are generally found on dedicated cable channels. However, magazine shows and infotainment programming also make an appearance on a range of other channels, including the GECs and some news channels, though they tend to be scheduled in the daytime and aimed at housewives and the elderly. Where questions of "modern living" and consumer-based lifestyles are perhaps most *nationally* prominent on Indian TV is on reality formats, which are a key feature of prime-time programming on GECs across the country, with regional GECs airing localized versions of international formats (often featuring local celebrities) such as *Big Brother*[17] and also carrying dubbed Hindi reality shows depicting the upmarket lifestyles of northern urbanites (McMillin 2001; Jensen and Oster 2009).

Given that cookery in India has been traditionally associated with housewives and, in professional urban households, is often performed by domestic workers, a landmark reality-lifestyle show has been the competitive cooking format *MasterChef India*, which is based on the UK *MasterChef* franchise. First airing on Star Plus at 9 p.m. on Saturday and Sunday in 2010, it has now run to its fourth season and produced a spin-off version, *Junior MasterChef*, in 2013, which also aired at prime time on the weekend. Meanwhile, one of the most popular "characters" on nonfiction Hindi GECs is the celebrity chef Sanjeev Kapoor, who was a judge on the third season of *MasterChef India*. Star Plus also aired another reality-lifestyle show in 2011, *Wife Bina Life* (Life without wife), in a prime-time slot during the weekend. Based on the British reality show *The Week the Women Went*, the show depicts ten husbands who have to manage their households and look after their children while their wives go on a luxury holiday for six weeks. Aside from these recent reality-based lifestyle forays into prime time, daytime schedules on the GECs, which are largely dominated by soap operas, also feature the odd magazine-style cookery show, health and well-being offerings, teleshopping, and also spiritual lifestyle advice shows, a genre we discuss extensively in chapter 6.

As noted above, the lion's share of glossy high-end lifestyle shows, however, are found on dedicated lifestyle channels as well as lifestyle-related youth channels such as MTV and Channel V. The top-rating lifestyle channels in India in 2011 were TLC (Discovery Networks Asia-Pacific), NDTV Good Times, and Travel XP (TAM 2011). As in Taiwan, these are niche channels targeting cosmopolitan English-speaking urbanites, with TLC India, like TLC Taiwan (chapter 4), largely offering British and U.S. lifestyle content such as Anthony Bourdain's travel and food show *No Reservations*. While based in Mumbai, Travel XP likewise aims for a transnational feel, producing "India-centric" travel shows that can be sold to a global audience. By contrast, NDTV Good Times's programming, which we discuss at length in chapter 5, largely consists of locally made shows featuring home-grown hosts and experts. Indeed, the trend on lifestyle channels is increasingly toward localization, with even the most global of lifestyle channels, TLC, recently developing Indian-based productions such as *Style Inc. with Aalim Hakim*, *Ravinder's Kitchen*, and *Trinny and Susannah's Makeover Mission India*. Here localization and format innovation is enabled by the large and growing nature of the lifestyle TV market in India. While lifestyle programming may only address 1.2 percent of the viewership (FICCI-KPMG 2014), the sheer size of the Indian audience (nearly half a billion viewers) and the fact that lifestyle audiences are seen as premium consumers by advertisers makes this a lucrative emergent market.

A key driver here is also India's large and growing youth population. In contrast to China's aging population, India is predicted to become the world's youngest country by 2020, with 64 percent of its population in the working-age group (Shivakumar 2013). Recognizing this, lifestyle producers are increasingly framing their offerings in terms of the youth market. NDTV Good Times, for instance, recently rebranded itself, changing its tagline from "Live the Good Times" to "Live Young." The channel is also increasingly producing programming in Hinglish (the playful blended "language" favored by savvy young urbanites) and using social media to connect with its audience.

Lifestyle channels have also started to move toward just-in-time targeted program offerings, in recognition that consumption of TV content on screens other than television, such as PCs, mobile phones, and tablets, is a growing phenomenon. There has been a rapid increase in online video viewership in recent years in India, with sixty million people having watched online videos on their PCs in 2013 (FICCI-KPMG 2014). Increasingly, broadcasters are looking to make their program offerings available on YouTube, and the top Hindi GECs Star Plus, Colours, Zee TV, and Sony Entertainment Television are among the ten most-accessed YouTube channels in India (FICCI-KPMG 2014). Interactivity with channels via social media—a nascent but growing phenomenon in India—has been driven in particular by reality TV, with shows increasingly moving from phone voting to voting via websites or mobile apps, while some channels have set up show-specific websites where users can more actively engage in contests and in some cases watch behind-the-scene action. It should be noted that such trends are still fairly limited, given the large social and geographic digital divide in India, with the 2011 census finding that while 20 percent of urban households and 5 percent of rural households now own a computer or laptop, just 1 percent of rural Indian households have an Internet connection (Shrinivasan 2012).

As our discussion above has foregrounded, the state of the Indian lifestyle TV industry has been shaped by three key characteristics. First, processes of deregulation have seen the rapid pluralization and opening up of the market since the 1990s to a range of international and local players. Given the relatively globalized nature of Indian TV programming, lifestyle or infotainment is a well-known genre in the industry, in contrast to China and Taiwan. Second, as in both China and Taiwan, the TV audience for lifestyle programming has become highly fragmented. This fragmentation is further complicated in India by significant linguistic, cultural, social, and political diversity and by distinct divisions along urban and regional-rural lines. As in Taiwan, globally recognizable lifestyle programming is primarily located on niche subscription cable and satellite channels targeted at young professionals living in urban centers. Low-budget magazine and infotainment programming, meanwhile, tends to be found on daytime TV on Hindi and regional GECs, though there is much less of an appetite for this kind of daytime life advice TV in India compared with China. Third, lifestyle television is increasingly being shaped by a strong trend to regionalization in India. For instance, programs on lifestyle channels and lifestyle-oriented reality formats in India are being reworked for regional audiences, reflecting a strong industry shift toward regionally differentiated programming that is supported by a growing local format production industry with an eye to not just indigenous but also diasporic national and international markets.

Conclusion: It's Lifestyle but Not as "We" Know It

In this chapter, we have sought to *situate* the emergence of lifestyle-oriented programming in China, Taiwan, and India by outlining the specific political, economic, and industry contexts that have shaped entertainment television in these countries and by offering a snapshot of their varied and complex televisual landscapes today. While, along with the wider region, these three industries have been shaped since the 1990s by growing commercialization, audience fragmentation, channel proliferation, and transnational flows of capital and content, each country has a highly distinctive industry that continues to be strongly shaped by national and local concerns.

Lifestyle programming here offers an interesting exemplar of the at-once transnational and still profoundly domestic nature of contemporary television. Life advice programming in various guises is a feature of scheduling in all three countries, with audiences in China, Taiwan, and India all having some access to transnational or transnational-style lifestyle fare. However, much life advice content is shaped by two interlinked trends: the localization of transnational trends, and locally specific audience demographics, with audiences increasingly divided along linguistic, cultural, and geographic lines (as is particularly the case in India and Taiwan). In all three countries, content also continues to be shaped by political forces: in China by a complex and at times paradoxical state-driven market engagement, in India by regional political interests, and in Taiwan by the entrenched antagonism between the two major political camps, which links to splits within the national audience along class, cultural, linguistic, and regional as well as political lines.[18] The nuances of the evolving TV landscape in these three countries speak, then, to the broader complexities of local and regional TV industries and cultural economies in Asia and their relation to both translocal and transnational media and cultural flows. In the next three chapters, we focus on how such flows have shaped audience understandings of city versus rural, the nation, the globe, and relations between self and other. Drawing from our interviews with viewers of lifestyle advice TV in China, India, and Taiwan, chapters 2, 3, and 4 focus on people's imaginative construction of place at a range of scales, from the perceived relation between regional localities and national metropolises to the complex relation between identification with a national homeland and the alluring vision of limitless global mobility.

TWO. Local versus Metropolitan Television in China
Stratification of Needs, Taste, and Spatial Imagination

Wang Weimin is a reporter for *Life Weekly* supplement of the *Shanghai Youth Daily*, a publication that describes itself as a "must-read for those who want the best quality life in the city."¹ The weekly supplement specializes in tracking the latest fashion, celebrities, and urban lifestyles in Shanghai. On July 27, 1996, Wang wrote a short commentary on a seemingly trivial matter. In "Women Running around in the Street Wearing Shoddily Made Sandals," Wang barely hides his contempt for these women displaying inferior taste, and lets it slip—presumably much to his regret—that these women are mostly rural migrants from Anhui and northern Jiangsu Provinces.

> These women wear shoddily made sandals and run around the streets of Shanghai advertising their own sense of fashion. Regional differences can be accounted for in terms of history, culture, and economy, and this difference can be embodied in the women from these places. Shanghai may be open to people who are unconventional, free-spirited, or uninhibited but we do not tolerate those who are uncouth, vulgar, and cheap. If you belong to the latter and prefer to run around in the streets wearing shoddily made sandals, you leave us with no choice but to call you a country bumpkin. (Wang 1996)

Wang's one-thousand-word article caught the attention of an Anhui reader, Xu Fei, who forwarded it to the editor of Anhui's provincial evening paper *Xin'an Evening Post*. On August 7, *Xin'an Evening Post* reproduced Wang's entire article, accompanied by a feisty editorial condemning the acrimony and arrogance displayed by the Shanghai reporter. Wang's article incurred the collective ire of Anhui citizens, and precipitated a minor cultural debate characterized by mutual resentment and hostility. The media of a number of other provinces such as Jiangsu and Henan, from where large numbers of labor migrants also travel to metropolitan cities such as Shanghai, joined in the debate. Xu Fei was scathing in his denouncement of the superiority displayed by Wang and his like, describing it as "typical of Shanghai people's colonial mentality and obsequiousness to the West," "wearing the fake garb of civilization" and "displaying nothing but their own place-based prejudices" (Xu 1996, 1).

Geographic literature concerned with the impact of economic reforms in China has made two points very clear. First, economic reforms over the past three decades have intensified socioeconomic stratification in China, and inequality, often measured in economic terms, is in fact intrinsically spatial. China's economic development policy has mostly adopted an inequitable approach giving propriety and preferential treatment to tier-one, coastal, and southern cities (C. Cartier 2013b). Second, rather than reducing spatial inequality, the era of economic reforms has created a new "geography of inequality" (Oakes and Schein 2006), consolidating the division between the urban and rural, the "last ultra-stable bipolar scales that resist deconstruction" (J. Wang 2005, 8). The debate between Shanghai and Anhui over the phenomenon of migrant women wearing cheap sandals is a debate surrounding geographically informed taste, fashion sensibility, and cultural capital. As the quote above demonstrates, the debate also highlights the distinctive form of each place's geographic imaginary of the other ("vulgar" Anhui; "arrogant" Shanghai). The meaning of such a debate cannot be fully understood without situating it in the larger context of the geography of inequality. With the advent of transnational capital into China, we have witnessed the emergence of metropolitan places—Shanghai, Guangdong, Shenzhen—as markers separating transnational spaces in China from those which are inland, rural, and relatively poor. These metropolitan places, which have experienced some of the most rapid economic growth in world history (Cartier 2001), have been imagined as a global forward-looking space inhabited by "successful people" (*chenggong renshi*), "white-collar beauties" (*bailing liren*), and "new rich" (*xin gui*). Mass media in China, particularly advertising, often use these terms to signify cosmopolitanism and urban middle-class consumption culture, and to promote the idea of success and upward social mobility. In these media narratives and images, coastal locations such as Shanghai, Shenzhen, Guangzhou, and Xiamen are magnetic places attracting individuals from China's northern, inland regions and provinces (Sun 2010).

Rural migrant women wearing cheap sandals running around in the streets of Shanghai also embody—literally—the contested relations between places shaped by various geographic scales. Social scientists working in the Chinese context have always understood China's spatial organization in terms of fixed scales of place—the world, the nation, the province, the municipality, the county, and the village. This scalar framework has also been fine-tuned by feminist geographers, who argue that the analysis of scale needs to be extended to that of the home and the body (Marston and Smith 2001). In the case of China, the consensus is that China has the longest history of scale-making in the world, and the Chinese state has always played a central and active role in various processes of fixing, maintaining, and regulating scale (Oakes and Schein 2006). On the other hand, China scholars, especially those in the business of documenting social and economic changes in the era of economic reforms, have shown that scale is never fixed and is in fact subject to change and active shaping and maintenance by various political, social, and economic forces (Oakes 1998, 1999; Cartier 2001, 2002). Furthermore, new modalities of scale can emerge to replace the old ones, and many social and economic activities in the reforms era are undertaken with the purposes of "transcending" and "jumping scales" for the sake of economic, social, and cultural gain (Sun 2012).

Metaprocesses in the era of economic reforms such as urbanization, migration, and modernization are the main prisms through which such scale-jumping activities are often viewed. And two hundred million internal migrants who have left their villages and traveled to Chinese cities despite the widespread urban discrimination against them testify to the strong desire and capacity of individuals to push the limits of scale. Anhui rural migrant women wearing cheap sandals may have done better for themselves in economic terms by coming to Shanghai than staying in the village (and they may have embraced what they consider to be an urban style with enthusiasm), but they have also brought themselves under the more direct and judgmental gaze of Shanghai cultural elites. In other words, while they have jumped scale by leaving the village, they are seen to be unable to shed the taste, sensibility, and lack of cultural capital one associates with the rural, the provincial, the "country bumpkin."

Although only five hundred kilometers apart in distance and both located in east China, Shanghai and Anhui present themselves as logical points of comparison and contrast. Separated by the Yangtze River, the dividing line between northern and southern China, they represent the difference between the coastal and the inland, south and north, urban and rural, metropolitan and rural/regional. As a tier-one city with a long history of economic development including in colonial times, Shanghai benefited from the central planning regime of the Maoist state, whose spatial organization ensured unfair advantage in the national distribution of natural resources. The city is blessed with the most modern infrastructural and administrative resources in the country (C. Cartier 2001) and has the highest concentration of middle-class consumers (C. Cartier 2013a). By contrast, rural Anhui is one of the largest sending zones of internal labor migrants, many of whom have gone to Shanghai. Shanghai people's spatial imagination of Anhui is that of poverty and backwardness (Sun 2002, 2005), whereas Anhui people's imagination of Shanghai is that of prosperity, cosmopolitanism, and—as evidenced in the vociferous criticism of Shanghai people's place-arrogance in the "sandal scandal"—cultural snobbery.

The "sandal scandal" points to the pivotal role of lifestyle media in the cultural economy of placemaking. It raises a few important questions, which existing media and popular cultural studies frameworks are ill equipped to address. How are media practices shaped by the cultural politics of scale? Do media work to fix and maintain scale, or do they also aim to jump and transcend scale? How does the "new geography of inequality" (Oakes and Schein 2006) structure and inform the business strategies, discourses, and forms of the media in a given place? What kind of needs and sensibilities are deemed to be place-appropriate and how do these principles help shape locality-appropriate taste, outlook, and geographic imagination?

As the previous chapter makes clear, the four-level structure of television in China and the vastly diverse nature of their *shenghuo*-themed programs point to the epistemological and methodological pitfalls of studying China's cultural production sector as a single-scaled, national phenomenon. Studies of Chinese television so far have not only betrayed an urban, technological, and class-based bias but have also largely ignored the formations of local media cultures below the scale of the province (Sun and Chio 2012). For instance, bearing the brunt of the growing spatial inequality between rural and urban, the inland and the coastal, and the smaller cities and booming metropolises, county-level and municipal-level terrestrial television has remained an invisible sector in Chinese television studies (Sun 2013). Comparative studies juxtaposing industry economics and cultural economy of placemaking between media entities of different scales are even scarcer.

This chapter explores the formats, structure of taste and needs, and spectrum of geographic imagination on Chinese television. It does so by pitting the shenghuo programs produced on two channels against each other: Channel Young in Shanghai, which is more globalized in format and outlook; and Bengbu Television (BBTV), a small, municipal-level, and terrestrially relayed television station in Bengbu City, Anhui Province. The case study draws on data from our four-year studies of Channel Young and Bengbu Television—consisting of interviews with senior managers and program producers, one-on-one in-depth interviews with television viewers, and extensive analysis of lifestyle programs from 2010 to 2013. In what follows, we first examine a number of ways in which Shanghai's Channel Young participates in the cultural economy of placemaking. How does Channel Young, "a Shanghai-based TV station that focuses purely on fashion and urban lifestyles, the only one of its kind in China" (Xu 2011), conjure up a sense of what Shanghai was, is, and should be like? We then turn to the priorities, needs, and place-specific concerns that inform the production of lifestyle programs on BBTV, and ask how the politics of scale is played out in programming that targets provincial and semirural viewers.

Lifestyle Programs on Shanghai TV: Between Good Value and Good Taste

Media and cultural studies literature interested in studying the culture of production points to the need to look at the vision and aspiration of individuals who are centrally involved in the production process (Du Gay et al. 1997). The CEO of Channel Young, Mr. Bao Xiaoqun, a Shanghai native in his forties, is a man of vision and aspiration. Having obtained his PhD in literature in France a few years ago, he returned to Shanghai, full of ideas about producing his own high-end lifestyle television programs in China that would match, both in quality and appeal, the themed lifestyle programs one finds on dedicated lifestyle channels on pay TV in the West. To Mr. Bao, if high-end lifestyle programs are to be produced in China, sophisticated Shanghai rather than materialist Beijing is the logical place to do so.

> It's hard to generalize, but people in Shanghai do pay more attention to the finer things in life. Unlike people in Beijing, people in Shanghai don't go for externalized, overt displays of luxury. Instead, they like finesse, details, and they know better than anyone else how to enjoy life. People in Beijing may have higher consumption power but they also have different consumption values. A Beijing person may equate price with style, so they would go for big brands such as Salvatore Ferragamo or Chanel. A Beijing person may wear a Dior jacket but a pair of Chinese peasant-style cloth shoes. You are not likely to see this kind of fashion disaster in Shanghai. A fashion-conscious person in Shanghai may choose her clothes from a tier-two retailer such as the Spanish Zara, but because

she knows how to match in terms of color, texture, and accessories, she looks more stylish, although in an understated way.²

It is clear that Mr. Bao views Shanghai as the natural leader in fashion and taste. While Wang Weimin (quoted at the start of this chapter) scoffs at cash-strapped rural migrants, Mr. Bao's object of derision is the cashed-up new rich in Beijing. Unfortunately for Mr. Bao, the middle-class Shanghai people whom he appreciates and understands, who know how to enjoy the finer things in life and have sophisticated taste in fashion and style, make up only a small percentage of the Shanghai population. People of refined taste are also the most elusive target audience group as far as lifestyle television programs are concerned. Watching a fashion show in Paris on Channel Young with us, one Chinese young man now working in an advertising company in Shanghai remarked that "those who watch this show cannot afford the fashion, whereas those who can afford it do not watch such shows." This is a reality that Mr. Bao and his colleagues cannot escape: Shanghai, like the rest of China, consists not only of a "consumer stratum" (*xiaofei jieceng*)—high-income earners who have the capacity to pursue a consumer lifestyle—but also the "wage-dependent stratum" (*gongxin jieceng*), who "needed to calculate on a daily basis how to make ends meet and whose pastimes were limited largely to viewing television or movies" (Ren 2013, 36). Much as he may detest their taste and aesthetic sensibility, catering to the needs of the latter, Mr. Bao realizes, constitutes the "bread and butter" of Channel Young's programs. This is a conundrum that confronts Mr. Bao on a daily basis:

> People with good education and cultivated taste do not watch free-to-air TV.... So the biggest problem I'm facing here is that I have to operate in a free-to-air type of competitive environment, so I can't produce high-end lifestyle TV such as the Oxygen Channel in the United States or FTV in France.... I'd like to produce cooking shows like Martha Stewart, but I know these won't work in China. The majority of our viewers are not interested in the techniques of cooking fine food; they are interested in shows that tell them where to buy a good bowl of wonton or plate of fried dumplings.... For most of our viewers, entertainment is more important than actual information.... I've thought about introducing competition cooking shows but I know that there won't be enough people watching it.... So you can see that my challenge is to juggle the need for high ratings and my own desire to produce professionally excellent but niche programs.

Mr. Bao's assessments are borne out by an independent survey of Channel Young's audience, which finds that 42.5 percent of the viewers value the entertainment dimension of the shows, 29.3 percent value the knowledge these shows provide, 21.5 percent appreciate the practicality of the advice on offer, and 6.7 percent like the topical nature of these shows (Shen 2009). The preference for entertainment over knowledge acquisition is, according to Mr. Bao, the hallmark of a lowbrow audience. As was mentioned more than once in our interviews with Mr. Bao and his staff, while Channel Young's ideal viewers are people between twenty-five and forty years old, mostly female, white-collar professionals with high incomes and a high level of education, the demographic of the actual audience is much more diverse. Our interviews with viewers suggest that Channel Young is watched by both men and women, white-collar professionals and suburban housewives, and those well over the age of forty. This diverse demographic composition may explain why as many as 51 percent of the viewers, when asked which kind of host they prefer to see in these shows, preferred a host who looks like an "ordinary person" (*ping min*), whereas only 17.5 percent surveyed preferred a host with style and elegance (Shen 2009). As we discuss in subsequent chapters, this is rather different to Taiwan and India, where celebrity is perceived, at least by producers, as key to the success of host-based programming no matter the class location of audiences.

Caught between the desire to produce high-end lifestyle shows and the reality of having to cater to the taste of the plebeian (or in Mr. Bao's words, "common people"—*ping min lao bai xing*), Channel Young has to cater to both a mass and a niche audience. This is where Mr. Bao differs from Wang Weimin, the fashion writer at the center of the "sandal scandal." Whereas Wang's position highlights class difference and unequal social relations between Shanghai cultural elites and rural migrant workers, Mr. Bao and Channel Young have to come up with strategies that pander to the sensibility of good value, on the one hand, and speak to the notion of good taste, on the other. It is often noted that in advertising for the latest brands and high-end consumer products, middle-class lifestyle and values are marketed in aspirational terms (Goodman 2008; Chen and Goodman 2013a), didactically teaching people how to consume and in doing so, "constructing notions of upward mobility" (Cartier 2013a, 39). But questions still remain as to how class difference or even class tensions are managed and negotiated in cultural terms in China. That overt strategies are often required is evidenced by the two-pronged modus operandi adopted by Channel Young. An examination of their approach is instructive; it gives us a glimpse into how Channel Young negotiates a complex and often paradoxical structure of taste by simultaneously connecting to the grassroots, on the one hand, and imposing a top-down projection of middle-class lifestyle aspirations, on the other.

The Cultural Economy of "Good Value"

In our conversations with producers of Channel Young's lowbrow shenghuo programs, the term *jie di qi* (staying close to the ground/grassroots) came up a few times. This term describes an ethos that is reflected in both the strategy of product branding and everyday decision-making in terms of style, televisual aesthetics, and content. The outcome of adopting this principle in production is a range of popular programs, which are heavily sponsored by advertisers and business entities and focus on shopping for value, and in doing so, ensure high ratings and hence advertising revenue. As we will demonstrate below, this strategy speaks to the desire for "good value," a collective ethos widely associated with Shanghai consumers. These programs encourage viewers to identify with Channel Young as a local channel for the Shanghainese, regardless of their socioeconomic status and level of sophistication. Although the relentless pursuit of ratings has driven many of Channel Young's programs into an early grave, a number of long-running shows have survived and proved to be the biggest earners of advertising dollars. These include programs covering a wide range of themes, such as cooking, shopping, fashion, beauty care and beauty products, and eating out, which offer advice, information, and guides for viewers who are looking for a good bargain, good value for money, and enjoy the pleasure of life while still living within one's means. (*Renqi Meishi* (Popular food), *Jin Ri Yinxiang* (Today's impression), *Zuoyou Shishang* (Fashion left and right), and *Shenghuo Wuyu* (Life stories) fall into this category. A few imported formats, including one based closely on Taiwan's *Nüren Wo Zui Da* (Queen) (see chapter 8), about women, fashion, and beauty care, also fall into this category.

Popular Food, a daily show, for instance, takes viewers to the streets in the city and suburbs, and shows them places to have a reasonably priced meal. One segment of the show, "Today's Search and Find" (October 22, 2010), takes viewers to a small café where "white-collar professionals," for the price of thirty-eight to forty-five yuan, can have a very good work lunch. The food sleuth, our reporter, dressed in casual and street-smart clothes, a mobile microphone in hand, jovially fronts up to patrons, puts them in the frame of the camera, asks a few quick questions about the food they are eating, and then moves on. Shot on location, with natural ambient sound, and in a friendly and

Figure 2.1. A reporter talks to punters about the food diners are eating on *Popular Food*, Channel Young, October 24, 2014.

casual atmosphere, *Popular Food* is typical of the lowbrow end of the consumer guide shenghuo programs on Shanghai Media Group's (SMG) Channel Young. The camera inevitably zooms in on the food on the plates, and then moves to customers who are asked by the reporter to give their verdicts on whether the café is good value for their money (see figure 2.1). Viewers are told, of course, where the café is and how to get there. The show clearly targets young professionals—a staple audience for Channel Young—who regularly go to cafés nearby their office for lunch.

Another long-running show catering to those looking for good value is *Today's Impression*, a consumer guide to fashion shopping. A regular segment of the show is called *Sale of the Day*, where a reporter will go to a sale, find out the price of fashion and clothing items that are discounted, and recommend them to viewers. The reporter talks to the salesperson, finds out about the price, and tells viewers how much money they can save after the discount. Conversations with the producers of these food and fashion programs point to the obvious commercial logic of their production. According to Wang Shuzhen, the producer of *Today's Impression*, fees received from the shops featured in these shows make up a considerable percentage of the show's income. These shops are prepared to pay Channel Young big sums in sponsorship for the customers the programs bring. According to a report on Channel Young that appeared in the *China Daily* newspaper, "every boutique store, restaurant or garment that it recommended attracts huge custom the next day, with customers lining up to buy into the fashion" (Xu 2011).

Aside from this commercial logic, staff members at Channel Young are keen to stress that the popularity of these shows lies in the fact that they do not set out to "teach" consumers about taste and style. They merely give you the permission to consume within your means and still get good value for your money. By doing so, they resonate with one aspect of consumption practice that Shanghai people relate to well: the art of enjoying life without spending too much money. For the pragmatic, price-sensitive Shanghai residents, "getting good value" (*he suan*) is rated much higher than conspicuous consumption.

But Shanghai people's desire for good value is not the same as wanting to buy the cheapest things. Many of our interviewees, including both Shanghai natives and recent migrants, noted that people in Shanghai have an eye for the fine things and are known for their attention to detail. To those interviewees who appreciate these Shanghai "traits," the descriptive words they used were "refinement" (*jingxi*) and "being particular" (*jiangjiu*). To those who do not appreciate them, the words used are "shrewd" (*jing*), "pragmatic" (*xianshi*), and "penny-pinching" (*jing da xi suan*). Duan Fang, thirty-four, from northern China, works in an advertising company in Shanghai. To her, Shanghai is a living paradox and its television programs feel quite Western in outlook, yet in spirit, they are not cosmopolitan:

> What do I feel about the programs on Shanghai TV? Well, I think that they conjure up the texture of ordinary folks' everyday lives and they really embody the spirit of "little people," but at the same time, you can tell that they also try to look foreign, well, yes, I mean Western. . . . How do I see their intention? Well, you can tell by the kinds of bourgeois sentiments [*qingdiao*] they demonstrate and their ways of rationalizing things [*shuofa*]. . . . Even though Shanghai is about ensuring the enjoyment of small things in everyday life, people here tend to feel superior. Shanghai TV is very different from national television. CCTV is much grander, looking at bigger issues and aiming to introduce important social values.

The paradoxical nature of Shanghai life—being able to enjoy the fine things in life while remaining deeply anchored in everyday life—is also noted by Jia

Min, a twenty-eight-year-old university lecturer who was born and brought up in Shanghai, and who sees this as central to Shanghai's appeal: "As a Shanghai person, I feel that Shanghai people love refined things and know how to enjoy life. People here do not necessarily chase luxury goods. Instead, if you walk around in the streets and back lanes in Shanghai, you will find that people appreciate things of good quality in everyday life."

A key aspect of these shows is their capacity to motivate viewers to act on and experiment with trying out "new" things. Our interviews with viewers in Shanghai suggest that it is quite common for a viewer to take the advice from these shows and "try it out." Yang Lin, a twenty-one-year-old university student from Hangzhou, now living in Shanghai, is one of these viewers. "I am always interested in trying out snacks with local flavor. These shows sometimes tell you which snack places sell what kind of specialty foods, especially in the areas of Temple Garden [Cheng Huang Miao] and Huaihai Road. Last week, they recommended a street specializing in snack places on Yunnan Road, so a few friends and myself looked it up on the Internet to figure out how to get there, and we went there on the weekend."

Mundane as it is, the activity of going out with friends, trying something new and different, and enjoying the comfort and pleasure of small material self-indulgences may well engender what the anthropologist Yunxiang Yan calls "a new kind of sociality" made possible by the arrival of consumerism. Such everyday consumption-based activities adopted by Chinese individuals, especially young people in big cities, encourage individual desires and aspirations, and are ideologically the polar opposite of what Yan calls the "organized sociality" typical of the prior socialist era, in which the state plays a central role (Yan 2009, 229–30).

Yi Ran, a twenty-four-year-old bank clerk, is from a rural township on the outskirts of town, and is now living in a flat purchased for her by her parents. To her, the informational and guidance value of these shows is plain to see:

> I think they do have quite an influence on how we spend money. Personally, I often watch these shows which recommend certain items of clothing as well as give suggestions on how to match accessories. . . . Yes, I have watched those shows where they grab someone on the street and offer him/her the opportunity for a quick makeover. . . . I found myself thinking: if I was there and if they approached me, I'd be in fact happy to participate. I think it would be fun to see how they dress me. But I wouldn't go so far as to register to become a contestant on their shows.

But it would be misleading to assume that these shows merely give practical consumer information by appealing to people's sense of good value. By immersing themselves in the material world of food, clothes, and other consumer goods, contributing to what Daniel Miller (2009) calls the "comfort of things," they also contribute on a quotidian basis to the formation of a normative idea of consumer citizenship. After all, in China, a good citizen is not only loyal to the Party and the nation but, equally importantly, also does his or her bit to spend money and engage in consumption, which is crucial to the sustained economic growth of the nation. At the same time, however, in the same way that the collectivist vision of socialism is not totally hegemonic, the ideology of consumer citizenship also has its skeptics and critics. Increasingly, it is in the quotidian decision of either going along with, ignoring, or critiquing consumer advice in the process of media consumption that individual subject positions are defined in the neoliberal economy. Our interviews suggest that not all consumers take on the assessment of price and their associated values wholesale. Thirty-year-old Yu Jia is a Shanghai native working in a bank specializing in lending and mortgages. Influenced by his wife's viewing habits, he has become quite familiar with these consumer advice shows. He acknowledges the practical value of these shows but is critical of their tendency to make assumptions about viewers' spending capacity: "These shows have introduced some consumer ethos. For instance, its constant mention of sales and discount, as if customers can always get good value for their money. But the reality is these shows keep enticing people to buy things they do not need and cannot afford. Some people don't realize that the prices are much higher than they can afford, even though they are supposed to be on discount and are not expensive by the guide's standard. They have gradually come to accept these prices as normal and reasonable, even if they are incompatible with their income."

The Importance of Good Taste

But Channel Young is not content with simply providing practical consumer guides. While Channel Young is considered a major commercial success, CEO Mr. Bao declared that its main mission was not to simply "pursue business numbers"; instead, "we want to influence the way the Chinese live" (J. Xu 2011). Here, Channel Young also wants to provide what cultural elites such as Mr. Bao and Mr. Wang think their viewers need. The aim here is a consciously pedagogical one: to lead viewers to identify, aspirationally, with the cultural taste, consumption values, and aesthetic standards befitting people from, to use Mr. Bao's words, "a higher social stratum." The popular, lowbrow shows discussed above take care of the station's "bottom line"; through their coverage of the "bread-and-butter" topics pertaining to everyday life, they appeal to a distinct consumer desire for good value. However, the real ambition of the channel is to advocate good taste rather than good value. According to Mr. Bao, Channel Young aims at "promoting good fashion and guiding ways of life" (*changdao shishang, yinling shenghuo*). Mr. Bao and his production team are active cultural intermediaries, consciously and conscientiously performing their role in defining, teaching, and constructing knowledge about what constitutes good taste, sophisticated fashion, and a desirable lifestyle. And to perform this role effectively, an array of symbolic resources—both Chinese and foreign—are marshaled.

One significant symbolic resource drawn upon by Mr. Bao and his team is the city's colonial past. Tropes of the glamorous cultural modernity of "old Shanghai," perpetuated in popular cultural icons and literary representations by modern-era writers such as Zhang Ailing (Eileen Chang) and contemporary ones such as Wang Anyi, hold a lasting fascination for cultural elites today. In the reforms era, images and icons of old Shanghai are endlessly reproduced to signify Shanghai's "classy past" (Donald and Zheng 2009, 504), a key dimension in the competitive market of placemaking. In 2002 Channel Young, then known as the Life Channel of Shanghai, made a fifty-two-episode documentary series titled *Shimao Waipo* (Fashionable granny). Through old footage, visual material, stories, and interviews with elderly Shanghai individuals who lived through the decades of the 1930s and 1940s, the series provided a nostalgic account of Shanghai's colonial past, its claim to feminine beauty, and its leadership in a bourgeois lifestyle associated with modernity. It also cashed in on Shanghai's reputation as the "Paris of the Orient" and the "paradise of Western adventurers." Narrated by a seventy-year-old granny, the retired but eminently fashionable Shanghai artist Zhou Liangliang, the series devotes each episode to one particular icon and aspect of the consumption practices in colonial Shanghai, evoking vividly the sound of the trolley buses in the Shanghai streets, the experience of visiting the four earliest big department stores on Nanjing Road, the place of mahogany furniture in Shanghai people's homes, old residents' memories of attending a Shanghai-style wedding, and the sounds and sensation of going to see a Shanghai opera. Zhou, the "fashionable granny" who narrates the series (see figure 2.2), has become a "certifiable carrier" of "middle-class or bourgeois life" (Donald and Zheng 2009, 504). The series was repeated in 2012 to 2013, bringing forth a renewed sense of pride

Figure 2.2. Zhou Liangliang hosts the Channel Young show *Fashionable Granny*, July 24, 2012.

and appreciation for Shanghai's bygone eras, and providing a historical context for the repeated claims of Shanghai as the capital of modern, bourgeois taste.

The discursive attempt to recuperate the spirit of an earlier, classier Shanghai is motivated by a widely held perception of the old Shanghai as a repository of bourgeois sentiments, taste, and cultural practices. For many viewers, watching Channel Young's programs simultaneously evoked and frustrated their desire to relive the glamour and sophistication associated with Shanghai in the 1920s, 1930s, and 1940s. Hong Sen, a twenty-five-year-old fashion designer and native of Shandong Province, believes that Shanghai owes its claim of cultural capital to its colonial past, which unfortunately is impossible to reproduce:

> I've read about people who lived in the old Shanghai. They were particular about what they wore; they looked up to Paris and London for inspiration in regard to style and elegance.... They pursued a much higher standard of beauty.... Even on winter days, women would wear *qipao* [cheongsam], with a high slit over the thigh. And if she came from a wealthy family, she might wear a fur stole over her shoulders.... If Shanghai had maintained that level of sophistication, its lifestyle programs would rival those of Paris and the UK. But today's Shanghai is not

Figure 2.3. Channel Young's *X Files* updates viewers with the latest fashion from Paris. This clip is a special on shopping in the Champs Élysées, July 31, 2010.

as refined as the old Shanghai, although its television does try to capture the essence of that spirit. The end result, to some degree, is some kind of compromise between the imaginary of the past and the reality of now.

If cultural elites and audiences in Shanghai look to the past for inspiration, they also selectively identify symbols of style and quality from outside China. Acutely aware of Shanghai's reputation as one of Asia's global cities, Channel Young sets its benchmark to be on par with Tokyo, Seoul, Taipei, Hong Kong, and farther afield to Europe, especially France. To both Mr. Bao and Hua Yang, producer of *X Dang'an* (X files), a high-end fashion show that focuses on the latest fashions and lifestyles in Europe, France has proven to be a constant source of inspiration (see figure 2.3). A Shanghai native and an elegant woman in her late thirties, Hua gives a clear sense of her vision behind some of Channel Young's "niche-audience" (*xiao zhong*) programs such as *X Files*.

> We may tell our viewers about how the French produce and consume red wine or what kind of garden people cultivate, or about their skating culture, but we hope that behind our accounts of their material culture, we are able to introduce certain attitudes, about how they spend time, use space, and how people relate to nature and to each other.... That's right—we hope to introduce the humanistic values that are associated with these material practices. Since these countries have experienced

modernity much earlier than us, we believe that these practices may have embodied their reflections and responses to modern life.... We are not saying that everything in these Western countries is better than us, but by giving them a different way of living a life, we hope that our viewers will think about questions such as what is beauty and what is important in life. We would like to "get away from the vulgar" [*tuo su*] and touch something in the hearts of our viewers. Even though a few of our programs don't have good ratings [*X Files* is scheduled at midnight], they are still worth pursuing. Mr. Bao and I are in agreement on this.

In the spirit of promoting excellence, refinement, and understated style, Channel Young actively promotes the brand names that embody these qualities, especially those from Europe, France in particular.

Viewers of these programs are not directly encouraged to go out and purchase these brands. Rather, they are offered exposure to a standard of living and an attitude to life that the channel's executives consider worth emulating. In other words, unlike the consumer-advice shows discussed above, which aim to encourage viewers to go out and spend money, this other group of programs is more aspirational in its modes of addressing the audience. Both operate, however, on the same assumption that, as Yunxiang Yan (2009, 227) observes, consuming properly and stylishly has become so important that consumption know-how itself has become a commodity. This know-how includes not only what to buy and where to consume but also, more importantly, what brand, style, and forms of consumption epitomize good taste. In the last week of October 2010, Channel Young's program *Wending Shijie* (A world of excellence) ran three stories on well-known brand names: the history and story of Hermes, a French accessories brand; Max Mara fashion, an Italian luxury fashion chain with French influence; and van Cleef & Arpels, a French jewelry brand. Combining biographic profiles of the vision and ambition of the individuals involved with the development of the brands, these stories consistently promote the idea of excellence, refinement, and meticulous attention to detail.

These shows, by the producers' own admission, do not rate well, but discerning viewers who do watch them appreciate their pedagogic value, as evidenced in the statement from Hong Sen, the twenty-five-year-old fashion designer quoted earlier: "These programs featuring high-end luxury brands separate audience members with good taste from those without. They also play an important educational role. Sure, these brands are expensive and most people who watch these shows can't afford them, but in the long run, they expose Chinese audiences to knowledge about fashion and design from New

York, Paris, and Milan. For a country that is late to develop its fashion industry, these shows are performing their duty to educate people."

Hua Yang, producer of *X Files*, concurs with this view but goes even further. She told us that Channel Young also introduces cultural trends—art, films, and literature—as well as material cultural practices from outside China. By consistently promoting the idea of elegance, real style, and good taste, Channel Young manages to reinforce and perpetuate a specific class position and contributes to the legitimation of the middle class in China through normalizing the values and lifestyle of the middle class in the realm of consumption and everyday practices. Channel Young's programs therefore are integral to the process of middle-class subjectification, where "questions of value, behaviour, and conduct" are placed within the everyday realm of consumption (Ren 2013, 40).

Life Channel on Bengbu Television: The Importance of Being Local

The above account of the multipronged approach of a metropolitan television channel reveals a stratified structure of consumer need, taste, and spatial imagination in Shanghai. To make sense of this structure within the context of the "new geography of inequality" (Oakes and Schein 2006), we need to compare and contrast the production, program content, and consumption of television at metropolitan and local levels. As the "sandal scandal" discussed at the beginning of this chapter indicates, a tier-three city in Anhui Province would present itself as a suitable location for comparison and contrast with Shanghai. By Chinese standards, Bengbu, located in the relatively less developed province of Anhui in Eastern China, is a small city. Consisting of a number of urban areas in the city center plus four peripheral towns and rural counties, totaling a population of around 3 to 3.6 million, Bengbu is one of the hundreds of inland, semirural, and less cosmopolitan cities in China. In comparison with coastal and southern provinces such as Guangdong and Zhejiang, Anhui Province exists in the national imagination as lagging behind the national average in terms of economic development, urbanization levels, and cosmopolitan outlook (Sun 2002).

Like residents in many similar-sized cities in China, Bengbu residents have free access to a bewildering number of television channels, including a dozen channels from CCTV, half a dozen channels from Anhui Television, and more than twenty satellite channels from television stations in twenty other provinces. On top of the free-to-air channels, they can also receive a selection of channels from other provinces and cities—including Shanghai Media Group's (SMG) Channel Young—with a digital set-top box. In addition, residents in Bengbu can access three local terrestrial channels from Bengbu TV (BBTV): the News Channel, the Public Affairs Channel, and the Life (shenghuo) Channel.

Our audience research in Bengbu indicates that BBTV has trouble attracting local young viewers, who have many alternatives. Shan Shan, a twenty-five-year-old bank clerk, is fairly typical of her generation:

> Nowadays with the Internet everywhere, we hardly watch TV. When we do, we watch it online. Watching programs on TV is annoying: you have to deal with ads and you have to be in front of the TV at a scheduled time. So why bother? The same content will be available online the very next morning. As for our preferred programs, we definitely go for entertainment programs, especially from Hunan TV and Jiangsu TV. Hunan TV's entertainment programs are popular with us, and so is Jiangsu TV's dating show *Fei Cheng Wu Rao* [If you are the one]. We don't watch health programs on BBTV. These are for old people. In fact, we don't even watch Anhui TV. They are all so drab and boring, and we are not interested in *yangsheng* [health and well-being].

Facing intense competition from national, metropolitan, and provincial television, and acutely aware of the less than cosmopolitan outlook of its viewers, BBTV knows too well that, to attract the largest possible local audience, it has to give them something that regional, metropolitan, and national television does not have. Furthermore, it has to achieve this goal with a very limited budget. Being a TV station in a relatively small city in an inland and economically "backward" province, it is unable to attract advertising from big businesses. In October 2010, when we conducted a series of interviews with the CEO, producers, editors, and hosts at BBTV, the station was in the middle of the transition from a public service model to a business and enterprise model. Han Song, the CEO of BBTV, explained that such transitions had been more or less completed at the national and provincial levels, and now county and municipal television stations all over the country had to follow suit.[3] While this is the case in theory, our conversations with program producers indicate that a strong ethos of public broadcasting still dominates at BBTV. Qing Xuedong, the producer of *Jiankang Ling Juli* (Zero distance to health), is given an annual budget of 900,000 yuan (roughly the equivalent of AU$150,000) and heads a team of ten staff. He sees his programs as primarily providing a public service. His editorial assistant, Ma Xiao, agrees: "Our self-positioning is that we are a public service channel, providing practical, useful information services to our local viewers. In order to do this, we must stay close to the grassroots [jie di qi]."

For producers at BBTV, "staying close to the grassroots" means that the decisions on the format and style of lifestyle programs in a small city must be shaped by the sensibility, taste, and needs of the majority of the local viewers. Qing, the producer of *Zero Distance to Health*, is aware that compared with provincial and metropolitan television, his programs lack style, drama, and narrative appeal. Although he puts this down partly to the lack of resources, he also believes that emulation of the more expensive formats and styles of presentation often seen in television elsewhere may be counterproductive from the point of view of maintaining cultural affinity with local viewers. Qing believes that there are considerable cultural differences between people in a big city and those in a small city. While television stations in big cities can run makeover shows featuring cosmetic surgeries and weight loss stories, small towns cannot afford them, and in any case, Qing believes that they would not work in small places. "If someone wants to get their nose done or eyelids folded, they would go through these procedures in secret so that their enhanced beauty appears natural. The notion of a makeover—showing the contrast between before and after—would be foreign to the people here, as it would defeat the purpose of the operation in the first place. It's harder to keep a secret and maintain anonymity in a small place, so we would be hard pressed to get someone to participate in the show even if we had the budget."

This producer's suspicion that the reality makeover format, now a "ubiquitous cultural phenomenon" (Lewis 2009, 1) and a decidedly globally recognizable television format, would not work with Bengbu audiences is instructive. It is not that viewers in Bengbu do not aspire to become more beautiful, thinner, or younger; it's just that they live in a place whose spatial scale determines that certain social and cultural practices are more preferable or acceptable than others. To recognize this point seems to offer producers at BBTV both a rationale for refusing to emulate metropolitan channels like Channel Young and as an incentive to have their ears close to the ground. In consideration of these local needs, BBTV has produced a type of television program that does not look like the lifestyle programs we see in Shanghai, on CCTV, or in the West. In fact, they seem to defy definition in terms of genre, format, and style, if we were to evoke the conventional style of lifestyle television as that category is internationally understood. BBTV therefore can be said to be a channel about life, not about style. From the point of view of producers as cultural intermediaries, Bengbu audiences need this type of information and service not because they aspire to acquire a more refined and elevated taste, sensibility, or outlook but rather because, as rights-bearing citizens and consumers, they require basic and adequate service and information.

Staying close to the grassroots also makes sense cost-wise. Under budget constraints, the only viable option is to stay resolutely local. Among BBTV's three channels, it is the Life Channel that hosts a regular suite of locality-specific shenghuo programs. One localizing strategy is the adoption of the local dialect. For instance, *Peng Jie Liao Shi* (Sister Peng's chitchat) features a middle-aged woman speaking, in the Bengbu dialect, direct to camera about the people and things that have either made the headlines of the newspaper or become household topics in the town. Peng is a relatively unknown host with the persona of an "ordinary housewife." By referring to her as *jie* (big sister) and her mode of discourse as *liao* (chitchat), the show reveals its intention to project a folksy and neighborly image. Combining a narrative account of local events (e.g., a dispute between neighbors, domestic violence, etc.) with her own commentaries, Sister Peng tries to make sense of the conflict and dispenses her personal points of view, all the time evoking common sense and fair judgment. Making its debut in 2010, *Sister Peng's Chitchat* has become, according to BBTV's own promotion, one of its highest-rating shows. Although most of our interviewees resonate with her points of view and the way she tells stories, Sister Peng's Bengbu dialect proves to be a polarizing factor. While the dialect endears itself to many viewers, who think it is more expressive of the local culture, at the same time it makes some viewers cringe. The response of Wang Li, a forty-two-year-old owner of a small shop, embodies this ambivalence.

> I think the show is very successful in reducing the distance between the host and us viewers. She speaks our dialect and talks about things happening around here. But the same time, I am not sure about her speaking Bengbu dialect.... It's not that I don't like people speaking Bengbu dialect to me, but I've always thought the dialect is for everyday conversations, not in the media.... I am used to hearing Mandarin on television, so it kind of feels weird hearing your own dialect all of a sudden.... It's not that I don't like Bengbu dialect; I just think that it doesn't sound good when it is spoken on the telly.

The use of language, accent, and dialect is always fraught with negotiations of unequal power relations. The ambivalence displayed by Bengbu viewers toward their own dialect being spoken on local television may be indicative of the stratified level of self-confidence demonstrated by places of different scales. When a person from a "small place" goes to a "big place," it is his/her responsibility to emulate the accent used in the bigger place. Bengbu viewers are not used to a TV host speaking their own local dialect, because authority, cosmopolitanism, and cultural capital is invested in Mandarin. To Bengbu viewers, using the Bengbu dialect on television has the adverse effect of reminding them too vividly of Bengbu's own lack of cosmopolitanism. In contrast, as discussed earlier in this chapter, ordinary Shanghai residents have no qualms about speaking their own dialect in front of the camera, and viewers of Channel Young, including both Shanghai locals and nonnative Shanghai dialect speakers, do not seem to be bothered by it. To many people in Shanghai, Shanghai is definitely a "cut above" all other places in China, including the Mandarin-speaking Beijing.

There is among TV industry professionals in Bengbu an acute awareness of how the socioeconomic status of the channel's viewership informs the type of information they seek out. Acting as cultural intermediaries, television producers decide that Bengbu viewers should be given information primarily concerning survival and basic livelihood. Rather than a vehicle for elevating taste and refashioning a more cosmopolitan lifestyle (as in the case of Shanghai's Channel Young), local television here sees itself first and foremost as a practical instrument of knowledge transmission. Acting according to this logic, in addition to using local dialect, BBTV also resorts to building a stable and loyal elderly audience cohort through its health and well-being–related programs. *Zero Distance to Health* is one such show. The show features a number of columns including "Let's Talk about Health," "Health News and Information," and "Expert Forum." A detailed breakdown of the show on an average day may provide some clues on the kind of topics the program deals in, hence explaining its popularity. On May 30, 2011, for instance, *Zero Distance to Health* starts with a story on the potentially hazardous nature of toys. Viewers are warned that a great proportion of toys for sale in the shops pose health risks of some kind. The program outlines, textbook style, complete with charts and tables, the risk to health associated with toys: unacceptably high levels of chemicals, lack of child-proof mechanisms in the design, and so on. It suggests that consumers look for clues for unsafe toys based on a number of factors, including color, smell, design, and labeling.

Following the story on dangerous toys is a story about how to correctly choose antibiotics, in view of a widely held assumption that newer and more expensive antibiotics deliver more effective outcomes. The program suggests, quoting doctors, that antibiotics of the generic kind, which may not be as expensive as new brands, may be more suitable or effective, so patients should learn to discern the appropriate antibiotics based on their function rather than their brand. The program then moves on to Health Hotline of the day, which includes a lesson—again delivered in a didactic textbook style—on the levels of radioactivity among various domestic electronic goods and appliances. Obviously addressing the anxiety among consumers about the level of radioactive exposure to everyday household goods, the program offers advice on how to minimize exposure, including, for instance, stay away from the microwave when it is operating, choose a fridge without digital functions, and hold the hair dryer a few inches away from the hair when using it.

Knowing that it is competing with the health programs of provincial, regional, and national television for the elderly audience, *Zero Distance to Health* ensures two things. The first is the simple strategy of making its content more accessible. In competition with the daily show *Yangsheng Tang* (*Yangsheng house*) of Beijing TV (the most popular health show on Chinese television), *Zero Distance to Health*, only fifteen minutes in length, is scheduled at 6:40 p.m. every day. The same content is also repeated the next morning. According to Ms. Wu, a seventy-eight-year-old retiree, this suits elderly viewers well: "We all have the habit of watching the national news bulletin at 7 p.m., so it is handy to watch fifteen minutes of *Zero Distance to Health* before the news. Also, the show is repeated the next day, so if you don't have the time to get all the information, you can always watch the repeat. *Yangsheng House* is about forty-five minutes, but *Zero Distance to Health* is shorter and often focuses on one single issue, so it's easy to follow. So, we watch both *Yangsheng House* and *Zero Distance to Health*."

More importantly, apart from viewer-friendly program scheduling, *Zero Distance to Health* also provides health-related information in a much simpler language that is easier to understand for elderly viewers. This is because Xiao Yu, the host of *Zero Distance to Health*, thinks that knowing the difference between the needs of audience in a big city and a small one is crucial:

> Most of our viewers are not as well educated as middle-class urbanites in the big cities. This means that the information they want may be considered very basic by the standard of big cities, and we have to ensure that the information we give them on television is clear, simple, and straightforward. For instance, a typical viewer in Shanghai who watches the local health program would already be familiar with the basic knowledge of how to live with diabetes. He or she would be seeking more advanced, specialized information on this topic so as to better manage their diabetic condition. But in Bengbu, we often get inquiries from viewers about what diabetes is and how to treat it.

To "sophisticated" Shanghai viewers, much of the material presented in *Zero Distance to Health* might come across as being crude and simplistic in the way it imparts health-related knowledge. But Bengbu viewers do not seem to find this a problem. In fact, some of our interviewees appreciate "being told what to do." Ms. Luo, a forty-seven-year-old school administrative staffer, thinks that TV programs offer timely dos and don'ts type of advice, which people "of our age" cannot ignore: "That show [*Zero Distance to Health*] is really practical. Many people have bad habits, and they need to realize that. For instance, people like to put too much MSG in their cooking. My mother-in-law does that, so I tell her what I learned from TV and not to put MSG into eggs (she thinks it makes eggs look nice and fluffy and taste good).... Yes, we have many wrong and unhealthy habits and we don't know that."

Nor do our interviewees seem to mind the repetitive and uncritical nature of the information provided in the shows. Some in fact believe that repetition is important for getting messages across. Ms. Wu, a seventy-eight-year-old retired school teacher, watches *Yangsheng House* on Beijing TV regularly and has a little notebook where she scribbles down useful tips and facts. She compared watching health programs to classroom teaching in the socialist decades: "Some information takes time to remember. For instance, old people with heart disease should be careful not to get angry, chilled, tired, or eat greasy, heavy meals. You hear these kinds of advice again and again, till you can finally remember it. Just like those years in the Cultural Revolution. You heard Chairman Mao's quotations day in and day out. Although you didn't really understand what was said at first, after a while, it became part of your thinking.... So repetition is good, especially for us old folks. We tend to be forgetful."

Ms. Wu's casual comparison of the effects of health-advice shows with citizens' interpellation by state propaganda in the Maoist era leads us to consider how these didactic programs could be seen to function as a "technology of the self" (Foucault 1977). First, these programs make viewers realize that their current health issues and problems are the consequences of their own "wrong" habits. Second, these programs never question the government's role in ensuring the safety standards of consumer items and its regulation of the pharmaceutical goods, nor do they ever discuss the wider social-environmental factors that put individuals' health at risk. Instead, they simply alert viewers to the potential hazards in consuming certain unsafe products, and regularly supply them with handy tips on how to avoid them. The message is rather clear. Given that unreliable and dangerous products and services abound, individuals must equip themselves with the necessary know-how for purposes of self-protection. Third, these programs urge consumers to take their health matters into their own hands, and they do so by encouraging viewers to reject fatalism and embrace hope. The idea that is consistently promoted is that as long as they are willing to act, good health or at least health improvement are within their reach.

Local Governing via Television: *Let Me Help You*

While BBTV's shenghuo producers are well aware of the range of upscale lifestyle formats available on Chinese television, they feel that the lifestyles promoted on these shows are not compatible with the everyday material standards familiar to Bengbu audiences. Bengbu audiences may mostly watch television for drama, spectacle, and entertainment, but their everyday needs—staying healthy, warding off poverty, and dealing with everyday living, including clothing, food, housing, and transportation (*yi shi zhu xing*)—take precedence. Tian Wei, the producer of *You Shi Wo Bang Nin* [Let me help you], believes that lifestyle shows in Bengbu must, first, satisfy the most essential needs of the viewers—health and everyday living—and, second, function as facilitators, enablers, and platforms for the resolution of the everyday concerns of ordinary people.

> Unlike the highly educated and technologically savvy middle class in the big cities who know how and where to get the information they need, our viewers rely on television for the information they need both as consumers and as citizens. Instead of competing with national and big-city television, we should just produce what they do not provide, but what our people need. It is not our place to lead the trend in fashion, or offer high-quality psychological counseling; we need to keep reminding ourselves that our core business is to meet the most basic, essential needs of our city. *Zero Distance to Health* and *Let Me Help You* are popular with viewers, because high-end television doesn't provide the knowledge we give them, or present this knowledge in the same format.

In order to fully appreciate BBTV's localizing initiatives, we now turn to *Let Me Help You*, one of the most popular programs on BBTV's life channel. Made on a shoestring budget, heavily subsidized by local businesses, and looking decidedly basic—some may say crude—in style, presentation, and content, the program aims to provide practical assistance to ordinary viewers with their problems and difficulties in everyday life.

Figure 2.4. Ms Xiao Yu, host of *Let Me Help You* on Bengbu TV, May 25, 2010.

In the first week of June 2011, *Let Me Help You*'s theme concerned a subject that preoccupies the minds of many young people and their parents at that time of the year: the university entrance examination. The program host Xiao Yu invited the director of Bengbu City's Recruitment Bureau into the studio, and in the form of a host-guest conversation, the director answered a range of questions concerning which form to fill in, eligibility requirements, steps to register online, and ways of checking examination marks. This was followed by a Q&A session during which anxious students and parents posed questions to the director by phone (the phone number was prominently displayed on the screen), text message, and QQ (a popular social media platform in China). During the Q&A, further information appeared on the screen in the form of a PowerPoint presentation detailing major rules, regulations, and policies regarding the examination.

Unlike Channel Young's informational and advice-oriented programs, which aim to be casual, light-hearted, and consumer-friendly, *Let Me Help You* is "no frills" in terms of aesthetics and style of presentation. Little attempt is made to turn the process of problem solving and information seeking into entertaining, visually appealing, or narratively engaging television. However, the show is popular despite this. And the popularity of this show lies partly in its capacity to bring figures of authority closer to ordinary people. Ms. Wu, a seventy-eight-year-old retired schoolteacher and viewer of the show, thinks "ordinary people" (*lao bai xing*) have trouble finding the right answers about government policies that concern them.

> People need to know answers to these questions but it's not easy to find them. For instance, how to join the New Rural Health Insurance Scheme, whose responsibility it is if your apartment leaks, how to fill out forms to enroll your kids in the university, what kind of chronic diseases are covered by the urban medicare system. This show often deals with policies that concern a lot of people. It does so by inviting officials into the studio, or going to their office and putting a microphone in front of them. This way, we get to find out the answers to our questions. How else can we access officials? We don't even know where to look for them!

In the following week, the program resumed its normal format, offering two stories that adopted a standard problem-investigation-intervention-resolution formula. In the first story, BBTV received a call from a resident in a semirural neighborhood in Bengbu about the disturbance caused by the noise of metal cutting from a nearby workshop. The reporter went to the scene and talked to the residents as well as the shop owner. She then got in touch with officials from the local Bureau of Industry and Commerce, in order to establish that the metal-cutting shop had breached the laws regarding the division between residential areas and business space—all on camera. The story ended with the closing of the workshop and local residents expressing satisfaction that the matter was now resolved.

While it is clear that BBTV functions as an intermediary between experts and the lay audience, here it is also mediating between the local government and local citizens. In the same way that viewers find it difficult to get hold of policy information, they find it equally hard to access people with specialist knowledge, especially in finance, medicine, and law. Twenty-six-year-old Li Jing, an employee in a construction company, believes that people in Bengbu are more in need of specialist knowledge than those in the big cities. "People here generally have less education, and we are not knowledgeable about things. For instance, we all want to buy an apartment, and there is a lot we need to know about various aspects of real estate in order to make the right decision, but we don't usually have this knowledge. So we try to use television as a way of learning about things." Quite a few interviewees told us that they liked the show because it has the means and power to embarrass unethical business entities and irresponsible bureaucrats, and shame them into fixing the problems that are either caused by them or should be fixed by them. Wang Ling, a middle-aged housewife, has absolute faith in the power of the media:

> Media is really powerful. Once you are on TV, you are exposed. Dodgy businesses and companies are scared of being exposed on telly. Media also has the power to scrutinize the behavior of unethical people and organizations.... Yes, I remember one example. The story I saw last week on the show was about some residents whose apartments leaked water. They went to the property management committee, which blamed the developer, and the developer blamed someone else. In the meantime, residents went to the media asking for help. The media turned up with a reporter and a camera, and the problem was solved pronto.... You see, this is how helpful they can be. Us ordinary people, we don't know who is responsible and where to find them, but television does, and they are keen to help!

Besides these problem-solving feature stories, *Let Me Help You* also has a "quick news" segment, providing a list of the most useful information for the local residents of Bengbu. For instance, on the sampled day, this segment included information about a new train station for the bullet train. While the host in the studio reads out information on the train timetable and ticket prices, the banner running across the bottom of the screen provided more useful—but unrelated—information in response to questions posed by viewers calling the show's information hotline. On that day, answers were provided to a number of questions, including how to register for subsidized housing, and what kind of evidence is acceptable to prove a theft and the identity of the thief. These were followed by an appeal for donations for a seven-year-old child who suffers from leukemia and needed a bone marrow transplant operation.

The types of help viewers seek from their local television station are deeply revealing of the new social environment that individuals must navigate in order to survive in postsocialist China. Having implemented the privatization of property, goods, and services in a wide range of sectors, the Chinese state, like its counterparts in liberal-democratic societies, increasingly prefers to govern "from afar" (Zhang and Ong 2008). Similar to lifestyle television elsewhere, lifestyle programs on Chinese television, as we discuss in detail in chapter 5, create a key pedagogic space to teach individuals how to make informed decisions. By promoting the discourse of self-responsibility, they embody the major ways in which individual choice functions as a "technique of governing" (Hoffman 2010, 145). At the same time, these information- and advice-oriented shows also exemplify unique ways in which local governments use television as an instrument of governing.

The ways in which television intervenes to help solve problems is instructive for understanding how television functions in a small Chinese city caught between "socialist legacies" and "neoliberal strategies" (Zhao 2008b). In comparison with the socialist mode of policy communication via the organizational channels of the workplace, and in contrast to the authoritarian model of media as propaganda, the governing of everyday life via television indeed represents a step away from the authoritarianism of prior eras. However, the presence of the state—embodied in local bureaucratic departments, neighborhood committees, and the police—remains central in these programs. Whether it is in the form of citizens seeking assistance in problem solving and conflict resolution, or consumers seeking information in order to improve their livelihoods and life chances, television is a ubiquitous and affordable mediation between the local government and ordinary citizens. In other words, while the central government is seen by local viewers as rulers from "afar" in the new neoliberal-socioeconomic order, local government and local television seem to take on a relationship that is best described as codependent and mutually sustaining. In fact, we can say that local government is forced to become more "up close and personal" with ordinary consumers and citizens *precisely because* the central government has distanced itself from the everyday life of the population. This codependent relationship is maintained and mediated by television. Or to put it in another way, local television has become an indispensable instrument of governing for the local government. Shows such as *Let Me Help You* follow a win-win formula, giving the "little people" a voice while assisting the local government in resolving myriad problems on a daily basis. While the "problem-solving via media" narrative formula has massive appeal to ordinary people, it also helps defuse social tension and ease grassroots' discontent with the government. This level of mediated codependency is largely missing from the high-end lifestyle programs on metropolitan and national television in China, as discussed in the first part of this chapter, as well as from lifestyle television in the West.

Conclusion

It is interesting to note that the producers of both Channel Young's lowbrow shenghuo programs and shenghuo programs on BBTV refer to the importance of *jie di qi* (staying close to the grassroots). As is evident in both Shanghai and Bengbu, being tuned to the needs of the grassroots means making place-appropriate and locality-specific decisions about the program content presented to viewers, as well as the style of presentation. This in turn translates into a dramatically stratified structure of consumption know-how between the two cities. Channel Young would not invest resources in making health programs as BBTV does. Similarly, BBTV would not consider it wise business sense to focus on fashion.

However, although staying close to the grassroots has proven to be a useful localizing strategy for both SMG and BBTV, there is one significant difference. For SMG's Channel Young, staying close to the grassroots is a business strategy that enables it to also "fly high." After all, it is the reliable revenue that is generated from its bread-and-butter, lowbrow type of programs that make the production of high-end fashion shows espousing cosmopolitan, European, and global taste and style possible. As this discussion makes clear, this two-pronged media practice has led to a multiscaled cultural imaginary of place. Taken in their entirety, the shenghuo programs on Channel Young project a cosmopolitan spatial imagination that is simultaneously local, national, regional, and global. In contrast, confronted with intense competition from provincial, regional, and national television, staying close to the grassroots is both means and end for BBTV. By giving local viewers what they cannot get elsewhere—pedagogically oriented and hyperlocal health programs for the elderly cohort and problem-solving assistance for citizens of all ages—BBTV is able to survive in a multiscalar media environment in which viewers' place imaginary is fragmented along the line of age, and in which the local audience's loyalty to local TV can by no means be guaranteed.

The juxtaposition of Channel Young and BBTV also points to the need to consider the implications of place-based and scale-determined stratification. This stratification not only sets some places apart as being less or more desirable than others in the popular imagination but also has come to shape the way in which cultural intermediaries operate. On the whole, citizens in Shanghai enjoy a better communication infrastructure, and are more skilled in harnessing information technologies, negotiating, and meeting their daily information needs. As a result, experts and cultural elites in Shanghai's TV industry can cater to "higher" needs, that is, the cultivation of good taste and sophisticated aesthetic sensibility. By contrast, in Bengbu, where residents in general may be less media-savvy, or where there may be less adequate provision of information of public interest, BBTV producers see it as more fitting to mediate between authorities and citizens, experts and lay individuals on a wide range of more pressing life matters.

Our discussion has gone some way toward addressing a significant lack in current work on Chinese television, which has to date maintained a relentless focus on national and metropolitan channels, and mostly neglected local-level television production and consumption. The political economy of scale determines that television channels at different levels not only choose to focus on different types of life matters but also have to adopt different language and modes of address. While due to the reality of channel specialization, lifestyle programs on national and metropolitan television can afford to address viewers mainly as consumers, viewers of the life programs on local television are encouraged to see themselves as citizens and members of the public whose interests and rights must be protected by their local stations. To viewers of local programs, television is part of a service-delivering public sector, as well as a consumer guide. Constituting the majority of the lifestyle programs on Chinese television in terms of quantity, these local programs may not be cosmopolitan in style but they resonate with local audiences due to their locally relevant content.

Our analysis in this chapter of the production, content, and consumption of lifestyle programs on a metropolitan channel and a tier-three local channel in China points to the need to recognize the value of the local and regional in the cultural economy of mediated placemaking and suggests that in this context the scale of place plays a pivotal role in shaping distinct formations of taste, outlook, and spatial imagination through a plethora of place-specific media forms. Unlike national and metropolitan television, which equate creativity and innovation with media practices, formats, and styles that "jump scale," municipal television's winning strategy lies, in contrast, in scale fixing and maintenance.

THREE. **Here, There, and Everywhere** Mediascapes, Geographic Imaginaries, and Indian Television

India very frankly breaks all the stereotypes, Western and other. India jumps. For example, you expect DTH [direct-to-home] to be very much an urban phenomenon. Where's the biggest growth happening? In the rural areas. Why? Because cable is not reaching them enough. They are prepared to come together as a community to pay that extra premium . . . but they are getting it directly from the sky. In India we used to wait for years to get a landline connection. . . . The revolution happened . . . so we jumped a whole phase. Even the man on the street who may not be earning much will have a cell phone connection. India is jumping a lot of levels. In terms of television, it's moving, India is the most dynamic market.—INTERVIEW WITH NIRET ALVA, Mumbai, November 27, 2010

The way we look at America through Hollywood or Australia or all first-world locations, there is a certain homogeneity that we find prevalent. In India the social structure is such that television is itself not a homogeneous medium. When we look at Hindi news television, even in that there are *televisions*, . . . which are targeting certain kind of people, certain sections of society in that immense viewership. . . . Television is penetrating very deep into Indian society. And it is doing two things; first it is empowering people with information, but it is also making people aware of the chasm between the haves and have-nots.—INTERVIEW WITH NILENDU SEN, Delhi, November 26, 2010

As we discussed in chapter 1, India today has a vast and unruly televisual landscape with a large array of broadcast and satellite channels available to rural and urban dwellers alike. Television as a cultural institution plays a particularly complex role in the context of a globalized, postcolonial nation-state marked by an endless plurality of TV markets, audiences, as well as, we would argue, "uses of television," to borrow John Hartley's phrase (Hartley 1999). In this chapter, we discuss the Indian television landscape in terms of its shifting role in shaping people's "imagined worlds," from the projected nationalism of Doordarshan in the 1980s and the hegemony of Hindi/Northern "national" imaginaries to the more recent pluralization and regionalization of television that has accompanied the commercialization and deregulation of the sector. A central dynamic here, as the two industry quotes above suggest, is the way in which the ever-changing Indian television landscape speaks to India's cultural complexity and geographic, social, and economic divisions. As in China (see chapter 2), these divisions have and continue to be often framed in urban-rural terms (as well as in terms of class and the lingering effects of caste). However, the comment at the beginning of this chapter by Niret Alva, producer of the Indian version of *Idol*, regarding India's phase-jumping tendencies suggests the difficulty of making easy socioeconomic or geographic assumptions in the Indian context. Like China, India's diverse geopolitical mediascape is one marked by significant spatial and social inequalities. However, while in the past, the urban Hindi North versus "rural South" was constructed as a clear hierarchy in terms of industry power, televisual territories, and communities of taste ("Southerners" have, for instance, often been caricatured as "Madrasis" or "country cousins"), in contemporary India the relationship between Northern metropolitan and so-called regional mediascapes has become more complex, shaped by interconnections and flows as much as divisions and hierarchies. For instance, with most of the Indian population continuing to live in rural areas (Ghosh 2012), as we discuss below, in recent years regional and local television has been one of the key areas of growth in an otherwise crowded media market, carrying the value-adding proposition of culturally and linguistically specific media content customized not just for large local audiences but for various "diasporic" audiences across India and the globe.

India's major metropolitan centers receive significant influxes of rural migrants (though not at the same rate as China, where more than half of the population are now city dwellers), while wealth tends to be clustered in Indian states with high levels of urbanization (Ghosh 2012). However, Northern cities like Mumbai, the home of Bollywood and the Hindi media entertainment industry, are also marked by significant local socioeconomic divides. Although the city is often pictured as an exuberant symbol of cosmopolitan media modernity, because of the real estate boom in the 2000s more than half the city's population now living in informal or "slum" housing, characterized by a "huge infrastructure deficit" in terms of potable water, legally supplied electricity, and sanitation (Jain 2010), though many slum-dwelling Mumbaikers are otherwise

Figure 3.1. Satellite dish amid the laundry in Mumbai's Dhobi Ghat (open-air laundry), in Dharavi, one of the largest slums in the world. Photo by Tania Lewis.

"connected" and technologically savvy, possessing cheap mobile phones, satellite dishes, and, increasingly, direct-to-home television (see figure 3.1).

In this chapter, we draw on multisited empirical research in order to offer a glimpse into the social and cultural complexity of India's varied mediascapes and imaginative geographies. While much of the scholarship on Indian television to date has focused on northern/Hindi and to a lesser extent English television (a powerful though elite, niche player in the Indian TV market), we sought to extend this discussion by engaging with audiences, industry, and programming in Southern India. As discussed in the introduction and chapter 1, we conducted research with industry professionals and with audiences in both Mumbai and the southern state of Karnataka (where Kannada is the main language), with many of our Kannada-speaking Northern audience members linked to the South by linguistic and cultural ties. Our concern was to emphasize the interconnections and *relationalities* that underpin Indian mediascapes, moving away from fixed notions of scale and territory and instead drawing upon geographer Ash Amin's work on the growing role of relational social ontologies of spatiality in a global context (Amin 2002).

In order to map the shifting spatial imaginaries of television in India, this chapter is structured as follows: the first section briefly maps the recent history of Indian television and in particular discusses the role of India's first and initially sole broadcaster, Doordarshan (a portmanteau of two Hindi words, meaning "seeing at a distance"), in constructing a national televisual imaginary. In the second section we discuss the sociogeographic divides that have hitherto shaped Indian television, particularly those between an urban, middle-class, Hindi elite and rural and non-Hindi-language audiences. We then move on in the third section to map the rise of regional television in India, a transition that has seen a dramatic shift in the dynamics of the Indian television landscape. Our final section returns to questions of "seeing at a distance," thinking through how visions of otherness on Indian lifestyle television produce new social and spatial ontologies not only in terms of a reimagined and revisioned sense of place and regionalism but also in terms of a growing sense of the *relational* and connected nature of locatedness and being in place. Here we argue for the need to delink questions of space and place in relation to Indian TV from territorial and scalar hierarchies, hierarchies that continue to structure the TV landscape in sites such as China, arguing that we need to understand people's everyday experience of, and engagements with, media worlds in contemporary India in terms of interconnected and "stretched" rather than fixed geographies.

Imagining Nationalisms: A Brief History of Television

William Mazzarella and Abhijit Roy have argued that the peculiar specificities of India's historical engagement with and shaping of television as a cultural technology continue to color present understandings and possibilities for television as social imaginary and practice (Roy 2008; Mazzarella 2012). Before we go on to discuss more recent developments in the geospatial and socioeconomic organization of television, in this first section we examine how various conceptions of nationalism and the nation-state have been key to understandings, constructions, and experiences of television in India. As noted in chapter 1, up until the early 1990s Doordarshan was the sole television channel. Prior to the embrace of satellite TV, Indian viewers were a captive audience for more than a decade, with Doordarshan as a state-supported broadcaster in the privileged position to shape their hopes, dreams, and conceptions of themselves as members of a modern postcolonial nation-state. Somewhat comparably to CCTV in China, Doordarshan embraced the opportunity to encourage Indian citizens "to imagine the nation entirely as a statist space" (Roy 2008, 31).

However, Doordarshan's move to a more unified set of policies and practices around "national integration" didn't come until the 1980s, when Indira Ghandi saw the political and democratic potential of a commercialized national broadcasting system, albeit Hindi speaking and based in Delhi (Rajagopal 2001). As the now well-known narrative of the rise of Indian broadcast TV goes, Ghandi's pro-business policies saw Doordarshan become increasingly dependent on advertising revenue and more attuned to large-scale consumer markets. At the same time, Indian television became spatially integrated, at least at the level of signal access, by the coordinated construction of the extensive national broadcast network, alongside a large increase in television's household penetration rate due to the opening up of a hitherto protected Indian market to cheap imported television sets (Jeffrey 2002).

This social and technological triumph over the sheer size and scale of India was celebrated in 1982 with the groundbreaking nationwide telecast of the Asian Games, arguably the first "event television" in India (Couldry 2002) and, as Roy argues, a key moment of "televisual nationalism" (Roy 2008, 37). The second pivotal moment was Doordarshan's highly successful experiments with entertainment-oriented programming in the 1980s, in particular Hindi serials, which the broadcaster used as a means of combining its concern with public pedagogy with a popular commercial agenda. Here Doordarshan's first big success story was the popular soap opera *Hum Log* (We people) (1984–85), a rather didactic show based on Latin America's highly successful model of the telenovela. Huge audiences across India followed the trials of this middle-class family, which included an alcoholic father and a daughter with feminist tendencies, with each episode ending with a piece of moral instruction offered up by the cinema veteran Ashok Kumar. The show was particularly interesting at the time as, while it was clearly pro-modernization, it also narrativized various fears and concerns about the onslaught of consumerism, materialism, and shifting social identities—marking television's emergent role in India as a key space for negotiating narratives of modernity.

While Doordarshan 1980s serials were enormously popular with a wide range of audiences, their claim to "televisual nationalism" needs to be strongly qualified, or rather recognized in strategic, conjunctural, and political terms. As Roy has argued, following the transition from a developmental modernity, in which the targeted public had been conceived of as predominantly rural, to an emerging consumerist modernity in the 1980s, the new public envisaged by state broadcasters was hardly an inclusive one (Roy 2008). Rather, it was a projection of a somewhat sanitized image of an urban Hindi middle class contained within the bounds of the home and within patriarchal familial structures (Roy 2008).

Alongside shows like *Hum Log*, Doordarshan also aired a number of very successful mythological or religious serials in the 1980s, such as *Ramayan*, the serialized version of the Hindi religious epic, which we discuss in chapter 6 on spiritual television. Such shows similarly offered a limited vision of nationalism, in this case projecting a culturally specific set of religious myths and values as the foundation for an imagined nationalism. As Rajagopal argues, despite its Hindu origins, the popular TV show marked "a new order of social connectivity, in a visual regime that now extended across the nation" (Rajagopal 2001, 31). The rise and success of Hindu nationalism lay in its ability to combine popular appeal through a vernacular return to traditionalism, with a liberalized economic agenda, which appealed to middle- and upper-class urbanites. However, in reality the anti-Muslim, pro-business foundations of its claims to a "unified" Hindu public marked a cultural populism that was divisive, "partial and contradictory" (Rajagopal 2001, 34).

While the 1980s saw such claims to nationalism made through the lens of a single national broadcaster, as we discussed in chapter 1, the deregulation of the industry in the 1990s and in particular the opening up of the market to private foreign satellite companies witnessed a dramatic transformation in the nature, scope, and scale of Indian television. The rather rapid transition from a nationalized state-television industry to a highly deregulated one has seen an exponential growth in the number of cable and satellite channels (somewhat similarly to the case in Taiwan; see chapter 1). The satellite revolution has not only meant a shift from "an era of scarcity" to (extreme) plenty (Ellis 2000, 39) but has also greatly expanded and extended the potential reach, scope, and scale of television in India, with major implications for its role in shaping geographic and social imaginaries.

For instance, while rural India continues to be served by Doordarshan (though with rather more emphasis on entertainment and on regional concerns than on "educational" television), the appearance of satellite dishes in rural villages, both communally shared and household-based, now means that rural viewers have access to a wide and highly diverse array of TV offerings, both "exotic" international programming (National Geographic, for instance, is a channel that many viewers in our study mentioned watching, from middle-class to poor urban viewers to villagers) as well as highly regional, linguistically and culturally "proximate" programming.

But what might be the wider implications of the growing penetration of commercial, entertainment-oriented television in India? If Doordarshan's programming tended to offer viewers rather limited, exclusionary visions of what it might mean to be a modern Indian citizen, the new commercial TV landscape arguably exposes audiences to a huge diversity of ways of living and being. What does this mean for people's sense of belonging and their imagined relation to place and cultural identity? In the next three sections, we discuss the growing complexity of mediated spatial and cultural imaginaries in India, first discussing the role of commercial media not only in displaying and relaying classed aspirations but also in mediating a sense of difference and disjuncture, before moving on to examine the growing role of regionalization and globalized translocal media and cultural processes in shaping India's evolving TV ecologies.

Aspirationalism and Disjuncture: Whose India Is on TV?

In *Shoveling Smoke*, a brilliant ethnographic study of the advertising industry in India, William Mazzarella argues that large-scale shifts brought about by economic deregulation and the opening up of once-protected Indian markets to foreign players from the 1980s onward laid the foundations for a new "social ontology of global consumerism" (Mazzarella 2003, 12), a transition crucially mediated by television. Where once Indian aspirations attached themselves to images of nation building, development, and raising up the poor, television and its associated commodity imagery brought in a new conception of collectivity that, while spearheaded by a class elite, legitimated itself via "the democratization of aspiration" (Mazzarella 2003, 98).

While, as we discussed in the introduction, economically the middle class represents a rather small percentage of the population, the Indian sociologist Leela Fernandes argues that the consumer middle class, and consumer-based aspirationalism more broadly, has come to play an important *symbolic* role within the national imaginary and state apparatus (Fernandes 2006). The popular reality game show *Kaun Banega Crorepati* (2000–present), which is produced in Mumbai as the Hindi version of the global format *Who Wants to Be a Millionaire*, could be read as one such example of a kind of collectivized national aspirationalism on Indian television (see figure 3.3). While our audience research underlines that people's taste in programming in India is highly diverse and often split along class, cultural, and linguistic lines, *Kaun Banega Crorepati* is one of the few popular factual shows that is universally lauded by rural audiences and middle-class urbanities alike (and invariably mentioned by TV executives as a moment of exemplary Indian reality programming).

Figure 3.2. Billboard at Star's Mumbai headquarters. Photo by Tania Lewis.

Figure 3.3. *Kaun Banega Crorepati*, the Indian (Hindi) version of *Who Wants to Be a Millionaire*.

Key to the show's cross-demographic popularity is the figure of Amitabh Bachchan, a stalwart of Hindi cinema who has transitioned highly successfully into the TV medium and appears in a range of advertisements for consumer products. Although he comes from a high-caste background and possessing huge wealth, his popularity stems from a persona that is marked by a kind of everyman quality, enabling many diverse Indian audiences to identity with Bachchan to some degree. The show's content also cleverly negotiates its highly disparate audience. Industry professionals and audience members alike connect its success to the fact that the show's producers appear to deliberately pick the most marginal and poor contestants to be on the show, from people hailing from villages in obscure parts of India to impoverished contestants lacking even the most basic markers of economic citizenship, such as bank accounts. As a poorer interviewee in Mumbai commented, "we watched because this season the participants came from a humble background." For viewers there is a sense of intense pleasure when such contestants win, and a number of viewers we interviewed commended the producers for the show's increasing focus on the "back stories" of such contestants and the stress on "rags to riches" narratives, which many saw as offering a shared set of aspirations for an otherwise disparate audience.

An easy reading here would be that the show's universal appeal—as a global reality format that celebrates the capitalist myth of instant success—confirms the triumph in postsocialist India of an aspirational culture premised primarily on monetary gain. Talking with viewers and industry professionals alike, however, the picture becomes not so much one of a collective embrace of get-rich-quick commercial culture but rather of a more complex and at times troubled sense of people's imagined relationship to such "national" aspirations. While *Kaun Banega Crorepati* is associated with a sense of hope, this is often contrasted with the "realities" of life in India and the fact that much of the other content on reality TV (such as *Bigg Boss*, the Hindi version of the global format *Big Brother*) is perceived by audiences, particularly poorer and rural villagers, as being too focused on a middle-class urban elite. For instance, a number of interviewees criticized *Bigg Boss*'s depiction of cosmopolitan lifestyles distant from their own ("someone who is poor cannot be like them"), while mocking the show's imitation of "Western" practices such as cooking in a shared kitchen when in "real life" urban Indian elites would have servants to cook for them. Further, *Kaun Banega Crorepati* was often framed in terms of aspirational narratives other than instant success and entrepreneurialism. For instance, viewers often discussed the show in terms of its educational and informational qualities ("it helps develop general knowledge"), linking the game show back to a long tradition on Indian television of educational quiz shows. Some households also emphasized the importance of the "recognition" of difference, seeing shows like *Kaun Banega Crorepati* and other reality formats such as the highly popular *Indian Idol* as giving national visibility to people who would normally have never made it to the small screen due to poverty, caste, and/or ethnicity.

While reality shows like *Kaun Banega Crorepati* have an undoubted potentially national reach, in a large, complex country marked by dramatic social and economic divides, they arguably foreground social divisions as much as they construct an imaginary national unity. Discussing the contemporary Indian TV landscape, Chadha and Kavoori state: "despite the medium's potential for facilitating a shared narrative, the television universe in India constitutes an increasingly divided terrain between the haves and the have-nots—paralleling the most fundamental trend within Indian society—so that it is not simply the real but also *the imagined worlds of citizens that are profoundly disparate and disconnected*" (Chadha and Kavoori 2012, 599, emphasis added).

Echoing elements of the metropolitan/regional divide evident in Chinese lifestyle programming, this sense of a growing disconnect between the lifestyles and "imagined worlds" of television was a recurrent theme in our interviews with poorer households, in both Mumbai and Tovinkere. For instance, Devkumar, a chauffeur, and his family live in a one-room dwelling on the outskirts of Mumbai, making considerable sacrifices to pay for one of their three children to go to an English-language school. Avid watchers of sitcoms, travel shows, and crime shows, Devkumar and his wife, however, were very critical of *faltu* (useless, of no value) programs such as reality and lifestyle shows that portray excessively aspirational lifestyles remote from their own everyday experience. As Devkumar put it: "In India, most are poor, 20–25 percent are better placed, in good positions. So these programs mostly show such better-placed persons. When people watch such programs, they feel . . . we don't have enough to eat, and when children watch such programs they start dreaming [or desiring]; dreaming is good, but it can hardly be true. Life on television and reality are different."

This sense of television's role in foregrounding difference and disjuncture as much as emphasizing collectivism and shared identification was also, perhaps somewhat surprisingly, a strong theme in our interviews with Mumbai- and Delhi-based industry professionals, who often spoke of a North–South divide in terms of cultural-linguistic (particularly Hindi-Tamil), urban and rural (see our discussion of China in chapter 2), and also class distinctions. A common distinction that Indian TV producers made in our discussions was between the "classes and the masses," and they were extremely aware that the majority of Indian TV viewers live lives far removed from the lifestyles depicted on lifestyle channels or on Hindi channels that air "popular" reality shows like *MasterChef India* and *Bigg Boss*. When we discussed shifting gender roles with a senior executive from Fremantle TV in Mumbai, he argued, for instance, that "if there is a modern India where the woman is stepping out, she is doing things and there are nuclear families.... In the smaller towns and cities, which is *really the larger India*, they are a lot more conservative and orthodox.... It is still deeply ingrained that the woman looks after the home, therefore there is only one bread earner within the family" (emphasis added).

Despite the somewhat caricatured depiction of small-town India as "not modern," there is at least a recognition here of the class limits and cultural specificities of Hindi/North Indian programming. Likewise, TV executives at the major lifestyle channels tended to emphasize the exclusive, *highly aspirational* nature of their programming and target audience. Indeed, as Rajiv Lakhsman, the host of the popular reality show *MTV Roadies* (the Indian version of the U.S. show *Road Rules*) and a TV producer with Colosseum Media, pointed out, the Indian ratings system itself has tended not to capture the viewing preferences of this very high-end socioeconomic category, as its focus (like AGB Nielsen's ratings system in Taiwan) has tended to be on lower and middling middle-class families: "Any household with a People-meter will be middle class, not even upper middle class.... It will have three kids, a joint family, will have three generations living together and will have one small car if at all. This is the socioeconomic category that the mainstream advertisers target. That's the reason youth television like *Roadies* or lifestyle shows don't even enter the radar because that's more of an urban elite consumption."

My TV: Language, Regionalism, and Imagined Belongings

Thus far in this chapter, we have highlighted the hitherto relative hegemony in India of urban-centered, middle-class, Northern/Hindi-oriented programming in laying claim to a national geospatial imaginary, both in the era of Doordarshan and in the post-1990s commercial context. However, India's pluralized postsatellite environment has heralded a diversity of new markets and audience, which have come to challenge the hegemony of Mumbai as both an entertainment center and also a site of national/cultural dominance. As the industry and audience quotes suggest above, claims to an imagined nationalism or sense of pan-Indian identity as projected from the North on to the rest of India are more problematic than ever within this space of diversity and disjuncture. A number of scholars have begun to map the complex and shifting terrain of Indian television in what might be seen as a postnational era, a key focus of which has been the rise of regional and localized forms of television. In the following sections, we discuss this shift to televisual "localisms" and the impact that this might have on conceptions of place, belonging, and relations between self and other. We suggest that the "vernacular" turn in television—marked as it is by complex relations to proximate and distant linguistic-cultural communities and to global-local flows of programming and formats—requires a rethinking of Indian television's geocultural landscape away from the fixed territorial understandings of place that underpinned Doordarshan's conception of "seeing at a distance" to a more *interconnected* and *relational* understanding of geographic imaginaries.

Since the early 1990s, there have been a growing number of regional players in the Indian TV landscape, with local production houses blossoming in smaller urban and regional centers (McMillin 2001; Moorti 2004; Sen and Roy 2014). Language has been a key aspect of the drive to regionalism within India's complex media landscape. Since India is a highly multiethnic, multilingual society, with thirty languages spoken by more than a million "native" speakers (Ministry of Home Affairs 2001), navigating daily life often means juggling two or more languages. As we noted above, Indian state television tended to privilege Hindi as a language of imagined nationalism, while "Hinglish" has an ongoing cultural cachet among the educated metropolitan middle classes. However, within the past decade there has also been a strong shift toward regionalizing language and programming. As Chadha and Kavoori note: "The recent burst of growth witnessed in the Indian television industry has largely come from the regional sector, which not only added 21 new channels compared to 4 for Hindi in 2009 but also experienced a sharp increase in advertising revenues, which grew by 29%. And, even though the growth of regional channels is uneven in that six key [official state] languages (i.e., Tamil, Telegu, Kannada, Bengali, Malayalam and Marathi) tend to be dominant, myriad other Indian languages have also dedicated channels and are growing at a much faster rate than the overall television market" (Chadha and Kavoori 2012, 598).

This growing complexity and array of linguistic localisms was foregrounded in an interview we conducted with the TV viewer Nivedita, a female IT engineer who had moved from the coastal port city of Mangalore to live and work in Bangalore, both cities in the southern state of Karnataka. A regular viewer of evening TV, Nivedita noted that whereas in Bangalore "local" programs and channels in the Kannada language (the state language of Karnataka) are popular, in Mangalore, people also watch programs in Konkani and Tulu (languages spoken along the western coast, including Goa), and also consume TV content in the Malayalam language, reflecting Mangalore's proximity to Malayalam-speaking Kerala, India's southernmost state. Alongside this engagement with "local" place-based programming, mobile urbanities such as Nivedita also often embrace more distant, "deterritorialized" programming such as that offered on Hindi GECs and English/Hindi-language lifestyle channels such as NDTV Good Times. Such practices echo the experiences of young professionals in provincial Chinese cities such as Bengbu who are likely to eschew down-home local programming in favor of the more cosmopolitan reality and lifestyle offerings emerging out of major media centers such as Shanghai and Beijing (see chapter 2). Nivedita, for instance, watches Hindi reality shows such as *MasterChef India* and English-language lifestyle shows aimed at a very niche audience and produced in Mumbai, such as the cookery-travel show *Highway on My Plate* (NDTV Good Times).

Increasingly, though, reality and lifestyle formats are themselves also being regionalized, with indigenized versions being produced by local private networks (McMillin 2001; Moorti 2004; Chadha and Kavoori 2012). Two of the recent big successes in terms of audience numbers (if not revenue) for regional television in Karnataka, for instance, have been the Kannada versions of *Bigg Boss* (itself a version of the Hindi reworking of *Big Brother*) and *Kaun Banega Crorepati* (*Who Wants to Be a Millionaire*). Both Kannada formats, like their Hindi counterparts, feature film stars as hosts, though hailing from the local Sandalwood industry rather than from Bollywood. For instance, one of the Bangalore TV producers and actors we interviewed, Akul Balaji, is also one of the participants in season 2 of the Kannada version of *Bigg Boss*, which started in June 2014. Hailing from a small town in the neighboring state of Andhra Pradesh (where Telugu, another major south Indian language, is the official language), Akul acts in Kannada reality TV, Kannada movies, and Telugu serials, reflecting the growing market for highly localized forms of entertainment programming and film (as well as the strong cross-currents between film and television in India).

The growing role of transnational formats on highly localized regional television suggests a complex and shifting relationship between constructions of place, language, cultural distinctiveness, and global-local cultural and capital flows. Looking at the range of shows on offer in Bangalore and the rest of Karnataka, or "RoK," as TV producers often categorize it, there is a strong similarity at least on a genre and format level to the TV offerings one might find in Delhi and Mumbai. Television schedules, for both RoK and city viewers, are dominated by the usual fare of news, serialized dramas, and film (Sandalwood and Bollywood), as well as both indigenized and Hindi versions of reality shows, though lifestyle shows oriented toward consumption, such as fashion, beauty, and "gadget" shows, tend to be aimed more at urban audiences.

However, while regional reality and lifestyle shows in Southern India, such as local game shows, cookery shows, dance contests, and singing competitions, may have elements of the look and feel of their Hindi counterparts—indeed, they may trade on such associations in their branding and market positioning—as Balaraj Naidu (nonfiction programming head at Zee Kannada) noted when we interviewed him in Bangalore, such international formats are often strongly regionalized to work in markets where audiences have distinctive linguistic and cultural affiliations and predilections. Naidu described the way that such localization occurs at every level, including marketing and the recruitment of participants. Thus while Zee Kannada has audiences across the country (with many of our Mumbai households watching Kannada-language TV produced in far-off Karnataka), as well as internationally, its marketing strategy is strongly localized. As Naidu notes:

> We conduct FGD [focus group discussion] in each district [across Karnataka] every month. . . . We play one of the episodes. For instance, any program that we would want to improve we show that, we get feedback, there would be Q&A sessions. We would also get the director, so it is interactive and immediate. . . . Such sessions would increase viewership, because the participants would watch and they would also tell others too. I also take the crew and actors to the districts; it would also be nice for them to interact with the audience. When there is such an event, we do marketing in the district like: loudspeakers in auto-rickshaws, hoardings, ads in local newspapers, and announcements on TV.

While reality formats such as game shows and talent shows are popular with RoK audiences, Naidu suggested that South Indian rural and regional contestants for competitive reality game shows like Zee Kannada's *Mummy No. 1* (see figure 3.4) are much more difficult to recruit than those from metropolitan centers. Similarly, Alok Sharma (a media professional in Mumbai whose family we interviewed), in discussing the recruitment of participants to the reality show *MTV Roadies*, commented: "If you look at participation, you will see shows have people from Bangalore, cities where youngsters are exposed to a different kind of lifestyle—kids are not coming from small towns." As Naidu noted: "The local version of *Minute to Win* was a flop because participation was not like the original [Western] one. Contestants here are not particularly

Figure 3.4. Zee Kannada's reality game show *Mummy No. 1*, a show that involves mothers competing to complete various tasks while being judged on their performances by their children.

open to share their experiences. They would be hesitant to share how much they earn, like: 'I'm an auto driver and I earn one hundred rupees or whatever' and come out with emotions; they have to be pestered a lot to make them say that, and by that time the episode will be over."

While local participants may be reluctant to engage in the kind of branded, high-energy performance of selfhood conventionally associated with transnational format television, regionalized formats nevertheless can be seen to entail complex identity performances that often articulate vernacular concerns to global cultural flows. Ramaswami Harindranath's work on Tamil cookery shows demonstrates complex creative negotiations between global, national, and vernacular cultural identities via lifestyle programming (Harindranath 2013). Likewise, Sujata Moorti's fascinating work on Tamil identity politics and reality programming on Tamil networks such as Sun and Jaya TV points to the way in which the space and form of format programming, with its logics of cultural mobility, enables nuanced performances of cosmopolitan microidentities framed in and through the local (Moorti 2004). The Sun network, for instance, is not only one of the largest regional networks in India but, like many of the so-called regional channels, it also has a significant diasporic audience, and lays claim to being the most popular Tamil-language channel in the world. Like many of the new regional networks, including its rival network Jaya, Sun is also politically backed, mixing strongly commercial imperatives with associations with (anti-Aryan/anti-Northern) Dravidian separatist politics. Both channels also have a strong focus on entertainment TV. Sun, for instance, offers multilingual versions of the major Hindi reality shows (for example, it broadcasts *Khatron Ke Khiladi*, the Hindi version of *Fear Factor*, dubbed in Telugu, Tamil, and Malayalam), while both channels produce an array of game shows, cookery programs, and talent shows.

Challenging assumptions that reality and lifestyle shows purely disseminate transnational consumerist values, Moorti argues that cheap, formatted television provides an ideal vehicle for enacting and engaging with the complex politics of Tamil separatism, as she contends these shows offer tests of "knowledge that is local and grounded, requiring a competency of the here-and-now, [that] is also suffused with markers of a cosmopolitan sensibility" (2004, 556). Discussing an hour-long show on Jaya TV called *Vay Jalam* (Word play), in which contestants have to come up with new words for "modern" terms with no Tamil equivalent, such as "cable television," Moorti describes the show's key premise as being a self-conscious performance and celebration of "vernacular identity," though a reflexive "localized" identity that attempts to creatively play with the notion of a Tamil modernity. At the same time, the show also emphasizes the importance of a kind of "transnational literacy," featuring a segment where families are asked to recognize the identities of various "Western" celebrities (2004, 559). While contestants often fail this test (with these "failures" accompanied by much humor), the transnational aesthetics and style of the host (who also often litters his speech with English words) and the set, alongside this flow of global celebrity images, many of which *are* no doubt familiar to Jaya's younger viewers, work to deterritorialize the oral, vernacular Tamil-ness performed on the show, thereby relocating Tamil identity within a self-consciously displaced space of cosmopolitan flow.

Further, as Moorti notes, on a number of Tamil-language quiz shows, Tamil culture is both represented and reinvented through a range of glossy touristic images connoting authenticity and heritage (see our discussion of Taiwan TV travelogues in chapter 4). As she suggests, "the reliance on a transnational regime of representation allows the vernacular to be presented as compatible with, not antagonistic to, global culture" (Moorti 2004, 560). At the same time, identity and relation to place are often reemphasized and fetishized within this regime. On the Tamil quiz show *Big Game*, hosted in Madurai, a city seen as the center of Tamil civilization, the show plays on its location, depicting a series of idealized images that suggest "a golden Tamil past" while the cosmopolitan host, who moves adeptly between speaking English and Tamil, repeatedly emphasizes his preference for Madurai over Chennai, the erstwhile capital of Tamil Nadu. This celebration of a kind of performative and negotiated sense of localism is repeatedly reinforced on the show, as demonstrated in the following exchange:

> HOST: How many years have you been a housewife?
> CONTESTANT: Thirteen years.
> HOST: How much longer would you like?
> CONTESTANT: Sixty years.
> HOST: Being married to the same man for so long, won't it be boring?
> CONTESTANT: You must ask him [the husband].
> HOST: So, is this a Tamil relationship or an Indian relationship?
> CONTESTANT: A Tamil relationship, a Madurai relationship. (Moorti 2004, 561)

India on My Plate: Displaced Visions, Imagined Others

A key element of mediated spatial and geographic engagements for Indian viewers is about not only proximate and local imaginaries but also distance and otherness. Thus far we have emphasized Indian television's disjunctures and disconnections, from exclusionary constructions of the national and of the northern urban middle classes to the reflexively diasporic micro-identities forged through cosmopolitan forms of regional TV. Much of our empirical work with producers and households has supported this construction of televisual heterogeneity. Indeed, difference was a key trope in our Indian interviews, with many viewers and industry professionals alike foregrounding the diversity of India's social and cultural landscape. While this sense of imagined difference was at times connected to tensions between the material realities of people's lives and the perceived unrealities of forms of highly aspirational television, many interviewees also remarked on the enabling capacities of television in providing glimpses into the worlds of others and opening up Indian viewers to a broader sense of diversity. Aanya, a student in Mumbai, commented on television's role in introducing an older generation to cultural difference through food:

> I remember one of the first cookery shows was *Khana Khazana* [a long-running TV show hosted by the celebrity chef Sanjeev Kapoor]—my mother learning to make good *idlis* [a savory breakfast cake traditionally eaten in Southern India] from there. We are Bengali [from the northeast] and *idlis* are not a part of our diet. Today's generation are more metropolitan in their outlook because they have lived in Bangalore,

Mumbai, Delhi; for them it is not such a problem adapting to different cuisines—they have friends from all over the place. If I go back to my parents' time, or my uncles and aunts, and [food] they are more used to . . . my father would expect rice and dhal and *sabzi* [vegetable curry].

Alok Sharma, the Mumbai-based media professional quoted above, likewise suggests that food television has helped "northerners" have a somewhat less narrow sense of "southern" identity than previously.

In India we have different food culture in different states. . . . That is something you get to learn from TV these days. Otherwise, earlier entire South India, that is, the India that starts south of Maharashtra [the state that is home to Mumbai], is Madras for every north Indian. So everybody is Madrasi [a term that has tended to have derogatory connotations in the pan-Indian context], even if they belong to Andhra Pradesh; everybody is Madrasi. But these days, things are changing; now people know what Malayalam is, what actual Madrasi is, what Andhra is.

Relatedly, there was a strong sense, in both poorer and better-off households, of television as a space of pedagogy in relation to exposing audiences to India's diversity. This was sometimes expressed in rather pragmatic terms: numerous interviewees, for instance, saw television as a gateway to linguistic skills. For instance, Archana's adult son, who lives in a poor household on the outskirts of Mumbai, commented on the benefits of television's multilingual programming for children, an issue that takes on particular significance in the context of growing privatization and inequities within education in India: "So they [children] communicate well (and learn fast). My son is six years old; he sometimes uses Hindi and Marathi in a sentence. He uses four languages in a sentence to communicate [the other two being Kannada and English]."

Likewise, Alok Sharma commented on his mother learning from TV, in the context of a broader discussion of the rise of food TV in India: "I thought a food channel would not work; although I was working for it, I was skeptical about it. It not only worked, I also realized a pattern in my mother's TV watching. In the afternoons, she is watching cookery shows in various languages that we don't even speak in our place. She is watching a Gujarati show—we don't speak Gujarati at home, but she understands Gujarati and Marathi—she is watching cookery shows in these two languages, she is learning and cooking from those languages."

The kinds of literacies instilled through engaging with difference on TV here encompass far more than the linguistic. Sharma also expressed a sense of surprise at the "cosmopolitan" nature and imaginative capacity of his mother's own viewing habits. His mother's engagement with "foreign" language cookery shows speaks to both the embodied, sensory dimensions of food TV and its relative ability to travel across cultural boundaries as a format, but it also foregrounds a key theme in our research: that people's engagement with television is marked not only by pleasures of identification and cultural proximity but also by an interest and engagement with "distant" places and practices. In our research in India, two of the key genres of lifestyle programming that people associated with a sense of "seeing at a distance"—genres almost universally embraced by the households in our study—were food tourism and travel shows, with cookery shows in particular often described by interviewees as a means of engaging with difference and otherness in India.

In his classic essay on the invention of Indian cookery books, Arjun Appadurai notes that, prior to the emergence of nineteenth-century household guides (aimed at the colonial elite) containing recipes, and the more widely dispersed cookbooks of the twentieth century, India did not have a gustatory or culinary tradition (Appadurai 1988). Instead, food was embedded in moral and medicinal discourses. In constructing India as a space of distinct and diverse culinary traditions, cookbooks enacted a doubled invention of culture and otherness. Similarly, food television in India today offers an education in both imagined cultural traditions and culinary-geographic diversity, often framed through a kind of touristic gaze or vision of cultural difference (Urry 2002). In what Niki Strange categorizes as the "tour-educative" genre of cookery shows (Strange 1998), popular shows like NDTV Good Times's *Highway on My Plate* (see figure 3.5) and *Zaika India Ka* (The flavor of India) take viewers on a journey to roadside restaurants around the country, critically assessing and re-creating dishes while discussing the specificity of local customs and cuisines.

These highly popular shows present cultural difference and diversity as something that can be readily accessed through food, a point often reiterated by viewers in our study. For instance, Alok Sharma's mother, Kalpana, saw food TV as offering people an education in cultural traditions other than their own. Discussing one show, she noted: "He [the chef] went to Kerala where they sell spices in boats. He tells you everything. I like all that; you get information about new places, new things, what people like in a certain place, what their lifestyle is. I watch more of these shows and less drama serials."

When we asked Kalpana if such shows encourage people to travel, to become tourists in India, she replied: "Yes, people must certainly be doing that. A person must have curiosity to do something new, they must have the desire

Figure 3.5. Imagined mobilities, cultural tourism, and "placing" cultural difference on NDTV Good Times's *Highway on My Plate*.

to see a thing to know what it is. We are vegetarian, but even if they show something non-vegetarian we still watch it, because we may be able to make something like it with soybean."

Kalpana emphasizes the way in which televisual imaginaries of distant cultures and places create a sense of both doing and knowing otherness, offering people an imaginary passport that often contrasted with the fact that many of the Indian viewers we spent time with rarely traveled, and if they did it was to return to their village rather than to travel for leisure. Sharmila (the wife of the chauffeur Devkumar, quoted above), who lives in informal housing on the outskirts of Mumbai, similarly states: "I like the programs that also show food in travel shows. It could be anywhere in India or even outside India like Switzerland or America. We are poor; we cannot afford to visit such places. We can travel, but only within Maharashtra. And it is nice to know about other cultures like the Chinese."

A university student in Mumbai who likewise was an avid watcher of travel shows but had seldom traveled commented on the fact that many Indian viewers have had very limited exposure to other parts of the country: "In India we are not exposed to so many places—let's say Northeast; we don't know most things about Northeast. We only know about a few states regularly projected by tourism, TV channels, Rajasthan, Kerala, or a few places like Darjeeling. But what about other places? These travel shows focus on unknown places. India-based shows will cover such places like Andaman or Lakshadweep."

As was strongly echoed in our Taiwanese interviewees' discussions of travel TV (chapter 4), what seems to be on offer here is the acquisition of a kind of touristic and geographic literacy or spatial consciousness, though one that may contrast with people's own material and domestic locatedness, habits, and practices. For instance, in our Indian household interviews, people often spoke with fluency about a range of cuisines, from international food to the "traditions" of other Indian regions. When quizzed on whether they cooked these foods, though, the answer was usually no, though some would jokingly note that they had prepared Maggi noodles, perhaps the most ubiquitous massified "foreign" food available in India. In Appadurai's essay on Indian cookbooks, he notes that as cultural manuals they offer a kind of nonthreatening imaginary engagement with otherness, enabling people to dabble in experiences of cultural/caste difference through culinary boundary crossing. In contrast to, say, the far more challenging practice of cross-cultural marriage, engaging with cross-cultural cooking and food (or indeed travel, via TV travel and cookery-tour genres) permits an experience of exoticness through "a variety of registers" as well as enabling "compartmentalization" (Appadurai 1988, 9). That is, one can "experiment" with and learn about difference through eating out or vicariously watching exotic dishes being prepared on TV in "strange," distant, but nevertheless Indian locales, while cooking and eating "traditional" food at home.

We would argue, however, that for many Indian households today, engaging with a range of imaginary and material "registers" in one's daily life is not just about compartmentalization but also involves a reflexive and relational engagement with close–distant spatialities and relations of self and other that are negotiated on a daily basis. As televisual citizens, Indian audiences regularly engage with the worlds of distant others while often negotiating their own complex "diasporic" identities through and across cultural and linguistic realms. A grandmother originally from Tovinkere but now living with her family in Mumbai watches Kannada cookery shows depicting "exotic" Punjabi locations and cuisines. A poor family in Mumbai, living in a one-room dwelling, enjoys the UK show *Man vs. Wild* in their "native" language courtesy of direct-to-home television. An IT professional in Bangalore downloads English-language shows from HBO for his own personal viewing while also watching Sandalwood films with his extended family. We would argue that such juxtapositions of proximity and distance, whereby being in place is negotiated through and with difference, mark an evolving media and cultural ecology. Here, older spatial and scalar logics jostle with new social ontologies in ways that challenge earlier national or governmental imperatives of "seeing at a distance," foregrounding instead a variegated media world characterized by a sense of both disjuncture and otherness and also connectedness and interdependence.

Conclusion: From Scale to Relationality

In this chapter, we have offered an overview of Indian television in terms of its shifting role in shaping people's "imagined worlds." In doing so we have been careful to avoid compressing the wider story of Indian television into a single-stranded narrative, and instead have emphasized the multifaceted and variegated nature of the communicative modernities at play in this extremely large media landscape. As Nilendu Sen's emphasis (in one of the quotes opening this chapter) on *televisions* suggests, the contemporary Indian TV "system," such as it is, is the messy and contingent product of multiple forces and cultural, political, and economic conjunctures: less a coherent "institution" than a space of interlinked local, regional, national, and transnational industries, markets, and audiences, in turn shaped by diverse political, linguistic, cultural, and sociodemographic variables. The recent and somewhat surprising rise of televisual regionalisms, tied to complex local political and cultural as well as economic logics, and marked by reflexive engagements with the provincial and the cosmopolitan, is one striking example of the difficulty of generalizing or indeed predicting developments within what is a constantly evolving mediascape.

Another key theme here has been the question of scale in vast media ecologies such as those of China and India, and the relationship between place and economic and sociocultural geographies of difference and otherness. In our chapter on China, we noted that national and metropolitan television, such as the programming offered by Shanghai's Channel Young, is marked by a strategic negotiation of urban "localism" as well as cosmopolitan engagements with scale jumping, providing a multiscaled cultural imaginary of place that stands in contrast to the workings of provincial television players such as Bengbu TV. While Bengbu TV's strategy for survival involves investing in forms of scale fixing and maintenance, however, as we noted, young aspirational provincial audience members often practice their own forms of scale jumping, engaging with cosmopolitan-inflected "national" programming such as the dating format *If You Are the One*.

A key difference between the contemporary Indian mediascape—globalized, postcolonial, weakly governmentalized—and that of China is clearly the central role of the state in China in attempting to regulate and articulate a national geospatial consciousness. In China, television, at least at an industry level, also continues to be marked by strong hierarchies and distinctions between urban and regional markets. As we've suggested, India's diverse mediascape has, as in China, been historically shaped by significant spatial and social inequalities, particularly between the urban middle classes and rural poor, and between a culturally hegemonic Hindi North and "the South." However, in recent years Hindi media hegemony has been challenged by the growing role of regional media, including television, throughout India. Indeed, Shanti Kumar goes so far as to say that regionalization—given huge potential markets in terms of audience numbers and the incentive of relatively low advertising costs—is now *the* central driver of media industries in India (Kumar 2014). Boosted by the affordances of digital technology, the televisual landscape in India is now both increasingly connected *and* decentered, regionalized and localized, so that audiences across the country, whether urban or rural, often negotiate an array of TV programs that defy simple categorizations regarding cultural identity, origin, or locality.

In the present-day context, these increasingly routine experiences of overlapping and interconnected spatialities in India suggest the need for a rather different model of understanding mediated geographic and social relations that goes beyond the scalar. As we've suggested, notions of connectivity and relationality become increasingly useful for understanding the kind of complex, quasi-postnational media space that characterizes India. Here the work of geographers such as Ash Amin (2002), who has sought to think about spatiality in a global context by moving beyond notions of scale, offers useful ways of understanding the current moment. In mapping recent shifts in conceptions of global spatiality, Amin critiques an "ontology of territorial containment and scalar nesting, as well as [more] traditional spatial distinctions between the local as near, everyday, and 'ours,' and the global as distant, institutionalised, or 'theirs'" (Amin 2002, 395). Here Amin is not arguing that scalar practices and institutions, associated in particular with forms of regulation and governance, no longer exist but rather that other logics are also at play in globalized spaces. Arguing for an understanding of spatial topology "that is marked by overlapping near-far relations and ... connections that are not reducible to scalar spaces" (2002, 386), his alternative framing of spatial ontology suggests moving away from notions of de- and reterritorialization underpinned by a priori notions of place and scales of power. Instead, he argues that we should understand place and the spatial as increasingly "virtual"; that is, characterized by "practices of varied geographical stretch" (386) whereby "the proximate and the remote [can coexist] at the same geographical level" (389). While scalar hierarchy is crucial in shaping television in China, in the context of the Indian TV landscape, Amin's delinking of space and place from territory and scalar hierarchies offers a useful way to understand the highly interconnected and relational nature of people's everyday experience of and engagements with media worlds. The regionalization of television in India, for instance, via indigenized "global" lifestyle and reality formats, can be seen to mark not so much the de- or reterritorialization of media space as "the erosion of the ontological distinction between place and space as 'placement' in multiple geographies of belonging becomes possible" (395). In the following chapter, we further investigate the unpredictable complexities of television audiences' experiences of the proximate, the remote, and "geographical stretch" by means of a case study on Taiwanese viewers' responses to the U.S.-owned channel TLC Taiwan.

FOUR. **Imagining Global Mobility** TLC Taiwan

In the preceding two chapters, we explored how geosocial divisions between regional and metropolitan areas in India and China are reflected in lifestyle television programming and audience responses to it. In this chapter, we extend our analysis of lifestyle television's role in shaping imaginative geographies out to a transnational scale by focusing on local viewer responses to the Travel and Living Channel in Taiwan (TLC Taiwan), which is owned by American Discovery Communications Inc. and run from Discovery Networks Asia-Pacific headquarters in Singapore. International cable channel TLC also operates in many other territories in Asia, including two of the other "tiger" economies with well-established middle classes—Singapore and Hong Kong—as well as India, Malaysia, Indonesia, the Philippines, Thailand, and Vietnam. Therefore, although our case study here is TLC Taiwan, our discussion has broader ramifications beyond the specificity of the Taiwanese context. While some aspects of our interviewees' engagements with TLC are undoubtedly locally specific, other aspects—especially their televisually mediated imagination of transnational mobility—may well be a more general feature of audience interpretations of Euro-American lifestyle channels like TLC in Asia. We present our case study of TLC Taiwan, then, as a snapshot of engagements by young, urban viewers in a late-capitalist East Asian society with TLC as transnational, Western-centric lifestyle television.

TLC Taiwan screens mainly imported English-language content. With a strong focus on Euro-American travel, cooking, makeover, and reality competition formats, TLC is the channel in Taiwan where lifestyle television appears most obviously and coherently as a genre. The channel provides the conduit into Taiwan for programs including *Queer Eye for the Straight Guy, Jamie at Home, How Do I Look?*, and *Extreme Makeover: Weight Loss Edition*. On the majority of Taiwanese channels where locally produced content dominates, lifestyle television does not appear in such generically cogent form; rather, disaggregated elements of it are dispersed through a range of other genres, notably in the ubiquitous Japanese-style variety talk shows and variety game shows (see chapter 1). This makes TLC Taiwan an obvious site to analyze in our project of tracing the impact of Euro-American lifestyle TV beyond the Anglophone West.

Our interviews with sixteen young, urban viewers of TLC Taiwan (six men, ten women) suggest that one of the most notable properties of this channel is the way it enables viewers to imagine a form of identity centered around the individual's *imagination of her or his own potential for transnational mobility*. Television has offered its viewers the means for imaginative travel ever since its popularization in the West in the mid-twentieth century (Morley 2000; Urry 2007, 169–70; Moores 2012, 1–25). But with the rise of a more intensively mobile society and the simultaneously increasing mediatization of everyday life, television, along with other ubiquitous visual media, comes to assume an even more significant role in enlarging the mobile imagination's field of operation (Appadurai 1996, 31). As Arjun Appadurai argues, in cultural globalization, televisual mediascapes "offer to those who experience and transform them ... a series of elements ... out of which scripts can be formed of imagined lives.... These scripts can and do get disaggregated into complex sets of metaphors by which people live as they help to constitute narratives of the Other and protonarratives of possible lives, fantasies that could become prolegomena to the desire for acquisition and movement" (1996, 35–36). Our interviews with Taiwanese viewers of TLC reveal that, as for the Korean and Japanese viewers of Western media studied by Youna Kim and Karen Kelsky, respectively, such media are "implicated in the imaginative pull towards mobility," offering viewers symbolic resources from which they assemble visions of not-yet-realized cosmopolitan selves (Kelsky 2001, 13–14; Kim 2011, 64).[1]

In a sense, whether or not such viewers' desire for mobility is ever realized is beside the point. What is foregrounded in these viewers' discussions of watching TLC Taiwan is their collective practice of *imagining* mobility and valuing the *potential* for movement—both geographic movement (internationalist desire) and, correlatively, social movement (class aspirationism). In light of this, a useful term for our discussion in this chapter is *motility*, defined by the sociologists Vincent Kaufmann, Manfred Max Bergman, and Dominique Joye as "the capacity of entities ... to be mobile in social and geographic space, or as the way in which entities access and appropriate the capacity for socio-spatial mobility according to their circumstances" (2004, 750). This final element, the "appropriation" of motility, is the one most pertinent to our discussion of viewers' interactions with TLC Taiwan, since it "refers to how agents ... *interpret* and act upon perceived or real access and skills. Appropriation is shaped by *needs, plans, aspirations and understandings* of agents, and it relates to *strategies, motives, values and habits*. Appropriation describes how agents consider, deem appropriate, and select specific options" (Kaufmann, Bergman, and Joye 2004, 750, emphasis added). In other words, appropriation refers to the point at which potential for movement is subjectively internalized; it is about what people *do* with the potential for mobility—perceived or actual—at the imaginative as much as the decision-making level. It is here, we argue, that viewer responses to the global imaginary conjured by TLC are properly located. In responding to TLC Taiwan, the viewers we interviewed are appropriating the idea of motility to imagine new forms of identity. As we will see in the program-based case study in the final part of this chapter, identification with motility may have implications for one's subjective relationship with one's own homeland, as much as for how one sees oneself in relation to the world beyond its shores.

TLC Taiwan: Someday, Somewhere Else
Founded in the United States in 1985, Discovery Communications Inc. initially focused on natural history, science, and hobbyist programs for U.S. audiences but has since become a major global producer of lifestyle and travel programming (Fürsich 2003, 136–37). Following the saturation of the U.S. cable market in the early 1990s, Discovery pursued a strategy of aggressive international expansion, and by 2012 some 37 percent of its more than US$4.4 million revenue derived from its international operations across the Asia Pacific (including each of the territories discussed in this book) as well as Europe, Latin America, the Middle East, and Africa (Fürsich 2003, 141; Discovery Communications 2013; Institute of Media and Communications Policy 2013). In her important critical analysis of the Discovery Channel as a global purveyor of nonfiction entertainment TV, Elfriede Fürsich observes that Discovery aims to produce "neutral" programming: framed as "quality," educational, and purged of potentially controversial content, thereby palatable to diverse international audiences (2003, 137–38). As Fürsich observes, travel shows translate particularly readily across national and cultural borders: their subject matter itself concerns border-crossing, and the genre appeals to a rising global middle

class for whom international travel is either an affordable commodity or a pleasurable fantasy (2003, 142). Discovery's Travel & Adventure channel was launched in 1998, then rebranded as Discovery Travel & Living in 2005 and again as TLC in 2010.

The Discovery Channel commenced operations in Taiwan in 1994 (Su and Cheng 2009, 9) and the Travel & Living Channel (Lüyou Shenghuo Pindao) was launched in 2003, prior to the 2010 rebrand as TLC (Hong 2012, 74).[2] In the early years, all of Discovery Taiwan's content was supplied by the central U.S. channel, but later, programs produced under contract in Taiwan and elsewhere in Asia also began to appear on Discovery's Taiwan channels (see below). Nonetheless, the overall feel of TLC Taiwan as described by the viewers we interviewed remains very clearly Western (the term used in Taiwan is *oumei*; literally, Euro-American). Underlining this, over a seven-day period in late February 2013, we found that 51 percent of TLC Taiwan's programs aired were from the United States, 16 percent were British, 16 percent Taiwanese, 7 percent Indian, 6.5 percent Canadian, and 3.5 percent Australian.[3] It is important to note here that the programs produced in Taiwan and India were made under contract to TLC or the Discovery Channel, were overwhelmingly in English, and adhered closely to the network's stringent stylistic guidelines so that their feel remained far closer to TLC's American-made shows than to popular local programming in either of these Asian countries. Ratings data reveal that TLC is favored by a specific demographic in Taiwan: in the final quarter of 2012, women outnumbered men three to two, and most viewers were full-time workers over twenty-five years of age with higher than average income.[4]

Some of the most popular programs watched by the viewers we interviewed in 2011 included *Project Runway*, *Queer Eye*, *Take Home Chef*, *Nigella Feasts*, *Jamie at Home*, *Passport to Europe*, *Man v. Food*, *America's Next Top Model*, and *Anthony Bourdain: No Reservations*. The emphasis is clearly on American and British cooking, travel, and reality-competition shows, with celebrities Jamie Oliver, Samantha Brown, Anthony Bourdain, and (especially) Curtis Stone frequently mentioned as targets for viewers' identification and desire, and as intermediaries between the Taiwanese audience and the alluring world of "Euro-America" that they saw as the channel's central subject. Reflecting this geocultural orientation, even Western cooking and makeover shows were often interpreted by our Taiwanese interviewees *as travel shows*: *Queer Eye* as a lesson about queer and metrosexual life in America; *Jamie at Home* as a showcase of exotic Western food ways that are interesting to see but too difficult to emulate in one's own home in Taiwan. In the words of Mr. Ding, a twenty-three-year-old master's student in Taipei: "I think TLC is . . . something that takes us . . . like, on a tour. I don't really define it . . . as a life channel . . . that teaches you how to cook or whatever."

In addition to "Western" (*oumei*), other terms frequently used by interviewees in characterizing the feel of TLC included relaxed (*qingsong*), casual (*suibian*), beautiful (*meihao*), luxurious (*haohua*), middle class (*zhongchan jieji*), fresh (*xinxian*), simple (*jiandan*), green (*lühua*), and leisure oriented (*xiuxian*). Mr. Han encapsulated the general feeling: "[TLC is all about] very simply, very relaxedly, very intuitively seeing and getting to know . . . different regions and different countries. . . . There's no way I can travel to every single place, so I get to see local life from [TLC's] point of view or [TLC's] angle. It's fun, fresh, and you get a different kind of information from it" (twenty-six, unemployed, Taipei). In one sense, TLC might be seen as simply offering its Taiwanese viewers the pleasures of escapism; the relaxed, affluent, and effortlessly fun world of "Euro-America" that it presents offers a soothing distraction from the pressures of everyday local life. Indeed, some viewers explicitly interpreted their enjoyment of the channel in this way: Mr. Han described how TLC had provided an emotional refuge during his recent two years' military service on the small, isolated island of Matzu: "I was really bored and depressed, so whenever I got the chance I'd watch TLC nonstop, to help me escape from . . . the environment I was in." Similarly, Mr. Zhou, a twenty-seven-year-old theater producer in Taipei, recalled turning to TLC during his lunch hour when working exhausting fourteen- to seventeen-hour days and six-day weeks in his former job at a large electronics corporation, to "get a bit of . . . rest for the soul." For Mr. Lin, meanwhile, "[TLC] feels more soothing [than Taiwanese channels]. . . . It's more green, more simple. . . . Like, you can live very simply, and you can be very at ease in your life. When I'm watching their shows I feel I'm far away from the hustle and bustle" (twenty-four, master's student, Taipei).

Some interviewees, like Ms. Cai, saw this aspect as connected specifically with their own position in urban, late-capitalist East Asia: "In East Asia, . . . there is more life pressure than in the West, and lots of work pressure, and we don't have . . . you know, like a month of vacation every year or whatever. So I guess we must have a greater longing, I mean people who want to find work-life balance would like this channel" (twenty-six, trading company employee, Taipei). In such interpretations, TLC presents Euro-America as a kind of soothing dream for viewers caught up in the high-pressure compressed modernity of an ex–tiger economy (Chang and Song 2010; Martin and Lewis 2012). Far from providing a how-to guide to global lifestyles to be followed in literal fashion, TLC's infotainment programming would in this view appear to have more in common with the genre of fantasy.

However, while the escapist function of TLC is clearly real, the significance of the channel's projection of a fantasy Euro-America also goes further than this. The viewers we interviewed were all urban-dwelling, twentysomething, tertiary-educated, middle-class people, and many presented themselves as consciously "internationalist" subjects (to borrow Karen Kelsky's [2001, 5–6] term). That is, they represented their interests, aspirations, values, and life plans as closely entwined with their hopes for traveling, studying, and/or working overseas, and they explicitly connected this outward orientation with their enjoyment of TLC. For example, twenty-six-year-old Ms. Zhu, who was studying Korean in Seoul and a keen viewer of *Take Home Chef, Jamie at Home, Passport to Europe,* and *Man v. Food,* represented her identity as structured almost entirely around her international orientation. With one sister married and living in South Africa, she described herself as coming from an "internationalized family." Ms. Zhu said she had always been interested in the world beyond Taiwan, and during her undergraduate years had acted as a volunteer guide for international students at her university, which enabled her to make foreign friends whom she now visited during her frequent international travels across Asia and Russia for recreation, study, and sporting competitions (she was also an elite athlete). She had previously gone out with two European boyfriends, one of her closest friends at the time of the interview was Iranian, and all of her good friends were either non-Taiwanese people or fellow Taiwanese students whose main point of connection with each other was their shared interest in overseas languages and cultures. Ms. Zhu felt that TLC "widens your field of vision," "opens Taiwan's eyes to the world," and provides a "bridge" between Taiwan and the rest of the world. She framed her own viewing of TLC as a logical extension of her cosmopolitan outlook, and felt that it helped her to realize what she framed as an ethical (as well as pleasurable) project of learning about and spreading understanding of global cultural diversity.

The twenty-seven-year-old medical technician Ms. Li, who had grown up in the small city of Taoyuan, about forty minutes from the capital Taipei, connected her TLC viewing practices with her own internationalist desires as follows:

> Right now I'm living in Taipei City, which is *OK*[5] I think; it's a relatively internationalized city, but . . . Taoyuan is less so. . . . In Taipei City you often see stuff like Italian restaurants, lots of different kinds of restaurants, but there are fewer in Taoyuan. I really hope to see Taiwan become more internationalized. . . . I personally also hope . . . to go to some kind of . . . more internationalized place to work; I think it would be pretty interesting.
>
> . . .

> I really like traveling, I like to go and look at different countries, different people, different cultures.... Through TLC we can find out about the customs of different countries; it's like it opens a window for us.... You feel like it's a small-scale global village.

In these comments Ms. Li, like Ms. Zhu, uses TLC as a means to construct herself as a certain type of internationalized person: a citizen of the "global village" projected by the channel. Thus TLC becomes a companion on her anticipated journey from provincial Taoyuan to internationalized Taipei and on again to an imagined future overseas destination. This becomes even clearer in her characterization of the type of person she feels would *not* enjoy watching TLC: "People who don't ever in their life want to leave Taiwan. Maybe they think the outside world has nothing to do with them, they just want to look after themselves and ... just their own family, that's enough. They just want to stay in Taiwan, and the rest of the world ... they don't care about." Ms. Li's tone implies a value judgment: unlike those small-minded folk who care only about their own immediate context and (mistakenly) see the world beyond Taiwan as irrelevant, watching TLC enables Ms. Li to see herself as a person who both recognizes and embodies the value of transnational connection and mobility.

Ms. Li's aspirationism in her anticipation of someday working overseas is an integral part of the outward orientation characteristic of this group of viewers. When discussing whether they ever had or would like to implement specific ideas presented on TLC shows, terms like *xia ci* (sometime), *yihou* (later), and *you yi tian* (someday) were common. For the most part, these viewers' social and geographic mobility was much more (perceived) potential than present actuality. Consider the following responses:

> I feel like what we're watching is a kind of "Oh ... someday." You often say, "Someday I want to go there too." For example if [the show] is about Spain, then, [I feel] I must go there someday. Or if it shows you somewhere really fun you'll be like, oh it looks gorgeous, I'll go there someday. It makes you look forward to it; a kind of ... hope, that someday you'll be able to do whatever. Actually it's the same with cooking, [you think], hey, I want to make that dish too, it looks delicious.... What I mean is, these shows create a lot of expectancy.... I think [they create] a *wish*.... A dream. (Ms. Peng, twenty-four, tech product manager, Taipei, planning graduate study in the United States)

> [You feel that] someday, when you have money, you might be able to do those things, it gives you ... an *image* ... of what you might want in the

future.... If you make money you'll be able to live that kind of a life. It's a way of thinking, a dream; it may not be realizable, but it paints a certain vision. (Mr. Chen, twenty-four, master's student, Taipei)

[TLC] really does give people a vision of something to hope for. Because I've tried watching it with my Ma and Pa, and they have *absolutely* no commentary to make on it, they won't say, "Wow, that looks great. I want to go there." It doesn't connect with them at all. My Pa will just be, like, "Wow, check out that massive fish!" [*Laughs*] But when I watch it with friends my own age, or with my boyfriend, I mean, since we're at the age where we still have lots of hopes for the future, we'll be like, "Wow, that's great, we must get a barbecue oven like that, and we must have a garden like that." It gives us a direction and a goal. (Ms. Qiu, twenty-five, government bureaucrat, Taipei)

Combined with the transnational orientation that TLC represents, this temporality of "oh, someday..." suggests that the channel is used by these young viewers for the imaginative elaboration of their own motility: their potential for (future) movement. The link between geographic and social mobility is clear in the responses above. The "someday" is specifically "someday, when you have money," and the lifestyles imagined in the future time and place are those of U.S.-style middle-class suburban life, complete with barbecue ovens and spacious backyards. Many interviewees told us that the Western-style recipes and domestic designs on TLC's lifestyle shows could not practically be emulated in the present: it was too hard to find the right ingredients, kitchens in Taiwan don't have ovens, apartments lack backyards, extensive renovation is impossible for renters and difficult even for owner-occupiers in densely populated apartment blocks. Rather, like the space of "Euro-America" itself, for these aspirational young viewers TLC's recipes and home designs became the province of an imagined future self who had achieved a level of social and geographic mobility that could, in the present, only be imagined.

The issue of class arose repeatedly in our conversations with these TLC viewers, as a majority of them were reflexively conscious of the classed character of the channel's mode of address, and several were openly critical of this aspect. Ms. Peng, for example, eloquently expressed her outrage at a show about a luxury yacht: "I was like, 'How can these people be so rich? They can just up and buy a yacht.' Sometimes I feel like yelling at them: 'What's going on, how come Europeans always get to be so rich? You just up and buy a huge yacht, with—with luxury fittings and all!' [*Laughs*]" (twenty-four, tech product manager, Taipei).

Such a response voices the other side of the Euro-America fantasy: a (postcolonial?) anger at the inequitable global distribution of wealth that appears, through TLC, to leave Westerners as a general category with levels of money, contentment, and material goods that can only be envied by this young Taiwanese viewer. On the other hand, other responses draw attention to how a preference for watching TLC works according to a Bourdieuian logic of taste as social distinction to shore up the identity of the viewer not just as an "internationalist" but also as someone with the high cultural capital appropriate to the upper middle class (Bourdieu 1984). For example, we heard stories of young, urban, university-educated acquaintances given to stating ostentatiously that TLC is the only TV channel that they watch. Mr. Zhou, too, made telling remarks about the kinds of people he thought would and would not watch TLC. The channel's viewers "would have an undergraduate degree or above.... They'd care about quality of life, and ... they'd like to try new things—like me, I'm a very curious person." When working in his former unhappy job at the electronics corporation, Mr. Zhou watched TLC alone during his lunchbreak, "because not a single one of my colleagues would have appreciated that kind of thing.... [They were] that kind of traditional ... office worker, petty and gossipy; who among them could possibly watch it?" And like Ms. Li, quoted above, Mr. Zhou attributed certain (negative) qualities to the type of people who *wouldn't* watch TLC: "People who watch *Night Market Life* [a high-rating Minnan-language soap opera] probably wouldn't watch [TLC], I'm guessing. [*Laughs*] Because ... I guess one would say it's the ... scope of their lives, I mean the things they *care* about are on the local village or neighborhood level, yeah. I mean even if they occasionally go overseas on holiday, I reckon they'd only go in a tour group" (twenty-seven, theater producer, Taipei).

Mr. Zhou's discussion of TLC and TV taste constructs two groups of (imagined) people. The first, in which he includes himself, watches TLC, is well educated, and is curious about "new things" and (by implication) about traveling independently outside of Taiwan. The second group of people, in which Mr. Zhou includes his former colleagues, does not watch TLC but probably watch Minnan dramas, and are "traditional," petty, and local rather than international in their concerns. They work in standard office jobs (unlike Mr. Zhou himself, who had finally left the electronics firm to work in the arts) and are group package tourists, not individual worldly travelers. The invocation of Minnan drama viewership as a shorthand signifier of working-class taste is a well-worn rhetorical strategy: Fang-chih Irene Yang has analyzed in detail how representations of this genre draw together associations of working-class identity, Minnan ethnicity, rural southern location, and feminine gender in an ideological molecule that expresses the denigration of each of these attributes in northern Taiwan's Mandarin-dominant, urban middle-class culture (Yang 2008). Mr. Zhou's response adds to this equation the variable of geographic mobility versus stasis. In his first imagined group, good taste and a middle-class identity are definitionally linked to TLC, transnational mobility, and a cosmopolitan orientation. In his second group, bad taste and petit-bourgeois or working-class identity are linked to local drama and Taiwan-boundedness.

A conversation between Ms. Wang (twenty-seven, video subtitler), Ms. Cai (twenty-six, trading company worker), Ms. Qiu (twenty-five, government bureaucrat), our research assistant Claire Tsai, and one of the authors further highlights TLC's status as signifier of "good" (trendy, urban, young, cosmopolitan, middle-class) taste, this time in the channel's uses in urban commercial space:

> MS. WANG: One thing I've really noticed is that some *bars*, or restaurants . . .
> CLAIRE: Ohh, yeah, American restaurants, all of the American restaurants near National Taiwan Normal University [NTNU] have TLC on the TV.
> MS. WANG: No matter when you go there, TLC is playing. It's really cool.
> MS. QIU: I think it's become the representative trendy channel. . . .
> FRAN: I'm just wondering why all the restaurants I go to have the TV tuned to ETTV News or something.
> MS. CAI: What restaurants do you go to?
> MS. QIU: You go to lunchbox buffets [*biandang dian*]??

TLC provides background visuals for the urban landscape of boutique bars, coffee shops, and cute accessories stores frequented by the student population, contributing to the definition of the university neighborhood as the sort of trendy, cosmopolitan place preferred by these young middle-class professional and student women. Just as Minnan dramas functioned as a byword for working-class "bad taste" in the exchange quoted above, in this case Fran's reference to sensationalist twenty-four-hour local news channels like ETTV was enough to alert these young women to the fact that she was frequenting the "wrong" sort of places: popular, cheap, decidedly un-trendy lunchbox buffets.

However, it is important to remain alert to television's inherent polysemy and capacity to evoke contradictory responses in different viewers. While for the educated, twentysomething viewers we interviewed in Taipei, TLC let them see themselves as motile subjects on the verge of upward (class) and outward (geographic) mobility, for other viewers the channel had virtually the opposite effect. Consider, for example, the following account from Mr. Ding, a twenty-three-year-old master's student in Taipei:

> My Pa bought a block of land in [far southern] Pingtung because of watching those shows on TLC.... He really wanted to live like them.... There are [some shows where they] go to a rural village, for example, yeah, and he really longed for that village life.... You see my Grandpa and his family are farmers, but my Pa moved to the city [after he grew up], to... urban Kaohsiung. And through... that channel, he realized he wanted to return to the farming life, so he bought a block of land that he hopes he can farm after he retires.... He loves to watch those travel shows, and he loves to go out to the country; my Ma and Pa both really like that [village life] feel.

Rather than reinforcing the global orientation claimed by Mr. Ding's own generation, for Mr. Ding senior TLC prompts a material reconnection with local lifeways remembered from childhood. From the point of view of audiences in the United States and Western Europe, TLC cooking and travel programs introducing the idyllic pleasures of rural and village life could be seen as presenting a nostalgic simulacrum, since such viewers are unlikely to retain personal memories of pre-urban, preindustrial culture. But Taiwan's compressed modernity, which saw the island's society shift from a largely agrarian to a postindustrial economy in a span of just forty-odd years, means that for Mr. Ding senior, TLC's programs recall a *personal* history of preindustrial life. While in the examples discussed above TLC represented a turning away from and in some cases a denigration of the Taiwan local, paradoxically, the standardized products of this U.S.-owned global media corporation enable Mr. Ding senior to enact an embodied critique of global, urban, late-modern culture. The aesthetic and spiritual value attributed to rural life in TLC shows has prompted Mr. Ding senior to revalue both his family history and rural south Taiwan as a social setting. But what exactly is entailed in reseeing one's home place through the lens of global media? We tackle this question, among others, in the following section through a case study of TLC's locally produced travel show, *Feng Taiwan* (Fun Taiwan).

Fun Taiwan: Glocal Me

Although Discovery's strategy has generally been to produce frictionless global edutainment (Fürsich 2003, 137–38), over the past decade Discovery Networks Asia-Pacific has begun to undertake some more "glocalized"

Figure 4.1. *Fun Taiwan*, season 5, May 27, 2011. Janet Hsieh introduces the mountain community of Nantou County: "It really is an adorable community."

productions, contracting local independent production houses to make programs to order for export across regional Asian markets (Su and Cheng 2009). *Fun Taiwan* is one such example: a travelogue launched in 2005 that ran to twelve seasons before spawning the spin-off *Fun Taiwan Challenge*, a reality competition format in its second season at the time of writing. Narrated and hosted in English by the lively, outgoing, Texas-born host Janet Hsieh, *Fun Taiwan* is a sixty-minute show produced by the Taipei production house Dongneng Yixiang under the close supervision of Discovery's Singapore headquarters. The show follows Janet to various locations around Taiwan, exploring local culture, trying local foods, and chatting with the locals in Minnan and Mandarin in her quest, as she puts it in a voice-over on the opening credits of earlier seasons, to "rediscover her heritage" (see figure 4.1). Janet's hosting style oscillates between bubbly and contemplative: in one scene she charms the locals with her girlish enthusiasm and naïveté about the finer points of local culture; in the next she launches into a pop-philosophical monologue on her spiritual experience of the landscape and folkways (see figure 4.2).

The concept for *Fun Taiwan* came from Discovery Networks Asia-Pacific's headquarters in Singapore, which in the early 2000s wanted to create more Asia-specific content for its regional channels.[6] Taiwan was chosen as the best location for a travel show for the expedient reasons that China was too large and Japan too far from the channel's regional headquarters, while Taiwan had the advantages of being close to Singapore, conveniently small, and

Figure 4.2. *Fun Taiwan,* season 11, June 3, 2011. The romantic-anthropological tourist gaze: Janet joins workers in the salt fields of southern Taiwan. Her voice-over in this scene muses, "Taking a step at a time across the salt fields in the sunset, I realize what a small drop I am in the bigger universe. The chaos from my mind purges as I surrender to this humility: a being as tiny as these salt grains; a speck on the earth."

geographically diverse. The making of the program was taken over by Dongneng in season 2 and Janet—then a student of Mandarin at National Taiwan Normal University—was discovered via a public audition, replacing the host of the first two seasons, Jia Pei-en. *Fun Taiwan* was initially trialed in Taiwan before being taken to overseas markets, and the show is now simultaneously broadcast on TLC in Taiwan and across the region. The show's central concept, according to the Dongneng employee we interviewed (see note 6), is "to look at Taiwan through a foreigner's eyes."

The "foreignness" of *Fun Taiwan* is palpable not only in its concept but also in its style. Like other Asia-produced TLC shows, the televisual form of *Fun Taiwan* is quite different from most popular local programming: Discovery's Singapore headquarters requires Dongneng to adhere to TLC's signature style of documentary realism and avoid the heavy use of postproduction effects and comedy that characterizes popular local travel shows. Achieving the required style and quality adds significant time to *Fun Taiwan*'s production schedule—estimated by Dongneng's director, Li Jingbai, at an extra fifteen days per episode compared to a local travel show (Su and Cheng 2009, 17).

Figure 4.3. Comic byplay, conviviality, variety-style effects, and a nonromanticized local scene on *Super Taste*, TVBS Entertainment, February 25, 2013.

Like all contracted Discovery productions, the program has a substantially higher budget than the local shows, an investment that can be recouped by Discovery from advertising sales across multiple national markets. Control of *Fun Taiwan* and its spin-offs remains very much in the hands of the global network: while the concept for each episode is generated by Dongneng, the ultimate say on what gets made and how it should look belongs to Discovery. This top-down structure is common across Discovery's Asian collaborations, and as Herng Su and Shu-Wen Cheng argue, marks a structural limitation to the localization process (2009, 23).

Before proceeding to our detailed analysis of audience responses to *Fun Taiwan*, it is useful to situate the show within the broader generic context of Taiwanese TV travelogues, since the ways in which this program differs from the popular local shows highlights important information about *Fun Taiwan*'s mode of address and the type of viewing subject it assumes. Popular at the time of our research but vastly different in style to *Fun Taiwan*, for example, was *Shi Shang Wan Jia* (Super taste), a local travelogue from TVBS Entertainment hosted by a team of young male comedians, focusing on eating, shopping, and sightseeing in different towns around the island. This show uses a comic mode of address and makes liberal use of postproduction effects (animations, sound effects, additional voice-over narration to enhance comic effect) (see figure 4.3). Gala TV (GTV)'s *Shijie Di Yi Deng* (World's number one), meanwhile, adheres to a similar style but introduces overseas locations. *Lüxing*

Yingyuan Tuan (Travel relief team), from Star Chinese, focuses on regional cuisines from around Taiwan. Hosted by an in-studio team with intercut segments filmed on location, this show takes one step further toward the variety genre. Other travel shows produced by local channels are more documentary in style, but overall there is a strong tendency to include comedy and variety elements, and *Fun Taiwan* sits toward the far naturalistic/documentary end of the spectrum. In the terms of John Urry's taxonomy of tourist gazes, if the local travel shows invite a convivial-collective tourist gaze, then *Fun Taiwan*'s form, style, and mode of address could be said to solicit a hybrid romantic-anthropological gaze (see figure 4.2). The show at once centers solitude and a "personal, semi-spiritual relationship with the object of the gaze" and locates its sights/sites interpretatively within a historical and cultural array of symbols and meanings (Urry and Larsen 2011, 19–20). *Fun Taiwan* presents Taiwan as an object of consumption for a young, middlebrow, internationalist "social tourist" gaze, perhaps somewhat similar to that centered in Lonely Planet's travel guides, but with the added element of Janet's "special" insider-outsider relationship with the sites presented.

In drawing comparisons between *Fun Taiwan* and local travel shows, some interviewees highlighted what they saw as the former's distancing effect. Mr. Ding, for example, compared Janet with Yan Jun and Yan Fu (known collectively as "2moro"), comedian cohosts of *Super Taste*, as follows: "Yan Jun and Yan Fu, they . . . they'll get very *involve*[d] in it, whereas I feel that Janet . . . doesn't feel as *involve*[d], I feel she's more . . . introducing [the place] from the perspective of a neutral, objective observer" (twenty-three, master's student, Taipei).

Mr. Ding explained that Yan Jun and Yan Fu seemed more involved than Janet primarily as a result of their highly skilled comedic interactions with local people. When introducing a place, they had no trouble slipping into the local patois and interacting effortlessly with the people they met, whose entertaining reactions and personalities become part of the show's central attraction, whereas Janet's presentation style and linguistic and social capacities—although impressive for someone raised overseas—held her at more of a distance from local life. Ms. Bai, a twenty-two-year-old student, expressed a similar idea by contrasting the different practices that *Fun Taiwan* foregrounds compared with the local travel shows: "I think that . . . [*Fun Taiwan*] is about looking at this place [*kan zhege difang*], whereas [Taiwanese travel shows] are about coming here to have fun [*wan zhege difang*]. . . . For example, . . . you might . . . just wander around: today I just want to slowly experience . . . this particular street, say. The [second] kind is, you arrive somewhere and other people say you should go to a certain shop or go wherever, then OK, I'll go to that shop. That's the basic difference."

The activity Ms. Bai selects as characteristic of a *Fun Taiwan*–style approach to a place—wandering alone to contemplatively "experience" a particular street—assumes a significantly higher level of cultural capital than the activity that she associates with the local shows: shopping for local specialties recommended by popular opinion. Moreover, *Fun Taiwan* centers *kan* (looking) rather than the *wan* (playing) that is centered in convivial-collective shows like *Super Taste*, thereby implying a more detached relationship with the place being presented. As the analysis of viewer responses below will demonstrate, this sense of distanciation arises not only from Janet's hosting style and *Fun Taiwan*'s distinctive stylistic features but also from the very specific spectator position that the show seems to offer to its Taiwanese viewers: that of an international(ist) subject "returning," as it were, to re-view her homeland.

Despite its intentional orientation toward overseas viewers and quite un-Taiwanese televisual style, *Fun Taiwan* has proven to be an unexpected hit within Taiwan, where its ratings have peaked at 0.2—which would be low for a GEC (general entertainment channel) but is high for this niche cable channel. The show has diversified into a range of other formats, including season 10, where Janet played tour guide to young foreign visitors in Taiwan; *Fun Asia* and *Fun USA*, which followed Janet's travels beyond Taiwan; and, since 2011, *Fun Taiwan Challenge*, an *Amazing Race*–style reality competition format hosted by Janet and made in collaboration with the Taiwan Tourism Board, where fifteen young international contestants race around Taiwan competing in various competitions for a cash prize (TLC Asia 2013). Janet herself has attained the status of major regional celebrity. The cheery ex-model has collaborated on several occasions with Taiwan's Tourism Board to produce short films promoting travel to Taiwan, and features regularly in fashion and lifestyle magazines across Malaysia, Singapore, and Hong Kong (Hong 2012, 74–76). Janet's star persona hinges on her identity as an ABT (American-born Taiwanese), and this insider-outsider status plays a key role in reconciling the localism of *Fun Taiwan*'s subject matter with the globalism of its style, mode of address, and institutional context as a TLC production. The show's global-local mix creates a complexly hybrid viewing position for its local audience, which is invited to re-see its homeland through the eyes of an international visitor and embrace local culture from a global perspective.

Several of the *Fun Taiwan* viewers we interviewed revealed that this unusual hybridity created initial confusion about the show's mode of address and target audience. In a typical statement, Ms. Bai related: "Originally I was like, is this [show] meant for Taiwanese people? It uses English, it takes a Chinese American host and uses English to introduce Taiwan, so I thought it must be meant for foreigners. But then I thought: hold on, but the people watching it are all Taiwanese. So back then, I totally rejected the program's design. I thought: if you want Taiwanese people to watch it, then why don't you just do it in Chinese, why do you insist on making it in English?" (twenty-two, student, Taipei).

Such responses are indicative of the program's muddying of the distinction between "foreigners" and "Taiwanese people."[7] Ms. Bai's friend Mr. Ma agreed, adding that he'd objected strongly to Janet's use of English to address a Taiwanese audience, since it reminded him of the way "some people like to insist on speaking English to you," which to him seemed pretentious and arrogant. However, most viewers with whom we spoke had overcome such initial hostility and come to enjoy the show's unusual mode of address. Indeed, we argue that the hybridity of the show's mode of address and its projection of a specific type of "glocal" (Taiwanese yet global) identity constitute some of its most meaningful features for the young, urban, "internationalist" TLC viewers we interviewed.

Interview responses indicated that *Fun Taiwan* enabled some viewers to take up a complexly split viewing position and cultural identification. In a particularly telling statement, Ms. Li, a twenty-seven-year-old medical technician, revealed: "Say for example I'm watching [*Fun Taiwan*] introduce a rural area in Taiwan's south, I'll say, 'Is that what it's really like?' I'll start to think back about how the south looked to me when I was there.... About 70 percent of me is watching to see if you've got it right, and 30 percent of me is imagining I'm a foreigner who's going to Taiwan and watching the show so I can plan where I want to go." In watching the show, Ms. Li experiences herself as a literally, mathematically split subject: 70 percent fact-checking local, 30 percent foreign visitor. Again, in Mr. Lin's words, *Fun Taiwan* implies the hope that "Taiwanese people could... look [at Taiwan] in a different way, not in the way of a local person." Just as the producers planned, then, the show seems effectively to present "Taiwan through a foreigner's eyes." It offers local viewers a new way of seeing, reassessing the local through identification with a global gaze and thereby reinforcing these young viewers' "internationalist" identity, as analyzed in the first part of this chapter.

Janet acts as the key intermediary to the internationalist-Taiwanese identification that the show invites. Janet's well-known life circumstances place her in between Taiwan and "Euro-America," and viewers' discussions of her persona repeatedly associated her with "foreignness." Mr. Zhou explained that "[Janet's] stand-out feature is that she's like a foreigner traveling in Taiwan, but that foreigner has a deep understanding of Taiwan"; and Mr. Lin felt that she "is willing to try anything, yeah, and she tries [new] things like a foreigner would, not like a Taiwanese girl." Mr. Ding thought that "the impression she gives you is of that kind of . . . Taiwanese girl that foreigners really like. . . . I think she's very free and easy, and for example, with eating weird foods, she'll . . . she'll be quite daring in . . . trying them. . . . For a . . . Taiwanese audience . . . actually she has a bit of a mixed-blood [*hunxue*] feel, even though she's not a mixed-blood" (twenty-three, master's student, Taipei).

The (imaginary) ethnic hybridity that Mr. Ding perceives in Janet resonates interestingly with Ms. Li's description, above, of her own split subjectivity in watching Janet's show, in that both conjure hybrid Taiwanese–foreign identity amalgams. As well as the repeated associations with foreignness (*waiguo*, which in Taiwanese usage is most often code for Westernness), the statements above also associate Janet with an outward orientation: she is seen as adventurous, bold, and willing to embrace new experiences. Such an orientation is itself associated with a "foreign"-style personality, in Mr. Lin's and Mr. Ding's statements; it also clearly echoes the young TLC viewers' *self*-representations in the accounts analyzed earlier in this chapter. Viewer identification with this aspect of Janet's character was made even more explicit in the way in which the very consciously internationalist Ms. Zhu—who had herself briefly considered auditioning for Janet's role on *Fun Taiwan*—expressed her admiration of the host: "[Janet]'s willing to learn different languages, she's even willing to learn some Indigenous languages. To me this is . . . a very important point. Because there are some foreigners who come to Taiwan . . . actually not necessarily [only] here, actually when foreigners go to any place they'll always face the issue of 'when in Rome' [*rujing sui su*]. Some people totally reject it; they think there's no need for them to learn [the local culture]" (twenty-six, student, Taipei/Seoul). For Ms. Zhu, Janet represents the very form of ethical cosmopolitanism—characterized by outward orientation, openness to foreign cultures, and a willingness to learn—that she herself strives to embody (see our discussion of Ms. Zhu's responses, above).

Mr. Chen also expressed an interesting form of identification with Janet's transnational, transcultural persona: "Before, at the start of the show, it would emphasize that [Janet] herself is a Taiwanese person, only she lived in America. And then she came back [to Taiwan] to 'find her roots,' yeah, like her identification with this place sort of called to her. And that calls you to watch the show, it makes you . . . it piques your interest" (twenty-four, master's student, Taipei). The term Mr. Chen used for "call" is *zhaohuan*; this is in fact a standard Chinese translation for Althusserian interpellation (Mr. Chen was studying for a master's in media studies). What he outlines here is a kind of interpellative chain: Janet recognizes herself in the call of Taiwan; and Mr. Chen recognizes himself in Janet's recognition. What is interesting, though, is that the element that calls out to Mr. Chen appears to be Janet's structurally *distanced* relationship with Taiwan: after all, she hears its call precisely because she has been away from it. And it is in Janet's reflexive return to Taiwan from a distant location that Mr. Chen somehow recognizes himself. Here, as in each of the above responses, transnational Janet works effectively—albeit apparently against the odds—as a target for the identification of these Taiwan-dwelling Taiwanese viewers. The transnational identity and reflexive relationship with Taiwan that for Janet are structural effects of her life circumstances seem to resonate with these viewers' "internationalist" imagination of their own relationships with both Taiwan and "Euro-America," despite the fact that these viewers have grown up and continue to live in Taiwan. Approaching Taiwan reflexively, as if from an international perspective, seems to come to them remarkably easily and pleasurably. Of course, people's relationships with place are never *not* mediated, to some degree—the places that are materially inhabited by the body and the social self are always also places that are symbolically represented to the inhabitant, whether through oral stories, performances, literary texts, electronic media products, or other means. What is new in a program like *Fun Taiwan*, then, is not the fact that it creates for the viewer a mediated or reflexive relationship with local place. Rather, the novel element is in the specific character of the perspective offered: the invitation to (re)view Taiwan from afar, and to (re)experience one's Taiwanese identity from the perspective of an explicitly transnational subjectivity. Through Janet, the program is able to effect symbolic reconciliation between the viewer's current material location, in Taiwan, and the global, mobile imaginary that is arguably TLC Taiwan's chief ideological product. It projects a form of identity that is global at heart and Taiwanese in its specifics: "glocal me."

Conclusion

In this chapter, we have framed TLC as an example of U.S.-style lifestyle programming being consumed in Taiwan to consolidate viewers' imagination of transnational mobility. We have argued that the channel works to shore up the mobile imaginary of young, urban, middle-class internationalist subjects, consolidating their consciousness of their own motility; that is, their (real or perceived) potential for future mobility both outward, toward the global, and upward, toward upper-middle-class consumer lifestyles. If, as Kaufmann, Bergman, and Joye argue, motility can be seen as a form of capital, then in thinking out new identities based on the capacity for social and geographic movement, these viewers are accumulating an immaterial form of "movement capital" (Kaufmann, Bergman, and Joye 2004, 752). It is in shoring up the value of such movement capital that lifestyle programming on TLC can be seen as contributing to the transformation of identities. In a broad sense, the imaginative function that we have seen TLC taking on for these Taiwanese viewers resonates with certain other Western-oriented lifestyle programming in the region. One example is Channel Young's *X Files*, discussed in chapter 2, with its quasi-documentary-style introduction of French fashion and lifestyle as a highly desirable form of cultural capital for young, urban Chinese audiences. In both cases, lifestyle television constructs an urban middle-class imaginary that is definitionally entwined with aspirations toward transnational mobility and consumer-cosmopolitanism.

However, in presenting this summary of some of the most obvious forms of identification enabled by TLC and its programs, it is also important to keep in mind the moments of ambivalence that punctuate viewer experiences of the channel. While for a younger generation of well-resourced urban viewers, TLC enables the imagination of oneself as a mobile global subject, nevertheless for an older generation with personal memories of rural and preindustrial life, the channel proves equally capable of prompting a (re)identification with intensely local lifeways. Even among the younger viewers we interviewed, moments of ambivalence about the global identity that TLC projects were common: recall one viewer's passionate resentment of the channel's persistent imaging of filthy-rich Westerners, and another viewer's disgust at the arrogance of *Fun Taiwan* in addressing a Taiwanese audience in English through an ABT host. Such moments highlight the push-pull effects of cultural globalization experienced at the subjective level: even for those who actively wish to elaborate mobile, internationalist identities, the process of negotiation with global forms may seldom be free from tension.

In the next chapter, we continue our discussion of the confluences of and contradictions between local and global forms through a focus on television experts in China and India, exploring how these figures hybridize local-, national-, and international-level models of popular lifestyle expertise.

FIVE. **Gurus, Babas, and Daren** Popular Experts on Indian and Chinese Advice TV

Placing the Popular Expert

Living in a stressful world as we do today, most conflicts and enmities are fostered by minds imbalanced by the pressures of everyday existence, the fight for survival in a fiercely competitive world and the strain of keeping up with the spiraling economic crises. By providing a vast store of information for healing the body, the mind and the soul, resource to such channel [*sic*] as Care World offers solutions to ease the existing strains and make for a more peaceable co-existence.—CARE WORLD 2013

While the look and feel of life advice programming varies considerably across South and East Asia, a central feature of these shows is the figure of the expert or life guru. Indian lifestyle shows invariably feature an array of "everyday experts" of some kind, whether celebrity chefs, wellness gurus, or more conventionally credentialed experts such as the doctors often interviewed, chat-show style, on magazine-style health shows. Similarly, in China, the figure of the popular expert is now a common feature not just of daytime TV schedules but increasingly also of evening television targeting a broader citizenry. At one end of the spectrum, glossy home makeover shows feature design experts passing on tips about taste and DIY skills to an emergent young, consumption-minded urban middle class. At the other, a plethora of low-budget health advice shows use a range of health and well-being experts to target China's growing aged population, interpellating them as self-managing citizens. In this chapter, we examine the proliferation of popular experts on contemporary television in India and China. Our central contention is that, as pivotal cultural intermediaries, these figures have come to play an increasingly important role today in promoting, shaping, and modeling particular styles of life conduct, selfhood, and citizenship (Lewis 2008). We argue that one of the key ways in which they function is as cultural intermediaries in Pierre Bourdieu's sense; that is, as tastemakers and shapers they function as crucial life guides in an increasingly aestheticized consumer market (Philips 2005; Redden 2008; Powell and Prasad 2010). Further, we suggest that, as in the West, the recent proliferation of popular experts on prime-time television "can be seen in terms of their role as an antidote to a growing sense of risk and doubt and as a source of new codes for living" (Lewis 2008, 12). That is, we are interested in the increasingly central role and status that these popular life advisors have as cultural authorities and guides within public life today and what the kinds of advice they offer and the manner in which they deliver it might tell us about the shifting nature of, and expectations around, norms of selfhood and citizenship in these two very complex social landscapes.

A growing number of scholars are interested in examining the phenomenon of the popular expert on prime-time television (Bonner 2003; Palmer 2004; Bell and Hollows 2005; Chakraborty 2007; Xu 2007; Lewis 2008; Ouellette and Hay 2008; Powell and Prasad 2010; Lewis, Martin, and Sun 2012). Much of this scholarship has focused on the Anglophone world and in particular the United States, United Kingdom, and Australia, and has tied the emergence of the figure of the TV expert to broader shifts in late modernity. For instance, media and cultural studies scholars have variously linked the rise of prime-time figures like celebrity chefs and makeover gurus to the contemporary "malestreaming" of a once feminized culture of self-help discourse (Brunsdon 2003; Hollows 2003; Lewis 2008), the growing marketization of domestic labor and skills pertaining to the presentation of self (Brunsdon 2003), the rise of neoliberal models of individualism and entrepreneurialism, and the growing role, under conditions of global capitalism, of class-inflected, "cosmopolitan" models of transnational consumption, taste, and aesthetic citizenship (Bell and Hollows 2005; Lewis 2008; Miller 2007; Ouellette and Hay 2008; Palmer 2004; Powell and Prasad 2010). In this chapter, we show that while elements of all these developments are being played out in India and China, in both countries the rise and role of the popular expert is tied to the very distinct trajectories of modernity that characterize these two societies, as well as to idiosyncratic cultural genealogies of expertise and to specific and variegated televisual cultures.

While the figure of the lifestyle expert is now globally recognizable, the growing popularity of this "new" form of expertise in India and China needs to be more broadly understood as "emerging out of a complex conjuncture of historical, social, and cultural developments" (Lewis 2008, 5). A central driver for the emergence of lifestyle experts in India is the rise of a new consumer middle class, with this growing sector of consumers providing a market for lifestyle advice not only on television but also across print media. But the emergence of everyday life gurus also speaks to the ways in which Indian citizens are finding themselves negotiating complex transitions in a compressed (late) modern social landscape. Here popular experts can be seen to act as cultural brokers, mediating between and offering how to guides for managing a range of competing modernities and associated life "options" in a shifting social, cultural, and economic context marked by complex coarticulations of, and negotiations between, secularism and spiritualism; entrepreneurial individualism versus duty to family and community; and a growing sense of emphasis on individuals and families as a site for the management of social and economic risk.

In China, lifestyle advisors of all sorts have been embraced with considerable enthusiasm. As the privatization and growing corporatization of the previously public sector has to a large extent turned the individual from a "workplace person" (*danwei ren*) and "institutionalized person" (*zhidu ren*) into a "social person" (*shehui ren*), it has also largely dissolved the mechanism of workplace socialization, ideological "thought work," and ethical guidance one associates with a socialist form of moral education. In its place, a market mechanism, consisting of commodified provisions of information and knowledge through, for instance, motivational publications on how to succeed, and television programs advising viewers of their lifestyle options, now assumes a primary pedagogic role, inducting consumers and citizens into a "new ethics of self-management and self-orientation" (Zhang and Ong 2008, 8).

As we have emphasized in earlier chapters, however, a number of crucial differences remain between India, China, and the liberal-democratic societies of the West. While China has dramatically transformed from a socialist to a largely capitalist economy, Chinese media operates within the context of neoliberal and deregulatory strategies, on the one hand, and a continuing and intensified (re)articulation of China's socialist legacies, on the other (Y. Zhao 2008b; Sun and Zhao 2009): what David Harvey calls "neoliberalism with Chinese characteristics" (Harvey 2005). Furthermore, three decades of marketization and privatization have resulted in China having changed from one of the most egalitarian societies to one of the most unequal societies in the world (C. Lee and Selden 2007; Sun and Guo 2013). As discussed in chapter 2, socioeconomic inequality and stratification manifest themselves in terms of income, consumption level, and life chances, played out in the divide between rural and urban residents; between the urban/rural underclass and the urban, upwardly mobile, well-educated middle class; and between inland, less-developed areas and regions and coastal, metropolitan places. Although it is the urban middle class that has shown most interest in the new lifestyle practices and choices brought to them by the process of cultural globalization and transnational movements, the Chinese television audience is still largely rural and poorly educated, occupying the lower echelons of China's socioeconomic order. Likewise, in India the consumption of lifestyle advice and expertise needs to be understood in the context of a country characterized by marked geographic, social, and economic divisions. These TV audiences are highly diverse, ranging from poor households living in informal slum dwellings, on the fringes of Mumbai with access to a large array of TV programming via unregistered cable connections, to educated English-speaking cosmopolitans who mainly interact with TV content via the Internet or subscription to high-end lifestyle channels.

What follows is a discussion of key sites of popular expertise on Indian and Chinese lifestyle advice TV. Our research is based on analyses of programming trends across the two countries as well as interviews with viewers and program producers in urban and regional areas. Based on this research, our aim is to analyze how the rise of life experts, on the one hand, taps into transnational shifts around lifestyle and selfhood and the rise of consumer middle classes, and on the other hand, points to the intensification of local points of difference vis-à-vis cultural negotiations of modernity and state-market-citizen relations, as well as growing social inequities in postsocialist, postwelfare environments.

From Aspirationalism to the Everyday:
Popular Experts on Television in India

Over the past ten years, Indian TV screens have become increasingly populated with a range of lifestyle experts. These figures need to be understood within a postcolonial context where systems of popular knowledge and belief have been in long-term dialogue with a range of Western modes of scientific and medical rationalism, U.S.-style models of self-help, self-improvement, and entrepreneurialism, and Indian religious, spiritual, and philosophical ontologies from Buddhism to Islam to Hinduism (Chakraborty 2007; Copeman and Ikegame 2012). Contemporary television has proven a particularly fertile place for a variety of forms of popular expertise to flourish, from more "traditional" figures such as yoga gurus (for example, Baba Ramdev, whom we discuss extensively in chapter 6), marriage brokers, and astrologers to newer icons of modernity such as food experts, gadget gurus, travel, taste, and fashion advisors, and a range of more "scientific" health and well-being experts, including popular psychologists and doctors (ayurvedic and allopathic) (Kasbekar 2006; Chakraborty 2007). While these figures are extremely diverse in terms of their modes of address and embodied expertise, the recent surge of interest in popular expertise speaks to significant shifts in lifestyle and selfhood in late modern India; transitions shaped by ongoing and in some cases intensifying differences around class, caste, gender, religious, and regional/local identity (Lakha 1999; Harindranath 2013). To provide a sense of this diversity in terms of both experts and audience engagement, in this next section we focus on two distinct areas in which popular experts have become prominent players on Indian TV: first, aspirational advice and secondly, rather more pragmatic, utilitarian forms of expertise.

ASPIRATIONAL ADVISORS

As we discussed in chapter 3, Indian social, cultural, and economic life has undergone a significant transformation since the 1980s, with the increasing marketization and deregulation of the economy seeing a growing emphasis on the symbolic significance of the aspiring consumer middle classes within the national imaginary (Mazzarella 2003; Fernandes 2006). One of the main spaces on Indian television where this kind of aspirational consumer culture is most celebrated and visible is on dedicated lifestyle cable channels. Aimed at aspiring middle- and upper-middle-class audiences, these include TLC India (the lightly localized version of Discovery's lifestyle channel, also popular with educated middle-class audiences in Taiwan, as we discussed in chapter 4) and a host of other glossy high-end channels such as NDTV Good Times, Travel XP, Zee Trendz, Fashion TV, and Zee Café. While many of these channels import large amounts of English programming, NDTV Good Times, one of the top lifestyle cable channels, offers a rather more interesting example of Indian lifestyle programming as it largely consists of locally made and, as we will see, at times highly culturally hybrid shows featuring home-grown hosts and experts.

Targeting well-heeled urban viewers and focusing on fitness, beauty, parenthood and marriage, cars and technology, travel, cookery, and pets, NDTV Good Times was launched by NDTV (formerly New Delhi Television) in 2007 and offers a range of locally produced, largely English-language lifestyle and advice programming. The channel produces a variety of lifestyle genres from highbrow "conversation" and advice shows (*One Life to Love*) to magazine-style travel (*The Single Female Traveler*), car (*All about My Car, Honey*) and pet shows (*Heavy Petting*), all featuring experts of some kind. It has also more recently moved into producing the odd reality-based lifestyle program such as *Daddy's Day In*, a fly-on-the-wall show about men attempting to run a household, and *Band Baajaa Bride* (BBB), a reality-makeover-style wedding format that we discuss below.

The channel's experts and hosts, while predominantly Indian, embody a mode of cosmopolitanism that badges them as members of a highly elite class. The channel also marks out its high-end status by featuring the odd French chef (to "demystify French cuisine" for culinary-minded viewers), as well as British Indian chefs, such as Manju Mahi, whose show *Cooking Isn't Rocket Science* aims to challenge the perception that British food lacks the finesse of gourmet cuisine. Although many popular cable channels aimed at young upwardly mobile urban cosmopolitans, such as MTV and Zee TV, increasingly offer programs in Hinglish, the expert-personalities on Good Times all speak English, often with a born-to-rule, "British English" accent, exhibiting a blend of privileged transnational and postcolonial embodiment. As Arati Singh, head of fashion (now channel head) at NDTV Goodtimes in Mumbai, notes, the use of English-speaking anchors and experts on Indian TV signifies that "our program[ing] is *very very very* aspirational."

The shows and their experts are for the most part also highly transnational in their mode of address and aesthetics, with many of the shows being Indian versions of recognizably Western lifestyle formats. The kinds of pedagogies and modes of expertise on offer here are quite varied: ranging from "straighter" consumer advice and magazine-style shows featuring an infotainment mode of address to the more embodied experiential expertise on display in the lifestyle-oriented food, wine, health, spa, and travel shows that dominate the channel, where viewers are often inducted by the anchor and the various experts she or he meets into "good" modes of consumption, cosmopolitan habitus, and taste. *Art Beat*, for instance, is a series where Noopur Tiwari, previously NDTV's Europe correspondent, travels to various European cities, introducing the audience to the work of famous artists such as Picasso and meeting locals and art experts. Filmed at various tourist sites, Tiwari offers viewers the opportunity to vicariously travel to famous European cities while also gaining extensive knowledge and cultural capital: on the show he provides extensive background history to the cities and artists profiled while various art experts and curators offer lessons in taste and interpretation.

At the infotainment end of the spectrum, *Gadget Guru* is one of Good Times' more popular shows, airing across the NDTV network. Introducing

Figure 5.1. Vikram Chandra (*left*) and Rajiv Makni (*right*), the hosts of *Gadget Guru*.

audiences to the newest high-tech consumer goods, the studio-based format offers a rather more playful take on consumer-advice programming, with the show aiming for the combination of irreverent humor and obsessive product knowledge that has made the British motoring show *Top Gear* such an international success. As on *Top Gear*, the show's "experts" include two highly confident key hosts and gadget obsessives: Vikram Chandra, ex–news anchor and current CEO of NDTV; and Rajiv Makni, an ex-model, technology journalist, and anchor of various other NDTV lifestyle shows. The two well-known host-personalities provide detailed, often highly critical rundowns on the gadgets they review. As such, they perform the role of idealized consumer citizens or what Grant David McCracken terms "super consumers"; that is, they are positioned as "exemplary figures [who have] have created the clear, coherent, and powerful selves that everyone seeks" (McCracken 2005). These two highly successful professional men thus promote the need for viewers to have the latest products at the same time as embodying a combination of informed consumer citizenship and entrepreneurial subjecthood (see figure 5.1).

At the highly aspirational end of Good Times' programming is *Custom Made for Vir Sanghvi*, a glossy show where well-known "foodie" and former newspaper editor Vir Sanghvi travels across India, in search of "bespoke" experiences of custom-made fashion, food, travel, and even spiritual offerings.[1] This is very high-end lifestyle programming, with Vir devoting one episode to exploring the top perfumers in India and having these "psychologists of smell, many of whom have trained in Paris, tailor scents for him according to their reading of his personality (see figure 5.2).

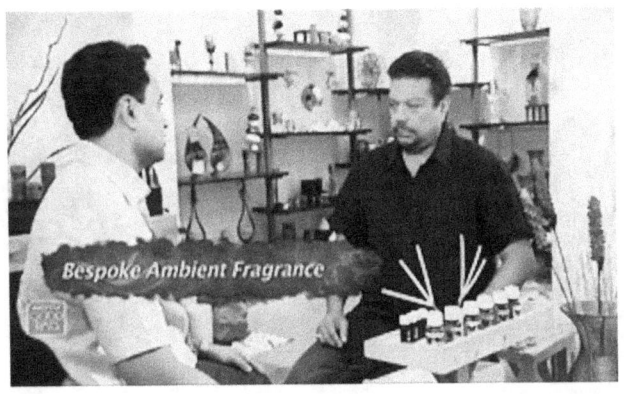

Figure 5.2. Vir Sanghvi (*right*) is introduced to the joys of bespoke perfume on *Custom Made for Vir Sanghvi*.

Another luxury-oriented lifestyle show of note on NDTV Good Times is *Royal Reservations*, hosted by Mahatma Gandhi's great-granddaughter, Amrita Gandhi. Taking the audience on a journey to royal palaces across India, our host, with the help of various experts and designers (and occasionally members of royal families themselves!), translates upper-class forms of taste and cultural capital into everyday modes of consumption by teaching the audience how to re-create royal lifestyles in their own homes. On one episode Gandhi visits "the chic city home of Princess Rajyashree of Bikaner, who tells us how to bring a piece of palace life into flats with three easy-to-do decor secrets [before we then] create, step by step, a bedroom fit for your inner Rajkumari [or princess]."[2] *Royal Reservations* thus has a consumer-oriented, lifestyle makeover dimension to it—offering the audience "a trunkful of royal inspiration to transform the way you live"—while Gandhi and her various guests, most of whom have upper-class British Indian accents and exhibit a sense of effortless style and taste, promote and embody upward mobility via particular regimes of aesthetically oriented consumption (see figure 5.3).

BROKERING CULTURE

Sanghvi, Gandhi, Tiwari, and the gadget gurus, like many of the anchors and experts featured on NDTV Good Times, present "soft" modes of lifestyle pedagogies that are as much embodied in their own highly confident, worldly forms of habitus and presentation of self as they are displayed through specific lessons in taste and savvy consumption. These shows address their audiences

Figure 5.3. The princess of Rampur (*center*), assisted by an unnamed cook, shows host Amrita Gandhi how to prepare for and host a soiree on an episode of *Royal Reservations* titled "Party like the Nizams" (former rulers of the state of Hyderabad).

as highly cosmopolitan, globe-trotting, and enterprising upper-middle-class subjects via depictions of lifestyles well beyond the reach of the majority of Indian viewers, begging the question of what kind of person actually watches the show. As Arati Singh, head of fashion (now channel head) at NDTV Good Times in Mumbai, comments: "We aim to be upper middle class, but you know and I know that the upper and upper middle class doesn't even watch that much television. So our numbers do come from the middle classes.... A lot of viewers come to just watch something that they can aspire to. I think India is looking for that. It's the same reason everybody enters the malls on Saturday and Sunday. I don't think they buy that much."[3]

Aspiration is a key element here; however, while the emergence of a "middle class" in India has been a recurrent theme in triumphalist neoliberal discourse, as we discuss in chapter 1, much care needs to be taken with how this term is used in the Indian context (Lakha 1999; Baviskar and Ray 2011). Disposable income may have risen considerably in India since 1990 for certain sectors of the population. There is, however, evidence of a growing gap between the poor and the increasingly wealthy urban upper middle classes, with the "new rich" constituting a small minority of Indians (*Times of India* 2011). In our interviews with lifestyle TV producers in Mumbai, there was a strong awareness of the potential disjuncture between the values and lifestyles promoted on their programming and the everyday lives of Indian viewers. NDTV Good Times's recent attempt to embrace reality formats—a mode of programming more associated with the "mass" audiences of the Hindi General Entertainment

Figure 5.4. Anchor Ambika Anand and fashion designer Sabyasachi Mukherjee (*center*) meet the bride, groom, and their respective mothers on *Band Baajaa Bride*.

Channels, who watch *Bigg Boss* (the Indian version of *Big Brother*)—suggests a recognition of the need to target a range of audiences across the Indian middle classes, as well as to speak to and engage viewers with a variety of cultural values. A case in point is the Good Times show *Band Baajaa Bride*, a highly culturally hybrid reality-makeover-style wedding format now into its fourth season. With a tagline that promises "A makeover for everything. Including fate," the show quite literally marries aspirationalism and consumer spectacle with a diversity of family values and religious traditions, with experts playing a key role as cultural intermediaries (see figure 5.4).

On *Band Baajaa Bride* a variety of hosts and experts "support" the bride, who is most often an educated professional, during her makeover, a process that is at times as much a negotiation of culture and religion as a style transformation. The show also includes a "mentor," in this case Sabyasachi Mukherjee, a male "design genius who with a single touch can transform the girl next door into a vintage diva."[4] *Band Baajaa Bride* also features a range of makeover gurus, from cosmetic dentists and physicians to more traditional adornment specialists and ceremonial face decorators. These various figures teach the bride everything from style, health, and lifestyle tips to how to make a cross-cultural, and sometimes cross-caste (though this is never openly discussed on the show), marriage work. With the help of the various gurus and the young stylish anchors (ex–male model Bharat Arora and attractive Good Times female fashion anchor Ambika Anand), the show deftly moves between a celebration of customary marriage traditions—advising and mentoring the bride, groom, and the parents along the way—and the bride's style makeover "journey." The anchors, sometimes dressed in Western clothes and sometimes in traditional garb, and brides, often wearing a *kurta*, move seamlessly between speaking in English and Hindi while discussing the "romance" that led up to the wedding—the partnerships are often the result of arranged marriages of some kind, which are still largely the norm in India (Titzmann 2011).

The bridal makeover typically involves a "traditional" transformation, whether being made over to look like the bride of Krishna or being dressed in a *kanjeevaram saree*, a lavish silk sari that hails from southern India. Through focusing on the apparently neutral realm of consumerism, beauty, and fashion, the anchors and various experts and consumer advisors on the show work to guide and mentor families, who come from a range of cultural and caste backgrounds and are juggling a range of aspirations and expectations. The experts here are in some ways classic cultural intermediaries in the Bourdieuian sense, teaching the show's participants and in turn audiences how to consume tastefully. However, their role on the show is also as cultural brokers in a broader sense: Sabyasachi Mukherjee's position as cultural and linguistic mentor, mediating between the bride-to-be's natal and marital families, is as important as or even more important than his fashion and style expertise.

In one episode, which Sabyasachi Mukherjee describes as his "greatest makeover challenge ever because this is about two families with completely contrasting culture coming together in holy matrimony," Mukherjee asks, "What happens when a Gujarati girl falls in love with a Bengali boy?" The audience of course knows exactly what is going to happen—a makeover—but in this case, the makeover process involves Mukherjee mentoring the bride in question and helping her to negotiate the wishes of the two families (see figures 5.5 and 5.6).

In the end this negotiation, however, within the confines of the reality format is less about a real engagement with different cultural conceptions and norms around ways of living and expectations around gender roles, a question of fashion and style, with the two mothers placated by "a Gujarati twist to a Bengali wedding." Thus, through a combination of prescriptive guidance and the "gift" of whitened teeth and luxurious handmade traditional clothes and jewelry, the show's team of experts assists the families and viewers in navigating a complex contemporary marriage culture in which Western-inflected desires for consumerism and romance are brought together with notions of fate and familial duty. The gloss of consumerist individualism here is largely underpinned by a patriarchal logic where the bride's "choices" are tied in the end to the needs and desires of family and tradition (Kapur 2009), and where

Figure 5.5. Accompanied on set by her mother (*right*) and mother-in-law, a Gujarati bride about to marry into a Bengali family tearfully shares her concerns with anchor Ambika Anand and fashion designer and "mentor" Sabyasachi Mukherjee (both out of shot) on *Band Baajaa Bride* (season 3 finale: "A Gujarati twist to a Bengali wedding").

Figure 5.6. Anchor Ambika Anand and fashion designer Sabyasachi Mukherjee from *Band Baajaa Bride* listen to and comment on the Gujarati bride's concerns (season 3 finale: "A Gujarati twist to a Bengali wedding").

the bride is largely positioned as an object of exchange rather than an agent of personal change.

EVERYDAY EXPERTS

While the glamorous end of Indian lifestyle television features celebrity hosts, expert-personalities with model looks, and references to Bollywood lifestyles (one of the brides on *Band Baajaa Bride* has her wedding filmed by a Bollywood filmmaker), a significant amount of the life advice programming watched by Indian audiences, and, as we will see, by Chinese viewers, is rather more "ordinary" and oriented toward more pragmatic and everyday forms of advice. As Rajiv Lakshman, the TV host of the hugely successful Indian reality show *MTV Roadies* (and CEO of a highly successful format production company), put it, "lifestyle, the way it is defined globally, is not a big player in India. . . . We have more existential issues than lifestyle issues."[5]

While in India the majority of lifestyle experts are found on dedicated lifestyle, health, and well-being cable channels, regional television is also increasingly offering localized advice programming targeted at urban and rural viewers, from competitive reality-style cookery shows featuring local celebrity chefs to magazine-style programming. As we discussed in chapter 3, there has been a strong push to regional television in recent years in India. As noted by Dr. Shiv Kumar, a senior executive at the regional channel Mahua TV, the recent drive to localize content has even seen high-end players like NDTV Good Times attempting to launch regional channels. Though, as he explains, the network fared poorly due to what he argues was a lack of connection to or knowledge of everyday life and of local customs and traditions. By contrast, Mahua TV, an emerging player in the regional market, produces highly localized low-budget forms of television aimed at Bhojpuri speakers located primarily in Eastern Uttar Pradesh and Bihar, a highly populated, impoverished state in Northern India where the majority of the population live in villages, though Dr. Kumar clarifies that the channel also has a significant international diasporic Bhojpuri audience (at the time of the interview in 2010 it had around 100,000 viewers).[6]

Given budgetary restrictions, Mahua TV has a limited though growing range of lifestyle and life advice programming, with one of the main programs featuring popular experts being the channel's daily breakfast show, *Bhihane Bhihane*.

> We have one show that is called *Good Morning Good Morning*. *Bhihane Bhihane* is the Bhojpuri version; the Hindi version is *Sabere Sabere*. It's

a breakfast show. There is a male anchor and a female anchor. They talk about the day today, what are the programs. There's a yoga segment. And we invite a guest from the local region . . . maybe a good singer, maybe a film celebrity, maybe a doctor, maybe a youth who has won a medal. . . . Our special thing is that whoever you are you have to sing a song.

As on Chinese regional television, the emphasis on this low-budget breakfast show is on pragmatic knowledges and forms of "everyday expertise," offered up by an array of fairly unglamorous, ordinary-looking local experts. Alongside its preoccupation with compulsory singing, the show offers various forms of daily advice, including travel advice, an astrology segment where viewers can call the show and get daily predictions, and health advice that one can practice at home. "We give alternative medicine advice. . . . So we say, sitting in your room you can get medicinal therapy . . . such as using tomatoes, using garlic for your gastric problems or your blood pressure."

A rather more Westernized format on Mahua TV is *Perfect Shrimati* (Perfect Mrs.), a show that aims to help "home-makers" bring their "efficiency to the fore" by both advising them and testing out their domestic skills, from household maintenance, health, and financial matters to managing relationships. Anchored by the well-known Bhojpuri actor and singer Aleet Anand, the housewives are given guidance by a panel of experts, including financial experts, doctors, interior designers, and chefs. A magazine-style format, the show moves between segments with experts visiting middle-class viewers in their homes, studio segments featuring various experts speaking with the host, and repeated segments throughout the show (tagged on screen as "expert advice" in English) featuring a mixture of male and female experts talking at length direct to camera about a range of topics, from how to manage peer pressure to discussions of spiritual well-being, and advice on makeover and health products (images of products frequently appear at the side of the screen while the show's host and experts are talking).

DIY EXPERTS

Alongside the show's naturalization of consumption, this juxtaposition of highly diverse forms of expertise and knowledge, from makeup to medical advice, can be read as part of "a growing 'informationalization' of everyday life, a process that has seen expertise become relatively democratized and presented in increasingly accessible forms" (Lewis 2008, 2). Increasingly on Indian TV, as on TV globally, fashion advisors and cookery experts—figures associated with more ordinary modes of knowledge and skills—are finding themselves being "placed in the same discursive category as other 'experts,' such as doctors, psychologists and dieticians" (Lewis 2008, 3). Going hand in hand with this apparent breakdown of the hierarchies between different forms of expertise under the sign of "lifestyle" is an implicit emphasis on viewers themselves as needing to become "experts" in their own lives. While on the one hand *Perfect Mrs.* engages with discussions of the role of religious and cultural traditions and customs in providing guidance and certainty in daily life, the show's roll call of diverse life experts suggests that optimal life management is a personal choice rather than a cultural or structural given. As recipients of an array of advice about everyday living, viewers are thus positioned as DIY selves tasked with perfecting or optimizing their lifestyles and also navigating daily lives marked by risk and uncertainty.

In our household interviews, and particularly in poorer households, lifestyle and advice shows such as cookery shows and yoga/spiritual shows were often seen in instrumental terms as potential sites for accruing useful free knowledge for managing day-to-day living, particularly in relation to health and education. For instance, Ramesh, a taxi driver who lived with his family on the outskirts of Mumbai in a neighborhood consisting of "extra-legally" constructed homes, was an avid TV viewer. He and his wife had direct-to-home (DTH) TV so that they could access a very wide range of channels, as well as channels with a multilingual option; their viewing habits were in certain ways similar to many of the other more middle-class Mumbai families we interviewed, ranging from serials to reality and lifestyle TV and astrology programs (Ramesh showed off an astrology ring he had bought from the Telebrand shopping channel).

He and his wife also watched a range of travel and cookery shows, including an evening food show (*Food at 9*) on Fox Traveller, which showcases cuisines from around India and the world. While Fox Traveller describes its audience as including "people who are hungry for new, bigger, better, and varied experiences; open to trying out even challenging things and wanting to visit the places and ideas that they see on the channel," Ramesh and his wife's interest in the show was more utilitarian than experiential. As Ramesh put it, "What is nice about *Food at 9* is in one hour they would show at least seven to eight dishes. They also show dishes that could be made without using a stove or gas... like green salad." Ramesh's wife often made dishes they'd learn from television, although they would substitute ingredients with locally available products. Their concern with the informational aspects of popular factual programming meant that they were critical of reality shows such as *Bigg Boss* that presented ways of living that were out of their reach. It is perhaps no surprise that they were not fans of the cooking show *MasterChef India*: "We cannot understand that show.... Because they have time limit to make a dish; someone like us who is interested in learning would find it difficult. It is a competition, not really for learning."

The multilingual options on DTH also enable Ramesh and his family to watch foreign pop docs, and reality and lifestyle shows on channels such as Discovery and Fox (which are often seen as "high end" in the Indian market and previously were only available via relatively costly subscriber fees). *Man vs. Wild* on the Discovery Channel is a favorite; interestingly, Ramesh reads the show primarily in terms of survival tips, noting somewhat paradoxically that Bear Grylls (the show's presenter, a "survival expert") has taught him things he didn't know about the healing properties of plants from his own home village. As he put it: "We get to know ayurveda-like information (via the show). It is a nice and informative show." Here we see a fascinating translation of a global entertainment format into a quite specific cultural and social context, marked by a highly utilitarian approach to televisual consumption.

Patil, a fifty-six-year-old government employee, and his wife similarly lived very modestly on the outskirts of Mumbai and also saw experts on television as providing crucial life guidance. Like Ramesh, Patil and his wife appreciated cookery shows that offered useful everyday tips such as how to make tasty meals from leftover food. Like many Indian families, they also watched a lot of spiritual programming, seeing TV *babas* or holy men as providing helpful life guidance: "you learn to be happy with what you have." Patil, who suffered from heart disease, also talked extensively about the health benefits of the yoga he learned from watching and practicing the *asanas* demonstrated by gurus every day on morning TV.

> In 2004 I had three artery blockages—72, 67 and 52 percent—and I heard that yoga would be helpful. When I was diagnosed, the doctor at the hospital suggested either angioplasty or bypass surgery. I consulted another doctor and he suggested yoga. And then I saw yoga on TV. I thought, instead of spending money, why not try yoga. I practiced it for three to four months and I started feeling better but could not get in to get a medical checkup. However, after six months I got examined, and the blockage was under 40 percent. Yoga was very helpful, you can stay fit. I am fifty-six.... But I feel like I am twenty. Sometimes I run to catch a bus! I practice yoga regularly. Earlier I used to practice for two hours, now only for thirty minutes as I have less time and have to go to work.

As we can see, Ramesh's and Patil's uses of television tend to be rather more pragmatic than aspirational: their interest lies in forms of life expertise, including spiritual advice (as we discuss in chapter 6, astrological and spiritual guides are increasingly positioned as life guides rather than "traditional" experts on Indian TV), that can help them with the daily struggles to cope with pressured lives and make do with limited access to resources. In this sense, the everyday expertise available on cable channels and regional programming can be seen as being oriented not only toward an audience of lower and middle classes but also to rural viewers and the working poor, a group who, depending on what part of India they live in and what kind of state government is in power at any point, are likely to have problems with access to housing, healthy food, adequate sanitation, and health care (which is largely privatized in India).

In the last two decades, state spending on health, for instance, has declined from 6–7 percent to 5 percent of total government spending, despite a large increase in the cost of treatment, while the health sector has become increasingly dominated by commercial players, with 80 percent of doctors in India today working in the private sector (Varman and Vikas 2007). The costs of health are thus increasingly borne by Indian citizens, with around 87 percent of health expenses covered by private financing and hospitalized Indians often having to take out loans or sell assets to pay for their treatment costs (Varman and Vikas 2007). Given these realities, increasing numbers of poor urban and rural Indians are avoiding seeking health care. In this context, as in China, the apparent democratization of life expertise, including health advice, via television and other media can be seen as being linked to a (neo)liberalization of the relation between the state and the socially marginal, with the poor increasingly expected to manage and take responsibility for once publically provided services such as education and health, while often having limited resources to do so. Television thus becomes a key site of access to advice, information, and support for those unable to afford privatized modes of service provision. The Indian health and well-being channel Care World nicely sums up this shift on its promotional website: "Care World satisfies the essential need of the affluent and the not so affluent, particularly the latter who can not invest in memberships and expensive spas and wellness institutes, who can not engage trainers and dietitians at exorbitant rates . . . by facilitating their access to fitness, well being and beauty by consulting just one channel and assimilating and absorbing the tips given by the experts in their respective fields."[7]

India clearly has a very different cultural history of citizenship and socialist statehood than China, but what they share are marked tensions and social divisions between groups with highly uneven access to the benefits of consumer citizenship. While, as we will see, life advice television has sought to fill the gap in state provision in China in a way that hasn't occurred to the same degree in India, as we've discussed, the rise of Indian lifestyle TV and its impact on ordinary people in both urban and rural areas and across class, caste, and religion does suggest that commercial and privatized expertise is playing a growing role in shaping citizenship and sociality. Here the role of lifestyle experts from chef-personalities and fashion designers to yoga and health and well-being gurus comes to fill not just a pragmatic, informational role; rather, they work to embody and enact a neoliberalized model of "consumer-citizenship" that reinforces and naturalizes an ethic of self-management and personal responsibility in the face of growing external risks and uncertainty (Lewis 2014).

Lifestyling Citizens: Chinese Popular Advice Television

As discussed in various chapters in this book, as the state has withdrawn from its previous welfare role, television programs advising viewers of their lifestyle options now assume a central pedagogic role in China. Given that television is both free and accessible to the majority of the population in China, including the remote and poor areas, it is not surprising that it has become the most favored medium for such an educational project.

Advice, guidance, and instructions on who to become, what to do, and how to live have become integral to the formation of what Zhang and Ong refer to as the space of the "new social" in China, defined by a "gap between state action and self-interested endeavours," the space that is vacated by the state and now taken over by "neoliberal tools of privatization" (Zhang and Ong 2008, 8). In what follows, we will examine two types of expertise on Chinese TV: First, we present the mode of advice prevalent on health-related lifestyle programs on local and regional television, which bear some similarities with the local and lower-end everyday-advice programming discussed in India. Second, we explore lifestyle programs from Shanghai Media Group (SMG), which represents a more global trend of democratizing authority and expertise similar to the aspirational cosmopolitanism evident on NDTV Good Times in India, though in both cases these modes of advice are significantly shaped by distinctly Chinese conceptions of knowledge, skill, and expertise. These two types of expertise (medical, health, and well-being, on the one hand, and fashion and everyday life, on the other) are chosen to showcase the internal diversity of popular expertise on Chinese television and differences in terms of format, mode of address, and geographic scale. However, they are by no means intended to represent the entire range of cultural intermediaries on Chinese television. Indeed, as is evidenced in other chapters, especially chapters 2, 7, and 8, such figures also come in the form of marriage and relationship counselors, parenting and child-rearing specialists, psychological and emotional therapists, career advisors, personal investment specialists, and travel guides.

SCIENTIFIC EXPERTISE, AUTHORITY, AND DIDACTIC TEACHING

Chinese life advice television features a range of very ordinary, everyday programming aimed at informing the populace. While often framed within an entertainment-based mode of address, Chinese life experts tend to be positioned as all-knowing authorities. Bengbu TV's (BBTV) "Health Hotline," for instance, represents a particular approach to teaching the science of everyday living that is best described as television *as* authority. In other words, television functions more or less as a blackboard in a classroom, adopting a top-down, one-way style of teaching and addressing the audience as students rather than as consumers or citizens. The information on the screen is presented as indisputable knowledge, whose authoritativeness comes from nowhere other than the sheer fact that it is on television. Viewers are encouraged to trust television's inherent capacity to bring them the most accurate, scientific, and useful information.

Along these lines, Xiao Yu, the host of Bengbu TV's *Zero Distance to Health*, sees her role as being to facilitate the transmission of expert knowledge from the specialist to the viewers (see figure 5.7). She may try to put the specialist's advice into more everyday language so that viewers can understand it better, but she always defers to their authority. In part, this is due to the fact that Bengbu is a small city, and the viewers are partly rural and partly small-town people, most of whom have never seen a specialist doctor. "Viewers in big cities are more educated about health topics. For instance, viewers of Shanghai TV may want to engage in a complex dialogue with the specialist or even question the advice given by experts, but for our viewers, doctors and specialists are authority figures. If I get into some kind of nuanced discussion with the doctor regarding the pros and cons of certain advice and treatments, our viewers may get confused, and we don't want that to happen."[8]

Every day, throughout China, hundreds of local and regional television channels such as BBTV's life channel impart a large amount of information to viewers—mostly semirural, of lower socioeconomic status, and possessing limited scientific knowledge—using this television-as-expert approach. Here Bengbu TV bears some similarity to Mahua TV in northern India, discussed

Figure 5.7. Host Xiao Yu (*right*) interviews and interprets the advice of a health expert on early warning signs of stroke on *Zero Distance to Health*, May 25, 2010. This is a daily show, aired at 6:40 p.m. each day and repeated the next morning, with each episode lasting fifteen minutes.

above. However, while Mahua TV uses competitions, reality, and other hybridized popular formats and employs local celebrities and personalities as "experts," BBTV's mode of presentation privileges quantity of information, clarity of messages, and effectiveness of communication over aesthetics and style, and aims to present as much information as clearly as possible within the shortest possible time, and at the minimum possible cost. In addition to the featured topics of the day, at the bottom of the screen BBTV's "Health Hotline" (a segment of *Zero Distance to Health*) also runs a rolling banner offering endless tips and advice for everyday living. On one episode, for instance, the rolling text tells viewers that kiwi fruit, grapes, and bananas help with sleep problems, and that beer should not be consumed simultaneously with vinegar.

As an incentive to viewers to tune in to the show, *Zero Distance to Health* also regularly runs quizzes for selected viewers, the winner of which receives a prize of substantial value. For instance, on April 28, 2011, a middle-aged woman viewer is stopped in the street and asked two questions: (1) at what times does the show go to air each week, and (2) what are the "five highs" that pose threats to health (answer: high blood pressure, high cholesterol, high blood sugar, high blood viscosity, and high urea content in the blood). When she answers both questions correctly, after much assistance from the host, she is presented with a shopping voucher for 358 yuan. It is clear by now that the pedagogic style on BBTV is by no means gentle, nor is it intended to be fun or entertaining, as many Indian lifestyle television programs aim to be. While experts on local Indian TV such as doctors often find themselves placed on a par with a range of other life advisors, from spiritualists and stylists to celebrity chefs, and (in studio-based formats) in dialogue with an argumentative audience, much of the television-assisted teaching and learning offered on China's down-home channels like BBTV treat viewers—old and young—as students, offering a mode of pedagogy that is didactic, authoritarian, and some would even say patronizing.

Discussing the role of health and medical professionals on television and in the print media, Jiang Xiaoyuan, a historian of science, is quoted as saying that such experts are seen to be scientists, who command a privileged and most respected place in the imagination of the Chinese people (Qiu 2010). Ordinary people have long been used to looking up to doctors and scientists, regarding them with awe and taking their words as gospel. The notion of challenging or doubting scientists has until recently been culturally unacceptable. This is particularly the case with rural, less-educated audiences. In comparison with their Western counterparts, the majority of the Chinese television audiences are more tolerant of a didactic, teacherly style of TV advice, due to a number of cultural and historical reasons, including a Confucianist emphasis on respecting the teacher, an authoritarian style of informing the national audience favored by the party propaganda machine, and a top-down mode of science education familiar to the Chinese people from the early phases of socialist modernization.

However, although the viewers we interviewed in Bengbu uniformly expressed an overriding trust in or even reverence for figures of expertise, some were keen to stress that they were not dupes. Asked if he trusts the advice given by the specialists who appear on *Zero Distance to Health*, Mr. Li Jing, a twenty-six-year-old company employee in Bengbu, said, "Yes, of course, I trust them. They are after all experts. That means that they are what they are because of their theoretical and practical knowledge." Asked whom he trusts most among hosts, experts, and guests on the show, Mr. Li said: "Of course, I'd trust the expert more, but that only means that I would give more thought to what they say. If what they say is useful to me, and makes sense to me, and proves to work in my case, then I trust them."

Some of our interviewees also questioned the authenticity of the image of the smiling, courteous doctors on television. Mr. Lu, a thirty-two-year-old office clerk, said that doctors on television are always nice, gentle, and patient, but in real life, most of them are not. "I feel that there is a big contrast between doctors on TV and the doctors you see in the hospital. The doctors I talk to, either face to face, or through telephone consultation, are mostly curt and impatient. This was certainly my experience when I took my kid to see a dentist. There is an element of 'show' with these television doctors."

Another commonly used format for presenting trustworthy information on Chinese television, particularly local television, is what we might call the television-plus-expert approach. A weekly segment on *Zero Distance to Health* called "Expert Forum" features a conversation between the anchor and a medical specialist on a particular health issue in front of a live studio audience, with topics ranging from the dietary regime of a diabetic patient and how to look out for signs of impending heart attack to ways of managing stress and anxiety for students and their parents before university entrance exams. This format is common in health and well-being programs on local, provincial, as well as metropolitan television. It is a combination of didactic classroom teaching and live interaction between the studio audience, the anchor, and the expert.

These shows usually feature the anchor in conversation with a specialist, whose professional credentials are both read out and listed on the screen at the beginning of the conversation. Viewers are assured that the information presented by this specialist is trustworthy, since the curriculum vitae presented to the audience details his or her academic training, scope of professional experience, title and rank, areas of expertise, as well as academic publications and professional accolades. Again, the attractiveness of such programs lies in the amount of information that is made available to viewers. Given that ordinary Chinese patients have limited access to doctors, and the doctors in public hospitals, often overworked and low-paid, are usually reluctant to go to great lengths to explain their diagnosis and treatment options to patients, such mediated doctor-patient dialogue proves to be hugely popular with television viewers. These figures, although they often seem to lack the style or charisma of celebrities or TV personalities, are nevertheless shrouded in the aura of the "expert" (*zhuanjia*).

RESTYLING THE SELF:
THE IDENTITY OF THE FASHION *DAREN*

If examples from regional programming so far have given the impression of a heavy-duty, didactic, and top-down form of educating and instructing the viewer, the lifestyle television programs on SMG's lifestyle channel, Channel

Young, seem to buck this trend. In comparison to those on local and regional TV, as discussed in chapter 2, lifestyle programs on Channel Young are more glamorous, lively, and stylish, catering to much younger, and predominantly female, urban professional viewers. The channel's high-rating shows include a makeover-themed reality show, *Meili Jiuyuan Tuan* (Beauty rescue team, which began as a copy of *Queer Eye for the Straight Guy*); *Xin Nüren Wo Zui Da* (New queen), a licensed format trade of the Taiwanese beauty and fashion advice show *Queen*, renamed *Ai Ni Ai Meili* (Love you, love beauty) in 2013 (the Taiwanese original is discussed in chapter 8); and seasonal shows such as *Vogue Wedding*. Such shows are charged with the task of making Channel Young a national leader in vogue and fashion (*yin ling shishang*) by keeping abreast of the latest trends of fashion and style from Taiwan, Hong Kong, Japan, South Korea, and Europe, particularly France and Italy.[9] With a bigger budget made possible through product sponsorship and advertising, Channel Young has more resources at its disposal than a local channel like BBTV, discussed above. Also, it often opts for coproducing many of its lifestyle shows with independent production companies. One cannot detect the earnest and serious pedagogic style one associates with China Central TV (CCTV), nor is information presented in the boring, textbook format one often sees in local, low-budget rural television like BBTV. Instead, the tone is light-hearted, joking, fun-oriented, and characterized by the kind of "manic and zany style" typical of Japanese/Taiwanese-style variety shows (Martin and Lewis 2012).

To be sure, Channel Young's lifestyle shows also feature experts prominently, but there are a number of major differences in the way expertise is framed here. First, as on Indian TV, the areas in which expertise is called for extend to every mundane aspect of everyday living, so much so that one can become an expert on anything. In contrast to Indian lifestyle TV, where fashion gurus and medical doctors alike are often referred to as "experts," most of SMG's lifestyle shows refrain from using the term *expert* (*zhuanjia*) and opt for more light-hearted, democratized labels, such as *daren*. This is an imported term that originated from the Japanese *tatsujin* (master) and arrived in China after 2010 via Taiwanese variety shows, where the term had already been in common use for several years. It describes someone with a particular, not necessarily professional, adeptness in something, for example *pinwei daren* (an expert on good taste) or *li yi daren* (an expert on manners). On a cooking show, the host might refer to Aunty Liu from the neighborhood as a "*daren* in making custard tarts"; on a consumer advice show teaching women the correct way of applying nail polish, Ms. Wang from a boutique cosmetic shop is introduced as a "*daren* in nail polish"; on another show on everyday life tips, a long-suffering victim of insomnia is described as a "daren in sleeping," since he has "become a specialist from his experience as a patient" (*jiu bing cheng yi*). In addition, one can become an expert on more intangible aspects of life, such as style and manners.

However, it has to be said that while such "neighborly" figures may be considered to be "comforting" for viewers of lifestyle shows in the West, not all viewers in China embrace these forms of ordinary expertise (Lewis 2008). Commenting on the frequent appearance of daren on Shanghai's lifestyle shows, Mrs. Yi, a fifty-one-year-old female technician, said, "These people don't have to be held accountable. They can say whatever they want, and make all sorts of claims." Mrs. Yi's husband, a fifty-year-old schoolteacher who joined her for the interview, agreed: "The daren phenomenon is a symptom of our society. Everyone wants to be famous, and have their five minutes' fame. And television promotes this idea of easy success. What it should promote is how hard it is to succeed, and give examples of individuals who try hard to succeed."

Our younger interviewees in Taiwan, too, sometimes expressed impatience with the explosion of what they saw as underqualified TV daren in recent years. But the younger viewers we interviewed in China seemed to welcome the fact that ordinary people may have something to offer. Ms. Xue Ting, a university graduate who recently got a job in a bank, thought that the key difference between an expert (zhuanjia) and a daren is that while experts may be knowledgeable in an area, a daren is simply someone who has a lot of experience in one particular aspect in everyday life. "A daren can be quite committed to something. He may not have lots of theories and he may not have solid scholarly background, but he may have lots of experience. Also, an expert has command of knowledge in a domain [*lingyu*] whereas a daren can be good at a tiny, specific thing, such as cleaning crabs or cleaning stains on clothes."

The second major difference between the health and well-being shows on national and local television and the lifestyle advice shows on Shanghai TV is that the figures of authority on Shanghai TV tend to be younger, transnational, and sometimes with unconventional gender presentation. The latter may reflect broader tendencies toward "a mixed gender address" on lifestyle TV globally (Attwood 2005, 90) and to a lesser extent a "queering" of reality television (Kavka 2004, 222) and its modes of expertise on fashion, style, cookery, and domestic makeover shows (Lewis 2007), a process also evident on Taiwanese television but to a much lesser extent on Indian TV (exceptions include the cosmopolitan youth programming found on Channel V and MTV, featuring camp figures such as VJ Andy, the host of the dating shows discussed in chapter 7). On Shanghai TV's version of Taiwan's *Queen, New Queen*, a show that provides gentle guidance on developing taste, aesthetic judgment,

Figure 5.8. "Teacher Kevin" on Channel Young provides fashion advice on *New Queen*, August 10, 2013.

and fashion sensibility, one teacher is simply called "Kevin" (Kevin Zhou): an effeminate, vivacious young man who is a mainstay of the Taiwanese original (see chapter 8), and a big part of its brand (see figure 5.8). As in the Taiwanese version, in Channel Young's *New Queen*, the girls seeking to receive fashion advice call him Teacher Kevin (*Kaiwen laoshi*). Discussion with audience members and TVBS Entertainment workers in Taiwan revealed that it is common knowledge that Kevin is in fact gay, although this fact is only ever alluded to quite indirectly in either version of the show. Performing a recognizably *Queer Eye*–style form of lifestyle-TV metrosexuality, Kevin gives his opinion on which handbag to match with which dress, and how the color of one's pants should match the style and color of one's blouse. If a participant in the studio makes a "wrong" fashion decision, Teacher Kevin feigns outrage, snatching the item off the girl and throwing it into the bin while often making witty justifications for his judgment, such as "that would be a really comfortable outfit for your mum!"

New Queen viewer Ms. You Wei, a thirty-year-old cashier in a bank, is somewhat baffled by Kevin's background: "Nobody seems to know where Kevin comes from; there is no introduction to his professional background, nor why he is qualified to give advice and comments." Despite this, most young, female, and cosmopolitan viewers in Shanghai—the intended audience of SMG's lifestyle show—seem to have no trouble accepting such authority figures. Transnational daren like Kevin resonate with *Queer Eye*'s Fab Five of the United States, as noted above, and are delivered to Shanghai audiences via the intermediary of Taiwanese TV culture, which is already familiar to many through the widespread piracy of Taiwanese variety shows, as well as the growing number of copies and licensed format trades, which *New Queen* exemplifies.

Indeed, Ms. Yi Ran, a twenty-four-year-old bank clerk, thinks that it is a good thing that there is now a wide range of aesthetic standards, and sees it as perfectly normal for effeminate men like Kevin to give fashion and style advice to young women: "No, I don't mind. I don't mind fashion teachers such as Kevin. I welcome the fact that they are happy and willing to teach girls how to put on makeup. I don't see anything wrong with them. I am not in the least disgusted by them."

Some young female interviewees went even further in their endorsement of Kevin as a teacher, despite the fact that Kevin, being young, effeminate, and playful, flies in the face of everything that mainstream cultural authority stands for. Ms. Bei Li, a twenty-five-year-old woman also working in a bank, lives with her parents, and, like her mother, is an avid viewer of Channel Young's fashion- and beauty-related shows:

> There is this guy called Kevin. In the show, he would go to people's apartments and give them advice on what to wear. I'd make sure not to miss this part of the show each time it's on. . . . My mum likes to watch it too. She really likes Kevin, and would never walk away from the TV when Kevin is on the screen. . . . Yes, I would take on Kevin's advice on what to wear. Kevin is good at giving advice to young women, although he sometimes does advise aunties and mums, too. . . . But my mum's wardrobe is not as stylish as those in the show, so she doesn't act on his advice. . . . [Laughs]

Male interviewees were less enthusiastic about his presence, although only a few, such as Mr. Shao Zhong, a twenty-seven-year-old police officer, openly expressed their disgust at the strong "homosexual undertones" of these shows: "I am really put off by these feminine men. I find them disgusting and offensive."

The third major difference between the experts on local and regional Chinese TV and Shanghai TV is that, in contrast to the one-way didacticism of the former, and true to the Taiwanese variety-show genre (see chapter 8), Shanghai TV's lifestyle advice shows adopt a playful, democratized mode of expertise. Shanghai TV's shows involve a significant amount of interaction—sometimes in the form of joking and bantering—between contestants/participants and experts, sometimes even allowing space for the daren to be challenged and teased. In one early episode of the *Queer Eye* copy, *Beauty Rescue Team*, on October 23, 2010, the makeover experts comprised one female fashion daren and two male masters of fashion taste, both of whom are pop singers, whose aesthetic sensibility and body language placed them on the metrosexual-to-gay end of the masculine self-presentation spectrum. The team set out to transform Xiao Hai, a young man in the IT industry. Xiao Hai was presented as spending a lot of time indoors, paying no attention to his clothes, and being shy about talking to girls, even though he was attracted to a girl he saw regularly walking down his street (that is, in today's youth slang, he was presented as a stereotypical *zhainan* 宅男: a male nerd or homebody, borrowed from the Japanese *otaku*). When the beauty rescue team knocked on his door and offered to help change his image, Xiao Hai initially said he was not interested, that he looked fine and didn't need anyone's help. The team, similar to Xiao Hai in age, then cajoled him into accepting that he needed to change both his appearance and his attitude in order to "get the girl." They dragged him out shopping for clothes, and much laughter, humor, and light-hearted banter, the team took him out onto the street, coaching him as to how to use eye contact, strike up a conversation with strangers, and chat up girls without being off-putting. As on shows like *Queer Eye* and the UK makeover format *What Not to Wear*, part of the show's drama rested on the fact that rather than accepting their judgments, Xiao Hai expressed his doubts freely. When the fashion daren took him to a menswear shop and got him to try on various styles of clothes, Xiao Hai said, "I'm not sure that suits me," to which his fashion advisor replied, "Well, look at me. We are the same age but you look so much duller in those clothes and that hairstyle. Trust me." Xiao Hai then decided to give it a try and—predictably enough—was happily surprised by the outcome of the makeover.

Another noteworthy practice on Shanghai TV's lifestyle programs is that some shows in fact do not feature experts at all but instead invest moral and ethical authority in the participant individuals, rather like the "super consumers" on NDTV Good Times's *Gadget Guru* discussed above. In a 2010 episode (October 9) of the show *Xin Shang Hunli* (Channel Young's weddings), a Shanghai bride and groom were featured because they had an environmentalist message to promote: the episode was rather literally titled "A Low Carbon Wedding." Instead of hiring a fleet of stretch limos, the bride, groom, bridesmaids, and groomsmen arrived on the lawn of a public park in a flotilla of bikes (see figure 5.9). Guests received invitation cards made from recycled milk cartons, complete with a subway ticket, urging them to catch public transport

Figure 5.9. The wedding couple and guests opt for sustainable transport on the "Low Carbon Wedding" episode of *Channel Young's Weddings*, October 9, 2010.

to the wedding. The host interviewed the bride and groom about the design of their wedding clothes and the furnishings of the wedding ceremony that, while all made from recycled material, looked very stylish and glamorous. Instead of giving a "red envelope" (cash gift) to the couple, guests presented them with a huge piece of hand-woven cloth, covered with well wishes from guests at the wedding and from curious passersby who, drawn to the spectacle, were also invited to write down their best wishes.

Through this performance of eco-consumerism, viewers learn new ways of recycling material, and a new morally and ethically charged aesthetic of consumption. The parents of the couple featured on the show confessed that they were a bit reluctant to go along with this idea, given that their children's wedding is a most significant moment and should not be treated frivolously. But they tell the host that they changed their mind after having witnessed the wedding, and are now convinced that their children have done the right thing. Guests were shown to be suitably impressed with the novel ideas behind the design, presentation, and ethos of the event, saying that they have learned a lot from this event, and they are going to think about how they will organize their own wedding and change their consumption practices.

In comparison with the Bengbu TV shows analyzed above, Shanghai TV's wedding show represents a much more democratized approach to consumer education via television. Although the couple has a decidedly moral message to push, aiming to educate the guests, family, and viewing public about the importance of an environmentally responsible lifestyle, the show does not come across as being "preachy," given that the couple's own act embodies the ethical position being advocated, and the manner of imparting tips for everyday living in an environmentally responsible way is gentle and mild. The role of the host on the show here is also worth considering. Rather than assuming the role of a "teaching assistant," who, alongside experts and specialists, promotes scientific knowledge and a certain ethical position, the host of this wedding show assumes the role of a curious learner, not afraid to ask ignorant questions and eager to discover and share new ways of doing things, again embodying and modeling a certain mode of engaged flexible selfhood and citizenship.

A few points can now be made about the figure of the expert or cultural intermediary in the Chinese context. First, the political role of these popular cultural intermediaries needs to be understood in the context of the shift from the government and the Communist Party to a growing focus on privatized expertise. A few decades ago, individuals could receive both practical and ethical guidance through the mechanism of workplace socialization and routine ideological "thought work." Now, despite the disappearance of party leaders, model workers, and the ubiquitous, well-meaning "aunty" figures from the residential neighborhood committee on one's street, people continue to seek guidance and advice, albeit in individuated ways. In other words, experts on Chinese television are not independent of the political and paternal agenda of the party-state but are important figures in China's "exemplary society" of the reforms era (Bakken 2000). Authorized, ultimately, by the state, and considered to possess higher levels of *suzhi* (human quality) compared with members of the public, these experts act to assist the smooth implementation of the state agenda under the changed conditions of the present.

Second, having said that, it is also true that notions of authority and expertise as practiced on Chinese television are deeply embedded in the negotiation between China's socialist past and its contemporary, market-driven cultural-economic logic. As Judith Farquhar and Qicheng Zhang observe in the context of health practices in China, power in the market reforms era most often appears as the "voice of the state-supported expert," who adopts a more "cajoling voice of a classically Foucauldian power/knowledge apparatus" rather than a coercive or violent politics (2012, 21). Although the figure of the popular cultural intermediary is new, in terms of modes of learning on the part of the audience and ways of teaching on the part of the expert, the past is never completely abandoned, nor is the present invented de novo. As we have argued, despite being encouraged to become neoliberal subjects, this specific historical context means that Chinese viewers continue to resonate with—rather than reject—the didacticism in today's lifestyle advice media.

Third, the juxtaposition of serious and authoritative figures such as doctors, scientists, and teachers with everyday life experts such as daren on Chinese television testifies not so much to a democratization of expertise, as found on Western lifestyle shows and to some extent Indian television, but to both the responsiveness and resilience of Chinese authoritarianism (Stockmann 2013, 254). As the Chinese people find themselves having to take on new attitudes, perspectives, and sensibilities, as well as scientific information and knowledge, the state and its media have also become more tolerant of alternative forms of knowledge production and transmission. The figure of the daren may not come across as equally "authoritative" as scientists, doctors, or psychologists with certifiable credentials, and the recognition of their expertise is highly mediated, short lived, and usually achieved on a small and—some might say—trivial scale. Nevertheless, these ordinary individuals, who otherwise might be "nobodies," embody a discounted (to borrow a word from Couldry [2010, 81]) but nevertheless auxiliary form of expertise that complements more authoritative modes of expertise, presenting a picture of diversity and complexity on Chinese television.

Conclusion

In this chapter, we have sought to paint a broad-brushstroke picture of the look and feel of expertise on Indian and Chinese lifestyle television, focusing in particular on the variations between modes of popular advice across socioeconomic groups, urban and rural audiences, and national and regional programming. As we've seen, both countries are negotiating complex transitions toward privatized, postsocialist societies, which, while played out in very different ways in the two nations, have seen a broad shift away from solely state-centered modes of governance toward a growing focus on consumer citizens as a key site of life management. This "responsibilization" of ordinary people has been accompanied by the proliferation of abstract, marketized knowledge systems for managing daily life, with commercial entertainment media playing a key role in shaping norms, taste, and aspirations around selfhood and citizenship, aided and abetted by a new echelon of life experts.

On Indian and Chinese TV, these figures include a range of popular and more traditional credentialed experts as well as exemplary versions of ordinary people, daren or "super consumers." As discussed, some of this expertise is geared toward the new consumer middle classes and is framed in aspirational and cosmopolitan terms. This aspirational expertise stands in contrast to the rather more ordinary life guidance provided by other forms of TV in China and India. Targeting both the lower to middling middle classes and the working poor in urban and rural locales, this everyday expertise provides ordinary people with guides for managing their lives in increasingly complex, pressured environments. In India, where television producers see viewers as being turned off by didactic or information-driven television, much of this expert discourse is packaged primarily as entertainment, with any emphasis on life optimization and/or "responsibilization" tending to be framed in softly pedagogical terms. In China, in contrast, while ordinary viewers are being asked to take responsibility for their health, lives, and families in a postsocialist "liberalized" setting, they are often addressed, particularly on regional and local television, in a rather paternalistic, top-down fashion. Here, the commercialization and privatization of life expertise can be seen, at least on an everyday, popular cultural level, as also being shaped by an authoritarian state-led culture.

Another key issue highlighted by the role of popular experts as life guides is, as we noted in relation to India, their place as cultural brokers, mediating between the multiple systems of modernity at play in these two societies. The wide range of different and at times contesting forms of expertise evident on both Chinese and Indian small screens suggests that these figures, rather than being simple harbingers of late capitalist modernity, embody complex articulations of residual and emergent social, cultural, and economic structures and value systems, speaking to our book's broader concern with the importance of understanding social transitions in the region via a multiple modernities approach. The next chapter picks up on and further develops this theme of historically embedded modernities through an analysis of what we term spiritual lifestyle television. Here we turn to contemporary lifestyle advice television based on religious, supernatural, and "traditional" belief in India and Taiwan to explore the complexly syncretic epistemologies that emerge there from the confluence of secular and nonsecular belief systems and late modern media cultures.

SIX. **Magical Modernities** Spiritual Advice TV in India and Taiwan

A century after it was put forward, Max Weber's claim that the secularization and rationalization of society—what he called the "disenchantment of the world"—was an irresistible, universal, and defining feature of modernity seems more dubious than ever (Weber [1919] 1946, [1922] 1963; Jenkins 2000, 12; Beck 2010, 19–46). Religions, both in collective institutional forms and in the newer styles of individualized "spirituality," are far from withering away. Rather than being eclipsed by (post)modernization, religions globally are adapting themselves energetically to both the marketplace and contemporary media forms (Roof 1993, 2001; Martelli and Cappello 2005; Hoover 2006; Pernia, Pascual, Rosel, and Kwon 2006; Clark 2007; Bahar 2009; Beck 2010; Ferjani 2010; Noonan 2011; Subijanto 2011; Gauthier and Uhl 2012). The emergence of new age and neospiritual movements across the world has also seen the reconfiguration of spirituality and religion as an individualized lifestyle "choice," making it increasingly difficult to exclude the spirit world from discussions of the secular (Redden 2002, 2011; Warrier 2004). Furthermore, as scholars including Colin Campbell and George Ritzer have argued, contra Weber, far from being a space of alienated rationalization, capitalism can itself be seen as a realm of enchantment, with advertising offering consumers no less magical solutions to worldly cares than those offered by old-style religion (Campbell 2005; Ritzer 2005).

If Weber's vision of Euro-American modernity has not been borne out in any straightforward way, then what of those "other" locales that were, for Weber, sites of "non-modernity"? In this chapter, we turn to contemporary lifestyle advice television based on religious, supernatural, and "traditional" belief systems in India and Taiwan to explore the complexly syncretic epistemologies that emerge there from the confluence of secular and nonsecular belief systems and late modern media cultures. In mainland China, although popular religion has been on the rise since the 1980s and there is significant religious continuity and traffic across the Taiwan Strait (Yang 2004), religious organizations are forbidden from using mass media to address their followers. Across the strait in Taiwan, however, religious TV is thriving. Similarly, while the Indian Ministry of Information and Broadcasting has taken some action against "superstition or blind belief" in advertising and programming content on private TV channels,[1] it would be hard to imagine television in India without spiritual guides and morning religious programming, and the ratings of religious channels have even surpassed those of music channels.[2]

Channel surfing in India and Taiwan, as in the United States and some parts of Europe, quickly reveals a contemporary media culture that is far from "disenchanted." A variety of gods and gurus, supernatural forces and sacred texts, narratives and rituals are presented to and interpreted for viewers to help them manage the challenges of personal morality, pressured and risky lives, questions of fate and fortune, and the search for transcendent meaning and collective affiliation in times of rapid social change. The varied examples we discuss in this chapter show that sacred entities and magical processes have made themselves very much at home in the realm of market capitalism in both India and Taiwan. Our argument is thus in many ways broadly comparable to those scholars who have analyzed mediated and marketized religion in Euro-American contexts (Roof 1993, 2001; Hoover 2006; Clark 2007; Beck 2010); however, the forms taken by mediated religion in the places we address are quite different. This is linked, first, to the modern histories of each place, especially the relations between religious groups, the (post)colonial state, and the media over the past half century. Second, issues of scale and the national must be taken into account. For instance, with India's huge range of languages and religions, religion and its representations are particularly significant vis-à-vis that nation's claims to both national secularism and cultural pluralism (Hansen 1999; Rajagopal 2001; Asthana 2008; Ohm 2011). Third, the televisual mediation of spiritual lifestyle advice is quite distinct in these two sites, drawing upon specific national histories of religious TV, and framed by distinct contemporary televisual cultures.

In this chapter, our key questions include: What is historically and locally specific about the interpenetration of religious, supernatural, and "traditional" belief systems and contemporary media cultures in India and Taiwan? How does the incorporation of elements from such belief systems shape the genre(s) of lifestyle advice TV in these two countries? How is religious lifestyle advice programming articulated to the specific contexts and contemporary contradictions of Indian and Taiwanese modernities? And, in what ways do these specific spiritually inflected negotiations of late modernity speak to more global questions regarding the role of magical thinking and spiritual beliefs in people's everyday lives in late capitalism?

From the *Ramayana* to Baba Ramdev: Religion, Spiritualism, and Television as "Electronic Shrine" in India

Whether visiting a regional center in the south or a major city in the north, or spending time in a rural village, it soon becomes evident that the secular and the spiritual are thoroughly entwined in India. Delhi, India's capital, located in the north of the country, is regularly brought to a standstill by religious festivals; saffron-robed swamis have been known to appear on reality TV alongside scantily clad B-list actors; superfamous Bollywood and TV actors such as *Who Wants to Be a Millionaire* host Amitabh Bachchan have shrines constructed in their honor, while the dominant form of domestic tourism is by far religious tourism, with 50 percent of package tours being to spiritual destinations (India Brand Equity Foundation 2003). In our interviews with thirty-four middle- and lower-middle-class households in Mumbai (in northwest India) and Tovinkere (a small village about 100 km northwest of Bangalore in southern India), religion was revealed to be a key feature of most people's lives, whether they were urban professionals, rural middle-class families, or poorer working households.

While the government represents itself as a secular liberal democracy, religion has played a powerful role in the unique form of negotiated state-based "secularism" that has developed in India. The European concept of secularism as a separation of religion from the state has been to a certain extent embedded in the country's system of governance since independence in 1947. Central to this has been a commitment to the protection of minorities, in a country characterized by tremendous religious and ethnic diversity as well as by a large Muslim population after partition. As Britta Ohm (2011) argues, in order to appear neutral and representative, the state has sought to distance itself from the Hindu majority, positioning religion as a private issue. On the other hand, images, symbols, and practices of Hinduism have long been central to mediated public culture in India (as we will discuss), including the manner in which many members of the government have dressed (Ohm 2011, 668). Further, the Bharatiya Janata Party (BJP, Indian People's Party), the parliamentarian wing of the Hindutva movement,[3] has been a major player in Indian politics and struggles over Indian nationalism, and is currently in power in a number of Indian states (Hansen 1999; Rajagopal 2001; Ohm 2011).

This complex imbrication of religion with state secularism, as well as economic liberalization, has also been played out in India's TV industry (Asthana 2008). As we have discussed in chapters 1 and 3, it was not until the 1980s that television started to be thought of as a national broadcast medium, with the reigning prime minister Indira Gandhi's pro-business policies seeing Doordarshan becoming increasingly commercial and dependent on advertising revenue. In the 1980s the broadcaster began experimenting with entertainment-oriented programming that combined a popular commercial agenda with a focus on social issues, having immense success with two key genres: the social interest soap opera (modeled after Latin America's telenovelas) and the mythological or religious serial. In relation to the latter genre, the show *Ramayana*, based on the Hindu epic of the same name, was hugely successful for Doordarshan, with the press at the time commenting on "*Ramayana* fever" and exclaiming that the streets were literally empty on Sunday mornings when the show was aired. Moreover, as the following press quote indicates, *Ramayana* also heralded television's distinctive positioning, at the time, in relation to everyday religious practices and as both a material and sacralized item in the home (see figure 6.1). "In many homes the watching of *Ramayana* has become a religious ritual and the television set . . . is garlanded, decorated with sandalwood paste and vermillion" (Melwani, quoted in Lutgendorf 1997, 224).

Ramayana not only saw the positioning of television as a kind of electronic shrine in domestic space; the inclusion of advertising on the show also heralded the normalization and legitimization of a kind of commercial spiritualism, or what Meera Nanda (2011) has referred to as "the God Market." As Britta Ohm argues, the blending of religious television with advertising saw spiritualism increasingly becoming privatized and tied "to social and economic aspiration and upward mobility" (Ohm 2011, 673).

Moving to the present day, while Ohm and other scholars argue that the religious sphere has become further commercialized and desacralized, Indians continue to be intensely religious, albeit in ways that blend spiritualism with lifestyle and consumption. While India has always had its share of mystics and shamans, over the past decade or so "new, urbane and sophisticated gurus have sprung up across the country—gurus who blend ancient wisdom and modern techniques to concoct a very contemporary spirituality" (Kasbekar 2006, 289), contributing to a process that Peter Jackson terms the "mediatisation of myth," a common trend across many contemporary Asian societies (Jackson 2009,

Figure 6.1. In many Indian homes the TV and the domestic shrine continue to be placed in close proximity, as we see in this household in contemporary Mumbai. Photo by Kiran Mulenahalli.

364). With the middle classes spending somewhere between 10 and 25 percent of their income on "spiritual pursuits" (Kasbekar 2006, 290), the religious market has become a significant dimension of India's cultural economy; in the publishing sector, for example, mythological retellings of classics such as the *Ramayana* and the *Mahabharata* are the biggest-selling genre in the country (Bal 2013). Thus, as Bhaskar Mukhopadhyay has observed, "Folk, vernacular, or 'traditional' culture is no longer experienced as part of the 'sacred' but is conceived, increasingly, as special kinds of artefacts, performances and representations. . . . This is the key to the understanding of not just the hybridized folk but the Indian vernacular modern as such. . . . Mass-media has made the gods more real, not less" (Mukhopadhyay 2006, 288).

And indeed, a key space where religious and spiritual advisors are flourishing is on commercial television. Indian audiences have access to a huge array of religious programming, from traditional Indian religious series (the original 1980s *Ramayana* TV series has been remade twice, in 2008 for NDTV Imagine and in 2012 for Zee TV) and classic mythological films to popular documentaries on Indian mythology, religion, and religious festivals around the country. What has been particularly marked over the past decade, however, is the proliferation of spiritual gurus and advisors on television, and the turn toward what we are calling spiritual lifestyle programming. Here, religious advice is increasingly married with life guidance more broadly, both in relation to fate and fortune and in relation to personal well-being and psychological issues.

As in Taiwan (discussed below), the televisual landscape in India is now populated by a number of religious cable channels, such as Aastha TV, Sanskar TV, Om Television, and Divya TV, to name a few, which offer twenty-four hours of spiritual programming, as well as channels like Pragya, which has branded itself in terms of wellness and lifestyle while, as we discuss below, clearly retaining a spiritual focus. TAM Media Research data indicate that the genre share of spiritual or devotional channels grew by over 25 percent between 2009 and 2012 (Gurtoo 2012). Spiritual programming is far from a niche cable offering, however, as religious programming is also featured on many of the general entertainment channels, especially in the morning slot. Tele-astrologers are a common sight on both Hindi (in particular, entertainment-oriented "news") channels and regional TV channels, where they often pay to have a slot featured on the channel (Talwar 2013), foregrounding the lucrative and highly commercialized nature of spiritual advice television in India.[4]

In this next section we discuss two key areas of spiritual lifestyle TV in India, which offer generative sites for comparison and contrast with the Taiwanese religious and spiritual programming discussed in the second half of this chapter. First, we focus on forms of TV (fortune-telling, astrology, home décor/*vaastu* shows) that aim to advise people in the areas of fate and fortune. Second, we discuss cable channels devoted to spiritual advice programming.

MANAGING FATE, FORTUNE, AND RISK: ANCIENT WISDOM
AND SOOTHSAYING ON THE SMALL SCREEN

Astrologers, tarot readers, fortune-tellers, experts in vaastu (an Indian version of Chinese feng shui), and mystical shamans of all kinds represent a common and increasingly popular feature of Indian programming across news and general entertainment channels as well as cable channels devoted to religious programming. While they draw on a range of belief systems and spiritual traditions, what is common to many of these mystical figures is their claim to offer life solutions and advice for dealing with an increasingly complex, stressful, and risky world.[5] In his book *A God of One's Own* (2010), Ulrich Beck argues that we live in a postsecular age in which, far from becoming more secular, religion and spiritualism are on the rise around the world but in ways increasingly tied to individual needs, desires, and biographies. One central role for spiritual advice within this context is to manage and minimize the risks that accompany living in a late modern era, where global and external concerns have increasingly become individualized and where life decisions—from what kind of house to buy and how to manage one's health to what to eat and to whom to marry—are seen as calculable life choices and investments in the self.

While mystics of all kinds have long played a role in Indian life, their growing popularity is linked with their self-promotion as figures that can assist with the stresses and strains of contemporary Indian life. Based on her fieldwork with astrologers and their primarily middle- and upper-middle-class clients in Banaras (Varanasi), Caterina Guenzi argues that in the context of a postliberalized India, the conception of destiny as *bhagya* (or one's "allotted share") has shifted to "a malleable resource, as an investment that can be increased, diminished, or wasted, depending on the choices that one makes in life" (Guenzi 2012, 41). Middle-class clients "confronted with new forms of social and spatial mobility" increasingly look to "astrologers [to] elaborate strategies and remedies for a better management of fortune" (Guenzi 2012, 41). As we will see, figures such as astrologers and other soothsayers increasingly frame their advice and remedies in terms of people's lifestyle choices and investments in family and the self; however, this advice is not necessarily framed purely in terms of internalized modes of individual empowerment (taking control of one's destiny) but rather often involves some degree of externalization of risk, of giving one's self over to larger forces, whether they be the alignment of the planets or the "science" of vaastu architecture and home décor.

One of the more popular forms of mystical or magical advice, particularly with regard to Hindu audiences, involves fortune-tellers or astrologers. Fortune-tellers on television tend to fall into two categories: On the more "traditional" side, we have male Brahmins who are not revered as holy men but whose credentials as gurus stem from their training, expertise, and lineage in ancient Hindu astrology. At the other end of the spectrum, we see a range of futurologists dabbling in more "global" arts like tarot and numerology—many of these are urban middle- to upper-middle-class women, who, like their counterparts in the West, have miraculously "discovered" their own psychic and mystic powers.[6] Fewer in number than traditional astrologers and mostly speaking in Hinglish or English to an urban audience, the credentials of the latter come not from their Brahminical lineage but mostly from their work with Bollywood celebrities.

By contrast, Hindu Vedic astrologers have a broader mass appeal and offer a more "traditional" mode of address, although as the journalist Ruchika Talwar points out, increasingly the "new breed" of Vedic astrologers are "flamboyant as well as hard-nosed entrepreneurs" (Talwar 2013). Sporting a saffron robe, a Hindu rosary (or prayer beads), and a ceremonial mark on the forehead, the expert-astrologer will often begin with a Vedic chant or discourse briefly on a mantra prior to making astrological predictions; the visual and aural settings of these Vedic astrology programs also bear religious overtones, featuring the chanting of mantras or graphic animations of holy symbols in the background. While many gurus offer generic astrological readings for the day, there are also a number of shows that blend astrology with health, psychological, and economic concerns, offering predictions geared to specific audience and lifestyle needs. On Zee Business, for instance, Sundeep Koachar (a self-professed "Astrologer, Anchor, Actor, Radio & TV presenter, Social worker, Author, Poet, Lyricist, and Dreamer"[7]), on a show called *Astronomics*, makes financial investment predictions for the day and offers one-on-one economic advice to audience members, while adopting a somewhat comic mode of address and often breaking into long motivational speeches. In the popular *Astro Uncle* (on the major Hindi news channel Aaj Tak), an amiable middle-aged host, Pawan Sinha (who is apparently not just an astrologer but also a healer, spiritual thinker, and a master in meditation skills[8]), offers general astrological advice as well as one-on-one feedback to audience call-ins on matters relating to parent/child relationships (see figures 6.2 and 6.3).

On one episode aired in July 2013, the show's female anchor, introducing the topic for the day in a playful conversational tone, talks about how her friend's four-year-old daughter is very irritable. Offering a "prediction" with a psychological edge, Astro Uncle explains that irritable children will not do well socially or academically, and face medical problems with their nervous system later in adult life. Here we are told that the planets *mangal* (Mars) and *rahu*[9] affect irritability and temper and that, while rahu's irritability is seasonal, mangal's irritability makes people self-absorbed and arrogant (see figure 6.2). The show then features a call-in from a woman who complains that her daughter is very irritable and often gets high fevers. Astro Uncle, reading her charts, suggests that since he can't see a lot of anger in the girl's constitution (as the moon is in the right place), her fever and irritability may be due to an abdominal or urinary infection. His advice here is both magical and modern—he tells the mother to book the child in for a medical checkup while also adding that the girl must wear a copper bangle and float a copper coin in a river.

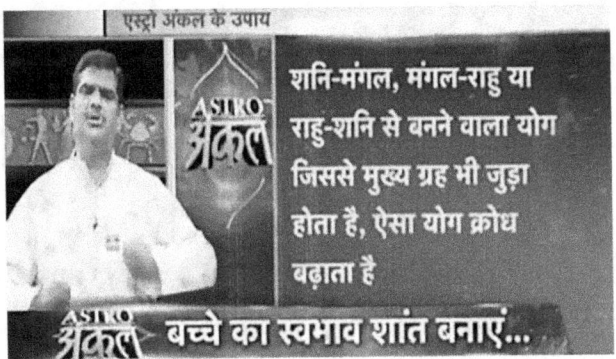

Figure 6.2. Pawan Sinha, resident astrologer on *Astro Uncle*, uses astrology to give psychological counseling for irritable children. In this episode, aired on July 27, 2013, the text in the panel reads, "The combination of Saturn-Mars, Mars-Rahu, and Rahu-Saturn in one's planetary alignment makes one prone to anger."

Figure 6.3. In this episode of *Astro Uncle* (June 30, 2013), Pawan Sinha claims that the material of the utensil from which a child eats affects their well-being. In this shot, parents are advised that children born under the Capricorn sign "whose palms show a high mound of Saturn will benefit from utensils made of silver and ceramic."

Figure 6.4. An image of Dr. Puneet Chawla, the star of *Live Vaastu*, taken from the opening titles to the show; the equivalent of a spiritual-religious "glamor shot," the opening credits of spiritual programs commonly depict the show's baba or expert using this kind of starry or haloed effect.

In contrast to the mass appeal of *Astro Uncle*, a range of tarot readers, numerologists, and vaastu experts offer rather more niche advice to middle- to upper-middle-class viewers. For example, Live India, a regional Hindi channel, has a dedicated show on the "ancient science" of vaastu called *Live Vaastu*, where a suit-wearing expert, Dr. Puneet Chawla, who looks more like an architect than a fortune-teller, responds to questions about the impact of vaastu—that is, household design and the placement of furnishings and objects—on a variety of life issues from troubled relationships to alcoholism to misbehaving pets (see figure 6.4).

Hosted (interchangeably) by a female and/or a male anchor, also wearing a Western suit, in a news-style studio setting, the show has segments featuring a split screen with Dr. Chawla on one side advising on the topic for the day and answering calls from viewers, while on the right side the audience is shown luxurious, Western-style home interiors or images of colors that should be avoided in certain parts of the house (see figure 6.5). Many of the viewers who call in are themselves highly knowledgeable about vaastu, suggesting a rather more democratized relationship to expertise than more traditional astrology shows, reflecting in part the educated and upper-middle-class status of the target audience. On one episode, for example, a caller rings in and explains

Figure 6.5. In this episode of *Live Vaastu* from February 2012, Dr. Chawla offers advice on what colors improve the energy of a house. In this clip (solution number 5), the audience is told to avoid the colors blue and black.

that, despite his gate and kitchen being in the "right" place from a vaastu perspective, his family has been faring badly. Dr. Chawla tells him to get the gate painted in a lighter color, and to put a mirror in the north side of the house so that it reflects back the energy of his kitchen, located in the southeast part of the house.

While *Live Vaastu*'s content deals with ancient Indian knowledge around the impact of cosmic forces on households, its mode of address is very cosmopolitan and aspirational. The show's resident vaastu expert is suave and well dressed, shifting between English and Hindi with ease. The advice given is very specific and often asked and answered in technical language while, unlike astrologers and other fortune-tellers, Dr. Chawla's answers do not venture into motivational or moralistic territory, though they are clearly aimed at improving fortune. On one episode, for instance, a viewer congratulates Dr. Chawla for making "the people and the country happy and prosperous" with his vaastu tips to improve people's lives. One of the more interesting components of the show is that every week features a prize-winning audience member, with Dr. Chawla visiting the winner's house and providing a complete vaastu reading and suggestions to improve the home (see figure 6.6). Referencing elements of the Western home makeover show and offering individually tailored lifestyle advice, *Live Vaastu* offers a mixture of magical risk management and consumerist self-expression to an educated, urbane, middle-class audience.

Figure 6.6. A segment of *Live Vaastu* where Dr. Chawla (compass in hand) visits an audience member's house to do a vaastu reading.

"MEET YOUR BETTER SELF":
RELIGIOUS TV AND NEOSPIRITUALISM

Alongside the growth in popularity of individual shows featuring astrologers and other soothsayers on Indian GECs and news channels, in recent years, with the deregulation of television and the huge growth in cable and satellite TV, like Taiwan (discussed below), India has seen the rise of channels dedicated purely to religious or spiritual programming. At recent count India now has forty-five such channels, with fifteen broadcast nationally.[10] Apart from Sanskar, which only offers telecasts of religious congregations, devotional songs, and extended religious orations, all other religious channels feature religiously inflected health and well-being programming alongside telecasts of gurus; these include magazine-style shows on yoga, ayurvedic therapy, astrology, and medical phone-ins.

The Hindi channel Aastha TV was the first spiritual channel to take the stage in India and continues to be the most popular. Of the top ten programs across religious channels, all but one are on Aastha TV, with the top three shows featuring the controversial yoga guru Baba Ramdev, whose trust now owns the entire channel. On the surface Aastha, with its impressive array of small-screen "saints and gurus,"[11] appears to be a fairly straightforward religious channel, albeit with the rather grandiose aim of "providing content, which fulfills the spiritual needs of the worldwide Asian Indian community."[12] However, as in the case of the Taiwanese Buddhist channel discussed below, yoga guru and owner Baba Ramdev's various prominent engagements with the major social, national, and political issues of the time, along with his business

Figure 6.7. Baba Ramdev as a holy man.

and technological savvy, mark the increasingly broad social role of (multi) mediatized religion, highly marketized forms of spiritualism, and religiously inflected development and business ventures in India (see figure 6.7).

The Aastha channel website describes itself as "India's Leading Socio-Spiritual-Cultural Television Network" rather than a religious channel.[13] Baba Ramdev has been prominently involved in political and social affairs, taking center stage in the 2012 anticorruption campaign in India when he marched to parliament, and voicing highly provocative ultraconservative views on homosexuality and AIDS. At the same time, Ramdev's guru status is inextricably tied to his success as an entrepreneur in both the religious and the well-being market. He owns a nationwide ayurvedic pharmacy network and a small Scottish island (where his trust is based); his claims that all kinds of modern ills (from stress to AIDS) can be treated by yoga and ayurvedic drugs (preferably bought from his pharmacies) underscore the aptness of Meera Nanda's description of contemporary religion in India as a "State-Temple-Corporate Complex" (Nanda 2011).

Ramdev has also been a very astute media player. As a guru who blends nationalist fervor with a fairly idiosyncratic take on Hindu doctrines, he is perhaps the most well-known of the current crop of contemporary spiritual guides on Indian television. Born to a poor farming family in rural north India, he claims to have earned a postgraduate degree in yoga and the *vedas* (knowledge), before retreating to a Himalayan cave as an ascetic. He subsequently came into prominence with a yoga program on the Aastha channel in 2003 and now has a presence on all major Hindi-language channels (news, religious, and GECs), as well as owning the Aastha channel itself. Unlike other babas and gurus, Ramdev has positioned himself as a man of the people, forgoing the status of a divine "god-man," and offering himself up instead as a crusader against the modern pharmaceutical industry (rather controversially calling for a ban on allopathic medicine), and the lifestyle ills of the modern world more broadly. While his teachings are premised on reintroducing ancient Vedic life principles to the Indian masses, his mode of instruction has been more practical than proselytizing. Ramdev has branded himself first and foremost as a yoga guru; he is best known for popularizing yoga among health-conscious Indians through his yoga *shivirs*, or mass yoga camps, which are attended by thousands of people and began to be televised in 1995 (see figures 6.8 and 6.9).

Ramdev's TV programs include yoga targeted at specific demographics and lifestyle issues, such as yoga for young women and recommended yoga asanas for losing weight (see figure 6.10). The baba's blend of ancient Hindu vedas with a health-oriented brand of yoga can be read as marking a broader Beckian shift to a privatized neospiritualism. Although as Chandrima Chakraborty points out, Ramdev also draws on discourses of nationalism, imagining a new disciplined India, with yoga seen as not just benefiting individuals but as building the nation's sociospiritual health (Chakraborty 2007). Yoga is thus constructed as a way of creating healthy citizens and contributing to the potency of the Indian nation via processes of individual self-care and spiritual discipline, with spiritualism shifting here from a mode of purely faith-based belief to being part of a broader "lifestyle" based on personal choice and self-fulfillment (Warrier 2004), an optimized combination of "physical, mental and spiritual health" that can be tailored to one's specific needs. As a TV executive we interviewed at NDTV Good Times put it, "We [our channel] don't have religion at all. We do yoga."

This neospiritual turn has also seen the rise of a number of lifestyle channels in India that are not necessarily categorized as religious channels, like Pragya, Care World, and Shakti TV, but that offer spiritually inflected forms of lifestyle programming: shows on yoga, meditation, psychology, ayurveda, and alternative medicine are interspersed with more secular lifestyle shows, such as cookery, parenting, relationship, and beauty shows. Pragya TV (*pra*

Figures 6.8 and 6.9. Baba Ramdev demonstrates a yoga pose for an audience of thousands at a yoga camp at Madhya Pradesh, May 5, 2012.

Figure 6.10. Yoga on YouTube: Ramdev as a health and fitness guide.

being Sanskrit for "moving forward" and *gyan* meaning "knowledge"), where we interviewed a couple of high-level executives at their head office in Gurgaon near New Delhi, is a particularly interesting case in point.[14] Calling itself a "well-being" channel and servicing a young (twenty-four to forty-five years old), educated, and aspirational upper-middle-class market with a 40:60 male-to-female audience split, the channel's tagline is "*Aapko milaye behtar aapse*," meaning "Meet your better self," while the channel's "philosophy" espouses a mix of self-development discourse, spiritualism, pop psychology, and antimaterialism, somewhat paradoxically combined with high-end lifestyle-oriented consumerism and an entrepreneurial edge.

In keeping with the channel's focus on inner well-being and its reflexive (if somewhat contradictory) take on materialism (according to their website, the "common man is our celebrity"), the low-key décor and location of the channel's headquarters stood in contrast to the glitz of high-end lifestyle channels like NDTV and Channel V we also visited. The channel nevertheless operates as a commercial affair and has corporate sponsorship; however, it is part of a much larger media conglomerate (The Century Group), giving it considerable leeway to turn down sponsors who don't fit with its "values." Under the banner of "social corporate responsibility," Pragya TV also conducts broader social programs including a yearly "event" where orphans visit elderly people in aged-care homes, and an annual week of tree planting. On closer inspection, however, these outreach programs appear to be fairly superficial photo opportunities or brand exercises rather than representing a deep ongoing commitment to community engagement and potential social change. Nevertheless, the two senior managers we spoke with, both of whom had worked for conventional commercial television prior to moving to Pragya, took pains to emphasize the uniqueness of working at the channel, which they saw as moving beyond a purely corporate model.[15] "Coming from a total entertainment background, I had other plans in mind, TRP [ratings] and all those other things. But later I started believing that I need to be serving people, something for which I have always had a secret desire. . . . When I read e-mails and SMSs [from Pragya's audience members] I realized these people are very attached to us. The channel business is purely business. Pragya is different. . . . We are changing lives and we are very happy."[16]

While the creative director spoke in rather reverent tones of the channel's "mission," the director of programming spoke rather more pragmatically of the channel's markets and target audiences, discussing for example a new feature program aimed at international audiences: "[The show] talks about how a soul works in your body, what kind of attention you should give to your soul, the soul as the universal power. This kind of content can be appreciated . . . if you are talking about the international market."[17]

Pragya's range of programming and content reflects this eclectic grab bag of concerns. The channel offers what might be seen as a cosmopolitan blend of neospiritualism, self-help, and self-improvement (the creative director spoke in the same breath of the teachings of the famous nineteenth-century Hindu monk Swami Vivekananda and the U.S. positive thinking guide *The Secret*); as well as lifestyle and consumer tips and information for optimizing every aspect of one's life, from parenting and home décor to beauty and health ("to channelize sensibilities, capacities and productivity of individuals," as the website puts it) (see figure 6.11). Morning programming tends to be focused more on the spiritual end of the channel's spectrum; here the schedule includes shows like *Dhyan Pragya* (Meditation knowledge), *Pragya Prabhat* (Knowledge morning), and *Vichar Sanjivni* (Elixir of thought), which aim to provide the audience with a kind of psychological/wellness "pep-talk" to get their day started, with the shows' guests offering a variety of advice on "science of meditation" and "religious teachings."

At the more secular lifestyle-oriented end of the spectrum, in the evenings Pragya also offers a number of magazine-style infotainment shows, often featuring audience call-ins. *Menz*, for instance, is a studio-based show focused on the stresses of being a man in contemporary India and providing advice on psychological, social, and physical well-being. In an episode in February 2012, the female host, Professor Navjot Sidhu (a media academic and TV host

Figure 6.11. "Wisdom comes with responsibility": Pragya TV website, featuring five categories of life advice videos, including beauty, relationships, good living, food (smart kitchen), and living wisely.

and producer), who is dressed in casual Western clothes and sports short hair, offers an in-depth introduction to the topic of concern: managing work–life balance. She then introduces Dr. Ankul Barar (a motivational speaker, tarot reader, Reiki master, and hypnotherapist), who reveals tips on meditation, acupressure, and deep breathing. *Just for Women* is a more glossy, fast-paced magazine show featuring two glamorous young anchors wearing casual kurtas rather than saris. Reflecting the complexity of the channel's neospiritual engagement with both "traditional" and secular lifestyle and consumerist culture, the show moves between reenactments of various lifestyle issues from hypertension to sibling rivalry; interviews with people with lifestyle problems; and advice relevant to the issue at hand from various experts, usually shot in their place of work. These shows nicely capture the way in which spiritual "holism" on Pragya TV has been refigured as a market-based privatized pursuit where the individual gets to pick and mix from a cornucopia of life skills, knowledge systems, and lifestyle products and services.

Pragya's shows thus epitomize Nandini Gooptu's argument that the new spiritualisms in India are increasingly tied to a neoliberalized notion of enterprise culture:

> Armed with the sacral power of Hindu religious systems and borrowing techniques from psychology and self-help literature as well as managerial practices in business, spiritualism in its present form concentrates on individual self-making on an unprecedented scale. Spiritualism and ideas of enterprise inflect each other and offer hopes of self-transformation and worldly success. Within an all-pervading environment which promotes aspirations, spiritual teachings purport to provide the actual tools with which individuals can realise their dreams and goals. Spiritualism thus assembles the essential components of enterprise culture through the amalgamation of aspiration and action. (Gooptu 2013, 16)

A final point to make about Pragya TV concerns its treatment of the many and varied "experts" it features on its programming. While specialists and authorities are central to most of its shows, they are often introduced fairly generically as "experts." In contrast to the emphasis placed on the training and lineage of the Brahmin astrologers discussed above, Pragya's programs don't necessarily pay much attention to the credentials of the life guides and gurus they feature. Here, as on many Western lifestyle shows, expertise is a democratized and marketable commodity that theoretically anyone can acquire, though a certain talent for performance and a degree of charisma are central to having a market edge (see our discussion in chapter 5).

Lieutenant Rita Gangwani, a former Indian army officer who features on Pragya's breaking show *Utho Jago* (Arise awaken), is a perfect exemplar of this kind of marketized, neospiritual "expertise" in India. A flamboyant, sari-wearing, middle-aged woman with fashionably bobbed hair, she is introduced on the show as an "image enhancer and personality architect," while her profile on the website for the "Humanity Healing Network" describes her as, among other things, a "Tea Leaf Reader, Tarot Reader, . . . Reiki and chios energy healer, . . . lifestyle coach, stylist, self taught face and body reader, Certified Dr. Silva's ultra mind training Graduate, and a successful Motivational speaker."[18] While clearly charisma and a certain personal authority (derived from her experience as an army officer) has been key to her success, her shopping list of "credentials" here speaks to the equivalency bestowed upon knowledge and training within a marketized system of lifestyle expertise.

This is not to overplay the distinctive nature of spiritual expertise in India, nor to exaggerate the role of calculative individualism in a nation where familial and ethnic ties are central to social life, and where many sections of the population strongly identify with religious faith and affiliation. While both Aastha and Pragya TV to a certain extent promote and celebrate forms of self-actualization, they do so in ways that often tie well-being and spiritual integration to the familial, communal, and national good. As noted above, Baba Ramdev's nation-building yoga camps, which involve large numbers of devotees practicing yoga en masse, focus on the identification and development of the "self" as an integral element to sustaining the communal harmony and spiritual well-being of the collective, with the individual here positioned as a continuation of the collective. Within Pragya's framework the self is, in certain ways, much more reflexive and individualized. However, the channel's "mission" is not purely "to enable individuals to meet their better self"; it also aims to "discipline and reform thoughts" and "to empower societies and nations," indicating that Pragya's notions of holistic well-being are characterized by both individual and collective elements in ways that are arguably not simply synonymous with the disciplined subjectivities associated with globalized forms of late capitalism or neoliberal forms of governmentality.

Religious and Supernatural Television in Taiwan: Magic and Modernity

In Taiwan, in contrast to India, both the proliferation of popular religions and the emergence of religious TV are relatively recent phenomena. Under Chiang Kai-shek, the island's Kuomintang (KMT) administration—like the Chinese Communist Party on the Chinese mainland—carried on the secular-scientific project of early twentieth-century Chinese intellectuals' cultural modernization movement (Madsen 2007, 28). Between the late 1940s and the late 1970s, the authoritarian party-state prevented the expansion of Buddhist and Daoist groups, co-opted local religious leaders and temples into the service of corrupt politics, criticized religious "superstitions," and promoted a self-serving form of neo-Confucianism designed to inculcate obedience to state authority (Madsen 2008, 296). The three TV channels in existence in this period, all KMT affiliated, carried no religious programming. The one exception was Christian groups and missionaries: the KMT allowed Catholic and Protestant churches to establish universities, hospitals, clinics, and welfare services in an attempt to pander to the United States, which provided financial aid and support for the regime (Madsen 2007, 43; 2008, 296). Local popular religion, meanwhile, retreated from public life and became confined to remote rural communities and the domestic sphere (Yang 2004, 213).

In the late 1970s, however, under Chiang Ching-kuo's leadership, a new cooperative relationship developed between the state and Buddhist and Daoist groups. In a context where rapid industrialization and urbanization were placing significant stress on the traditional family-based social support system, the state began to make use of these religious organizations' willingness to provide welfare services (Madsen 2007, 33–34; 2008, 317–18). For example, in the late 1970s the KMT donated land to the Tzu Chi Buddhist organization—whose TV channel, Da Ai, we discuss in detail below—to build a multimillion-dollar general hospital on the island's underresourced eastern coast (Madsen 2007, 34). This marks an important step in Tzu Chi's rise to its current position as the most significant and efficacious nongovernment welfare provider in Taiwan, taking the lead, along with other Buddhist and Daoist groups, from the Christian groups who had been given a head start on modern institution building (Madsen 2008, 296).

It was after the lifting of martial law in 1987, though, that the boom in popular religion really gained momentum (Yang 2004, 213; C. Huang 2009, 33). In this period, all kinds of civil associations blossomed at the same time as media censorship significantly relaxed and a flourishing commodity culture entrenched market logic as a pervasive cultural force. Against this background, popular local religion of all sorts experienced a renaissance, and by the 1990s religious, spiritual, and supernatural themes featured regularly in locally produced TV content (Yang 2004, 223).

Robert P. Weller observes two notable trends across both Taiwan and China since the 1980s: first, the growth of popular religious practices that center the individual's needs (such as ghost worship and spirit medium cults); second, the growth of large-scale, universalizing religious organizations (such as the Tzu Chi Buddhist organization, analyzed below) (Weller 1999, 83–84). Weller links both of these seemingly contradictory tendencies to the social effects of market logic. Simultaneously, old conventions and normative beliefs are stripped away—activating an existing individualist streak in traditional Chinese religion, where the magical powers of ghosts and spirits can be commissioned for personal advantage—while the formation of new communal bonds is also necessitated, as exemplified in the rational-ethical megasects of institutional Buddhism and Daoism. The examples we will analyze below—popular commercial feng shui advice shows and Tzu Chi's Da Ai TV channel—illustrate both of the trends Weller identifies.

Among the two-hundred-odd channels operating in Taiwan at the time of writing, there are seven cable channels run by religious organizations and dedicated to religious-themed programming; six of these are Buddhist,[19] one Christian.[20] In addition to these dedicated channels, TV content based on supernatural and traditional beliefs and practices is also scattered through popular entertainment programs screened on the general commercial

Figure 6.12. *Feng Shui Matters*, January 23, 2012. Xiao Zhen and Li Peizhen read letters from viewers asking for advice on the use of feng shui to solve financial and employment problems.

channels, notably in talk and variety shows themed on fate, fortune-telling, and feng shui.[21] It is this latter genre to which we now turn.

FENG SHUI MATTERS:

MAGICAL WAYS OF DEALING WITH MODERNITY

Fengshui! You guanxi (Feng shui matters), a sixty-minute show that screens on the Videoland (Weilai) cable network on Saturdays and Sundays at 10 p.m., provides a good example of the TV adaptation of a popular individualistic supernatural belief system (Weller 1999, 83–105). Popular among married women over twenty-five, both working women and housewives, across a wide range of income levels, the show is hosted by two attractive, fashionable, and lively young female celebrities, Hu Yingzhen (Xiao Zhen) and Li Peizhen (see figure 6.12).[22]

They are joined by a male feng shui consultant—at the time of writing, this role was taken by the portly, middle-aged Hsieh Yuanjin, an expert in feng shui, fortune-telling, and auspicious names, and also available for public consultation via his "Centre for Fortune Research."[23] In terms of genre, *Feng Shui Matters* blends elements of the variety/talk-show format with the celebrity home makeover genre. Typical of populist television in Taiwan today (and like Sinicized variety shows throughout the region), it is marked stylistically by the heavy use of postproduction graphic and audio effects, comic mode of address,

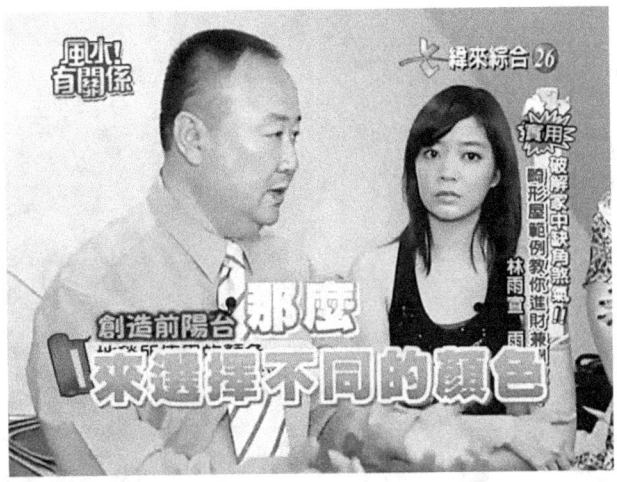

Figure 6.13. *Feng Shui Matters*, June 2, 2013. Master Hsieh Yuanjin advises the underemployed actress Lin Yuxuan on how choosing the right colored rug can bring her more work.

and energetic, informal group interactions originally adapted from Japanese formats (Martin 2013). Each episode sees the hosts accompany the feng shui master to the home of a minor media celebrity to solicit the master's advice on how the apartment's feng shui could be improved to bring its occupants better luck (see figures 6.13–6.15). Offering magical solutions to contemporary problems, *Feng Shui Matters* represents an excellent example of how a premodern system of enchantment adapts itself to late modern social life and media culture (see figure 6.16).

The central theme of the advice given in *Feng Shui Matters* is that of bringing more luck—that is, increased wealth—into the households of the makeover-ees. While this is no doubt a timeless theme in Chinese societies, many of the situations presented as warranting feng shui intervention are also, as on Indian spiritual TV, specifically connected with late capitalist urban life and its discontents. For example, a common topic concerns how to disperse the "evil-spirit energy" (*shaqi*) that emanates from inauspicious structures visible from apartment windows. In one episode (figure 6.13), the underemployed actress Lin's chronic hormonal imbalance is explained as a result of evil-spirit energy emanating from the sharp corner of a women's hospital next door. In an episode screened on January 23, 2012, meanwhile, evil-spirit energy is said to arise from four roof-top cooling towers with the shape of traditional medicine jars, visible from the living room window (see figure 6.17). In dense

Figures 6.14 and 6.15. *Feng Shui Matters*, June 2, 2013. Inauspicious versus auspicious furniture arrangement: before (*top*) and after Lin Yuxuan's feng shui makeover.

Figure 6.16. *Feng Shui Matters*, June 2, 2013. Enchanted modernity: advice on the correct treatment of gods' likenesses in the home.

Figure 6.17. *Feng Shui Matters*, January 23, 2012. Evil spirits are generated by dense urban living.

urban environments like those in which the majority of people live in Taiwan, evil spirits seem virtually unavoidable. It is tempting to interpret the feng shui master's declarations to this effect as an encoded critique of the risks to well-being inherent in contemporary urban life.

The episode just discussed commences with an in-studio scene where the anchors read out a series of letters from ordinary female viewers describing their current luckless condition and the hope that some feng shui adjustments could help them turn things around (see figure 6.12). Ms. Chen in Taichung has worked diligently for years yet has never had a pay raise, while her heavy overtime load has affected both her health and her relationship with her boyfriend. In Toufen, Mother Lin's husband, brother-in-law, and sister-in-law have all become unemployed, plunging the family into anxiety and financial disarray. Ms. Wang from Yungho is a single mother with a sixteen-year-old son; despite her hard work in raising him, he constantly argues and fights with her, and they are also suffering from money problems. The show frames these as "women's problems" arising from the growing burden placed on women as a result of increasing paid employment and ongoing domestic care duties. But what are highlighted here are in fact employment conditions that affect both women and men in the current labor market. In 2011–12, economic growth significantly slowed in Taiwan as a result of the economic decline in Europe and the United States. Ms. Chen's delayed pay raise, Mother Lin's unemployed relatives, and Ms. Wang's cash-flow problems are likely to be local symptoms of the situation in the wider world of global capitalism. Again, though, rather than framing these issues in economic or social terms, the remedies the master suggests are magical ones: when situating your stove, observe the five taboos of the kitchen god; deflect evil spirits with plastic window film; and so on.

As these examples show, like *Live Vaastu* discussed earlier, *Feng Shui Matters* imbues magic into late modern social structures and processes. However, in contrast to the positioning of vaastu in technical terms as an ancient "science" in that program, *Feng Shui Matters*'s epistemology is largely antirational, with supernatural forces invoked as both the cause and the antidote for human misfortune.[24] Its strongly individualized framework, adapted from premodern supernatural beliefs and practices (Weller 1999, 89–91), does suggest a certain resonance with contemporary global trends in both religion and life advice media (Roof 1993, 2001; Hoover and Park 2005; Hoover 2006; Beck 2010; Noonan 2011). However, unlike the Euro-American discourse of the individualized "spiritual seeker," which centers on a quest for abstract inner meaning, the televisual feng shui discourse focuses on external aims. As the discussion above suggests, it is possible to infer an encoded critique of the risks of modernity in a program like *Feng Shui Matters*, with the feng shui discourse offering a kind of magical antidote to the harsh social and economic realities facing individuals in Taiwan's late capitalist society. Rather than seek political or state-based solutions to problems like unemployment, poor working conditions, the gendered division of labor, health risks, and urban overcrowding, viewers are directed to address the spirit world instead. Hence, the feng shui discourse's response to late modern risks is ultimately microtactical and adaptive. This lack of an overt universalizing moral critique of modern processes and structures stands in significant contrast with the Buddhist channel discussed below. As we will see, Da Ai TV offers much more of a macrolevel critique of the harms of (post)industrial society, promoting a collective, other-focused response to contemporary problems. Through its advancement of generalized spiritual principles for leading a good life, it also articulates a critical counternarrative of modernity itself.

THE TZU CHI FOUNDATION AND DA AI TV: MODERN WAYS OF BEING BUDDHIST

Da Ai (Great Love) is the television station of the Buddhist Compassion Relief Tzu Chi Foundation, a lay organization with monastic leadership founded by the renegade nun Cheng Yen in 1966. From its humble beginning as a group of housewives compelled by Cheng Yen's humanitarian quest to spread compassionate relief to the needy, Tzu Chi has grown rapidly since the late 1980s to become the largest formal association in Taiwan today, with an expanding membership among diasporic Taiwanese worldwide (Huang 2009, 1). Membership estimates range from five to ten million globally (Huang 2009, 1; O'Neill 2010, 57), and as many as 20 percent of Taiwan's population are Tzu Chi members, with membership concentrated in the middle classes (Weller 1999, 97; Liao 2012, 42). Interestingly, the organization's membership is around 80 percent female, in distinction to institutional Buddhism's historically masculinist character (Weller 1999, 93). The anthropologist Hwei-Syin Lu observes that Tzu Chi's philosophy sacralizes Minnan and Hakka women's traditional caring roles within the family, encouraging them to generalize their maternal love outward toward society at large, and with the nun Cheng Yen at the helm, "the underlying structure of the Tzu Chi voluntary group may be viewed as the 'mother-centered-family'" (Lu 1998, 546).[25]

The total value of Tzu Chi's assets is estimated in billions of dollars (Madsen 2007, 36). In Taiwan, Tzu Chi runs a massive island-wide recycling program, six hospitals, a university with a standard medical school, a technical college, and several kindergartens and schools (Madsen 2007; Huang 2008; Lin,

Shu, and Chan 2010). The organization has branches in over forty-five countries, as well as Tzu Chi kindergartens, schools, free clinics, and an international bone marrow registry; its humanitarian missions, begun in 1991, have been carried out in more than seventy countries (Madsen 2007; Huang 2008; Lin, Shu, and Chan 2010).[26]

Da Ai TV, which commenced operations in 1998, runs two channels—one for Taiwan and Asia, one for the rest of the world—and in 2010 Tzu Chi claimed its signal could reach 79 percent of the world's population via twelve satellites (O'Neill 2010, 55–56). In 2005 Da Ai moved to its current center of operations in northern Taipei, built on land donated by the owner of a software company (O'Neill 2010, 60). The multistory tower is a state-of-the-art facility, where the latest technology—Da Ai was the first channel in Taiwan to go completely digital—is housed in spotless, austerely stylish surrounds highlighted with high-end environmentally sustainable finishes (bamboo features heavily).[27] It is staffed by Da Ai's five-hundred-plus employees in modest, conservative dress with shoes removed, Buddhist temple style. Da Ai is funded from a number of sources: sales from Tzu Chi's recycling plants, monthly donations from the 100,000 "Friends of Da Ai," donations from commercial companies in exchange for brief acknowledgment on air, and DVD sales (O'Neill 2010, 61).[28]

It is important to note that, rather than representing simply a "hangover" form of premodern religiosity in the contemporary period, Tzu Chi is in many important respects a paradigmatically modern enterprise. As Richard Madsen, a leading scholar of the sociology of religion in Taiwan, argues, first, it is a direct descendent of the socially engaged, humanist Buddhism that developed in early twentieth-century China in response to social problems arising from modernization driven by imperialism (Madsen 2007, 22–23). Second, Tzu Chi addresses the concerns of a culturally modernized urban middle class in a (post)industrial society (Madsen 2007, 45–48; 2008, 295–96). Third, Tzu Chi tends toward a rational-ethical religiosity characterized by a demythologization of traditional beliefs, a devaluation of ritual, a dilution of hierarchy, and a bureaucratization of organization (Huang 2008, 40–82; Madsen 2008, 298). Rather than centering ritualized speech and performance imbued with magical significance (as is more the case in the popular feng shui example above), Tzu Chi focuses on the elucidation of "abstract, general principles that allow for many fine distinctions, can lead to many different conclusions, and can legitimate many different personal choices" (Madsen 2008, 308). A preference for rational-ethical religiosity, Madsen observes, is characteristic of middle-class professionals in specialized decision-making roles in the contemporary period (Madsen 2008, 308–9). In these ways, Tzu Chi reconciles elements of historically entrenched Buddhist belief systems with the specific cultural, economic, and institutional conditions attending Taiwanese late modernity.

On the other hand, Tzu Chi's modernity is an enchanted and anti-individualist one. As C. Julia Huang elaborates in her detailed study of the organization, Cheng Yen's appeal to her female followers in Taiwan is based on charismatic authority (Ritzer 2005, 54–56; Huang 2008). Referred to within the organization as *Shangren* (Exalted one), Cheng Yen, not the individual follower, is the central locus of spiritual insight. For her followers, the Buddha seems less the personal, individualized "god of one's own" that Ulrich Beck argues characterizes our individualized, "post-secular age" than a god experienced *through Cheng Yen* (Huang 2008; Beck 2010). Further, as several scholars have noted, rather than "diluting" the sacred through outwardly secular-seeming worldly engagement, Cheng Yen imbues this-worldly activity with sacred significance (Madsen 2007, 39–40). Hwei-syin Lu, for example, observes how Cheng Yen often exalts the female volunteers in Tzu Chi's social programs as the "thousand eyes and one thousand hands of Kuan Yin Bodhisattva" (Lu 1998, 542). Also, in contrast with the feng shui example discussed above, and the neospiritualism promoted by Pragya TV in India, the modern religiosity embodied by Tzu Chi actively decenters the wants of the individual, rather than aiming toward personal well-being. Emphasizing followers' collective involvement, a focus on the needs of others, and a relation with Buddha that is mediated by Cheng Yen as spiritual leader, in important respects Tzu Chi stands at a significant distance from Beck's concept of religious individualization (Beck 2010).

Tzu Chi's TV channel Da Ai makes three kinds of programming—voice of Dharma (scriptural teaching), documentary, and culture and education—and its schedule, which features solely content produced in-house, reflects these key genres.[29] The Da Ai day begins at 4:30 a.m. with an hour-long prayer. The daily schedule includes programs based on prayer, sermons by Cheng Yen, and scriptural exegesis, with an emphasis on relating Buddhist teachings to everyday life situations, as well as Da Ai news bulletins, documentary magazine formats exploring Tzu Chi's humanitarian work abroad, Da Ai drama series (soap operas based on the true-life stories of Tzu Chi members), a range of talk shows focusing on morality and interpersonal ethics, vegetarian cooking shows, medical advice shows based on traditional Chinese medicine, and children's moral and environmental education shows. Da Ai's audience demographics are skewed toward the middle-aged and elderly, and reflecting Tzu Chi's membership, the channel overall is more popular with women than men.[30]

DA AI'S REFLEXIVE CRITIQUE OF MODERNITY

Da Ai's mission is encapsulated in a simple phrase, *bao zhen dao shan*: report truth and guide [people] toward improvement.[31] If a defining feature of lifestyle television is the aim of instructing the viewer on how best to live in late modernity, then in a very broad sense, all of Da Ai's informational-educational (info-ed) programming—like that found on the other religious channels—is concerned with a lifestyle project, albeit one far removed from the individualized and consumerist emphasis of much commercial lifestyle media in Taiwan and abroad.[32] Illustrating this distance from a consumerist ethos, a critical environmentalism is a very central part of Tzu Chi's spirit and practices. It is embodied most clearly in the organization's huge recycling program in Taiwan, and a related set of concerns are evident in Da Ai's TV programming.

Renjian Puti (Boddhi among the people) is a fifteen-minute program made every morning and subtitled in both English and Chinese for local and international audiences; it airs at 7:45 p.m. The show's ratings are lower than for the populist *Feng Shui Matters!*, discussed above (0.07 compared with 0.10 in mid-2013), and *Boddhi among the People* is most popular among married, nonworking women over forty-five, in a midrange income bracket (compared with *Feng Shui Matters*'s viewer base, which along with nonworking married women also includes younger, working women).[33] Narrated by the Dharma Master nun Cheng Yen in her Taiwanese-accented Mandarin, the show cross-cuts between news footage of current world events, visuals of recent Tzu Chi activities, and her direct address to the camera from behind a pulpit. On May 15, 2013, the daily theme was "Purifying our Minds for a World of Peace and Harmony." The viewer is told that people should cleanse their minds and return to a simpler lifestyle in order to reduce carbon emissions—"when our minds are purified, the world will be purified" (see figure 6.18). Cheng Yen's words mount a specifically Buddhist critique of modernity's excesses, translating environmentalism into the language of the sutras and the sutras into environmentalism.

Related themes are common in Da Ai programs. For example, Da Ai's Friday night documentary/talk-show series, *Juexing Niandai* (The age of enlightenment), featured an episode titled "Shi Zai Tai Duo" (There's too much food, February 10, 2010). Guests included the manager of a food bank where excess food is recycled, a Tzu Chi volunteer who had just returned from missions to help famine-stricken people in North Korea and southwestern China, and a Tzu Chi medical expert who advised on eating more modest, healthier portions—noting also that Buddhist vegetarianism is a low-carbon option. While the mode here is more secular than Cheng Yen's address in *Boddhi among the People*, the humanitarian-environmentalist-health project

Figure 6.18. The venerable Dharma Master Cheng Yen with an environmental message, *Boddhi among the People*, May 15, 2013.

of reducing food consumption and waste is linked with the Buddhist precept of renouncing desires—again, a critique of industrial modernity's excesses is made by means of a modernized articulation of traditional religion.

DA AI'S ADAPTIVE RESPONSE TO LATE MODERN SOCIAL LIFE: WOMEN, THE FAMILY, AND TAIWANESE CAPITALISM

The articulation of a modern, rational-ethical version of Buddhist thought and morality to late modern problems is seen throughout Da Ai's programming, extending beyond health and environmental topics to other areas, including family relations and changing gender roles. On these topics, though, the approach is less directly critical and more adaptive, with Da Ai programming forging links between Buddhist moral ideals and the continuing desirability of the social values and gendered practices that have underpinned the development of Taiwan's capitalist modernity. An example can be found in *San Dai zhi Jian* (Between generations), a weekly thirty-minute talk/advice show screened on Sundays at 5 p.m. With ratings on par with those of *Boddhi among the People*, the program is most popular among married women between forty-five and sixty-four, both workers and housewives, in a mid-income bracket. *Between Generations* is hosted by a trio of female presenters representing three generations in a family (see figure 6.19).[34]

Each episode begins with a dramatization in which the twentysomething youngest woman (Pinky) solicits advice from her mother (Li Ali) and

MAGICAL MODERNITIES / 187

Figure 6.19. The opening image of *Between Generations*.

Grandma on marriage- and family-related issues. Her mother then interviews an "ordinary couple" of Tzu Chi followers about their negotiation of this issue in their own family—wherever possible steering the conversation around to the desirability of applying Cheng Yen's moral wisdom to wife–husband relations.

On February 24, 2013, as part of "A 13-part Course on Happy Marriage," *Between Generations* aired an episode titled "Realizing the Dream of Starting a Business." The episode presented several scenarios in which women participated in small businesses at different points in the history of modern Taiwanese capitalism, with an emphasis on how they reconciled their business activities with the affective labor morally required of them within the family. The episode presented a capitalist economy based on family-run small- and medium-sized enterprises (SMEs) as the common-sense context of women's lives; women's task was not to criticize the harms inherent in the system but to act within that context based on Tzu Chi's interpretation of correct moral precepts. Like the episode of *Feng Shui Matters* analyzed above, this episode of *Between Generations* offered advice to contemporary women managing personal and familial financial stress resulting from external developments in global capitalism. Here, however, consistent with Tzu Chi's broader orientation, the advice offered is based on generalized rational-ethical principles rather than magical solutions.

Figure 6.20. *Between Generations*, February 24, 2013. A cross-generational discussion of the social effects of the global financial crisis.

The episode opens with a dramatization of daughter Pinky discussing the morning paper's financial news with her father and grandmother in the family's living room, marked as a middle-class space by the "tasteful" wood finishes and understated contemporary design of the furniture, and the conspicuous display of books (see figure 6.20). Pinky reports that financial experts are divided as to whether or not the world economy is beginning to rally again post–global financial crisis (GFC). She gives an example of people directly affected by the crisis: friends in her own generation who left stable, high-paying jobs in the United States to start businesses in China, only to find themselves bankrupted by the global economic downturn. The grandmother then narrates a flashback to when she and her husband ran a family manufacturing business in their youth, when her husband woke up at 3:30 a.m. to begin work and she took on a supporting role, packaging and shipping the goods, which often left her with bleeding and severely cramped fingers. An intertitle text sums up: "Grandma says: Starting from nothing to run your own business can only be done one arduous step at a time."

We then cut to a shot of Pinky's mother, Li Ali, in the interview studio. The viewer is introduced to the present-day working-class couple Li will interview,

Figure 6.21. *Between Generations*, February 24, 2013. Li Ali interviews Yunyin and Rongli about the relationship challenges of running a family business. The scrolls behind the couple display words from a Buddhist hymn: "Pure mind; generous heart."

wife Yunyin and husband Rongli (figure 6.20). Accompanied by romantic snapshots of the couple, a gentle female voice-over narrates the story of how Yunyin achieved her dream of running her own hair salon with her husband's help, despite significant cash-flow problems that also put their marriage to the test. Explicitly linking Yunyin's decidedly modern, entrepreneurial small-business dream with Buddhist moral virtue, the voice-over instructs: "The setback didn't defeat them; rather, they helped and uncomplainingly supported each other even more. . . . They not only realized the dream of starting a business, but also embarked together onto Tzu Chi's Bodhisattva path. Prayerfully grasping the Exalted One's dharma, together they took action to help even more people."

Crucially for our proposal that such an example illustrates Da Ai's religious and moral disciplining of feminine subjecthood in the context of Taiwanese capitalist modernity, the stories related in the episode thus far represent a potted history of women's involvement in Taiwan's economic development since the 1960s, and link the story of the island's economic modernization with the theme of married women's moral virtue. Fostered by the KMT developmental state, Taiwan's postwar economic growth was driven to a large extent by small to medium-sized family-owned enterprises, including home-based establishments—like the one Grandma recalls—that manufactured parts literally in the family living room (Hsiung 1996; Yu and Su 2009, 391–92). Married women worked in these businesses for little or no pay at the same time as caring for young children, which has led the feminist labor anthropologist Ping-Chun Hsiung to argue that far from economic modernization dissolving women's subjection to traditional familial roles, "the satellite factory system represents the latest version of the Chinese family—a locus where capitalist logic and patriarchal practices intersect" (Hsiung 1996, 13).

However, in *Between Generations*, this history is given a markedly different ideological inflection as a result of the central emphasis on Tzu Chi's version of Buddhist morality. Far from critiquing women's subjection in the process of capitalist modernization, this episode *naturalizes* Taiwanese women's subjection to the logics of both capitalist development and patriarchal family structure as their moral duty. Pinky's hardworking grandmothers are described as happily suppressing their personal interests in order to better support their husbands' entrepreneurial ventures, enacting a modernized, Buddhism-inflected version of traditional feminine virtue.[35] This history is linked with the situation of contemporary Taiwanese women through Pinky's and Yunyin's stories. The story that Pinky relates frames today's Taiwanese women participating in the postindustrial economy through transnational ventures. Raised in Taiwan, working in white-collar jobs in the United States, and investing in China, the friends Pinky describes exemplify flexible citizenship (Ong 1999) and an economy marked by deepening transnational interconnection—but despite these differences, the episode implies, such women are no less in need of Tzu Chi's moral guidance on proper feminine roles. In contrast, the small-scale, local-level entrepreneurship of guest interviewee Yunyin is structurally similar to the family businesses of Pinky's grandparents, with the significant distinction that Yunyin's dream was of a business not in manufacturing but in the service sector, which has for two decades dominated Taiwan's domestic economy (DGBAS 2010).

Overall, this episode takes on the task of (re)interpreting the meaning of contemporary Taiwanese women's late-modern entrepreneurial "dreams." By insistently emphasizing the need for mutual support between wife and husband, it places wives' business ventures firmly into the context of their familial roles. Through the example of Yunyin, it locates personal fulfillment not just in women's entrepreneurial activity but also, more importantly, in both their affective labor within the family and their involvement in Tzu Chi's collective-altruistic religious mission.

This episode of *Between Generations* thus works to link some of the social values that underpin Taiwan's capitalist economy with Buddhist moral ideals.

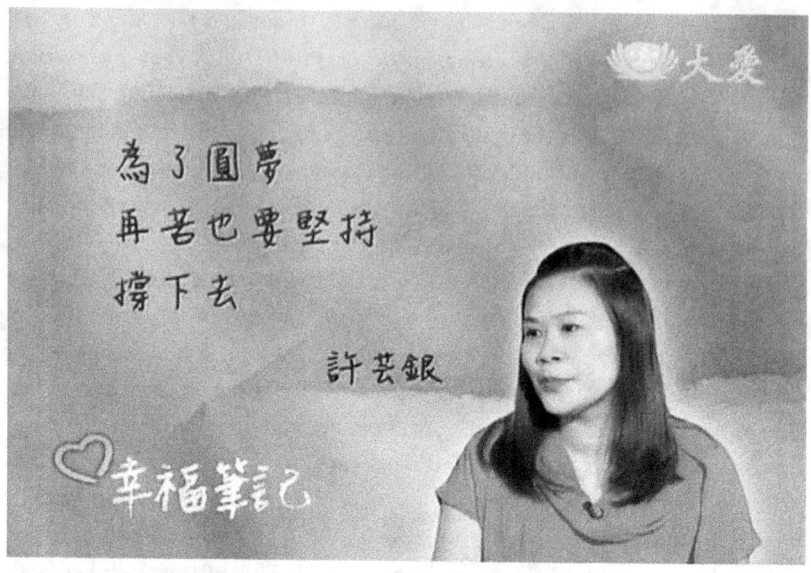

Figure 6.22. *Between Generations*, February 24, 2013. Buddhist-inflected motivational business advice.

Yunyin and Rongli have been through tough economic times, especially when Yunyin's elder brother became seriously ill, meaning that she had to divide her energies between the salon and helping care for her brother, exacerbating the salon's financial problems. The couple explains how they weathered the tough times by reducing and simplifying their food consumption. The program then cuts to an intertitle summarizing Yunyin's message: "To realize your dream, you must persevere no matter how tough things get" (see figure 6.22). This sequence manages—seemingly against the odds—to link Buddhist virtue with a kind of individualizing, late capitalist motivational rhetoric. Rongli and Yunyin's descriptions of their spartan daily meals during the tough economic times carry connotations of the Buddhist moral virtues of appetite restraint and asceticism. Yunyin's narrative also plays on the historically entrenched cultural virtue of feminine self-sacrifice, which in the Tzu Chi vision ultimately benefits not just the members of a woman's own family (as in its traditional articulation) but also the members of the wider society. At the same time, Yunyin's hair salon represents not just a business venture but also a personal "dream," a "sense of achievement," and the power of individual self-motivation against the odds. These ideas resonate strongly with a globally prominent lifestyle TV script in which entrepreneurial ventures are represented as an opportunity for personal fulfillment (Lewis 2011b). This sequence thus manages to reconcile Buddhist moral virtue with an individualizing motivational rhetoric that in turn blends easily with the historically entrenched cultural valuation of entrepreneurism and small family business in the context of Taiwanese capitalist modernity.

Conclusion: Postsecular Modernities

As we noted in the introduction to this chapter, the Weberian concept of a secular modernity is becoming more and more suspect as a normative frame, given the proliferation of contemporary neospiritual movements around the world and their inextricable imbrication with civic and political culture. The deregulation of television in both India and Taiwan, along with the freeing up of religious expression since the late 1970s in the case of Taiwan, has seen the proliferation of programming geared to both ordinary forms of supernatural belief and more organized, institutional forms of religion. The growing popularity of saints, gurus, and fortune-tellers is clearly more than simply a case of providing an outlet for preexisting traditions of religion, magic, and spiritualism. Beck's thesis about religion in an age of cosmopolitanism is, to an extent, borne out in some of the examples we have analyzed: the rise of the risk society and the growth of reflexive individualization have proved fertile ground for a shift away from conventional religious affiliations to the framing of spiritual "belonging" as a lifestyle option articulated in choice- rather than faith-based terms (Beck 2010). Illustrating this, in her study of the devotees of the famed Indian guru Mata Amritanandamayi, Maya Warrier comments:

> Devotees rejoice in the knowledge that the Mata recognizes the variety in their individual needs, attitudes and preferences. They believe that in her spiritual ministrations, the Mata "descends" to each one's spiritual level, and handles each individual case differently, instead of expecting all devotees to conform to a uniform and standardized body of spiritual practice. What we see here is an intensely interiorized and private form of faith which defines the religious life as an inner horizon predicated not upon external authorization but upon the personal choice and self fulfilment of each individual (Warrier 2003, 247).

In India, this apparent turn to individualized and customized forms of spirituality has seen the rise of what we have termed spiritual lifestyle television. As we discussed above, the small screen in India has been marked by an explosion of gurus of all kinds, and many of these figures are a far cry from traditional spiritual leaders, blending ancient vedas with a hodgepodge of other belief systems and claims to credentials, from pop psychology to astrology. Up to a certain point, these figures can be placed on a continuum with the kinds of lifestyle experts and so-called gurus found on Western lifestyle shows, in the sense that they are increasingly positioned and branded within a broader field of life advisors (personal stylists, home décor specialists, fashion designers, etc.) and possess a kind of market equivalency with such figures. This is particularly the case with some of the more "secular" lifestyle shows discussed above, aimed at cosmopolitan middle-class audiences, such as *Live Vaastu* where magical thinking has become scienticized and tied to calculative ends. Likewise in Taiwan, both commercial feng shui advice programming and organized religion as represented by the Da Ai channel can be viewed as responding to late modern risks by means of reinvented traditions. While Da Ai, at first glance, might appear to represent the antithesis of cultural modernity, on the contrary we have argued that it exemplifies an indicatively modern form and outlook, with its organized bureaucratic structure and generalized rational-ethical belief system.

However, in important respects Da Ai stands at a significant distance from Beck's concept of highly individualized, consumption-based systems of individualized spiritualism (Beck 2010). In addressing the risks connected with the environment (local-urban or planetary), economic and working life, and health, among other issues, the Da Ai channel's lifestyle advice shows include an explicit metalevel critique of some of late modernity's most obvious harms—overconsumption, environmental destruction, inequitable social relations, and callous individualism. In doing so, Da Ai contrasts markedly with the more laissez-faire individualism and models of consumer citizenship implicit in more "lifestyled" spiritual shows. But insofar as it critiques modernity's excesses by means of a thoroughly modernized, rational-ethical religion and organization, it mounts its critique, in significant part, on modernity's own terms.

In contrast, while magical advice shows such as India's *Astro Uncle* and Taiwan's *Feng Shui Matters* respond to very concrete contemporary concerns, such as the pragmatics of minimizing individual economic risk in late capitalism, they represent an antirational, ritual-magical epistemology in late modern media culture. However, these shows largely locate the magical within contemporary structures of choice-based consumerism, underlining again that consumer culture is a highly malleable space, easily able to accommodate discourses of enchantment alongside those of rationalism.

Another point of complication vis-à-vis Beck's argument that religion is becoming increasingly privatized and individualized is the strong and ongoing element of collectivism underpinning both Indian and Taiwanese religious movements. Baba Ramdev's mass televised yoga camps, held at locations around India, represent more than just a gathering of health-seeking individuals; as we have noted, they also link the corporeal and spiritual practices of participants and audience members to a *national* body through a transpersonal engagement with the spiritual, social, and physical health of the nation. Likewise, Da Ai is strongly collectivist-altruistic in orientation, with the benevolent actions of Tzu Chi members framed as an extension and transsubstantiation of Cheng Yen's teachings and directives. Such developments can be read as examples of the complex and distinctly modern articulations of civic responsibility emerging in contemporary South and East Asian countries, with hybrid social-philanthropic/corporate/religious organizations like the Pragya channel in India and Tzu Chi in Taiwan stressing, to varying degrees, personal moral citizenship, public responsibility, and cosmopolitan conceptions of the global and social "goods" (Srinivas 2010). In the next chapter we examine another space marked by complex negotiations of individualization, marketized social relations, and civic (and familial) duty: the fraught realm of love and relationships. While, like spirituality, the space of love might seem to inhabit a realm beyond the logics of late modern struggles, we argue that contemporary TV shows focused on love, marriage, and dating offer a privileged perspective from which one can gain an understanding of the local specificities of cultural negotiations of modernity.

SEVEN. **Risky Romance** Navigating Late Modern Identities and Relationships on Indian and Chinese Lifestyle TV

> The absoluteness conveyed by the experience of love at first sight has faded away into the cool hedonism of leisure consumption and the rationalized search for the most suitable partner.—EVA ILLOUZ, *Consuming the Romantic Utopia*

While media excursions into the wilds of relationships and romance in China and India have conventionally been the preserve of film, soap operas, and TV drama, in recent years TV audiences in both countries have been exposed to a growing number of reality and lifestyle shows focused on dating, marriage, parenting, and love relationships. While, like spirituality, the affective and intangible space of love would seem to inhabit a realm beyond the logics of late modern struggles, in *Why Love Hurts* Eva Illouz (2012) argues that, on the contrary, the study of love offers a privileged perspective from which one can gain an understanding of the process of late modernity. Gender identities and gender struggles in the field of love, she contends, perform "the institutional and cultural core dilemmas and ambivalence of modernity" (Illouz 2012, 9).

In this chapter we look at the field of love as it is explored in lifestyle and reality shows, focusing not just on dating and partner choice but more broadly on intimacy and interpersonal relationships. Our key contention is that popular factual shows dealing with the rocky terrain of interpersonal relationships offer a particularly rich site for examining the complexity of contemporary negotiations of identity, risk, and individualization in China and India, encompassing as they do questions of contemporary gendered and familial identities, class, caste, social mobility, and religion in highly transitional social landscapes. Drawing on a range of examples from game show–based dating formats to reality shows dealing with love and romance to more advice-oriented formats, our analysis focuses on the complex negotiations played out between various competing values and ideals around lifestyle, selfhood, and relationships in two large and diverse nations undergoing huge social and economic change. How are these struggles expressed in the forms and narratives of dating programming in these two countries, and through the various life "tests" such shows often set for the hapless contestants? The aspirational middle classes now play an iconic role in the "liberalizing" social, cultural, and economic landscapes of India in particular, but also in China (Mazzarella 2003; Fernandes 2006, 30; Goodman 2008; Baviskar and Ray 2011; Chen and Goodman 2013b; Ren 2013). In light of this, how do these shows navigate the contradictions between apparent forms of gender empowerment and marketized aspirations toward social and cultural fluidity, versus the realities of powerful ongoing gendered social and economic inequities, and the continued cultural potency of familial and communitarian notions of duty? What "freedoms," risks, and anxieties accompany the rise of "new" forms of intimacy linked to calculative, choice-based models of selfhood (Bignell 2005; T. Miller 2007; Ouellette and Hay 2008) where people and relationships are increasingly framed as sites of (potential) economic and brand value (Hearn 2009), or what Skeggs and Wood term "economies of personhood" within late capitalism (Skeggs and Wood 2012, 52)?

Love, Dating, and Risk in India and China

Sociological and cultural studies scholarship largely treats matters of the erotic not as an innate expression of individual experience but one structured by the contingencies of broader social relations (Foucault 1979; Giddens 1992; Luhmann 1998). For instance, Eva Illouz in her book *Consuming the Romantic Utopia: Love and the Cultural Contradictions of Capitalism* argues that the affective medium of love has become increasingly tied to the logics of the market. Not just a cultural commodity, romantic love has been reconfigured as "rational, self-interested, strategic and profit-maximising . . . so that romantic relationships are conceived and managed in the categories of the utilitarian and instrumentalist ethos that lies at the heart of the capitalist economic system" (Illouz 1997, 188). David Shumway's *Modern Love: Romance, Intimacy, and the Marriage Crisis* (2003) complicates this argument somewhat, noting that prior to the late eighteenth century, when questions of desire and choice started to come into play in the marriage arena, marriage was tied to financial concerns of property and alliance. Indeed, he suggests that romance and the late twenty-first-century ideal of "intimacy" in part offered spaces of escape from the social fragmentation and alienations of capitalism. However, what is key here for both Illouz and Shumway is that the rise of modern love, romance, and intimacy is, at the same time, part and parcel of broader shifts in late modernity and capitalism; in particular, the discourse of modern love marks the dissolution of earlier social relations and obligations and the growing individualization and privatization of marriage.

Similar patterns of individualization are arguably being increasingly played out in South and East Asia. With the growing influence of late liberal global economics and, to varied degrees, the cultural logics of liberal capitalism in India and China, the landscape of love, sex, and interpersonal relationships is becoming an intensified site of struggle between vernacular beliefs and expectations and marketized, "romantic," and consumer-based individualistic logics (Mazzarella 2003; Yan 2009; Kleinman et al. 2011). Arranged marriages of some kind still dominate in India; as Fritzi-Marie Titzmann points out, 90 percent of Indian marriages can still be seen as "arranged" even if this increasingly represents a continuum rather than an opposition between love and arranged marriage (Titzmann 2011). On the other hand, they are now much less frequent in China, although it remains the norm for parents to have some influence in sons' and daughters' choices of spouse. However, in both India and China broader shifts in social and economic relations over the past decade or so and the emergence of a growing consumer middle class have seen significant contestations and renegotiations of conceptions of love and relationships, particularly for sections of the more globalized middle classes and those working in globalized labor circuits (Ramasubramanian and Jain 2009).

These tensions are further heightened by an increased sense of privatization and individualization of "choice" around lifestyle and love. In postsocialist China, now widely considered to be a high-risk society, this is is particularly the case. Here economic reform and privatization have seen the state redirecting responsibility and redistributing risk (Ren 2013). While this shift of responsibility to the individual has created personal freedom "in planning one's life in the face of new contingencies" (Ong 2008, 186), at the same time it creates extra feelings of vulnerability, as every decision one makes comes with a sense of potential risk. In India, economic neoliberalism has to some extent flourished, and there as in China, for certain sections of the urbanized middle classes—the target audience for much of the programming discussed in this chapter—experiences of insecure and flexible labor have seen a growing focus on privatized investments in the self as a means of managing and minimizing risk (for example, through paying for one's own training course, or investing in a subscription to a commercial dating agency). Nandini Gooptu (2013) argues that Indian middle-class citizens increasingly see themselves rather than the state as responsible for their own personal security and success.

Increasingly for both Chinese citizens and certain sectors of the Indian population, then, there is a sense of a reframing of personal responsibilities and freedoms according to what Ulrich Beck (1992) calls "individualization," a shift that carries with it a key paradox. On the one hand, privatization has removed individuals—or "disembedded" them—from prescribed social norms and commitments associated with socialism, thereby affording individuals a hitherto unavailable space of personal freedom to experiment with different modes of self-formation. On the other hand, individuals are feeling the pressure to "re-embed" themselves into new types of social commitments, which prescribe new normative ideals, including those concerning marriage, gender roles, and personal fulfillment, and which often involve negotiating ongoing ties to familial and civic duty.

Given the pressures on both Indian and Chinese citizens to negotiate a range of lifestyle, identity, and value "choices" in the field of love and intimacy, what role might popular factual and life advice television be playing in shaping and promoting particular norms and values around interpersonal relationships? How does commercial television narrate and navigate questions of both freedom and risk, disembedded modes of individualism, and questions of "duty" to others? What ongoing roles might class, culture, gender, and family have in television's negotiation of modern relationships?

The Dating Game: Aspirationalism, Risk, and Marketized Selfhood in India

In recent years, dating shows of all stripes and persuasions have flourished on Chinese and Indian TV and, in both countries, have often been accompanied by considerable controversy. Central and recurrent concerns in many of these shows are, on the one hand, with the presentation of self (an issue that of course comes to the fore in the dating market) and, on the other hand, with the issue of status. Thus, while these shows may gesture toward romantic notions of love and finding "the one," much of the focus is on how contestants present, package, and add value to themselves in the dating market, with questions of social, cultural, and material status as a key underlying (albeit sometimes unspoken) parameter by which contestants judge each other. A prospective

Figure 7.1. The host meets with female contestants on an episode of *Splitsvilla*, season 4, episode 3, December 17, 2010.

spouse's status, of course, becomes harder to judge away from the familial space of matchmaking and within the relatively democratized and performative arena of mediatized dating, leading to much anxiety, which is often played out on these shows.

In India, where, as we have discussed throughout this book, reality TV has been very popular since the 2000s, the past decade has seen the emergence of a range of flamboyant entertainment-oriented dating-, relationship-, and marriage-related reality programming. One of the shows mentioned by many of the viewers in our Mumbai study (usually in highly dismissive terms) was *Splitsvilla* (see figure 7.1). Aired on MTV India since 2008 and based on the American dating reality show *Flavor of Love*, the show revolves around a group of young men and women housed together in a mansion who compete in a date-and-dump world to make alliances with each other in order to stay on the show and win the final cash prize. In the rather more *desi*-ized or "Indianized" show *Swaymwar*, contestants compete in a range of individual talent contests and emotional compatibility tests to win the hand of a featured celebrity. With more mass appeal for a general Hindi-speaking audience, rather than the middle-class youth audience usually targeted by dating shows, the latter show claims that it is reviving a mythic practice of royal matchmaking where a princess would choose her spouse in a courtly competition between princes, albeit in a competitive reality format bearing strong similarities to the American format *The Bachelor*.

Figure 7.2. A woman catches her partner in a moment of infidelity on *Emotional Atyachaar*, season 4, episode 24, June 16, 2013.

Another show much discussed (and often loathed) by the Indian viewers we interviewed is *Emotional Atyachaar*, an Indian version of the U.S. format *Cheaters* in which people doubting their partner's fidelity volunteer the partner for a loyalty test (see figure 7.2). *Emotional Atyachaar* is one of a number of shows on Indian TV aimed at "testing" relationships. *Perfect Couple* is an *Amazing Race*–style travel adventure format where the couple's success depends on their intuitive connection and mutual compatibility. Meanwhile in *Love Lockup*, a couple (usually minor celebrities) on the brink of relationship breakdown is locked up in a house under twenty-four-hour surveillance to sort out their differences and see whether their relationship can survive under pressure.

One of the dating shows popular with urban middle-class Hindi youth, which we will discuss in some detail here, is Channel V's *Dare2Date*. Branding itself as an antiromance show, *Dare2Date* employs a humorous reality format in which contestants are matched up with people who are the complete opposite of their "ideal date." An educated, English-speaking woman from Mumbai is thus matched up with a cashed-up man hailing from a rural political family who arrives at the date in a limousine with his driver; a free-spirited nonresident Indian man born in the United States is matched with a docile middle-class girl who does voluntary social work.

Hosted by VJ Andy, a British-born Indian actor who has also been a contestant on *Bigg Boss* (the Indian version of *Big Brother*), the show's humor derives

Figure 7.3. VJ Andy (*left*) interrogates a contestant on *Dare2Date*, season 3, episode 31, November 24, 2014. The quote in the pop-up graphic translates as "this third-class citizen desires a high-class wife."

from often marked differences in social status and cultural background, with contestants having to present and defend themselves to their prospective dates, often with amusing results. Shepherding the couples through their unlikely dating encounters, VJ Andy is positioned in the show as a kind of ironic matchmaker or cupid; well known as gay in a country that in 2013 once again made homosexual sex a criminal offence,[1] he embodies a certain kind of progressivism for a new generation of Indian youth. As such he bears something in common with the queer hosts of Anglo-American reality shows like *Queer Eye for the Straight Guy* (Lewis 2007).

While *Dare2Date* as a whole turns love into a risky adventure and a space of play, potentially challenging social mores around relationships, as a role model for viewers and a mediator between broader community concerns and the world of television, VJ Andy can also be seen as policing social norms, particularly around class (see figure 7.3). When contestants make a social or cultural faux pas, Andy invariably responds with a tongue-in-cheek comment, shooting an incredulous look to the camera, with many of his comments presented to the audience via onscreen graphics. Andy's cutting judgments and satirical remarks (delivered with a nod and a wink to the audience) are seldom about contestants' character flaws as individuals but rather are concerned with misjudgments in their self-presentation. Whether this relates to their mispronunciation of English words or to outlandish claims to being a fashion model, his "critique" tends to relate not to personality but to concerns around the *performance* of social identity, and in particular the possession (or lack thereof) of a kind of cultural or performative capital, or what Illouz terms in relation to love relationships "communicative capital" (Illouz 1997, 287). While not explicitly foregrounded on the show, the possession or not of this kind of self-knowing, performative capital is implicitly linked to the social and cultural status of contestants.

Channel V's reality show *LoveNet* similarly explores the question of performative selfhood, though from a rather different angle. The premise of the show is to set up real-life meetings between people who have developed a "relationship" on Internet chat portals. Offering cautionary tales from the world of online dating, the show is about revealing the facades that people create to project an idealized image of themselves. The show plays on concerns around the gap between performed modes of selfhood and the realities of people's social backgrounds. As Zulfia Waris, the Channel V executive who conceptualized this show, explained it to us: "The concept was . . . do you really think the person you have been chatting with for the last few years is what he is? He says he is from Bombay, living in Malabar Hill, has a swanky car, green eyes, and looks like Richard Gere. Come, meet him, he actually lives in a small by-lane in Bombay, in a little two by two room, he doesn't speak English, he translates it by typing, and he has been romantically involved with not just you but five others, meet them too."[2]

As on *Dare2Date*, *LoveNet* again draws on elements of *Queer Eye*, though without the same degree of humor or playfulness. Like the Fab Five who descend on the home of clueless straight men, *LoveNet*'s two young cosmopolitan male and female hosts invade the homes of unsuspecting daters, with the datee in tow. The main part of the show consists of a detective-style investigation, where both the datees and host snoop into the private lives of the other person, looking for clues as to the "real" lifestyles and selves of daters through talking to their friends and family and examining personal belongings in their bedrooms, often, as per the Fab Five, donning gloves to examine household items such as dirty hairbrushes or discarded clothes. In the final section of the program, the dates meet each other for the first time, with the meetings, not surprisingly, often ending in confrontations. In an attempt to present themselves as morally and socially superior, each person reveals evidence about the other while the show's hosts decide which party has represented themselves more falsely.

As the show's title *LoveNet* suggests, the realm of dating is portrayed here not so much as a space of freedom as a combative arena of risk and mistrust where people are not what they seem. Dating here becomes an allegory for the challenges and anxieties of dealing with a modern world of shifting social relations, with the show offering a rather conservative take on gender and relationships. The implication is that rather than dabble in the aspirational world of online dating, one is better off engaging in the rather safer realm of semiarranged relationships (a theme in other dating shows in India, as we discuss below), where one's partner is likely to come from a similar social background as oneself. Thus, in one episode where a young man who has pretended to have money and cultural capital is found to be poor but clearly aspirational, the show's host and his proposed upper-middle-class date laugh at the English-language course materials they find in his flat. In response to the revelation that he has lied about his abilities to speak English, he retaliates by commenting on his upper-class date's messy home: "not only do you not do domestic work, you can't even supervise the maid properly." Here the participant foregrounds the social tensions evident on a show that, like *Dare2Date*, while outwardly dealing with love and romance is in fact preoccupied with social and cultural status and with the risks involved in encountering social "others."

Channel V's popular reality dating shows *Dare2Date* and *LoveNet*, while both offering by turns humorous and playful takes on looking for love in contemporary India, present a rather bleak picture. Rather than embracing the perceived "freedoms" of romance, the two shows portray the dating realm as something that has become a calculative space of exchange in which selfhood is packaged, bought, and sold. As the shows' "buyer beware" message suggests, these programs in some ways offer a critique of marketized relationships and of the notion of selves as brands. At the same time, however, the shows themselves valorize a particular kind of interiorized, critical, and performative self (Skeggs and Wood 2009)—the savvy and reflective middle-class subject embodied by figures like VJ Andy and the attractive cosmopolitan hosts of *LoveNet*. While "queered" figures like VJ Andy might be read as troubling gender and social identity in India, these shows nevertheless offer a rather normative take on gender and social status, somewhat paradoxically encouraging a certain degree of aspirationalism while at the same time cautioning viewers on the dangers of overstepping the boundaries of class. These shows thus superficially celebrate a kind of liberalized and globalized world of choice-based love and romance while remaining steeped in concerns around class, caste, and cultural compatibility, themes that as we discuss later in this chapter are dealt with explicitly in a range of Indian shows that attempt to "marry" or reconcile questions of romantic love with familial concerns.

Chinese Dating Shows: Between the Party Line and the Bottom Line

One of the more popular genres dealing with love and romance in China in recent years has been the studio-based dating-game-show format. Arriving on Chinese television in the early 1990s, these shows challenged the monopoly of television drama serials in terms of output, ratings, and advertising revenue (Bai and Song 2015). The earliest dating show on Chinese television was Beijing TV's *Jinwan Women Xiangshi* (We are meeting tonight) in 1991 (Fang 2011). But the genre did not capture the imagination of the national audience until the late 1990s, when China's provincial television went national via satellite. In 1998 *Meigui zhi Yue* (Rose date) appeared on Hunan Satellite TV (Fang 2011), China's most enterprising provincial television channel, known for its innovative entertainment formats including the *Super Girl* talent quest (Sun 2007). Over recent years, Chinese television has been inundated with dating shows, including Shandong Satellite TV's *Aiqing Lai Qiaomen* (Love comes knocking), Hunan Satellite TV's *Women Yuehui ba* (Take me out), and Shanghai Media Group's *Yinwei Aiqing* (Because of love). But it is Jiangsu Satellite TV's *Fei Cheng Wu Rao* (If you are the one), launched in 2010, that has proven to be most enduring in popularity. Its annual advertising income has reached 0.4 billion RMB, and on average, the twelve minutes of advertising time within each episode is bought at the price of 200,000 RMB per fifteen seconds, the highest advertising price on any variety and entertainment show on Chinese television (Fang 2011). Meng Fei, the main host of the show, has become a household name across the nation and beyond while the popularity of the format has led to numerous copycat versions, ensuring a war among provincial satellite channels. These include Zhejiang Satellite TV's *Wei Ai Xiang Qian Chong* (Charge ahead in the name of love) and Yangzhou Satellite TV's *Xiang Qin Xiang Ai* (Dating for love). According to one Chinese journalist's rough estimate, there are currently up to thirty dating shows airing on Chinese television (Fang 2011).

If You Are the One is a high-end studio production with a focus on spectacle, glamour, and fashion (see figure 7.4). It is not only popular with domestic viewers across all ages and social strata but has also attracted a great number of non-Chinese and diasporic Chinese viewers. Potential contestants are recruited from both inside and outside China, although Chinese nationals form the staple of contestants. In recent years, to meet growing demand outside China, intermittent episodes have been produced on location in a variety of cities in the United States and Australia for simultaneous worldwide screening. Australia's Special Broadcasting Service (SBS) bought the copyright and has been broadcasting the show since 2013. The format presents five male

Figure 7.4. Three female contestants field questions from the bachelor on *If You Are the One*, July 14, 2013.

bachelors to a lineup of twenty-four glamorous female guests. After each male hopeful introduces himself to the audience and his potential dates, we are then presented with various video clips (on his "background," what he wants in a woman, and what his friends think of him), interspersed with in-studio interactions. The female contestants then decide whether to dismiss the candidate by switching their podium light off. The man who survives three rounds of "voting" gains the right to vie for the heart of his dream girl.

A highly entertaining format, the popularity of this show derives from the humorous and often brutally frank conversations between guests and hosts. However, the show is also arguably popular because it taps into Chinese young people's shifting attitudes toward love, sex, and marriage, and in particular the kind of calculative, individualist, and materialist turn illustrated in our discussion of Indian dating shows above. In its earlier stage, the show made little attempt to censor some of its contestants' more mercenary attitudes in selecting a mate. Featuring young women talking bluntly, and sometimes cruelly, about what they like and do not like about a man, the show both shocked and resonated with the audience, who know too well that, brutal as they may be, these remarks are reflections of the growing influence of materialistic values in the society. Among these brutally honest remarks, the most famous ones were made by Ma Nuo, now dubbed the "BMW girl," who has become a household name in China for her declaration on television: "I'd rather sit in a rich man's

BMW crying than sit on the back of someone's bike smiling." Also well known is Zhu Zhengfang, dubbed the "big house girl," who famously declared on one episode: "Only my boyfriend can touch my hand; anyone else who wants to touch it has to pay 200,000 yuan" (Chen 2011, 47).

Having captured the imagination of the national audience with the blunt social commentaries made by its contestants, the show nevertheless incurred the ire of the Chinese government. In fact, *If You Are the One* was a prime target of the government crackdown in 2011 (discussed in chapter 1), which aimed to "clean up the screen" (Bai 2015). Initially criticizing it for blatantly promoting materialistic and selfish values, China's State Administration of Radio, Film and Television (SARFT) requested the show either raise its moral standards or risk being suspended. Succumbing to pressure, the show went through a few cosmetic changes, adding rural migrant workers, Communist Party–school academics, and other economically unattractive or marginalized social identities to the lists of participants, in order to defuse the accusations of commodifying human relationships and wealth worship.

SARFT's reactions to entertainment programs on Chinese television is a form of moral panic with "Chinese characteristics," with the party-state stepping in to assume the role of arbitrating and defining vulgarity, bad taste, and unhealthy sentiment. The source of this panic is, however, not so much an innate, aggrieved moral sensibility as a new realization that instead of constituting an ideologically safer zone that avoids, elides, or camouflages the conflict between the rich and the poor, entertainment media can in fact accentuate class tensions. By contrast, while the Indian dating shows discussed above promote a certain degree of aspirationalism, they also emphasize to viewers the dangers of overstepping the boundaries of class, and offer a more normative take on gender and social status than the rather more unruly calculative and competitive individualism on display in the early version of *If You Are the One*.

It was precisely the fear of contestants' controversial statements giving visibility to class-related social conflicts that led dating shows such as *If You Are the One* to become the most controversial entertainment genre on provincial satellite television. The Chinese party-state, though content to govern "from afar" most of the time (Zhang and Ong 2008), does not hesitate to revert to more hands-on authoritarian media practices and communication strategies that one associates with socialism when the need is seen to arise. While wanting to promote a kind of neoliberalized privatized sense of personal responsibility, it at the same time also wants to enforce strong limits around the "freedoms" that might go with that by imposing its definition of vulgarity and moral propriety on matters connected with marriage and love. In the eyes of the party-state, individuals with low levels of *suzhi* (quality) such as the "BMW girl" and the "big house girl" should not be rewarded with the status of celebrity; instead, they should be condemned.

The various "tests" and identity performances required of the young participants on Indian and Chinese dating shows like *Dare2Date* and *If You Are the One* speak to the broader anxieties of and pressures on a new generation of Chinese and Indian youth negotiating a very different social, cultural, and economic landscape from that of their parents, with such tensions reflected in the morally inflected media controversies that dating shows have produced in both countries. While older generations, especially those living in rural India, might have been raised in extended patriarchal families, young people are now exposed to a range of different models for living and conducting relationships, including dual-income families and single households, which are on the rise (Raja 2014). Cultural difference and caste, however, continue to play an important role in framing customs and practices around marriage and family relations in India. In China, meanwhile, marriage was effectively modernized by the outlawing of many traditional marriage practices by the Marriage Law of 1950 (Davis 2014), and the one-child policy implemented in 1979 instigated a continuing trend toward smaller family size (Hu and Scott 2014). However, the extent to which diminishing household size reflects a full-scale nuclearization of the Chinese family, and whether shifting practices of marriage and family in fact reflect thoroughgoing ideological detraditionalization, are topics that are energetically debated (Cartier 1995; Hu and Scott 2014). More direct material pressures, too, impact significantly on people's experiences of marriage. For urban dwellers, skyrocketing real estate prices following the marketization of housing add an additional layer of financial stress to the negotiation of marriage contracts, with young men struggling to afford the apartment that they are widely expected to provide for the newlywed couple, and young women and their families forced to make ever more calculating choices about prospective husbands based on their savings and earning capacity (Hong Fincher 2014; Zhang and Sun 2014). Meanwhile, the reforms era has witnessed a decline in married women's workforce participation as the state encourages women "back to the family" in times of rising unemployment, with some commentators seeing reversals in gender equality in the contemporary period indicating a retraditionalization of women's roles (Rofel 1999; Cook and Dong 2011; Hong Fincher 2014). In China, then, while the outward form of families may be shifting, older-style familial ideologies may continue to linger not far from the surface, and may even be revived under the new social and economic conditions of the present. In India we see a complex set of developments; recent census data indicate that, contrary to widespread belief, the percentage of nuclear families has actually dropped in urban areas, a development that, as in China, is likely to be linked to job pressures and real estate costs, with generations of families opting to stay together, as well as to new types of "nuclear" family arrangements, with dual-income couples relying on a live-in parent for child care (Raja 2014). Alongside a growing number of single households (linked to a rising rate of divorce, delayed marriage, and an increased number of people choosing to remain single), India's new household patterns suggest not so much a retraditionalization of family and marriage structures as a plurality of late modern familial and nonfamilial household arrangements. Thus in both countries, albeit in different ways, the contemporary moment is marked by new and intensified ideological contradictions, collective anxieties, and material stresses around love and marriage, arising along with the far-reaching social and economic transformations that are in process in each of these societies.

Legitimizing Romance: Families and Dating on Indian TV

Given the contexts sketched above, the shifting material conditions and cultural mores around love and relationships foregrounded by shows like *Dare2Date* and *If You Are the One* have not surprisingly led to a sense of anxiety and risk for parents and youth alike in approaching marriage (Zhang and Sun 2014). Here, dating shows are particularly interesting as many of them represent an imaginary space "outside" of the logic of family where peers (the audience, other contestants, and the hosts) play an important role, although family members are also sometimes called upon to comment on and vouch for the character of dating hopefuls.

As we have argued, however, while these shows focus on partner choice and performative selfhood in the marketized space of love and dating, they also often exhibit considerable unease about the kind of "posttraditional" turn implied by the individualized ethos of dating. Here we want to discuss some key shows in India that attempt to negotiate the slippery terrain of contemporary love by bringing the family back into the dating equation, albeit in posttraditional ways. In turn, in the following section we discuss the place of family on Chinese shows.

In India, *Date My Folks*, a spinoff from the success of *Dare2Date*, offers a very different take on romance to its Channel V counterpart, inverting the dating format with the *parents* of the datee concerned going on a date with two prospective candidates. Hosted again by the ubiquitous VJ Andy, the parents featured on *Date My Folks* are depicted as fair and generous types who are keen to find a suitable match for their child. They also invariably claim that they can make a better choice of partner on behalf of their child, who is often seen as likely to be swayed by superficial qualities such as good looks rather than the social background, character, and values of prospective partners.

The show opens with the parents listing their criteria for an ideal partner, which are then contrasted with their offspring's. The device of cross-cutting interviews with family members and the prospective partner often highlights conflicting values and ideals and creates significant dramatic tension regarding the show's resolution. While a family member (usually the mother) then goes on a date with the two candidates for prospective partners, both VJ Andy and the datee secretly watch the proceedings via a hidden camera. During the date, family members evaluate the contestants in terms of their lifestyle, social background, and personality, often asking probing and highly personal questions about their attitudes toward relationships and moral standards in matters of love. The show's narrative comes to a close with a final date in which the parents watch their child (again via a hidden camera) on a date with their chosen candidate and assess the suitability of their choice.

While much of *Date My Folks* is played for laughs, the issue of reconciling individual choice with parental authority takes a rather more serious if melodramatic turn on another popular Channel V show called *Love Kiya to Darna Kiya* (Why fear when you love). Shot in a low-budget, vérité style, in this show people in serious but secret long-term relationships, even marriages, confess about these relationships to their parents and try to reconcile them to it (see figure 7.5). The young couples living away from their families have kept the truth hidden from their families but wish to come clean about their choice via the confessional medium of television. As Channel V puts it: "Why is love treated like a crime? Why do we hide it from our parents, from society, from the world? [Channel V] are putting an end to this. How far is too far? How much does your relationship really matter? Is your family a price you're willing to pay for it?"

The show thus depicts itself as dealing with both sides of the equation and, similarly to American philanthropic reality shows like *Extreme Makeover: Home Edition*, purports to offer a kind of positive intervention in people's lives (Ouellette and Hay 2008). The format of the show is structured as follows: The couples first make a plan to bring their parents for a visit to the city, and then surreptitiously introduce them to their partners without initially revealing who they are. After meeting and interacting via a social activity, such as a shopping trip, and once the couple feel that their parents have had ample

Figure 7.5. A "fly on the wall" scene from *Why Fear When You Love* where we witness a distraught young man disclosing to his family his two-year relationship with a woman from another caste, episode 7, August 4, 2011.

time to know and judge the person, the final meeting for the "big reveal" is set up. Both the couple and their families congregate at a set location where the couple attempts to subtly open up discussion and reveal their situation to their families. When their children confess to serious relationships or marriages, the results are often highly dramatic, invariably leading to confrontations and even violence. In their introductory profile at the beginning of the program, couples often voice their fears about their parents' likely objections to the social status and/or caste/religion of their partner, and this is often the primary reason for their concealment of the relationship. At the moment of confession, we usually see their fears proven well founded as the parents express concerns about the noncompatibility of the relationship. The parents typically argue that while they like the chosen partner as a person, they nevertheless see social background as an insurmountable barrier. Many of the parents on the show appear fairly permissive of the lifestyle and career ambitions of the young people concerned, and their permissiveness at times seems to show some tacit acceptance of fleeting romantic entanglements. But most parents ultimately consider the decision for offspring to marry as rightfully theirs to make according to social considerations of marrying within the same social rank, whether of caste, region, or religion.

Although *Date My Folks* and *Why Fear When You Love* are very different styles of reality programming, they both address head-on the social and cultural upheaval associated with shifts toward individualization in India. For a new generation of Indian youth, particularly those in the urban middle classes, partner choice is increasingly being shaped by individual and psychologized concepts such as "personality" and "compatibility" rather than older family-based criteria such as caste and religion (Titzmann 2011), and it is now not uncommon for children from more liberal Indian families to challenge their families' partner selection (Ramasubramanian and Jain 2009). These growing "freedoms," at least for the economically and socially mobile, are reflected in the increasing mediatization of the domain of love, not only on television but also the Internet.

As Titzmann's work on the online matrimonial market in India shows, marriage websites have been on the rise since the late 1990s, with most online matchmaking sites being in English, indicating a privileged niche group of users who are young (eighteen to twenty-five), tertiary educated, and urban (Titzmann 2011). However, as on the reality dating shows discussed here, while on the one hand these new forms of matchmaking represent a growing emphasis on individualized partner choice, they also reflect a concern with managing the risks associated with nonfamilial matchmaking, in particular the fear of being paired with someone socially or culturally incompatible. Thus, newspapers like the *Times of India*, along with matrimonial sites like SimplyMarry.com, offer a range of *swayamvaras* (self-chosen spouses) categorized along linguistic/caste lines, for example Brahmin swayamvaras or Punjabi swayamvaras. Shows like *Date My Folks* and *Why Fear When You Love* reflect an attempt to recognize and to a certain extent negotiate an individualized "free market" of love, but as the invariable not-so-happy ending of the latter show suggests, they often continue to emphasise familial concerns and engage with questions of duty and obligation.

Real Families: Navigating Risk and Relationships on Chinese Reality TV

Despite the growing individualization of social relations in China (Yan 2009), as in India, decisions about whether someone is a suitable lifetime mate are often made in negotiation with elder members of the family. A number of reality-style shows have emerged in China that attempt to manage and mediate the intergenerational tensions produced by this conflict between individualizing formations of selfhood and the continuing power of parental opinion in marriage practices. Channel Young's *Zhangmuniang Kan Nüxu* (Mother-in-law eyes her son-in-law) is a good example (see figure 7.6).

Figure 7.6. "Mum number 1" judges a prospective son-in-law the wrong height to suit her daughter on *Mother-in-Law Eyes Her Son-in-Law*, May 15, 2011.

In this show, the prospective boyfriend is subject to the interrogative and judgmental standards of his prospective mother-in-law. Integrating studio panel discussion with reality segments, *Mother-in-Law Eyes Her Son-in-Law* is a dating show with a twist, for, as in our Indian example above, it is not just the dynamics between the two young people that is under the spotlight. The show usually starts by laying out the potential problems or challenges associated with the prospective fiancé, and it centers around the conflicts and compromises between the mother and daughter surrounding the question of how to respond to and deal with these problems. For instance, on July 13, 2013, in an episode titled "For the Sake of Love," the prospective fiancé, a hairdresser, comes with two issues: first, he cannot allow anyone, including his girlfriend, to sit on his bed for fear of germs; and second, he feels that he has to bring into the new relationship a pet dog that belonged to his previous girlfriend.

A discussion between the mother and daughter in response to these issues takes places in an ensuing segment of the show called "In the Secret Room" (*mishi*). This involves the camera following the mother and daughter into an enclosed space, where they have a supposedly confidential discussion about the candidate and work out their differences regarding the suitability of the prospective fiancé. Mothers are often cool-headed and "objective" about their daughter's boyfriend, and their assessments are made on the basis of whether the daughter's life will be properly taken care of in the next thirty to forty years. Not wanting to risk having any regrets, mothers, especially Shanghai mothers, who are known for their focus on pragmatic matters, try to warn their daughters of the danger of following the heart rather than the mind. At the same time, the show also plays up the intense emotional bond between the mother and the daughter. And it is precisely these dynamics between conflict and emotional connection that make such shows compulsive viewing.

Although the mother-in-law often comes across in this show as domineering, the last words are usually reserved for the experts. Typically, the show features two "teachers" (*laoshi*)—a psychologist and a counselor (symptomatic of the prominence of didactic pop-psychological advice on reality advice TV in China; see chapter 8). Invited to sit in and watch the conflicts unfold for a while, these experts step in at the appropriate moment, asking questions, analyzing the issues at hand, and mediating between the mother, daughter, and the daughter's prospective fiancé. Not wanting to take sides yet often willing to play the devil's advocate, experts good-humoredly challenge each of the three parties to reflect on their often "irrational" views and behaviors, thereby helping them work toward making a decision that everyone can live with. To this end, in the episode mentioned above they asked the prospective fiancé, "You said that you can't stand the idea of people bringing germs into your apartment, but how come you are not worried about germs, since your job involves touching people's hair on a daily basis?" The young woman is also challenged: "If you can't trust him about not going back to his former girlfriend, how will you manage knowing that every day, as a hairdresser, he will be in close physical contact with many attractive young women?" And to the mother-in-law, the advice is to "look at the big picture, and try to understand that young people are here for the sake of love."

Here, then, television steps in to help people navigate personal, intergenerational, and familial tensions and risks in the postsocialist era. If in the Maoist era, much of individuals' fate was determined by the action of the state, in the reforms era, by contrast, when individuals increasingly have to make their own choices as well as live with their consequences, a "revolution from within," to use Barbara Cruikshank's phrase (1996, 231), has to take place to accommodate and equip people for this dramatic shift. Life advice television like the examples analyzed here takes on the task of advancing that internal revolution.

Another reality show that affords us a glimpse of the impact of moral and ethical privatization on individuals in postsocialist China is Channel Young's *Balinghou Juchang* (The post-80 theater) ("post-80" designating the younger generation, born after 1980). Unabashedly melodramatic, shows such as *The*

Post-80 Theatre tap into postsocialist Chinese viewers' need for moral orientation and emotional anchorage and a growing interest in reality programs that show ordinary people making decisions in everyday situations.

An episode titled "Mum, over 50, Goes for Plastic Surgery" (screened on April 22, 2011) offers a good illustration. Presented in a studio format with interspersed videos of their lives, the show features five people: a young couple, one parent of each, and a female host. What is of particular interest here is that it is the mother rather than the younger couple who is the focus of moral scrutiny. The segment starts with the female member of the couple, Yan Yan, hearing that her widow mum, who is in her fifties, has decided to undergo a series of plastic surgeries, including a nose job, breast enhancement, and a facelift. Yan Yan is incredulous of her mum's decision and manages to drag her into a TV studio instead of the clinic so that the TV host can "talk some sense" into her. Upon being quizzed by the TV host, Yan Yan's mother says that she has decided to have plastic surgery because she wants to make herself attractive for her in-law—the widowed father of Yan Yan's husband, Zhang Yuan—with whom she has fallen in love. Zhang Yuan, unbeknownst to his wife, supports the romance between his father and his mother-in-law but is angry to discover that his father has in the meantime fallen for a younger woman. Zhang Yuan is furious with his father not because of his emotional infidelity but instead because his father's change of heart and possible marriage to the younger woman would mean the family assets and property would go to a stranger "outside the family." Meanwhile, Yan Yan's mother is devastated because her in-law confesses to prefer the younger woman to her. Anxious to keep the family assets intact, Zhang Yuan does his best to prove to everyone that the younger woman his father is to marry is in fact a gold digger, discrediting her declaration of love. In the meantime, Yan Yan's mother is too heartbroken to consider forgiving her lover. But she still wants to undergo plastic surgery, as planned, but now in the hope of regaining her confidence as a woman.

As this episode illustrates, as individuals venture into the uncharted waters of interacting with familial, spousal, and sexual relationships at a time in which both traditional and socialist values and practices in these domains have become radically unsettled, people seek guidance to negotiate their bearings in the new moral-sexual-economic order. Interviews with producers of the show indicate that while the story is "true," the people who appear on this reality show are actors, and much of the footage shot outside the studio is in fact a dramatization of events. In dramatized real-life stories such as this on Chinese TV, characters are depicted making decisions and choices following their own individual principle of managing risk, with the sense that external norms have become uncertain and perhaps ineffective. It is precisely in this sense that Aihwa Ong conceptualizes privatization as "fundamentally an ethical relationship to oneself, in the sense of one's relationship to the self, to others, to things, and to one's fate." This process requires individuals to "work on themselves, stylize their personalities, and hone their skills," in order to maximize their capacity to "proliferate connections and access to power" (Ong 2008, 184–85), even in the sphere of love and romance.

Alongside reality shows dramatizing the fraught decision-making processes that accompany privatization, Chinese television has also produced an array of rather more pragmatic programming offering advice on marriage and relationships, from *Qinggan Da Caijue* (Verdict on feelings) on Hebei Satellite TV and *Wo Gai Zenme Ban* (What should I do) on Yunnan Satellite TV, to *Aiqing Baowei Zhan* (In defense of love) and *Dasheng Shuo Chulai* (Say it out loud) on Chongqing Satellite TV. Although there are some slight variations among these shows in terms of format and presentation, on the whole, these are talk shows with a live studio audience, consisting of a panel of experts, a host, and a couple whose relationship is in trouble and desperately in need of help.

In contrast to much of Indian entertainment television (except perhaps for some of Doordarshan's rural, pedagogically oriented programming), these Chinese life advice formats not only offer entertainment in the form of narrative pleasure, pathos, and voyeurism but, more significantly, fulfill an important ideological task assigned to the Chinese entertainment industries by the state: to "provide moral education in the form of entertainment" (*yu jiao yu le*) by demonstrating exemplary norms and thereby teaching viewers appropriate methods of coping with the contradictions of cultural modernization (Bakken 2000). In other words, although much that used to be guaranteed by the state has been redefined as personal decisions, choices, and risks, on these shows the process of ethical self-training embarked on by individuals still takes place within the parameters informed by the moral and ideological legacies of socialism. These programs espouse moral advice that promotes what Ong calls the "Chinese version of self-proprietorship," which is not the product of political liberalism but is "fostered by conditions produced at the intersection of market freedom and political authoritarianism" (Ong 2008, 183). Unlike *If You Are the One*, these shows aim to reduce rather than spectacularize social conflicts, and condemn rather than showcase selfish and materialistic values. Lacking the competitive and sometimes combative elements of a show like *If You Are the One*, their main aim is to mediate and resolve conflict, not amplify it. They constitute a politically "safe" zone wherein tensions between classes, genders, and generations are defused rather than exacerbated. For the audience as well as the individuals appearing as guests on these shows, television functions as a virtual classroom, whereby they learn the politico-morally correct ways of navigating the uncertain terrain of feelings and emotion. We now turn to a specific example from Chongqing Satellite TV to see how this normative ethical position is taught.

Broadcast on Chongqing Satellite TV at 10 p.m. each Tuesday, the fifty-minute show *Say It Out Loud* is described on its own official website as a program dedicated to "resolving dilemmas and reducing pressure" (*shi huo, jian ya*). Its objective is to "adopt a lively and endearing style, guide (*yinling*) the Chinese people, and help them figure out how to think, how to feel, and how to live." On June 3, 2014, *Say It Out Loud* featured a young couple whose relationship was in trouble. Ke'er, a twenty-four-year-old office worker, has been living with her boyfriend Luo Jie for a couple of years, and the couple is planning to get married soon. However, Luo Jie's mother comes to stay for three months. After her departure, Luo seems to have gone cold on the idea of getting married. Ke'er is not happy about this change in her boyfriend, so the couple comes onto the show in the hope of some mediation and resolution. In conversations with the panel of experts (a well-known actress, a marriage counselor, a psychological counselor, and a media commentator), viewers learn that Ke'er does not know how to do housework, nor does she think she should. "To be a wife is to be loved," she says, and as for housework, that's the job of a maid. Luo Jie, on the other hand, seems weighed down by the unattractive prospect of a married life filled with the pressure of work and the burden of housework. Having his mother stay for three months and help out with housework has driven home the fact that he is getting a raw deal out of this relationship.

The central role of intermediaries such as emotional and psychological counselors makes these shows far more directly didactic than *If You Are the One*. Anchored in more conservative morality and cultural values, the aim of shows like *Say It Out Loud* is to guide as well as to entertain, with the intermediary figures featured drawing heavily on revived traditional values pertaining to gender roles, family, and moral virtues. In the case of the episode of *Say It Out Loud* discussed above, the "experts" step in to diagnose the problem, offer advice, provide moral critique, and, above all, help improve the suzhi (human quality) of overly self-centered individuals like Ke'er.

Tu Lei, perhaps China's most well-known media commentator and host of relationship-counseling shows (see figure 7.7), appears as a guest on the panel. After Ke'er receives a thorough dressing-down for her selfish behavior from Chen Sisi, a well-known actress, Tu's interrogation of Ke'er gets straight to the

Figure 7.7. Tu Lei, the best-known commentator on relationships on Chinese television, gives bride-to-be Ke'er a dressing-down on *Say It Out Loud*, June 3, 2014.

point. Pointing to her boyfriend, Tu asks Ke'er: "When he is sick, have you looked after him? When he is stressed out, have you comforted him?" "Your problem is that you only know how to enjoy life, but you don't know how to do hard work." Tu Lei not only problematizes Ke'er's behavior but also offers a diagnosis of what causes it. His words hit the increasingly defensive Ke'er with surgical sharpness:

> Have you thought about why he is reluctant to marry you? It's not just because you can't make beds or you don't want to wash dishes. You have a more serious problem: you have had a bad upbringing [*jiajiao*]. . . . You were rude to his mother, and you only talk about what you want. . . . Of course, this lack of proper upbringing is not all your fault; your parents are also to blame. Nowadays, a lot of parents only do the "bringing up" part, but fail to do the "educating" part. Because of this bad upbringing, you now behave like a shameless rascal [*pi zi*]. What you must realize is that when you were young and outrageous, people may have thought you were cute; but now you are an adult, and if you still behave like a

child, you will fill people with repulsion. People change, and their roles change, too. You need to grow up.

This dressing-down articulates extremely direct pedagogical instruction in the rules of "proper" feminine gender vis-à-vis normative life stages (we return to this topic in chapter 8). But in the eyes of the experts, neither is Luo Jie entirely blameless. He has spoiled his girlfriend rotten and has not taken any action to change the dynamics of the relationship. Again, Tu Lei's advice to him is served as a bitter medicine: "You may think that you've already caught the fish, but your job is not done. If you want this relationship to work, you must be a father as well as a husband. Your problem is that she won't change by herself; you will have to make her change. It's your job to teach her. Maybe you could see this as a blessing in disguise, and learn to derive some sense of achievement from having successfully transformed her."

Despite the didactic, sharp, and acerbic lectures served out by the panelists—or perhaps because of them—the couple seems to emerge feeling enlightened. They appear to accept the advice given to them and resolve to give their relationship another chance by earnestly reforming their behavior. The studio audience is also given the chance to voice its opinion. They are asked to vote: do they hope the couple stay together (yes), or do they think the couple should go their separate ways (no)? Not surprisingly, 80 percent vote yes. In fact, most episodes in these shows have a "happy ending": the couple in trouble emerges from the show feeling confident that they can see a way out of their problem and remain committed to staying together.

In assessing the moral landscape inhabited by the Chinese people in the reforms era, Kleinman et al. observe that the Chinese individual is socialized indirectly by the state, and directly by the family, to understand the "very real limits of their small freedoms as well as a responsibility to live a divided life with great alertness to the boundaries that one does not trespass" (2011, 286). If Kleinman et al. are right, life advice TV shows play a key role not only in showing individuals such as Ke'er and the audience what these "small freedoms" constitute but, more importantly, in reinforcing in them, on a daily basis, an alertness to the boundaries beyond which they must not trespass.

Conclusion

Our concern in this chapter has been to examine the ways in which the dilemmas and risks of modern love, marriage, and intimate relationships are interrogated on contemporary Indian and Chinese reality and lifestyle shows.

We have discussed how the notion of dating, in particular, is a site of tension as it unleashes a concept of romantic love enmeshed with ideas of freedom of partner choice, emotional compatibility, unique individuality, and nonmarital sexual relationships in social contexts where traditional values and practices around marriage and family remain influential. However, the shows we have analyzed here speak to and respond in very different ways to the growing marketization of love (Illouz 1997, 2012) and the rise of choice-based consumer identities in China and India, illustrating distinct modes of cultural modernity in the two countries.

On the one hand, we have seen the dating subjects on *If You Are the One*, *Dare2Date*, and *LoveNet* undertake emotional labors of personality cultivation and performance in order to project often idealized images of themselves within a "free" market of love that is implicitly structured by social status. On the other hand, in both China and India we also see a range of reality shows that illustrate the tensions between privatized logics of enterprising selfhood and residual (and in China's case, re-emergent), gendered familial norms.

In India, where as in China familial social relations continue to shape and constrain the shift toward an enterprise culture of selfhood, we see reality shows like *Date My Folks* and *Why Fear When You Love* quite literally attempting to "marry" an individualized ideology of choice, romance, and associated liberal notions of "freedom" with the material realities of familial-inflected social relations. In such an environment, arguably it is reality dating shows like *Why Fear When You Love* and *Date My Folks*, in which the parents are as much the focus of the show as the would-be lovers, that offer the most nuanced and "realistic" insights into the state of contemporary love, in a context where emergent trends toward individualization and enterprise still largely occur in articulation with cultural and familial norms and logics.

In China, meanwhile, the space of love, marriage, and relationships has become a new ideological frontier on which battles between neoliberal logic and socialist legacy, and between the stability-maintenance agenda of the state and profit-chasing drives of the market, are fought—as we saw in the media controversy over, and the state's intervention in, the case of *If You Are the One*. Further, while for the past century, individualism and the formation of the modern family have posed robust challenges to traditional values, in the postsocialist period, neotraditionalist ideas about the self, gender roles, and family have reemerged to provide a means of re-embedding individuals into a set of readjusted moral, ideological, and political imperatives at a time of dramatic economic and social transformation. On shows like *Mother-in-Law Eyes Her Son-in-Law* and *The Post-80 Theatre* we see dramatizations of these complex negotiations around individualism, consumerism, and re-emerging older-style ideas about the self, gender roles, and family. In contrast, life advice shows like *Say It Out Loud* constitute a politically "safe" zone wherein tensions between classes, genders, and generations are defused rather than exacerbated. Here television functions as a virtual classroom supported by an array of cultural intermediaries, providing the means to navigate the uncertain terrain of feelings and intimate relationships through the presentation of politico-morally correct exemplary norms.

This array of reality shows focused on intimacy and love functions as metaphor and metonym of both India and China's unique and contradictory trajectories toward individualization. Our discussion has revealed how these shows, like much contemporary lifestyle and reality TV in South Asia and East Asia, offer popularly inflected insights into the risks, ambivalences, and social upheavals associated with negotiating modernities at the microlevel of individual everyday life. In the next chapter, we extend this investigation though a focus on the related issue of the production, regulation, and negotiation of gender norms on Chinese-language life advice TV from China and Taiwan.

EIGHT. **A Self to Believe In** Negotiating Femininities in Sinophone Lifestyle Advice TV

Given the pervasive cultural associations of femininity with physicality, mutability, and consumption across both Euro-American and Asian contexts, one might say there is a particular affinity between the topic of "women" and lifestyle makeover formats that dramatize the transformation of physical appearance through consumption—whether of fashion, cosmetics, or cosmetic surgery. The feminist film theorist Mary Ann Doane proposes that in film as in Western culture more broadly, woman has historically been associated with the surface rather than the putative depths of the image, to the extent that "femininity itself . . . is constructed as a mask—as the decorative layer which conceals a non-identity" (Doane 1999, 138). However, while observing that the manipulation of women's appearance is indeed central to the Euro-American makeover genre, Brenda Weber argues that far from exposing the masquerade of feminine gender—the "non-identity" beneath the performance—programs like *The Swan*, *Extreme Makeover*, and *What Not to Wear* strenuously police gender normativity in the name of authentic identity. Such shows paradoxically promise to release an inner feminine essence—and a newly self-confident "me"—that "was there all along" and yet is only accessible through stylistic intervention (Weber 2009, 127–70).

A range of adaptations of Euro-American women's makeover formats is currently being produced in China, including cosmetic surgery reality shows such as *Hui Guniang yu Tian'e* (Cinderella and the swan, Shandong Qilu TV), with concepts modeled quite closely on the U.S. programs (Hua 2013, 177–84). Wen Hua's extensive ethnographic study of Chinese women undertaking cosmetic surgery investigates the broader social context for this upsurge of televisual interest in feminine perfectibility (Hua 2013). She observes that the cosmetic surgery recipients she interviewed "seemed to regard their bodies as a collection of raw materials through which one can construct one's own true self" (6). This recalls the logic of physical manipulation producing authentic feminine selfhood that Weber observes in Euro-American women's makeover formats; and as we will see below, a similar logic is also echoed in Chinese women's makeover TV beyond the cosmetic surgery subgenre. Elsewhere in the Sinophone mediasphere, in the distinct genre of Taiwanese-style women's variety-talk shows, women's beauty, fashion, and makeover topics also constitute a major theme. These Taiwanese programs and their copies in China and Singapore similarly focus on constructing "better" feminine selfhood through stylistic manipulation. How, then, are these various forms of lifestyle advice and makeover TV both reflecting and contributing to available formations of feminine identity? How are such programs simultaneously produced out of cross-fertilization with globally and regionally mobile forms, and marked by the specificity of their more immediate historical, social, and cultural production contexts?

To address these questions, this chapter presents two case studies of women's advice shows from China and Taiwan, as well as a discussion of audience responses. We begin with a study of the gendered dimensions of China's *Gou Shishang* (Pretty trendy), a reality makeover show produced by one of the channels of the state broadcaster (CCTV-2) offering guidance to "ordinary" female guests suffering from stylistic and personal problems. *Pretty Trendy* is a reality makeover format that engages a panel of experts, including a psychologist and stylists, to teach contestants the cultural capital they need to transform themselves both inwardly and outwardly, culminating in a dramatized "reveal" at the end of each episode. Although it is a product of one of the Chinese Communist Party's main media organs, in terms of style and format, *Pretty Trendy*—like many Chinese programs today—is clearly influenced in some respects by Euro-American reality makeover TV. We argue that *Pretty Trendy* pursues a three-sided pedagogical project. First and most obviously, it educates the viewer in good taste and fashion consumption, idealizing a particular formation of urban, middle-class consumer-femininity. Second, it educates the viewer in pop psychology, naturalizing a "deep," individualized, interior self as the subject's most precious possession. Third, it represents and polices the proper embodiment of normative feminine life stages. Since for women, social consensus structures these stages into quite a precise calendar in which marriage, childbirth, and child-rearing are central events, the types of feminine identity imagined by the program—no matter how stylistically cosmopolitan and psychologically individualized—ultimately reinforce the postsocialist gender essentialism that women's life and identity are definitionally entwined with marital and familial roles.

Our second example is an allied yet distinct genre: comedic variety-talk fashion and beauty guides for unmarried urban working women. This genre, which originated in Taiwan through cross-fertilization with the Japanese TV variety genre, is now proliferating in both mainland China and Singapore (see chapters 1 and 5), and is popular right across the transnational Sinophone mediasphere. Programs like *Nüren Wo Zui Da* (Queen), the Taiwanese show we analyze here, center an emergent feminine identity based on urban residence, unmarried status, individualistic attitude, high level of education, white-collar employment, and penchant for beauty and fashion consumption. These attributes index material transformations in the conditions of many young women's lives in Taiwan, Singapore, urban coastal China, and elsewhere across East Asia. We show that while in the broadest sense, *Pretty Trendy* and *Queen* share several characteristics in common—especially a tension between individualized and familial femininities; an omnipresent popular discourse on creating "a self to believe in" through fashion and beauty; and an idealization of urban, middle-class consumer-femininities—they also differ in a number of important ways connected to genre, tone, and pedagogy. In particular, we argue that while *Pretty Trendy* reinforces postsocialist gender essentialism through its fairly straightforward policing of normative feminine life stages connected with familial roles, in several respects—not least, for its viewers—*Queen* is a highly polysemic text that *at once supports and challenges* the gender normativity of such familialism.

Post-Mao China: (Re)privatizing Femininity

In China, the end of Marxist-Leninist-Maoist socialism and the emergence of a market economy since 1978 have had far-reaching implications both for women's economic and cultural experience and for the ways in which femininity is produced as a set of cultural assumptions in public culture. With the dismantling of the old centralized socialist economy, many women have taken up new roles in the privatizing economy, and women's conduct in these professional roles is among the subjects addressed in the reality makeover format that we discuss below (Hershatter 2007, 68–69; Chen 2008). However, the post-Mao period has also witnessed a widening gendered wage gap and an overall drop in urban married women's labor force participation—which under Mao was among the highest in the world—as they are encouraged back to the family as the state withdraws from elderly, infant, and child care (Hershatter 2007, 64–78; Cook and Dong 2011, 949). The transition from the "iron rice-bowl" of state-assigned lifetime employment to market capitalism has brought with it, overall, significantly increased risks for urban women, as they grapple with ferocious competition for jobs in the context of increasingly sexist employment practices, including discrimination in hiring based on female applicants' levels of conventional beauty, and a tendency for firms to preferentially hire and retain male workers in times of rising unemployment (Cook and Dong 2011; Hua 2013, 147–64).

As well as thoroughly transforming the structural conditions of women's working lives, market capitalism has also created new formations of feminine gender identity based not on political background or work-unit ties but rather on labor-market value and recreational consumption (Chen 2008; Yan 2010; Kim 2011; Wu 2012). Lisa Rofel illustrates that "a sea-change has swept through China in the last fifteen years: to replace socialist experimentation with the 'universal human nature' imagined as the essential ingredient of cosmopolitan worldliness. This model of human nature has the desiring subject at its core: the individual who operates through sexual, material, and affective self-interest" (2007, 3). Consumption, argues Rofel, becomes a "postsocialist technology of the self," constructing—especially for young women, who are posed as the ultimate consumers—a self based on possessive individualism and acquisitive consumption (Rofel 2007, 118, 112). Whereas socialism constructed class identity and political engagement as the defining factors in citizens' social being, the public culture that emerged along with China's market economy constructs a universal human nature based on individualized desire. To simplify somewhat, the privatization of state enterprise is paralleled by the privatization of selfhood and the rise of a "self-animating, self-staging subject": an entrepreneur of the self motivated by private accumulation and self-interest (Hoffman 2006; L. Zhang and Ong 2008, 1).

Following a spate of new translations of Freud's major works in the mid-1980s and the processing of related ideas into pop psychology, this new "universal human nature" has often been inflected by versions of psychoanalytic theory. As Fran Martin has observed elsewhere about Freudian theory's role in the 1980s cultural ferment: "In the postsocialist Chinese context, the 'deep structures' of the human psyche that Freudianism proposed were able ... to work collusively with the re-emergent discourse of humanist individualism in challenging the functionalist collectivism of [the old Marxist-Leninist-Maoist] official state ideology" (Martin 2010, 79). During the 1980s, representations of psychologized selfhood functioned as a challenge to state discourse's lack of an adequately complex theory of the human subject. However, as we will see, by the second decade of the new millennium the psychologized self has become a tool wielded enthusiastically by the state's own media organs in producing exemplary norms for regulating the conduct of the citizenry (Bakken 2000; Yang 2014).

The postsocialist ideal of the individualized, self-making subject exercises an allure for women as well as men (Rofel 2007, 111–34). However, the culture of postsocialism has produced contradictory effects in discourses on gendered personhood. Rofel notes that concurrent with the rise of the universalized desiring subject, post-Mao public culture also produced a discourse on woman as "naturally" focused on motherhood, wedded love, and family care (Rofel 1999, 217–56)—a cultural imaginary in sync with the state's withdrawal of support for social reproduction and the consequent relocation of this burden back into the household (Cook and Dong 2011, 949–51). This "privatizing" discourse that associates femininity with domesticity, as Hua observes (2013, 93–98, 112), can be seen as a renewed appeal to prerevolutionary gender tropes, including the old adage of *nan zhu wai, nü zhu nei* (the man's sphere is the exterior; the woman's, the interior [of the household]). The soft, nurturing feminine "nature" thought to have been repressed by Maoist feminism, is now at last "free" to express itself through increased gender differentiation in everyday behavior and self-presentation (Croll 1995, 153–55). However, Rofel observes that the state itself, far from receding on all fronts, is collusive in promulgating this discourse, through its regulation of marriage, childbirth, and child-rearing, "actively involv[ing] itself in naturalizing femininity and masculinity" (Rofel 1999, 219). This accords with Leta Hong Fincher's in-depth study of the resurgence of gender inequality in the reforms era, in which she demonstrates how state media have promulgated a discourse stigmatizing so-called leftover women—a caricature of educated, professional women who remain unmarried at age thirty—thereby encouraging women to stick closely to a normative, marriage- and family-centered life course (Hong Fincher 2014).

In her study of Chinese women undertaking cosmetic surgery, Hua links the surgery trend with the broad cultural shift identified by Rofel (1999), whereby women have become defined through their physical features rather than their ideological stance, class background, and labor performance, as had been the case for previous generations (Hua 2013, 14). The (re)eroticization and commodification of feminine beauty in the reforms era intimately links to "a new culture of sexuality . . . within which attractive and sexualized female images are emphasized and the erotic female body is consumed" (16). Hua points to an increasingly gender-biased job market that openly favors conventionally beautiful women as an important motivation for many of those who undergo cosmetic surgery, underlining the very real material value of "physical capital" for women in China today (75–98).

The wider social and historical contexts surveyed above are all clearly reflected in popular TV today, including dating shows (see chapter 7), cosmetic surgery shows, and fashion and beauty advice shows. Here, "experts," from surgeons to psychologists to stylists, instruct women on how to remake themselves to embody the currently valorized formation of beauty and "soft" femininity in sync with naturalized, family-centric life stages while at the same time understanding themselves as free, entrepreneurial postsocialist subjects. The televisual promotion of individualized, physicalized, familialized consumer-femininity is common to both state and commercial channels, although it takes different forms in each, with the state broadcaster tending to adopt a more directly didactic, less playful style. It is in this context that we now turn to this chapter's first case study, CCTV-2's reality makeover show *Pretty Trendy*.

CCTV-2'S *PRETTY TRENDY*

Gou Shishang—whose title puns on "really [*gou*] fashionable" and "buying [*gou*] fashion," and which we freely translate as "pretty trendy"—is described by its producer as CCTV's first-ever original fashion and consumption reality show.[1] The popular fifty-minute program, sponsored by China's New Silk Road Fashion Organization (the nation's largest modeling agency) and Harper's Bazaar China, commenced broadcast on December 31, 2010, and at the time of writing, airs in a 7:30 prime-time slot on Friday evenings (Zhao 2012). The program also has an interactive Internet version, *Wo Yao Gou Shishang* (I want to be pretty trendy), linked from the program's website and networked with Weibo (China's Twitter-like microblogging platform), allowing viewers to win prizes and directly seek expert advice on their own stylistic problems.[2] That site is also cross-linked with CCTV's extensive online shopping mall, which sells everything from fashion and accessories to sporting goods, toys, food, and electronics.[3]

The TV version of *Pretty Trendy* is hosted by the thirtysomething veteran male TV host Gao Bo along with a younger and less well-known female "fashion assistant," Zhang Jing. Each episode features two ordinary women contestants who have been selected as makeover subjects based on specific problems they are experiencing linked to their self-presentation in everyday life: for example, they have trouble meeting suitable men, they are stuck in a stylistic

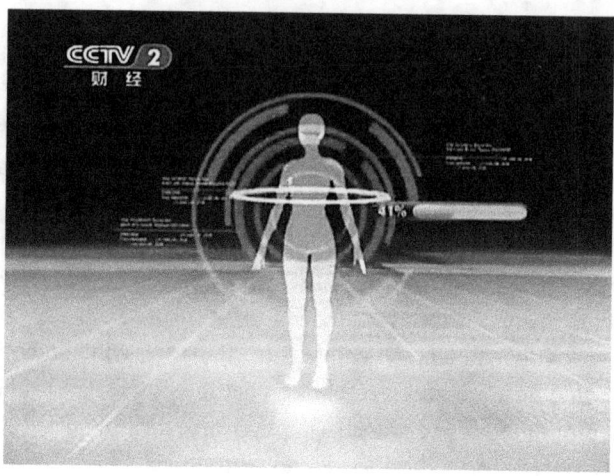

Figure 8.1. *Pretty Trendy*'s "fashion scanner" graphic.

rut that is affecting their career advancement, they are crippled by shyness in social situations, they are tomboyish or fail to embody conventional feminine graces, and so on. Each woman tells her story, aided by two friends, family members, or colleagues. These acquaintances bring along some items belonging to the makeover-ee that symbolize her "old self" (inappropriate shoes, a dowdy purse, ugly sportswear, etc.), and she is invited to say good-bye to the associated aspects of herself by releasing the items into a clear plastic vacuum-tube that sucks them up and away. A psychologist offers expert advice on how the contestant's stylistic problems are symptoms of some deeper psychic issue: frequently a lack of belief in herself (*zixin*) and a tendency to cling to old stylistic habits for a "sense of security" (*anquan gan*). In the subsequent "fashion scanner" segment (whose concept and graphic presentation clearly draw on Euro-American reality makeover formats like *Snog Marry Avoid*), stylists give advice on preferable hair and clothing styles, offering models for emulation drawn from Chinese and international celebrity culture (see figure 8.1). There follows a "challenge" segment: contestants are given specific tasks designed to help in their self-transformations—for example, a shopping trip to test their fashion sense, or a sports or social challenge to test their self-confidence. Contestants' performances in the challenges are then judged by the experts. Finally, a professional hair-makeup-clothing makeover off-camera precedes the final "reveal" of each contestant's new look—both to the viewer, and, most dramatically, to the contestant herself in a ceremonially unveiled mirror. In some episodes, the studio audience then votes on whose transformation has been most complete.

The program's slogan—recited by Gao Bo at the start of every episode—is "fashion reshapes the self; self-confidence changes one's life" (*shishang chongsu ziwo, zixin gaibian rensheng*). CCTV's international arm (CNTV) elaborates on this slogan as follows: "The program chooses people who are yearning to change themselves and hoping to take up the fashionable life, thoroughly revealing the process of their self-perfection. . . . It helps them to understand life, to become good at living, and to love life. The ugly duckling can become a swan, Cinderella can claim her glass slipper. Anyone aiming for the fashionable life hopes for the wonder of a glamorous self-transformation. *Pretty Trendy* has created a stage for just that, allowing you to follow fashion step-by-step to reshape a fashionable self."[4]

Two repeated concepts stand out from these statements—fashion (*shishang*) and selfhood (*ziwo*)—and the program's central concept is very clear: through a proper understanding of fashion, feminine selfhood can be remodeled in more desirable form. As Hua observes, terms for "fashion" as used in contemporary China (*shimao, shishang*) index quite specific cultural imaginaries that have emerged as an effect of economic reform; in particular, the new ideal of urban middle-class consumer-selfhood. Thus, the shimao (fashionable) urban female consumer is the antithesis of the *tuqi* (hick, drab, tacky) laboring woman (Hua 2013, 117). In addition to its remarkably candid pedagogical project of teaching women how to embody this new feminine ideal, the program is also notable for the *depth* of transformation it imagines. For this is no merely superficial style makeover: the process of becoming fashionable is nothing less than a wholesale renovation of the heart and mind and a remaking of the individual self (ziwo). The program's extension of its transformational project inward into the core of the self is achieved through the emphasis on personalized psychological advice, whereby contestants' stylistic and behavioral "flaws"—namely, deviations from the ideal of fashionable, middle-class consumer-femininity—are related back to deep-seated psychic issues, responsibility for which is placed squarely on the individual. Examples from specific episodes will help to illustrate these points.

On July 7, 2013, *Pretty Trendy*'s theme was "All kitted out to realize their dream" (*weile mengxiang zhengzhuang dai fa*). The first contestant, thirty-six-year-old Pan Mengting, is a school canteen worker in a provincial town with a keen interest in fashion and a lifelong dream of becoming a famous model. However, not conventionally beautiful and slightly plump, she has long

Figure 8.2. Before shot of Pan on *Pretty Trendy*, July 7, 2013.

endured the ridicule of her coworkers and family for clinging to her modeling dream and wearing girlish, frilly, and revealing outfits deemed inappropriate to her age, build, occupation, and identity as a wife and mother (see figure 8.2).

Two specific regulatory projects are evident in this episode that also typify the program as a whole. First, we will discuss the program's *psychologization, individualization, and "responsibilization" of the classed subject.* In a typical example, in presenting her advice to Pan, the well-known radio psychologist Qing Yin interprets Pan's "cheap" clothing taste as an example of her low self-esteem and lack of self-respect: in short, of her failure to recognize her self as a possession to be valued above all things. She advises Pan to seek self-respect elsewhere than in her fashion obsession, and to take greater efforts in finding someone to love: "You don't love anyone, and you don't love yourself, either. This is quite disastrous." It is only through the inner pursuits of self-respect, self-acceptance, and love, Qing advises—her "caring" smile and carefully modulated voice failing to mask a steely didacticism—that Pan will be able to find true fulfillment. Qing's brutal final assessment (based on Pan's selection of a sheer, patterned dress with spaghetti straps as her "new me" outfit on a shopping trip challenge) is that Pan must have completely given up on herself. "If I were those clothes, I would be thinking: I am so unworthy of you," says (pretty, educated, expensively dressed) Qing, causing Pan to dash away tears, which she explains are the result of frustration at not understanding how she "should" have chosen the outfit (see figure 8.3). Pan's preference for styles that to Qing appear self-evidently tacky is interpreted as Pan's unconscious

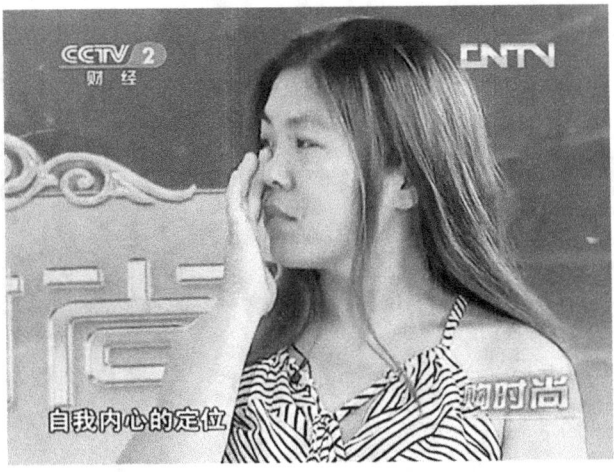

Figure 8.3. Pan wipes away tears as psychologist Qing Yin berates her for her lack of self-belief as purportedly revealed in her dress choice.

self-deprecation: the structural effects of social stratification and class habitus are disavowed through individualizing pop psychology, as responsibility for producing a form of selfhood appropriate to middle-class, marketized urban culture is sheeted squarely home to the individual. The tears that Pan sheds, then, may partly be tears of class humiliation: what is revealed in this scene is the shameful gulf separating her own cherished aesthetic sensibility from the one idealized in the experts' version of good taste. The stylists' remodeling of Pan in what they term "simpler" hair and clothing styles is directed at removing the tuqi elements of her look (unevenly dyed flyaway hair, fussy detailing, loud colors, etc.), and produces a sleeker and, unsurprisingly, recognizably more cosmopolitan, middle-class image (see figure 8.4). This episode's rather brutal staging of the attempt to discipline a provincial working-class woman's taste—and selfhood—in line with urban middle-class ideals supports Janice Hua Xu's argument that such consumer-oriented lifestyle programs both embody and reinforce deepening class stratification in postsocialist Chinese society (Xu 2007, 375; Yang 2014).

The individualization, psychologization, and "responsibilization" of the subject and the attribution of interior causes for stylistic problems are omnipresent throughout *Pretty Trendy*, underscoring the high symbolic stakes it places on its refashioning project. Fashion style is not "just" style but an index of the psychological health, social viability, and ethicality of the feminine self. The repeated references to the unique individual "self" (ziwo) and the ethical

Figure 8.4. Self-confrontation: Pan's reveal.

imperative to believe in and be true to it performatively materialize the postsocialist model of the self-making subject as the ultimate locus of meaning. This is visually literalized through the staging of the self-confrontation at the end of the show, when the "reveal" is given added drama by the fact that this is the first time that the contestant "meets her new self," in a mirror (see figure 8.4). These scenes proffer a literalized enactment of the project of reflexive identity formation that is at the core of this program, whereby the individual woman is given ultimate responsibility for securing her own happiness and well-being through proper attention to her self. Such a discourse is evident right across the program: time and again, the extrinsic reasons offered by contestants for their own stylistic and/or social problems (color-blindness, overwork, the demands of parenting, a limited social circle, being new to urban life) are explained away by psychologists, concerned family members, and hosts as merely excuses for the contestant's underlying lack of belief in herself (zixin). The program demands not only that contestants learn to "believe in themselves" in the pop-psychological, self-empowerment sense of the phrase but also that they learn to *believe in the self* as a central structuring concept for interpreting personal experience and social life.

The serious-mindedness with which *Pretty Trendy* approaches the question of women's inner selfhood perhaps also reflects China's current regulatory environment. In January 2012 the State Administration of Radio, Film and Television (SARFT) brought into force an edict restricting "entertainment" programs and encouraging TV channels to produce educative content that was "harmonious, healthy, and mainstream" (Sun 2012, 14; see also chapter 1). In his master's thesis on the current situation of lifestyle TV in China, Xiaofan Sun proposes that this genre—exemplified in *Pretty Trendy*—offers a new frame in which educational and entertainment values can be effectively melded, teaching "healthy, harmonious, mainstream" values in formats entertaining enough to draw good ratings (X. Sun 2012, 14–15). *Pretty Trendy*'s project of regulating not just women's exterior beauty but also their inner "psychological health" is precisely what commentators in China point to as marking the show's educational and moral "healthiness," in accord with SARFT's edict (Gao 2011; X. Sun 2012, 15; Meng 2013).

The second regulatory project that the program takes on concerns its *policing of life-stage-appropriate feminine style and behavior*. In the episode discussed above, a central aspect of Pan's "problem," as diagnosed especially by her colleague and brother (see figures 8.5 and 8.6), is the way in which her love for a youthful fashion style conflicts with social expectations connected with her age and maternal status. Aside from being stylistically incompatible with the idealized image of urban middle-class sophistication, the types of outfits that Pan favors say "girl," whereas Pan occupies the ascribed identity of "woman." Her addiction to the wrong kind of fashion means that she fails to approximate normative standards for self-presentation by "respectable" wives and mothers. This episode, like many others, dramatizes the "correcting" of feminine self-presentation in accord with life stage and familial roles.

The episode that aired on April 14, 2013, for example, titled "Chenggong, Heshi Cheng Jia?" (You've found success; but when will you found a family?), focused on the topical issue of female PhD graduates unable to find husbands in a marriage market where men prefer to "marry down." In doing so, this episode indirectly cites the widespread "leftover women" discourse that encourages educated, professional women toward "timely" marriage by means of public shaming (Hong Fincher 2014). Gao Bo introduces the two contestants, a thirty-eight-year-old accounting PhD and a thirty-three-year-old doctor of meteorology, with a spiel that praises their academic achievements while framing their unmarried status as self-evident tragedy. The first contestant's inability to attract a husband is linked with her preference for exercising with elderly people in public parks, considered an inappropriate social activity for her time of life. "Do you feel that your life is lacking a certain vitality?" asks Gao Bo. "Like a sunset years feeling?" The second contestant, meanwhile, is criticized for her dowdy hair and clothing style; in particular, a pair of tartan

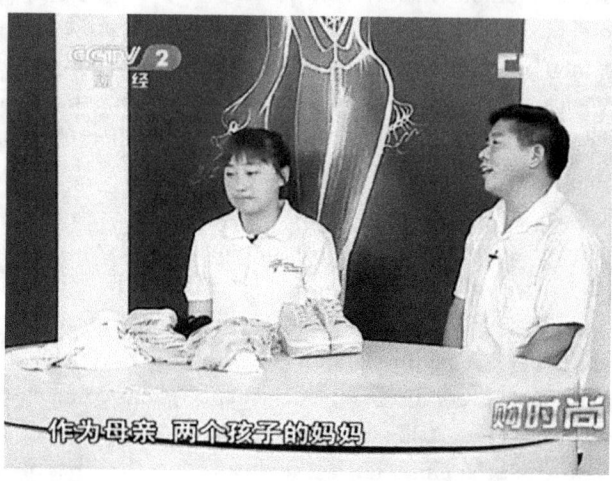

Figures 8.5 and 8.6. Pan's colleague and elder brother offer samples of Pan's inappropriately girlish garments for elimination by vacuum tube. Pan's brother says: "As a mother, as Mum to two kids, she should be focused on her family."

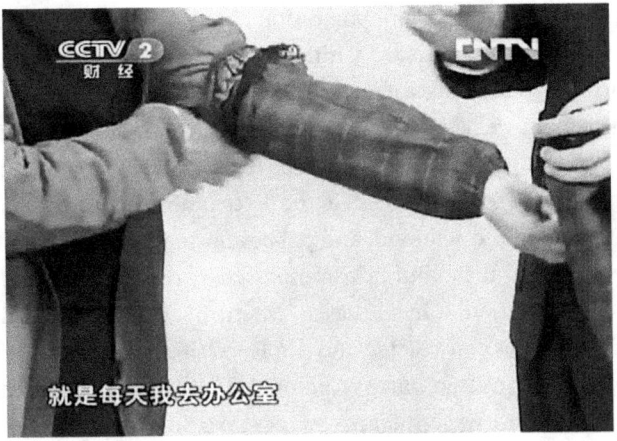

Figure 8.7. Anachronistic and "housewifely" sleeve protectors on *Pretty Trendy*, April 14, 2013.

sleeve protectors that she likes to wear in her research lab (see figure 8.7). Her three younger dormmates describe these as "something that would be more at home in a housewife's kitchen," while Gao Bo plays it for laughs, mocking their anachronism: "It's quite some years since I've seen anything like these. . . . Yes, I'm old enough to remember them. Accountants and people like that used to wear the blue ones, right?" The sleeve protectors are thus linked not only to a "housewifely" identity inappropriate for a single woman but also to the "backwardness" of the China of twenty or thirty years ago.

Illustrating a similar preoccupation with policing life-stage-appropriate behavior, on June 16, 2013, a whole episode was devoted to correcting the stylistic mistakes of two young mothers. These include a twenty-seven-year-old who is often mistaken for an eighteen-year-old and is anxious because she prefers a studentesque clothing style and can't get the hang of the sophisticated fashion looks in the downtown business district where she has recently begun working. A stylist—the chief corporate image planner for Harper's Bazaar China, Shi Yan—advises this contestant: "You've had your baby now; your new role is that of a *mama*. You should show more feminine gentleness [*wenwan*]." In her advice, Shi sums up the program's line on age-appropriate style for women: "You've held on to the dream that you're still a little girl. But your identity—and everything about you—is all changing. At the appropriate age, you must dress according to the appropriate image. *That* is the meaning of correct, good taste." In *Pretty Trendy*'s vision, then, good taste for women involves not only a grasp of urban, cosmopolitan fashion aesthetics and an unwavering belief in the self as one's most important possession but also a clear understanding of the styles and behaviors required at different times of a woman's life, as defined by the normative landmarks of marriage and child-rearing.

In this section, we have tried to demonstrate how CCTV-2's *Pretty Trendy* develops a pedagogical project that overtly idealizes urban, middle-class consumer femininity; proselytizes faith in the determining importance of individualized, psychologized selfhood; and polices normative feminine life stages, thereby reinforcing the cultural "common sense" of essentialized gender in the postsocialist period. It inculcates an emergent concept of a feminine self whose subjectivity is constructed and displayed through the conjoined projects of "tasteful" consumption, psychologized "self-belief," and familial role (Xu 2007, 373). Before we move on to our next example, we would like to make some further observations about the tone of this pedagogical project. For there appears to be a stark disjuncture between a high level of "democratization" in *Pretty Trendy*'s representation of the sphere of consumer choices, on the one hand, and a highly authoritarian style of providing advice and guidance, on the other. Although lifestyle advice programs such as this illustrate the triumph of entertainment-oriented media practices over older traditions of political propaganda, the manner in which everyday skills and personal orientations are taught seems no less authoritarian and coercive. Viewers continue to receive didactic, judgmental, and patronizing instructions, albeit from "experts" on television instead of directly from the workplace party secretary or state-endorsed political role models. In other words, lifestyle experts not only function as cultural intermediaries but are also charged with the task of governing by proxy, pushing a range of moral and ethical positions that accommodate the postsocialist state's style of governance. In this case, the program's active (re)domestication, privatization, and "responsibilization" of the feminine subject supports the state's shifting of the burden of family care onto the shoulders of individual wives and mothers, and its unleashing of a market capitalist system where individual citizens must be made responsible for their own economic fate. The difference between *Pretty Trendy*'s "hearts-and-minds" approach and the far less psychologized, less authoritatively pedagogical mode of the Taiwanese-style genre discussed below highlights a certain cultural-historical continuity in CCTV's preference for reforming the "whole person" (Meng 2013), as our discussion above of the program's fit with SARFT's encouragement of "harmonious, healthy, mainstream" fare also underlines.

But if on the one hand a program like *Pretty Trendy* executes the ideological project of the reforms-era party-state, then on the other hand, in terms of genre, style, and concept, the similarities between *Pretty Trendy* and Euro-American women's reality-makeover formats are equally noteworthy. Indeed, in its earnest, authoritarian pedagogy of a feminine selfhood based on self-belief, self-motivation, the pursuit of happiness, and loyalty to the "natural woman" within, *Pretty Trendy* reveals an uncanny convergence between a CCP state-led project of subject (re)making and the neoliberal-style "new you" projects of U.S. women's reality makeover formats, as analyzed by Weber and others (Heller 2007; Lewis 2009; Quellette and Hay 2008; Weber 2009, 127–70).

However, lest this example give the impression that Chinese lifestyle television is dominated by a didactic, top-down style of viewer education, it is worth noting that the lifestyle programs on Shanghai Television's lifestyle channel, "Channel Young," buck this trend. In comparison to those on CCTV, lifestyle programs on Channel Young—including *Meili Jiuyuan Tuan* (Beauty rescue team), which began as a copy of *Queer Eye for the Straight Guy*; *Xin Nüren Wo Zui Da* (New queen), renamed *Ai Ni Ai Meili* (Love you, love beauty) in 2013, a licensed format trade of the Taiwanese beauty and fashion advice show *Queen*, analyzed below (see also chapter 5); and seasonal shows such as *Vogue Wedding*—are much more lively and playful, catering to younger, predominantly female, urban professional viewers. On Channel Young, one can barely detect the earnest pedagogical style one associates with CCTV. Instead, the tone is light-hearted and playful, and has a distinct element of the "zany style" that is typical of Taiwanese-style variety shows across East and Southeast Asia (Lewis, Martin, and Sun 2012).

In the following section, we follow this second type of women's lifestyle advice TV "back to the source" by focusing attention on the text and audience reception of the leader in the field, the long-running Taiwanese variety-talk show *Nüren Wo Zui Da* (Queen), which has provided inspiration for a plethora of copies across Taiwan, mainland China, and Singapore. As we will see, while some elements are clearly common to both genres—notably, the naturalization of middle-class consumer femininity and a postfeminist discourse of building "a self to believe in" through fashion—there are also very significant differences between these two types of programs. In particular, we argue that whereas *Pretty Trendy* naturalizes normative feminine life stages and familial identities, *Queen* centers on the idea of the unmarried, freewheeling, urban working woman, an image that—especially in its embodiment in the unconventional middle-aged celebrity host, Lan Xinmei—offers imaginative resources for viewers to envisage alternatives to a normative feminine life course.

Taiwan after the Economic Miracle: Postfamilial Femininities?

The "compressed" history of Taiwan's industrialization and deindustrialization since the 1960s, together with the far-reaching social and cultural transformations following the lifting of martial law in 1987 (see the introduction), have entailed specific effects vis-à-vis social experiences and cultural representations of feminine gender. On the one hand, as elsewhere in the transnational Sinophone world and beyond, the social experiences of industrialization, urbanization, and family nuclearization challenge the ideological dominance of women's identity as defined by "traditional" familial roles. On the other hand, industrial capitalism by no means does away with the conceptual link between femininity and family, and in the case of Taiwan some have argued that it proceeds *in collusion* with the modernizing patriarchal family, rather than dissolving the power of that system (see our discussion in chapter 6). Meanwhile, the impact of feminism and women's rising levels of education over the past three decades produce the conditions for a robust critique of women's subjection to patriarchal authority, both in the family and within the culture more broadly.

In this section, guided by some of the central preoccupations of the Taiwanese women's lifestyle advice TV to be analyzed below, we focus on the emergent contradiction between women's identity as individualized agents of consumption and labor, on the one hand, and on the other hand their subjection to ongoing social pressures to embody familial identities in the domestic sphere. The tension between these two models of femininity is everywhere evident in Taiwanese popular television. It crystallizes particularly in the figure of the *qingshounü*—an educated, unmarried, urban, middle-class, working woman in her midtwenties to thirties—who appears across a range of programs and genres, from idol dramas to variety shows.[5]

Macrosociological indicators support popular television's promotion of the idea that such women constitute a significant and growing demographic in Taiwan today. The rate of unmarried women's workforce participation has been virtually identical to that of unmarried men for several consecutive years, although women's paid employment drops off markedly after marriage, while men's rises (DGBAS 2011). Meanwhile, marriage rates are significantly declining and there is a strong trend toward "late" marriage and childbirth: in 2009 the average age for women's first marriage was 28.9 (*China Post* 2010; DGBAS 2012). Analyses of these trends highlight the material factors accounting for the waning appeal of marriage for young women. The impacts of feminism and women's increased education place younger women's increasingly post-traditional view of gender roles into direct conflict with older-style familial ideologies that place the major burden for the care of other family members onto the wife's shoulders.[6] This, plus the availability of paid employment enabling women to support themselves independently, combines to make the opportunity-cost of marriage significantly higher for women (especially educated women) than for men (Jones 2007, 463). These trends over recent decades toward delayed marriage and nonmarriage among women are among the most notable sociodemographic developments not only in Taiwan but also in many neighboring nations including urban coastal China and Singapore, among others—and this may partially explain the popularity of Taiwanese media focusing on unmarried urban career women among audiences in these neighboring nations (Jones 2007; Y-h. Chen 2009).

However, numerous studies of Taiwanese society across a range of fields indicate the persistent material and ideological centrality of the family that, far from withering away under current conditions of capitalist modernity, has tended to persist by shaping capitalist imperatives to its own ends. Studies in the anthropology of work illustrate how the prominent structures of the family firm and the family-based satellite factory system, in their extraction of value from female family members' unpaid labor, regenerate old-style patriarchal family values and structures in and through the logic of capitalism (Greenhalgh 1994; Hsiung 1996; Lee 2004). Sociological research has revealed that while on the level of everyday practice people's ties with the older-style extended family are indeed weakening, nonetheless on an ideological level the values associated with familialism—the symbolic importance of the "ancestral chain"; filial piety (entailing the necessity to marry and produce children)—tend to persist, whether as directly held beliefs or in ambivalent negotiation with more individualist desires (Thornton and Lin 1994, 396–411; Farris 2004; Yi and Lin 2009; Chang and Song 2010). Recent work on gender representation in Taiwanese commercial television genres, too, shows the persistence in locally produced variety shows of old-style, patriarchal familialist frameworks, albeit disguised in the individualizing, pop-feminist rhetoric of women's "empowerment" (Lin 2011). In the following section, we present a study of the text and reception of the popular Taiwanese women's fashion and beauty advice show *Queen*, in order to illustrate how women's lifestyle advice TV both reflects and contributes to the ongoing public-cultural processing of such gendered contradictions within (and beyond) Taiwan today.

TVBS-G'S QUEEN

Queen, whose Chinese title literally translated means "A woman, I am the greatest," is a high-rating variety-style show produced since 2003 for the moderately popular cable TV channel TVBS Entertainment, and is seen by this

Figure 8.8. A starlet models what not to wear to a job interview 1: mockingly described as a "saucy secretary" look, *Queen,* July 26, 2010.

channel, which targets a female audience, as its flagship program.⁷ The show's success has spawned a monthly beauty magazine of the same name, and in 2010, product sales from the program's website plus sales of the magazine reputedly generated revenue of NT$350 million (over US$12 million) (Wang 2010). Screened in Taiwan on weeknights at 9–10 p.m. with multiple repeats, *Queen* offers tips on feminine-coded topics like fashion, beauty, and shopping, with forays into other life skills such as what to wear for a job interview (see figures 8.8, 8.9, and 8.10), self-defense, yoga, and healthy eating. Staged on a pink set with a comedic mode of address from the middle-aged singer/comedian hostess Lan Xinmei (Pauline Lan; see figure 8.11), *Queen* features a regular team of expert "teachers" (laoshi and *daren*; see chapter 5) giving advice to a group of twentysomething C-list starlets, known as the "women's corps" (addressed on the show as "classmates") (see figure 8.12). Members of this panel are seen by the producers as a stand-in for the "ordinary" viewer at home, replacing a previous Q&A format to pose questions on the viewer's behalf, and acting the part of clueless young women in order to give the viewer an identificatory anchor.⁸

Important for our analysis below, a key factor differentiating *Queen*'s mode of address from that of *Pretty Trendy* is that while *Pretty Trendy* addresses women across a wide range of familial statuses, including older married women and those with children (Gao 2011), *Queen* centers on the figure of

240 / CHAPTER EIGHT

Figure 8.9. A starlet models what not to wear to a job interview: described rather scathingly as a "bar hostess" look, *Queen*, July 26, 2010.

Figure 8.10. Made-over starlets model what to wear to a job interview, *Queen*, July 26, 2010: semimockingly described as a "Japanese trade delegation PA" look.

Figure 8.11. Lan Xinmei (*right*), host of *Queen*, January 20, 2012.

Figure 8.12. Starlets of the "women's army" perform "ordinary" young femininity, *Queen*, September 29, 2010.

the unmarried woman and strongly downplays women's familial roles. This is done both through the show's regular topics of discussion—which very rarely focus on women's familial duties—and through the persona of the host, Lan Xinmei, who is famous for being an unconventional woman who has remained unmarried, glamorous, and youthfully beautiful right into her late forties. In our interviews with fifteen *Queen* viewers in Taipei in 2011 (aged twenty-two to twenty-three; twelve women, three men), interviewees concurred that the style of femininity shown in the program is that of the qingshounü (young-mature woman): a recently invented identity that is based on unmarried status, urban residence, white-collar work, and investment in the project of the self (Martin 2016b).

Whereas the most obvious generic relative for *Pretty Trendy* is the Euro-American reality makeover genre, *Queen*'s genealogy leads back, rather, to the Japanese-style variety show (see chapter 1). In Taiwan, there has emerged an array of locally produced variety-hybrid programs overtly targeting female viewers, part of a broader trend in Taiwan toward proliferating female-targeted infotainment TV (Martin 2016a).[9] Many of these programs, including *Queen*, are aired across prime-time and late-night slots, for working women, as well as in the traditional morning slots for "women's television."

As the first highly successful program in the variety/talk/beauty advice subgenre, *Queen* has inspired multiple copies both in Taiwan and abroad. Highlighting Taiwan's role as a central source of television formats for PR China, at the time of writing, no less than three copies of the program are screening on satellite entertainment channels on the Chinese mainland (Keane 2004b).[10] Meanwhile, Singapore's MediaCorp has produced two copies of the show to date—although a MediaCorp employee we interviewed admitted the difficulty of producing something as attractive to audiences as the Taiwanese original, which she attributed to Singaporeans' less fluent command of Mandarin, hence an inability to replicate the witty repartee (and our Singaporean interviewees concurred on the blandness of MediaCorp's copies of this and other Taiwanese variety shows).[11] The Taiwanese original is widely viewed across the region via both satellite channels and informal Internet downloads, via streaming sites like Sugoideas.com and mainland Chinese torrent sites like bt.hliang.com, which archive vast quantities of Taiwanese idol dramas and variety shows. *Queen* is particularly popular in Malaysia and Singapore, where the original is aired on the TVBS Asia cable channel, and Lan Xinmei visits these countries annually on promotional tours.[12] The show's popularity among diasporic Sinophone audiences is also evident in Australia, where dedicated shops selling *Queen*-endorsed beauty products can be found in both Sydney and Melbourne

Figure 8.13. A shop dedicated to selling products endorsed by *Queen* on Broadway, Sydney. Photo by Fran Martin.

(see figure 8.13). The styles of femininity we analyze in the following pages, then, must properly be seen as transnational. *Queen*'s promotion of particular beauty and fashion styles alongside its symbolic negotiation of emergent forms of feminine identity speak to women far beyond Taiwan, right across the Sinophone world.

Negotiating Class through Plural Address. One particular 2010 episode, spontaneously cited by several of the *Queen* viewers whom we interviewed in Taiwan, brings out clearly the complex negotiations around class that necessarily underlie a program like *Queen*, which seeks to capture a very broad target audience (defined by TVBS-G as women between twenty-five and forty-four years of age, regardless of class, income level, or occupation).[13] On September 29, 2010, *Queen* screened the first of a two-part special titled "The Ladies Are Here!" This episode had the women's corps panelists play the part of naïve young things eager to maximize their chances of "marrying into a grand household" (that is, marrying a wealthier man). In this they were offered

Figure 8.14. Sun Yunyun (*left*) and Sun Yingying (*right*) as templates of high-class "fashionable ladies" (*shishang mingyuan*), *Queen*, September 29, 2010.

as role models two special guests: wealthy socialite sisters Sun Yunyun and Sun Yingying, daughters of a major commercial family of mainland Chinese descent, who modeled classy fashion that was then translated by the regular stylists into a list of tips for "ordinary" girls (see figure 8.14). The kind of sleek, sexy, cosmopolitan taste the Sun sisters display is exhibited as a contrast to the girlish vulgarity of the starlets of the "women's corps." The tension between the upper-crust guests and the starlets as representative of "ordinary girls" is strongly played up: the setup requires individual members of the panel to perform an (incorrect) approximation of "high-class fashion," only to be corrected by the Sun sisters.

Yet interpreting this episode as a simple directive to emulate the Sun sisters' birthright of high-class habitus would be a mistake, for the setup often reveals itself as not wholly serious. When Lan Xinmei asks the panel at the beginning, "Who wants to become a lady?" the starlets clamor, "Me, me!" with strong Taiwanese accents and comically exaggerated fervor. Throughout, they perform naïve vulgarity and "getting it wrong" with a playfulness that makes being young, female, and vulgar look like a lot of fun—a kind of glamour in itself (see figure 8.12). Their collective girly chatter about shopping, collecting, and

A SELF TO BELIEVE IN / 245

wearing cute and trendy accessories, however poorly selected, evokes a localist girls' public culture that seems at least partly separated from "serious" worries about proper behavior and one's social status in the eyes of wider society.

Indeed, the doubleness of this episode's mode of address was part of its design, with a playful critique of the Sun sisters' taste and manner implied in a number of comic jibes made by Lan Xinmei and the women's corps. According to TVBS-G's own audience surveys, this double mode of address enabled part of the audience to side with the Sun sisters, and part with the cast's gentle criticism of the ideal that the Suns represent, thus maximizing audience appeal.[14] One of our interviewees—offended by Sun Yunyun's condescending fashion advice to Zi Gongmi, a starlet in the women's corps whom she admired—remarked: "Sun Yunyun told [the starlets] how they should dress in order to be fashionable. So it turned into, like, she was set up as the representative of 'fashion.' I think that notion is pretty weird. Oh, so what the famous ladies wear is called *fashion*. What are other people, then, chopped liver? [*Na qita ren suan shenme ne?*]" (Ms. Peng, twenty-four, tech product manager, Taipei). Such comments appear to demonstrate this episode's success in making readily accessible an oppositional reading of its framing of the Sun sisters as templates of ideal femininity.

Indeed, our interviews with viewers of *Queen* suggest that the collective-democratic sociality staged through its variety-genre form may constitute the program's attraction as much as—for some, even more than—its instructional content. For example: "I think it has a really upbeat atmosphere. They're always laughing out loud. [*Laughs*] And then sometimes it's a little coarse, as well. A little crude. I don't feel distanced from it. I feel it's more friendly, more similar to myself. The guests are always getting slagged off [*tucao*]. They straight-out take the piss, they'll say, 'God you look crap in that,' 'Old bag [*asang*], and stuff. I mean . . . it's just like between friends" (Ms. Ning, thirty-two, unemployed, Taipei outer suburb). "[*Queen*] fits into a certain category of program: the feeling is of a tangle of people messing around together [*yi qun ren gao cheng yi tuan*]. [*Laughs*] Those people—they're always there together like that, every day. . . . It's a very Taiwanese style of program. . . . What it wants to do is create a sense that it's close to the ordinary people, close to your everyday life" (Ms. Peng).

That a working-class woman like Ms. Ning can feel that the intentionally colloquial performances by Lan and the others make the program's participants feel "similar to myself" and "like a group of friends" (a concept that Ms. Ning emphasized throughout our discussion) surely indicates a triumph for the producers in their attempt to maintain broad appeal. The witty phrase that Ms. Peng invents to encapsulate this defining feature of *Queen* and the variety genre more broadly, translated literally, means something like "a group of people messing themselves up into a clump": it implies a cluster of people who entwine themselves into a friendly morass. What stands out is the "stickiness" that binds the presenters together, as well as the longevity of the entanglement that enables the viewer to become part of the tangle: "they're always there together like that, every day," and their entwinement is what one enjoys and, by virtue of their "ordinary" mode of address, remotely participates in (see Holden and Ergül 2006, 112).

Queen can thus be seen as fractured throughout by a certain tension: between the aspiration toward improvement contained in its *instructional content* (moral improvement, class betterment, taste education), and the spirited revelry in contemporary local girls' culture foregrounded in its comic-variety *generic form*. In comparison with both the American makeover television analyzed extensively by Brenda Weber and the mainland Chinese program *Pretty Trendy* analyzed in the first part of this chapter, *Queen* presents a much "softer" pedagogy: the "before-body" represented by the merry starlets is not wholly abject but seems to remain an inhabitable and possibly even attractive subject-position. Full surrender to the style experts is not so harshly demanded, and emphasis seems to be placed not so much on revealing and expressing a formerly "blocked" authentic interior self—"you, only better"—as on offering optional possibilities for small-scale adjustments to external appearance (Weber 2009, 1–35). In marked distinction to *Pretty Trendy*, *Queen* centers not on the deep, individualized self of psychological discourse but rather on the playful collectivity of feminine sociality.

Queen's overt polysemy and hybrid mode of address—accommodating both working-class and middle-class taste cultures, genre preferences, and formations of gendered habitus—thus significantly complicates attempts to interpret the class character of the style(s) of femininity it promotes. On one hand, it is undeniable that *Queen*, like *Pretty Trendy*, broadly idealizes a form of urban consumer femininity based on middle- to upper-class (*gaoji*) fashion style. On the other hand, however, the program also actively makes available opportunities for viewers to identify with more "ordinary" or "vulgar" (*diji*) formations of gendered habitus, and to criticize the elitism of the "classy" style that is ostensibly offered as a template for emulation. If we were to venture comparisons with Euro-American examples in related genres, we might say that while the earnest pedagogy of self-improvement in the service of self-confidence seen in *Pretty Trendy* adapts key elements of a program like *What Not to Wear* (Meng 2013), then the screen time given over to performances of likeable vulgarity in *Queen* perhaps shares a little more in common with shows like *Ladette to Lady* or *Australian Princess*. Especially in the pair of episodes analyzed above, the way in which the "classy" ideal offered for emulation is partially undercut by light mockery also suggests a certain resonance with those Anglophone formats.

The Young-Mature Woman and Lan Xinmei's Makeover of Middle Age. In the first part of this chapter, we argued that while China's *Pretty Trendy* is in many respects similar to Euro-American reality-makeover formats that naturalize an individualized, psychologized feminine self, it also pursues a parallel project of policing normative feminine life stages that are organized centrally around familial roles, especially wife and mother. How, then, does our Taiwanese example, *Queen*, relate to such a tension between individualized versus familial feminine identities? Elsewhere, Martin presents a detailed analysis of the model of femininity that the Taiwanese viewers we interviewed concur is projected by *Queen* (Martin 2016b). This is the figure of the qingshounü—literally, "young-mature woman"—a new identity invented by Taiwanese commercial and media culture over recent years. The urban, unmarried qingshounü's investment in the project of her self is indicatively expressed through her consumption of fashion and beauty products. A central character in the current wave of "pink" Taiwanese idol dramas as well as variety formats like *Queen*, the qingshounü "lives for herself," although in some representations, she is wracked with anxiety about her unmarried state. As noted above, this media imaginary responds to real macrosocial trends in Taiwan and elsewhere in the region—especially women's increasing education and labor force participation, declining marriage rates, and delays in first marriage—and a program like *Queen* could be seen as a response by commercial media to the public-cultural topicality of an emergent concept of "postfamilial" feminine gender identity.

It is perhaps tempting, then, to position the topicality of the qingshounü as a marker of the historical advance of women's individualization—an East Asian echo of Ulrich Beck and Elisabeth Beck-Gernsheim's individualized woman living a "life of her own" (2002). Alternatively, one might see the qingshounü identity as indicative of the global spread of a neoliberal discourse of the self-mastering, self-fulfilling feminine subject, a trend that is often critiqued in women's lifestyle genres on U.S. and UK television (Lewis 2008; Ouellette and Hay 2008; Sherman 2008; Weber 2009). However, the meanings of *Queen* as engaged by its viewers are more complex than these lines of analysis alone can suggest, for the *Queen* viewers we interviewed tended to assume that the self-making, individualized form of femininity emblematized by the qingshounü concept had a strongly *time-limited* character. If such an identity is available to women at all, it is available only in the "window of opportunity" between the end of schooling and marriage, after which point the structural constraints of the uneven division of domestic and caring labor mean that a woman's focus almost inevitably shifts away from the project of her self, and toward her family-care duties. As thirty-year old, upper-middle-class Ms. Guo mused when asked about who she thought would be the typical *Queen* viewer:

> When someone's identity roles increase, then the topics she's concerned about will also increase in number. For example, before you have kids, how would you ever consider which brand of booster seat you should buy? Or, before your parents have gotten old, how could you have considered which is preferable, an old people's home or a live-in Filipina nurse? . . . As your roles increase, the things you care about also increase, so your attention to this one particular sphere [of beauty and fashion] will become dissipated. . . . So of course, I think that young girls, because their identities are few, and their roles are few, . . . will be attracted by this kind of program.

Ms. Guo—herself a wife and expectant mother—makes very clear exactly what kind of duties are most likely increasingly to occupy a woman's mind as she moves from the qingshounü stage into her thirties: the examples she cites are those of child care and elderly care, two of the main familial carework responsibilities shouldered by Taiwanese wives.[15] Rather than fundamentally challenging adult women's familial identity, then, the qingshounü concept as our interviewees understood it rethinks the content of the premarital life stage, imagining it as a zone of increased economic, personal, and sexual autonomy, and *temporary* individualization. Thus, like the version of the self-entrepreneurial feminine subject that we analyzed above in China's *Pretty Trendy*, the Taiwanese qingshounü concept diverges from the vision conjured by theories of female individualization insofar as it, too, does not displace but cohabits with a parallel vision of women's identity as determined by familial roles.

Nonetheless, while our Taiwanese interviewees collectively thought that the qingshounü identity projected by *Queen* would *usually* be available only temporarily to (unmarried) women, the program itself centers on a remarkable exception to this rule in the figure of the host, Lan Xinmei. As we observed above, despite her age Lan embodies for some viewers some of the key markers of qingshounü identity. We now go further, to suggest that in important aspects of her star persona, Lan can be seen as modeling quite a radical revisioning of normative feminine life stages and familial identities.

Several interviewees were enthusiastic in their appreciation of the alternative gendered life course that Lan models. For example, Ms. Li painted a vivid picture of the kind of glamorous, urban life that she imagined Lan leading:

> Lan Xinmei, I really like her feel. She's very independent, and that has allowed her to accumulate a lot of capital, and make herself look beautiful. [*Laughs*] . . . I do envy her, a bit. . . . I think she's great. [*Laughs*] Just that she's made so much money, so she can live a happy life, and have tons of friends, and go drinking all the time. And then, yeah, she doesn't need to have a steady boyfriend. She doesn't need a steady husband, yeah! She just gets together with boyfriends when she feels like it. So I think she's great. [*Laughs*] (twenty-four, student, Taipei)

As this response indicates, Lan's persona is directly countertraditionalist—even radical—in aspects of its sex-gender ideology. The form of "postfamilial" femininity that Lan models in her glamorously unmarried state in middle age is certainly not a dominant one on Taiwanese television, where even popular idol dramas focusing on young urban career women usually underscore a familial context for their protagonists, and a majority of variety TV targeting women over thirty assumes the viewer's married-and-maternal status (Liu and Chen 2003; Lin 2011; Martin 2013). In modeling an individualized or nonfamilial (older) woman, Lan is therefore not rendered ordinary but held up as a remarkable exception.

The allure of Lan's alternative rendition of middle-aged femininity spreads beyond Taiwan: for our Singaporean interviewees, the type of gender identity that Lan embodies (daring, sexy, independent, fashion and beauty obsessed) was several times interpreted as a "typically Taiwanese" formation, marked off from more conservative, less "flashy" formations of Singaporean-Chinese femininity. Two fiftysomething Singaporean nonworking "aunties," Mrs. Y and Mrs. E, made a very positive assessment of Lan's persona, with explicit reference to her reconfiguration of the normative wife-and-mother role:

> MRS. Y: I like [Lan Xinmei], she's really pretty and you can't tell how old she is; you can't tell that she preserves her looks very skillfully.
> MRS. E: . . . I think she's about our age.
> MRS. Y: Yes, yes. And . . . she tried to have a child but failed. . . .
> MRS. E: Artificially, you mean?

MRS. Y: Yes, yes.

MRS. E: Oh, she's married, I didn't realize.

MRS. Y: She's not! . . . I know she tried [insemination] twice but failed. . . . You see? So, she's pretty impressive. . . . She's very classy. She's that really *modern* type, not the pure-woman type. . . . [The show] should be for all women. . . . I really hope it will continue.

The story of Lan's attempted artificial insemination that Mrs. Y cites so approvingly here is common knowledge among her fans—Lan discussed it openly on *Queen* at the time—and was also referred to frequently by our interviewees in Taiwan. Although Lan's attempts ultimately failed, nonetheless her intention to create a husbandless, fatherless family poses a significant symbolic challenge to the moral authority of the patrilineal, patriarchal ideal. This challenge was not lost on viewers: one interviewee in Taiwan recalled that her own vocal approval of Lan's attempted single motherhood sparked an argument with her own father, who insisted on the immorality of such a project.[16]

Lan also enacts reconfigurations of family and feminine familial identity in other ways as well. For example, she has publicly "adopted" a group of younger, unmarried media celebrities as her "children": the group lives together at Lan's house, and these adoptees—who include Wu Yilin (nicknamed Xiao Man), the regular hair stylist on *Queen*—relate to Lan socially as a mother figure.[17] Lan emphasizes in interviews that the quality she most values in her "children" is filial piety (*xiaoshun*) toward their own birth parents (Lan Xinmei, *Kangxi Laile*, October 17, 2012). The assemblage that Lan has created, then, is a form of remade family that cites elements of normative familialist discourses (the value of filial piety; a hierarchical relationship between parent and children) while radically reconfiguring the content and meaning of "family" itself (lack of a husband/father role; chosen rather than biological relationships). And as with Lan's artificial insemination project, her chosen family project also resonated strongly with some of *Queen*'s female viewers. In Taiwan, working-class Ms. Ning (thirty-two) spoke at length about her enjoyment at seeing the "real" love and care Lan shows for her group of experts—particularly the hairstylist (Lan's "daughter") Xiao Man, whose neck is disfigured by a burn scar, and who related on *Queen* the story of her physical abuse by a former boyfriend, eliciting Lan's tears and later, a special gift of a necklace given by Lan to Xiao Man. Here, the emotional resonance of mother-daughter love and care is transplanted onto the relationship between Lan and her chosen family, at once creating an intense identificatory response in the viewer, and symbolically rewriting the meaning of feminine familial identities.

Lan Xinmei's star persona provides a radically alternative model of middle-aged femininity, one that steps assertively outside normative social-sexual morality in its eschewal of marriage and its extension of self- and friendship-focused life attitudes well into middle age. The enthusiastic appreciation of these elements of Lan's persona by some of the young women we interviewed certainly suggests that such a powerful media imaginary plays a significant part in viewers' lives, reinforcing misgivings about women's subjection to familial-marital imperatives and offering symbolic resources for the reflexive imagination of alternative futures.

Conclusion

In this chapter, we have examined two quite different examples of women's lifestyle advice and makeover television from two different locations within the Sinophone mediasphere. Both China's *Pretty Trendy* and Taiwan's *Queen* pursue a broadly similar project of localizing transnational genres to teach viewers about how to embody urban, middle-class consumer femininity; both promulgate a popular discourse about women's "self-belief" or "confidence" as gained through fashion and beauty consumption. Nonetheless, there are significant differences between the examples that are worth recapping as we conclude this chapter.

In terms of genre and style, CCTV-2's *Pretty Trendy* draws most clearly from Euro-American reality-makeover formats, while TVBS-G's *Queen* draws instead from the Japanese-style comic-variety genre. As we have tried to show, these generic affiliations have very significant implications for the pedagogy and tone of each program. *Pretty Trendy*'s tone is quite strongly authoritarian, revealing an intriguing convergence between U.S.-style TV makeover projects and the aims and style of the Chinese Communist Party's central broadcaster. *Queen*'s pedagogy is "softer," diluted by a relatively democratized mode of address arising both from the program's variety-talk genre and TVBS-G's wish to speak effectively to a wide range of viewers with varying spending power, tastes, and class habitus. Also related to generic form, *Pretty Trendy* promotes a psychologized model of the individual feminine self, whereas *Queen* foregrounds the pleasures of feminine sociality; *Pretty Trendy* centers on "real, ordinary" women (to be corrected) whereas *Queen* focuses on both female celebrities (to be emulated) and glamorized versions of "ordinary girls" (as anchors for viewer identification). While both programs idealize urban, middle-class consumer femininity, *Queen*, unlike *Pretty Trendy*, incorporates clear cues for the viewer to critique the ideal it represents. Whereas through its selection of topics and contestants, *Pretty Trendy* addresses a wide range of women vis-à-vis marital and maternal status, from student-aged single girls to married middle-aged women with children, in its topics and the personae of its host and many of its presenters, *Queen* focuses more specifically on unmarried women. But both programs manage to incorporate *both* the idea of female individualization as a social and personal good *and* the assumption that women's identity is—and/or should be—centrally defined by familial role. However, we have argued that especially in the star persona of its unconventional host, Lan Xinmei, *Queen* tends simultaneously to challenge the normativity of women's identity as defined by family-related life stages, whereas *Pretty Trendy* straightforwardly polices and enforces those norms. Overall, then, notwithstanding the broad similarities in their pedagogical projects, a comic variety-talk show like *Queen* reveals itself as a far more polysemic, "open" text than an earnest reality-makeover format like *Pretty Trendy*.

It is worth underlining in closing that the styles represented by each of these programs constitute important trends across the wider Sinophone mediasphere. In particular, we must keep in mind that *Queen*-style copies are now proliferating not only in Southeast Asia but also on mainland Chinese commercial entertainment channels (see chapter 5), so that mainland audiences have access to both of the styles of programming we have analyzed in this chapter. The two case studies discussed in this chapter have been chosen not as representative of the whole of women's lifestyle advice television in each place—which is in any case far too diverse and internally contradictory to afford selection of one representative example per country—but rather because we see each program as indicative of emergent cultural patterns. China's *Pretty Trendy* speaks to the state's ongoing project of remaking subjectivity and citizenship through the exaltation of consumption, middle-class urban identity, naturalized gender roles, and a psychologized, individualized, and "responsibilized" model of the subject. Although the majority of "women's television" in Taiwan—especially dramas and talk shows—continue to naturalize women's marital and familial identities, *Queen*'s high popularity, both within and beyond Taiwan, indicates that its challenges to the tenacious cultural link between women and family have touched a nerve across today's Sinophone world. Given all this, our analysis of the central structures, assumptions, and preoccupations of these programs has offered insight into emergent formulations of gender culture that we can expect will continue to be influential far beyond the lifetimes of the programs themselves.

CONCLUSION. Negotiating Modernities through
Lifestyle Television

In this book, we have traversed a wide and varied televisual territory, from downhome, Bhojpuri-language life advice TV in India to glossy, high-end English-language lifestyle programming in Taiwan, and from globally recognizable formats such as Indian and Chinese reality dating shows (*Dare2Date*, *If You Are the One*) to more culturally specific examples like Taiwan's Da Ai channel, whose shows offer Buddhist-inflected principles for leading a good life. We have also drawn on a wide range of approaches to analyzing television, from textual and discourse analysis to audience-based qualitative approaches and political economy. While the methods and sites we have chosen and the programming we have examined are diverse, throughout, we have been centrally concerned with developing what Nick Couldry has described as "socially oriented media theory" (Couldry 2012, 8). In particular, we have sought to demonstrate how lifestyle advice television in South and East Asia speaks to the question of how to live optimally under late modern conditions; that is, the way this type of programming both reflects and intervenes in the public imagination of how to *manage modernities* at the level of everyday life, often in the context of intensified and compressed social, cultural, political, and economic change (Chang 2010).

As we have seen, such engagements are enacted in quite different ways in different sites, with lifestyle advice offered on a wide range of programming (from reality programming to variety shows), which in turn are often shaped by distinct local-regional televisual cultures and modes of address. Where Chinese regional TV offers rather straitlaced pedagogical fare on how to become a self-managing citizen, more globalized Chinese formats aimed at young cosmopolitan urbanites, such as *If You Are the One*, offer a rather more playfully theatrical take on the risks of late modernity and individualization, where the "search for love" is turned into a calculative and commodified spectacle. In Taiwan, where, for reasons connected with local media and political histories, audiences have little interest in blatantly educational television, the question of how to cope with the pressures of late modern existence is often explored through entertainment-oriented variety genres. One example of this is the beauty and fashion format of *Queen*, where the complexities of gendered individualization are enacted through highly reflexive, quasi-ironic forms of identity performance and play. While Indian general entertainment channels feature an abundance of lifestyle experts and gurus offering a wide range of advice, from spiritual to financial, glossy Western-style lifestyle programs tend to be found on dedicated lifestyle channels oriented to a fairly niche audience. As we've shown, a key mainstream site in which questions of lifestyle and cultural modernity are also negotiated on Indian television is on reality shows.

Generic diversity aside, what all these modes of programming arguably share is an increasingly reflexive and *ethicalized* sense of everyday existence where, as Nikolas Rose puts it, the focus on understanding one's life as a style or ethic involves "the obligation to *shape a life*" through a series of "choices" (Rose 1989, 261, emphasis added). Identity as a social project is central to such processes. We have tried to demonstrate how in each site, despite their very distinct television industries and formations of cultural modernity, lifestyle advice television constitutes an important reflection of and agent for subjectification, mediating between emergent and residual social norms and, in particular, playing a crucial role in inciting capacities for self-government through discourses and practices of self-improvement (Zhang and Ong 2008, 16). Lifestyle programming thus offers blueprints for being and living for the increasingly self-reflexive subjects of consumer modernity. Taken as a whole, the diverse array of programs, formats, and genres we have considered, in the rich contexts of their production and consumption, can be seen to function as mechanisms for symbolically processing the emergent forms of risk and opportunity, precarity and promise that characterize the unfolding of late modern social life across East and South Asia. Our various site-specific studies have illustrated the copresence—and indeed the increasing, sometimes paradoxical convergence—of commercial with governmental logics, of regulatory regimes with free-market structures, and of consumption-based selfhood with civic forms of identity. Lifestyle advice television emerges from this study as a platform on which the societies under discussion explore some of the sharpest contradictions of emergent late modernities in Asia and, to a certain extent, also globally: mobility versus stasis, collective association versus individual aspiration, authoritarian rule versus democratic participation, "freedom" versus duty.

Reflections on Methodological Cosmopolitanism

As we discussed in detail in our introductory chapter, a key aspiration in the research project on which this book is based was to advance the project of "provincializing" Western-centric television studies by relativizing the Euro-American cultural and theoretical norms that have historically shaped this field (Chakrabarty 2007). Our sustained attention to contemporary TV cultures in our Asian focus sites, then, underlines our engagement with a wider intellectual strategy that Ulrich Beck and Edgar Grande have called *methodological cosmopolitanism*: "an approach which takes the varieties of modernity and their global interdependencies as a starting point for theoretical reflection and empirical research" (Beck and Grande 2010, 412). Following such an approach, one of this book's central endeavors has been to balance our understanding of the enduring nationalness (and often, localness) of television in our focus sites (Turner 2009b; Flew and Waisbord 2015) with close attention to the effects of transnational structures and processes. These include, at the level of ideology, globally extensive appeals to individualization, self-responsibilization, and consumer-citizenship; and, at the level of form, lifestyle television itself as a series of localized formats and genres marked by links, of varying strengths, to transnational media trends.

We have been interested in part in exploring the extent to which examples of life advice television in Asia can be linked to certain common experiences shared across (late) modern states operating within a global capitalist economy. At the same time, our in-depth research on media sites marked by very different speeds and experiences of modernity has also prompted us to ask how these multiple experiences and social ontologies might speak back to and transform conventional understandings of the mediated relations between politics, social identities, and citizenship. By definition, methodological cosmopolitanism "not only includes the other's experiences of and perspectives on modernization but corrects and redefines the self-understanding of European modernity" (Beck and Grande 2010, 424). In the realm of media studies, then, such an approach must move beyond geocultural exceptionalism to underline the necessity of rethinking our broader understanding of how media work in the world today in light of non-Euro-American exemplars.

Below, we synthesize some of the key findings arising from our case studies in order to make explicit how these exemplify patterns that are distinct from Western European and North American examples. As we hope will be clear, the point of this is not to support some argument for the absolute "otherness" of East and South Asian TV cultures: if nothing else, our discussions in the preceding chapters have surely demonstrated that television today is far too transnationally networked and transculturally interconnected to shore up such an essentialist fantasy. Rather, the purpose of drawing attention to the points at which our examples diverge from the Euro-American ones that have to date largely been taken as normative in the field is to underline the contingency and context dependence of *all* examples, and thereby to "correct and redefine the self understanding" of lifestyle television studies itself (Beck and Grande 2010, 424). Given, as Beck and Grande note, the "global interdependencies" of modernities, and in light of China and India now becoming major players in transnational television (and broader entertainment) industries, we want now to reflect on a set of broad questions including: What is specific about the kinds of mediated civic spaces emerging in Asian postcolonial, postdevelopmental, and postsocialist nations grappling with the potentials and challenges of commercial global media? How does the evolution of lifestyle TV in these sites speak to changing relationships between popular media, audiences, and social, moral, and political engagement in the world today? And how might the experiences of these states impact on our thinking about media modernities more broadly?

Provincializing Neoliberalism

First, as we discussed in our introductory chapter, in the Euro-American scholarship, lifestyle television's entreaties to take individual responsibility for one's own physical and mental well-being, to emulate middle-class habitus, and to reconceptualize citizenship in terms of consumption—its oft-discussed "neoliberal" cultural characteristics—have all been widely understood, to date, as normatively linked with the existence of a certain type of state: an advanced capitalist democracy in the process of transformation from a welfare state model to a neoliberal mode of economic, civic, and social governance. The existence of this type of state forms the presumptive background to the concepts of "second modernity" and "post-traditional society" (Giddens 1991; Beck 1992) and the "risk culture" that attends these, precipitating the new cultural dominance of reflexive life-planning, reflexive identity, and the self-governing citizen (Rose 1989, 1996; Beck 1992). However, the examples analyzed in the foregoing chapters have demonstrated that media entreaties to enact and identify with self-responsibilization, consumer-citizenship, and middle-class habitus—including the idealization of mobile, cosmopolitan selfhood—are in fact not contingent upon the existence of this type of state but are also seen in lifestyle advice television produced in the postdevelopmental capitalist democracies of both Taiwan and India, and also in China, a socialist transition society governed by an authoritarian state (Harvey 2005; Ong 2007; Beck and Grande 2010; Y. Yan 2010; Dirlik 2012).

In citing the term *neoliberal* to refer to media idealizations of self-responsibilization, consumer-citizenship, and middle-class habitus, we emphasize that we are aware of the limitations of "neoliberalism" as a term that has become a kind of catchall to refer to any and all of the workings of late capitalism, and that can have a highly normative edge, often glossing over the complexity, plurality, and context-dependence of relations between abstract state systems, social collectives, and individuals. Our emphasis on *provincializing* the term, then, encodes a double significance. It refers both to our concern with *locating*, and thereby limiting the universalizing claims of "neoliberalism" as a supposedly global political rationality, and to our desire to emphasize the deeply socially embedded and differentiated character of subject formation on the ground.

In India, as we have noted, there is considerable debate over the relevance and utility of viewing the country's complex postsocialist society through a purely marketized or neoliberal lens, given the enduring legacy of the Nehruvian state, the coexistence of various competing and contrastive economic structures and logics (neoliberal, public sector, subsistence agriculture), and, in certain domains, the proliferation rather than decline of state welfare interventions over the past decade (Münster and Strümpell 2014). Nevertheless, the country has undergone dramatic changes since opening up to global markets in the early 1990s, with media highly privatized and (to a large extent) deregulated and shaped by a complex mix of global, regional, and local flows. The degree to which this has been accompanied by a widespread "neoliberal" *social* revolution at a grassroots level is, however, more debatable. Through our engagement with programming and audiences across a range of sites in rural and urban India, and in poor as well as more solidly middle-class urban neighborhoods, it has become clear that social experience and identity are highly stratified and continue to be shaped by a variety of cultural logics. While young English-speaking urbanites may embrace elements of the globalized enterprise culture and self-development ethos enacted on high-end glossy lifestyle shows, for many of the non-English-speaking viewers we interviewed, their everyday experiences and sense of selfhood continue also to be strongly shaped by complex intersections of caste, ethnicity, gender, and class, as well as place-specific state, political, and economic factors (such as the Tamil identity politics played out on Sun TV's game shows). Here our findings are similar to those of Steve Derné (2008), whose fieldwork in provincial India in the 1990s and 2000s indicates that economic liberalization and the widespread circulation of transnational, cosmopolitan culture and media in India over the past two decades has not necessarily transformed the lives and social practices of the majority of Indians.

In China, as we have seen, the pop-factual televisual field is defined by a tension and constant negotiation between the top-down directives of the state, which uses television as a means of shaping the culture of the populace; and commercial forces, which use popular entertainment as a means of profit-making through advertising. The formation of a strong and stable middle class—including people's subjective identification with middle-class identity, which is encouraged through the state discourse on *suzhi* (human quality), reflected in many of the Chinese programs we have discussed—is seen by the leadership as a useful means of buttressing social stability during the turbulent process of economic and cultural "marketization." Televisual entreaties to self-responsibilization make as much sense for a postsocialist state like China as for Western European and Australasian post–welfare states: in both cases, the withdrawal of the central government from the care of the citizenry in key arenas like health and education leaves a gap to be filled by popular media. In local-level television in provincial China, however, as we have seen, television often works in conjunction with rather than replacing the state, so that socialist structural legacies and neoliberal logics are complexly intertwined. Even in China's metropolitan and provincial-level commercial entertainment television channels, where we might expect the imprint of the state to be weaker, the nation's strong, central media regulation means that this is not necessarily the case. Here, too, lifestyle television effects cultural translations of what are essentially state projects of population governance rather more directly than is the case in Western post–welfare states. This results from the fact that under the guidelines of the State Administration of Press, Publication, Radio, Film and Television (SAPPRFT), if a program can be officially classified as "educational," then it escapes certain direct restrictions imposed by the state on "entertainment"-category TV. Hence, China's commercial entertainment channels use "educational" lifestyle advice formats somewhat strategically, as a way of producing high-rating (semi)entertainment content that nonetheless keeps the censors happy by effectively furthering the state's agenda of moral education.

As Li Zhang and Aihwa Ong have argued, while the Chinese state has clearly rejected many key structures and practices of neoliberal economics, nevertheless many of the *cultural* strategies introduced along with privatization in the reforms era seem strongly congruent with neoliberal thinking, leading to a "cross between privatization and socialist rule [that] is not a 'deviant' form but a particular articulation of neoliberalism" (Zhang and Ong 2008, 2; see also Harvey 2005; Dirlik 2012). Chinese lifestyle television's entreaties to its viewers to take individual responsibility for their own well-being, to embody indicatively middle-class tastes and norms not just superficially but as a core project of moral personhood, and to understand citizenship in terms of consumption exemplify the Chinese articulation of neoliberal thinking in the media realm. As we discuss below, in the forms of public pedagogy they exemplify, they also contain significant echoes of China's past, encoding certain moral and ideological legacies of socialism. Such examples of neoliberal-style media culture from the Chinese postsocialist state demonstrate that the link between these particular representational strategies and the capitalist, democratic ex–welfare state is not of absolute or definitional importance; in doing so, they help us to provincialize the European articulation of neoliberalism that has often been taken as normative.

The State-Television Apparatus

Second and relatedly, our examples have shown that lifestyle television may be used by states rather *directly*, in population governance projects, rather than acting as a *replacement* for state management of citizens' lives. If in Euro-American social theory, neoliberalism in the cultural domain equates to the "responsibilization," "consumerization," and intensified individualization of the citizenry as the state withdraws from welfare and social life more broadly, then in China, this is only partly replicated. On the one hand, the postsocialist state *has* withdrawn from welfare provision in ways analogous to the European post–welfare state. But as Lisa Rofel (2007), Børge Bakken (2000) and others have argued, in China the neoliberal project *is itself a state-directed one*, centrally planned and executed through state media and media regulation through SAPPRFT. Recall, for example, our discussion of examples from China's central state broadcaster, CCTV, in chapter 8. In CCTV-2's reality-makeover show

Pretty Trendy, we saw highly moralistic, psychologizing, and shaming demands made on contestants by expert mentors to "believe in themselves" and to "remake" themselves for success in career and marriage markets along the lines of the enterprise self. In tone, content, and style, this example revealed remarkable resonances with certain forms of North American personal makeover television. And yet, far from representing the withering-away of the state's regulatory function, to be replaced by purely commercial forces, this CCTV-2 program speaks as the "throat and tongue" of the Chinese party-state itself. In this case, lifestyle TV's neoliberal-style entreaties work as a cultural implementation of the state's governmental imperatives rather than as a commercial replacement for the state's regulation of citizens' lives. Such an observation contributes to the important project in China studies, identified by Ralph Litzinger, of complicating "simplistic views of neoliberalism as the unfettered exercise of market logics, *outside of the state*" (2008, 233, emphasis added).

This example, as with the China examples more generally, also reveals the extent to which contemporary forms of media and culture continue to operate, here, in the shadow of a previous era. Despite the radical transformation of Chinese social life over the past three decades along with economic reform, in China's "exemplary society" (Bakken 2000) we detect a certain continuity between the function of contemporary TV experts and socialist-era forms of state pedagogy based on the public, state-led modeling of exemplary conduct, for example in the old "model worker" and "model citizen" campaigns. We see here, then, not a radical, epochal transformation but an uneven, partial, and gradual process where the cultural forms of the present overlap in sometimes unexpected ways with those of earlier modern eras. Clearly this mode of media governance is very different from the kind of fully devolved governmentality enacted on U.S. reality television, as analyzed by James Hay and Laurie Ouellette in their 2008 book, *Better Living through Reality TV: Television and Post-Welfare Citizenship*. By contrast, the media-state apparatus that underlies the production of Chinese lifestyle television today continues to carry within it important aspects of the logics of centralized statehood and socialist population management.

Complicating Individualization: Gender, Family, Religion

Third, our examples have shown how popular television reveals distinct varieties and degrees of individualization, especially in relation to gendered freedoms versus duties. Across examples from China, India, and Taiwan, chapters

7 and 8 demonstrate the way in which appeals to individual romantic and sexual freedom are shaped by the continuing power of calls to family duty, particularly for women.

In India, the prevalence of *saas bahu* (mother-in-law/daughter-in-law) soaps on television marks the persistence within much of mainstream media of normative associations between women and familial roles, while ongoing taboos around representations of female nudity reflect a continuing emphasis on femininity as a highly policed moral site. At the same time, Indian reality and lifestyle shows dealing with love, marriage, and dating, aimed at young aspiring middle-class urbanites, *are* increasingly confronting the major social and cultural upheavals associated with shifts to individualization, with shows like *Dare2Date*, discussed in chapter 7, playfully attempting to negotiate the tension between the ongoing hegemony of "traditional," ascribed modes of identity associated with class, caste, ethnicity, and gender and a "posttraditional" self associated with consumption-based individualization. As Henrikke Donner's work on middle-class Indian women and media representations of the family likewise suggests, while gendered identities are to some extent being remade in "the contexts of globalisation, post-liberalisation and neo-liberal ideologies" in India, this is occurring in ambiguous and paradoxical ways (Donner 2008). Thus, while she notes the "increased significance of privacy, conjugality and individualism among urbanites," she also points out, for instance, that "patrilocal residence, arranged marriages and lifelong unions still constitute normative discourses, and are often reinvigorated" in middle-class urban life, as well as in and through Indian media depictions of family and relationships (Donner 2008, 181–82).

Likewise, an underlying presumption of the moral rightness of familial roles and duties for women is pervasive—albeit also strongly contested in certain examples—in Taiwanese lifestyle television. As we have seen, in contrast to that of China, Taiwan's television industry is structured almost entirely by commercial forces, which leads to a much "lighter" tone and approach, with far less China-style earnest didacticism (if we see it at all, it features on the religious programming discussed in chapter 6: arguably, modern religions, not the state, provide the loudest moral voice on Taiwanese television). Illustrating the distinctive path to female individualization in the advanced capitalist society of this East Asian ex–tiger economy, in the Taiwanese example in chapter 8, we showed how the idealized popular media imaginary of the qingshounü or "young-mature" (unmarried) woman does not represent a straightforward exemplification of the European theory of female individualization as living "a life of one's own" (Beck and Beck-Gernsheim 2002).

Rather, it bespeaks the cultural prominence of *temporary* individualization and *imagined* individualization (see also Martin 2016b). As also with our discussion of the televisual mediation of tensions between brides' and wives' desires for greater personal autonomy and their continuing subjection to familial roles and duties in Chinese and Indian dating and relationship advice shows (chapter 7), this reveals a form of partial female individualization that is fundamentally conditioned by the continuing power of locally specific ideologies and familial practices.

In the case of China, this resonates interestingly with Yunxiang Yan's observation of the paradox that "the individualization process in China does give the individual more mobility, choice and freedom, but it does so with little institutional protection and support from the state. To seek a new safety net, or to re-embed, the Chinese individual is forced to fall back on the family and personal network or *guanxi*, the same point where disembedment begins" (Y. Yan 2009, 288). Yan's broader point about the relative lack of institutional protection for individuals in postsocialist China is underscored in many of our Chinese examples, which illustrate that not only the family and guanxi networks but also popular media play a role in proffering "safety nets"—practical advice, information, and general life guidance—to help individuals manage emergent forms of social risk. Indeed, we have tried to show how both the re-embedment and dis-embedment processes are impossible and incomplete without the working of media production and consumption. In other words, media practices in production and consumption are not external to or crudely "reflective" of these processes; rather, they constitute integral aspects of these processes per se.

But the examples discussed above also underline the fact that with regard to the Chinese path to individualization, the option of "falling back on the family," in Yan's phrase, has a sharply *gendered* dimension, insofar as historically embedded family structures and practices tend to be patriarchal in organization. As our discussion in chapter 8 illustrates, China's transition from the socialist system to market capitalism has entailed increased gendered risks for women, as they face sexist employment practices that include the state's encouragement of working women to return to family-care work and family-focused identities in times of rising unemployment. As we have seen, in this context, lifestyle advice television plays an active role in buttressing the idea that an urban working woman's self-presentation and identity should be based primarily on her familial roles ("dressing like a mother" at work, for example). All of this not only underlines a broad point about the sociocultural specificity of individualization processes beyond Euro-America but also, more particularly, it highlights the *gendered* specificities of partial, temporary, and imagined individualization in these contexts.

Relatedly, in chapter 6 we observed the hybridization of individualist with markedly collectivist elements in the forms of late modern religion instantiated in TV examples from India and Taiwan. The mass spectacle of Baba Ramdev's nation-building yoga camps, the overt emphasis in both Indian and Taiwanese examples on the dissolution of individual desire in the service of collective engagement, and, in the case of Taiwan's Tzu Chi movement and its TV channel Da Ai, a relation with Buddha that is mediated by Cheng Yen as spiritual leader place these instances at a significant distance from the highly individualized forms of spirituality on which Beck has focused in his theorization of late modern religion as the search for "a god of one's own" (Beck 2010). However, once again what is interesting here is the way in which these elements of cultural specificity often cohabitate with other elements that are more familiar in Euro-American examples: these include the increasing commercialization, mediatization, and modern bureaucratic administration of religion; and appeals to modern-style abstract rational-ethical principles rather than (or as well as) supernatural forces and entities and magical ritual. Discourses of spiritual individualization and self-development, then, are often linked with apparently dissonant cultural logics of collectivism and subservience to religious hierarchy, underlining the ways in which India's and Taiwan's media modernities embody distinctive dialectics of enchantment and enterprise.

The Middle Classes in South and East Asia

Fourth, another key limit point that our analyses reveal in relation to normative Euro-American conceptions of lifestyled, late modern selfhood is the issue of class. Much of the extant Western research on lifestyle and reality TV posits that the so-called individualized, posttraditional "lifestyled" self is inherently a classed subject, often exemplifying a normative, bourgeois model of identity (Bonner 2003; Palmer 2004, 2008; Lewis 2008; Skeggs 2005; Powell and Prasad 2010). While the rise of media and technology in both South and East Asia is often assumed to be associated with a "middle-class revolution" (Robison and Goodman 1996), who is it that constitutes this new middle class? As we have discussed in the preceding chapters, there are significant limits to the material and economic support for claims of a region-wide middle-class revolution, especially given the growing social and economic inequalities in many parts of the region. Further, claims to a "new" middle class raise questions about how members of this social group might be positioned in relation to earlier social and political formations and power structures. What does it mean to speak of social class in postsocialist China versus late capitalist Taiwan, or in an India still shaped by colonial, cultural, and caste-based hierarchies? How well does European social theory's association between a rising middle class and democratic, secularizing, and liberalizing impulses translate into contexts shaped by such different historical, cultural, and political formations?

As we have seen, while there are certain shared characteristics and experiences across our South and East Asian sites, class—in particular, what we have been terming here as "middle-class" identity—is often articulated through lifestyle media in quite distinct ways, highlighting how classed social identity is "placed" in different ways in different contexts, both as a material and economic reality and as a discursive construct. Furthermore, this process of emplacement often involves complex negotiations between global cosmopolitan, national, and more "ordinary," localized conceptions of class. In India, a recurrent theme, voiced by TV producers and audiences alike, is that lifestyle media, while providing a highly diverse populace with glimpses into the worlds of others, foregrounds extremes of social distinction and hierarchy inflected by caste, gender, cultural, and geographic differences. Poorer interviewees often complained of the large disparities between the material realities of their own lives (as well as their cultural backgrounds and belief systems) and the highly aspirational, globalized lifestyles and modes of consumption depicted on shows like *Bigg Boss* and *MasterChef India*. While the emergence of newly rich, consumer "middle classes" across South and East Asia is a key tenet of triumphalist neoliberal discourse, those who self-identified as middle class in our Indian study, from chauffeurs and media producers to government employees, often lived extremely modestly compared with Western middle-class households. Although these viewers may enjoy watching consumer advice, travel, and food shows depicting high-end cuisine, they rarely traveled (except to visit the family village and to undertake the odd religious pilgrimage), often lived in very small dwellings with basic furnishings and a single television set, and were for the most part unable to afford to eat out regularly at restaurants. As noted in our introduction, while much has been made of the rise of the new middle classes in postliberalization India, as in China, there is evidence of growing disparities between rich and poor, while, using income-based definitions, the "actual" middle class, economically speaking, remains a very small segment of the population.

Nevertheless, as we have seen, the *imaginary* of "middle classness" does function as a key aspirational concept in Indian public culture, one that is intimately bound to the nation-state's conception of itself as a liberalizing global power. As Leela Fernandes notes, although "the emerging liberalizing or 'new' middle class is not identical with a generalized sociological description of the middle class" (2006, xviii), nevertheless, idealized depictions of middle-class taste and habitus function as symbolically important sites of social aspiration, particularly for those lower middle classes in small towns and rural areas who seek the cultural capital to enter into middle-class culture. However, while most of the households, including the poorer families in our study, identified as "middle class," their social identities, values, and belief systems were clearly shaped by a range of influences including nonsecular and distinctive culturally embedded logics. As our examination of a wide range of lifestyle media has indicated, the middle class as a social category in India does not necessarily align in any straightforward way with European-style secular, liberal democratic conceptions of modern middle-class identity. Its classed social ontologies are highly distinct, coarticulated as they are with gender, caste, culture, and religion as well as with older middle-class formations, reflecting the ongoing legacy of the colonial and socialist state.

Although in China the notion of the "middle class" is an elusive, contested, and vaguely defined concept (Chen and Goodman 2013a), in practice, it describes a social group comprising urban-dwelling people with higher income, higher education, and higher occupational prestige than the largely rural wider population (Li 2013). But since this group is too proportionally small to represent a real shift to middle-class culture, some argue that such a class exists more in discourse than in actual social structure (Lin 2015). However, as we touched on above, despite the obvious ambiguity surrounding the term, one thing is certain: the middle class in China is considered by the state to be simultaneously a destabilizing and a stabilizing force, with the former concern reflected in the state's anxiety over culturally liberal shows like *If You Are the One*. On the one hand, the leadership worries about a possible association between a strong middle class and the development of civil society, and the concomitant identification with Western-style liberal democratic values (as seen in the Tian'anmen democracy movement, led by urban intellectuals). For this reason, the middle classes represent a potentially oppositional force to the Chinese state. On the other hand, post-Tian'anmen, as beneficiaries of state-authorized uneven development, the middle classes rely on the state to protect their economic interests and privileged social positions. Although it displays exemplary cosmopolitan aspirationalism and yearnings for globally inflected cultural capital, as played out through certain forms of lifestyle media, such tendencies are not necessarily accompanied by a critical political stance. On the contrary, this class demonstrates a propensity for political apathy, conservatism, and a willingness to play along with the state in its management of unequal class relations. Especially following the 1989 political crackdown and the accelerated economic liberalization instituted in its wake, the middle class's democratizing potential has been effectively diffused by that class's economic reliance on the state's stability. Middle-class identity in China today, then, is framed by a complex double entanglement in culturally and economically liberalizing and politically illiberal logics.

As our discussions of Indian and Chinese lifestyle TV in this book have shown, the varied roles of religion, authoritarian statehood, locally specific family structures, and caste logics in shaping distinctive class dynamics in these developing economies present major challenges to classic European social theory's assumption that the rise of the middle class is intrinsically linked with secularizing and liberalizing impulses and the emergence of a coherent and deliberative, proto-democratic public sphere.

Placing Media Modernities

Fifth, and last, our work on lifestyle television in these three Asian sites has foregrounded questions concerning the relations between place, media geographies, and social identity. Implicit in the concept of methodological cosmopolitanism is a certain set of relations to space and place: Beck and Grande's (2010) understanding of cosmopolitanism as marking a dialogic tension between the self and a "global other" implies a universal connectedness but also a place from which one connects with others, a locatedness. A central concern of our book, and a key framing device for chapters 3 through 5, has been with the cultural politics of space, place, and location in relation to lifestyle television's framing of imaginaries of self and other, emplacement and mobility. Our focus has been to think about locatedness in terms of specific media geographies, in particular the *placed* nature (and place-*producing* elements) of television, but also sociocultural geographies; that is, questions of identity and social and cultural location, and of geolocated social status and "differential power" (Knauft 2002, 33).

Our research presented in this book demonstrates how the rise of consumer middle classes and the associated transformations in culturally available conceptualizations of lifestyle and selfhood have profoundly shaped the aspirational horizons and life imaginaries of television viewers from Taipei to Bangalore to Shanghai. At the same time, our analyses of sites of TV production and consumption have highlighted growing social and geographic inequities in China and India in particular. Here, our in-depth audience studies suggest that television not only extends people's horizons of experience but also foregrounds tensions vis-à-vis state-market-citizen relations, underlining growing inequities in these postsocialist, postdevelopmentalist, and postcolonial contexts. Such inequities are seen, for example, in nonmetropolitan China, where television has become a key site of access to advice, information, and support for those unable to afford increasingly privatized modes of service provision. A central contradiction of lifestyle TV as a vehicle of consumer modernity, then, is that while it promotes aspirations that are often out of the reach of ordinary citizens, thus foregrounding growing divisions between the new rich and increasingly marginalized "others," at the same time, in some settings, it also assumes a kind of (privatized or semiprivatized) public service role, buttressing state structures to shape viewers as dutiful self-managing citizens.

While China and India clearly have distinct developmental histories of modernity and statehood, they share contemporary social formations marked by major tensions and divisions between groups, with different sectors of the population having highly uneven access to the benefits of consumer citizenship. As our examination of television as a cultural technology in China indicates, lifestyle television is part of a highly stratified and uneven cultural economy of place-making, where "tier-one" cities are economically and culturally privileged over their regional counterparts. As we have seen, this process of privilege extends into the workings of social aspiration, which is strongly articulated to place and social identity. For instance, while producers at Shanghai TV see their viewers as having a Shanghainese sensibility of sorts, they are also addressed as cosmopolitan consumers possessing a multiscaled cultural imaginary: simultaneously local, national, regional, and global (indeed, paradoxically, one of the markers of *local* Shanghainese identity is precisely the imputed ability to be at home with cosmopolitanism). By contrast, provincial audiences, particularly elderly viewers, are constructed primarily as *citizens* rather than consumers, whose imaginative horizons are shaped by highly localized content, even as technological and regulatory developments grant them potential access to the more cosmopolitan visions of metropolitan channels.

The central relevance of geographic scale in understanding the television industry in China today is linked with the nation's long, embedded history of scalar social and political organization. China is known to have the world's oldest and most enduring system of territorial-scale hierarchy (Oakes and Schein 2006). In the socialist era, the state was the major, if not the only, force in the process of fixing, maintaining, or changing this hierarchy, but in recent decades, this process has become subject to other forms of power in addition to the state. In the era of economic reforms, China's lifestyle television, produced by local, provincial, and national stations, mirrors and reinforces this scalar hierarchy, on the one hand, while also displacing and transgressing it, on the other. Television content producers plan, produce, and distribute content based on not where the city is located but which tier category the city falls into, be it tier-one metropolitan cities like Beijing and Shanghai, or tier-two, provincial capital cities like Hefei and Nanjing, or tier-three cities like Bengbu and Kaifeng. In a competitive media environment, the economic viability of a television channel is determined by the extent to which it makes scale-appropriate decisions in terms of its audience's taste, lifestyle, consumption power, and consumption habits. At the same time, however, television executives also know that it is precisely the creative impulse to challenge the existing scale hierarchy and extend people's spatial imaginary that gives one channel the competitive edge over another. It is in the process of negotiating this tension between scale fixing and scale jumping in a hierarchical, scalar media geography that we see the distinctive spatial politics of Chinese television industries today.

Indian spatial politics are likewise shaped by a degree of hierarchy between metropolitan and nonmetropolitan locales. However, we have suggested that India's television industry is also structured by somewhat distinctive media geographies. Specifically, we have drawn on Ash Amin's relational, stretched conception of space to suggest that both India's media industry and the experience of media by Indian audiences are framed not only by scalar politics but increasingly also by the pluralized and interconnected nature of locatedness and being in place (Amin 2002). As we noted, to a far greater extent than is the case in China with its Mandarin-centric state language policy (Zhang and Guo 2012), a major growth area in Indian television is regionalism, with the TV industry showing a growing interest in tailoring content to local concerns and regional languages. However, as we show, Indian audiences (such as Mumbai-based Kannada-speaking viewers) often consume culturally proximate programming at a distance, while so-called regional television increasingly features highly localized versions of Hindi formats that are themselves Indianized versions of transnational formats. These examples suggest a complex and shifting relationship between constructions of place, language, cultural distinctiveness, and translocal cultural and capital flows. Thus, while geographic, social, and cultural locations strongly frame people's everyday engagements with media worlds in contemporary India, the experience of locatedness is increasingly produced through interconnected and "stretched" rather than fixed geographies. Although new content delivery systems like online video streaming and the national reach of provincial and metropolitan channels now also enable viewers in China, potentially at least, to transcend the fixed geography of their physical location, nevertheless the greater degree and wider variety of culturally and linguistically marked regionalisms in Indian television content arguably further exacerbate the disjunctive, "stretching" effects of translocal television consumption in India as compared to China.

This reflexive experience of media geographies and imagined otherness was also very much in evidence in our research on Euro-American-style programming in Taiwan, but at a highly aspirational level, with the glossy, high-end programming on TLC interpellating viewers as culturally and socially mobile subjects. As with the popular Indian travel-cookery show *Highway on My Plate* (see chapter 3), TLC shows such as *Fun Taiwan*, which positions Taiwan itself as an exoticized tourist destination and teaches its young, middle-class urban audience "to look at Taiwan through a foreigner's eyes," contribute to the development of a kind of critical geographic literacy or spatial consciousness. Indeed, as the concept of telemodernities suggests, a recurrent theme across our study was this sense of a split or divided consciousness: of the complex capacities of television in enabling viewers to aspire to a kind of "world citizen" identity, but often in ways that simultaneously highlight their local-level cultural and social embedding. In a different example, slum-dwelling Mumbaikars who were "connected" and technologically savvy—possessing cheap mobile phones, satellite dishes, and, increasingly, direct-to-home television—referred to themselves as "middle class" and spoke of their aspirations for social and material mobility. At the same time, they drew attention to the gap between the aspirational lifestyles projected on television and their own material realities of limited opportunities in the face of the growing privatization of citizenship (education, health, etc.). Compared to upper-middle-class viewers, lifestyle television's clarion call to "self-management" and "self-improvement" is received in a rather different light by these slum-dwelling viewers struggling with the uneven and often brutal nature of India's transition to capitalist modernity.

The transformational narratives of lifestyle TV, while populated with aspirational ideals of individualized, empowered selfhood, calculative consumption, and optimized interpersonal relationships, tend to produce a "lifestyled" self that is reflexively rearticulated to, and re-embedded into, extant social, cultural, and material conditions and hierarchies. We might understand this as a kind of *negotiated cosmopolitanism*: an aspiration toward and yearning for an imagined global or metropolitan experience and identity, but one that is fundamentally shaped by the constraints of locatedness and social inequity. As we noted in our introduction, throughout this book we have taken the locational specificity of people's modern aspirations, and their connection with differential power, as axiomatic. The point to emphasize is that the relation between place and one's potential for imagining a "global other" are very differently enabled at different sites, suggesting the limitations of excessively generalized theories of the power of a mediated global imaginary.

Having challenged the claims to universality of some of the key tenets of influential Western-centric theories of lifestyle television and media modernity in the five points raised above, then, how might we open up different conceptualizations of media modernities that would enable a range of more flexible and located approaches? Crucial here is a *pluralized* understanding of the complex and varied articulations of modernity, as captured in Kyung-Sup Chang's taxonomy of "compressed modernity," from the rapid industrialization and democratization of South Korea and East Asia's other tiger economies (poster nations for rapid-onset modernity) to the protracted and "ultra complex" experiences of system transition that characterizes China in the reforms era (Chang 2010, 457). Central to understanding these variegated articulations of compressed modernity is a double vision that we have tried to keep in view throughout our analyses: on the one hand, a recognition of spatially shared and temporally condensed *global* political, economic, and cultural processes and practices; and, on the other hand, an appreciation of the fact that "nation-states continue to be the dominant regulatory unit of economic life and sociopolitical citizenship" (Chang 2010, 451).

How, then, might the distinctive embodied experiences of media modernities in China, India, and Taiwan, as explored in the chapters of this book, impact on our thinking about media modernities more broadly? Rather than enabling us to blithely generalize about the impacts of "global" popular media on "local" audiences, these distinctive media ontologies remind us of the need to always pay close attention to the way in which media content, media audiences, and mediated civic spaces are each shaped in idiosyncratic ways by endogenous forces. If the study of lifestyle television is, at its heart, a study of the production of the mundane, then research on how this media form articulates with the social experience of its audiences must necessarily come to grips with both the translocally networked and the materially embedded nature not just of television but also of everyday life itself in the late modern world.

NOTES

INTRODUCTION

1. In relation to television in China, such a multiperspectival approach has been pioneered, in different ways, by a series of earlier works (e.g., Lull 1992; Zha 1995; Zhu and Berry 2009; Zhu 2012); these works and others are discussed in chapter 1.

2. It is generally believed that societies with a Gini coefficient of more than 0.40 are at increased risk of social unrest (Goodman 2013).

3. We were aiming initially to base all the audience interviews in domestic settings, but for a range of logistical and cultural reasons we were able to conduct household-based interviews only in India.

ONE. Lifestyle Television in Context

1. For detailed histories of the structural evolution of the current broadcasting system, see Guo 2007; X. Chen 2010; and Zhou 2012 (especially chapter 3).

2. In 2009 these ranked second, third, fifth, seventh, eighth, and ninth in nationwide ratings (F. Wu 2010, 119).

3. The *China TV Rating Yearbook* of 2012 lists sixteen Chinese productions aired on provincial satellite channels based on such trades in 2011, mainly talent shows (e.g., Fremantle Media's *X Factor*), variety/light entertainment (e.g., ITV's *Surprise Surprise*), game shows (e.g., BBC One's *This Time Tomorrow*), and marriage/dating shows (e.g., Endemol's *The Marriage Ref*) (Wang 2012, 198).

4. Interview with Mr. Bao Xiaoqun, CEO of Channel Young, Shanghai, China, October 20, 2010. Further quotations from Mr. Bao are from this interview.

5. The ten top channels by market share in descending order for 2012 were FTV (terrestrial), San Lih Taiwan (cable), CTV (terrestrial), TVBS News (cable), San Lih News (cable), ETTV News (cable), TTV (terrestrial), FTV News (cable), CtiTV News (cable), San Lih Urban (cable) (Taipei Media Agencies Association 2013, 12–14).

6. See http://www.niotv.com for detailed schedule and channel information.

7. Thanks to Taiwanese media industries scholar Ti Wei for his discussion with us on these points.

8. Governments may, however, influence news through the purchase of "product placement" of the government line in news content (Kuang 2011, 75–76).

9. Fran Martin's interview with Mr. Wang, Taipei, Taiwan, June 15, 2010. Wang used the English word *lifestyle*.

10. Material in this section is drawn from Fran Martin's interview with Christine Che, former deputy manager of programming and now cultural programming researcher at CTS, Taipei, Taiwan, June 14, 2010.

11. Interview with Christine Che.

12. For example, on Saturday, September 3, 2011, FTV's popular variety show *Zhu Ge Hui She* (Zhu Ge club) rated at 3.63, slightly higher than TTV's idol drama *Xiaozi Nühai Xiang Qian Chong* (Office girls) the following Sunday (3.48) but below both FTV's idol drama *Xinbing Riji zhi Tezhan Yingxiong* (Rookie's diary) (4.86) on the previous Friday and the top-rating weeknight drama in the same week, San Lih's local drama *Jia He Wan Shi Xing* (The harmonious family; 5.02). See *China Times* 2011.

13. Interview with Christine Che; Fran Martin's interview with Harry Hu, CTS executive vice president, Taipei, Taiwan, June 14, 2010.

14. Tania Lewis's interview with Niret Alva, Miditech, Mumbai, India, November 27, 2010.

15. For instance, Doordarshan complained to the Competition Commission of India in 2012 that the total number of people meters installed was only eight thousand and that those meters were installed only in urban areas, excluding the rural audience from being considered (*Times of India* 2013).

16. A recent scam in West Bengal featuring the Saradha Group, which owns eighteen newspapers and TV channels, revealed ownership links to the state's ruling Trinamool Congress party, with the media group essentially acting as a direct voice for government.

17. Following the huge success of the Hindi version of *Big Brother* (*Bigg Boss*), various regional versions have emerged including *Bigg Boss Bangla* (the Bengali-language version of Bigg Boss) and *Bigg Boss Kannada*.

18. These are the "pan-blue" camp, including the KMT, with its support for economic unification with China, and the "pan-green" camp, including the DPP, with its Taiwanese nativist politics and anti-unification stance.

TWO. Local versus Metropolitan Television in China

1. The website of *Life Weekly* is http://www.why.com.cn/epublish/node32682/.

2. Wanning Sun's interview with Mr. Bao Xiaoqun, CEO of Channel Young, Shanghai, October 20, 2010.

3. Wanning Sun's interview with Mr. Han Song, CEO of BBTV, Beijing, October 12, 2010.

FOUR. Imagining Global Mobility

1. For a discussion that incorporates analysis of the gendered dimensions of these Taiwanese TLC viewers' imaginative engagements with the channel, see Martin 2016a.

2. It seems that while Travel & Adventure was not rebranded as Travel & Living in Euro-American markets until 2005, Travel & Living was already airing on the

Asia-Pacific network in 2003. It therefore appears that the new name took effect earlier for Discovery Network Asia-Pacific.

3. These figures are derived from TLC Taiwan's schedule in the week of February 17–23, 2013. Percentages reflect the number of programs aired from each country, including repeats, rather than hours of airtime (although the vast majority of programs are sixty minutes long). In cases where the channel airs TLC or Discovery Channel content made by local production houses outside the United States, these programs are attributed to the country of production (for example, *Fun Taiwan*, *Lady in the House*, and *Maggie's Magic Menus* are counted as Taiwanese, while *Go Asia with Anita Kapoor* and *Oh My Gold!* are attributed to India).

4. Ratings information courtesy of AGB Nielsen Taiwan, private data purchase. The income of TLC viewers clustered above NT$90,000 per month, whereas average monthly earnings in October 2012 were around NT$41,000 per month.

5. Words in italics in interviewee quotations were spoken in English. The interviews were in Mandarin and have been translated by Fran Martin.

6. This and other background information on the program in this section are from an interview conducted by Fran Martin with Mr. A. (pseudonym), a program planner at Dongneng Yixiang, in Taipei on March 6, 2011.

7. Such responses probably also channel a degree of preexisting cultural hostility to the ABT/ABC identity. One interviewee described "most ABCs" as "stuck-up" (though he exempted Janet from this category); see also Mr. Ma's comments.

FIVE. Gurus, Babas, and Daren

Epigraph: Promotional blurb on the website for the Indian health and well-being channel Care World. See http://www.careworldtv.com/about-us/channel-profile/.

1. Alongside his status as a food critic and bon vivant, Vir Sanghvi, an Oxford-educated journalist who won the prestigious Rajiv Gandhi Journalism Award in 2008, has edited national dailies, published numerous books, and hosted various TV shows, including the well-known panel debate show *A Question of Answers*.

2. See the description for episode 5, accessed January 29, 2014, http://royalreservations.ndtv.com/royal-reservation/.

3. Interview with Arati Singh, Mumbai, India, December 12, 2010.

4. See the show's main page, accessed January 10, 2014, http://goodtimes.ndtv.com/bandbaajabride/default.aspx.

5. Interview with Rajiv Lakshman, Mumbai, India, November 30, 2010.

6. Interview with Dr. Shiv Kumar, Gurgaon, India, November 26, 2010.

7. See its channel profile, accessed January 23, 2014, http://www.careworldtv.com/about-us/channel-profile.

8. Interview with Xiao Yu, Bengbu, China, October 11, 2010.

9. This strategy of self-positioning is very clear from our conversations with a dozen producers, assistant producers, and strategists of lifestyle programs on SMG. Wanning Sun's interview with Channel Young's CEO Mr. Bao Xiaoqun also reinforces this. Interviews took place in Shanghai in October 2010.

SIX. Magical Modernities

1. See the letter sent by the Government of India Ministry of Information and Broadcasting on November 29, 2011, under the Cable Television Networks Act (1995) reminding TV channels of their obligation to adhere to the code (http://mib.nic.in/ShowDocs.aspx). In June 2013 the ministry took stern action and sent out a notice to channels to pull back shows and advertorials with superstitious content; see "Govt Cracks Down on Baba & Guru Shows on Indian TV," June 18, www.indiantelevision.com/headlines/y2k13/jun/jun94.php.

2. See "Chrome Data: Religious Channels Lead the Chart in Week 52," December 30, 2013, http://www.indiantelevision.com/headlines/y2k13/dec/dec124.php.

3. *Hindutva* has become an umbrella term for capturing the rise of Hindu nationalism as a major cultural, religious, and political force in India over the past couple of decades, with the destruction of the Babri Masjid mosque in 1992 seen as a watershed moment in the emergence of the movement.

4. A recent public litigation filed in the Delhi High Court marks broader public concerns over the money-making aspects of astrology-based TV shows with channels seen to be potentially compromising their ethics and breaching broadcast rules, in particular the Drugs and Magic Remedies (Objectionable Advertisements) Act of 1955, which limits the advertisement of drugs or magic talismans for the treatment and prevention of disease (*Hindu* 2014).

5. Vedic astrological charts are drawn up by the family priest for everyone at their birth, placing the planets in twelve different houses, according to their position in the sky at their time of birth. Vedic scriptures present a complex and detailed ontology connecting all observable aspects of the universe—the sensorial, vegetal, mineral, aural, linguistic. Each star sign is allocated with certain alphabets that are to be used for names for the newborn, and specific gemstones are prescribed depending on the planetary alignments. Although individual astrologers may take some liberties with their readings and remedies, most of their ideas would be grounded in some basic fundamentals stated in the scriptures.

6. For example, Sunita Menon, the tarot reader to Bollywood celebrities and resident astrologer on the erstwhile Kosmiic Chat, is an ex–flight attendant who discovered her psychic and tarot skills with her mentor in Ireland.

7. See Sundeep Koachar's personal website, accessed March 25, 2013, http://sundeepkoachar.com/.

8. See the website for Pawan Sinha's ashram and "charitable trust," accessed March 12, 2013, http://paavanchintandhara.com/.

9. Rahu is not a visible luminary but is mathematically calculated as a shadow planet that causes solar and lunar eclipses.

10. Alongside the scores of national and regional Hindu channels, Arihant, Jinvani, and Paras TV are Jain channels, while there is also a Lord Buddha TV. Of the Christian channels on offer, Aseervatham, Blessing (both South India–oriented), and Angel TV appear to be locally owned, while Shalom and God TV are internationally run. The Muslim channel Peace TV was banned a few years ago ostensibly for its lack of a license, and Quran TV (from Saudi Arabia) is no longer offered; instead, more watered-

down "Islamic culture" channels, such as ZeeSalaam, are now available to Indian audiences, and recently the Shia Muslim channel WIN TV has been launched.

11. For their profiles, see http://www.aasthatv.com/index.php/saints-gurus, accessed March 3, 2013.

12. See http://www.aasthatv.com/index.php/about-us, accessed March 3, 2013.

13. Despite its public branding as a spiritual rather than a religious channel, Aastha has a strongly proselytizing element and, drawing upon its significant income stream, has launched a subsidiary channel called Aastha Bhajan just for devotional songs. See website for "spiritual-cultural Channel" Aastha TV, accessed January 20, 2013, http://www.aasthatv.com/index.php/home.

14. See website for "Wellness Channel" Pragya TV, accessed March 1, 2013, http://www.pragyatv.com/About-Pragya.aspx.

15. A very similar positive comparison was made by a staffer we interviewed at the Da Ai channel in Taiwan, discussed later in the chapter, who had also come from previous employment in commercial television to a religious channel whose mission she saw as more ethically meaningful. Interview with Ms. B. (pseudonym), senior staffer in Da Ai's programming department, June 15, 2010.

16. Interview with Anil Rishii, creative director at Pragya TV, Gurgaon, November 26, 2010.

17. Interview with Shivani Agrawal Pragya, director of programming at Pragya TV, Gurgaon, November 26, 2010.

18. See Rita Gangwani's page on the Humanity Healing website, accessed March 25, 2013, http://community.humanityhealing.net/profile/RetdlieutRitagangwani.

19. The Buddhist channels represent some of Taiwan's largest religious organizations, notably Renjian Weishi (Beautiful Life Television, BLTV), run by the Buddha's Light Mountain organization; and Da Ai (Great Love), run by the Tzu Chi Compassionate Relief Foundation. These represent two of the four largest Buddhist organizations in Taiwan; a third, Dharma Drum Mountain, runs a web TV channel. The major religious organizations have also launched a range of smartphone apps, enabling followers to catch up on missed TV episodes or reflect on the master's aphorisms on the go.

20. The Christian channel, Hao Xiaoxi (Good TV), describes itself as the first worldwide Chinese Christian channel, promotes "family values," and runs daughter channels in Hong Kong and North America. See Good TV website, accessed November 25, 2015, http://www.goodtv.tv/about.

21. The Wei Xin channel (WXTV), associated with the Hsien Fo Zen Buddhist temple, is dedicated to exegeses of feng shui and the geomancy of the *I Ching* (*Book of Changes*). However, its programs mainly take the form of classes or sermons with a dharma master lecturing on abstract principles in direct address to camera in a static setting. This stands in contrast to the reality TV influence and focus on everyday applications that characterize the commercial feng shui advice show discussed in the next section, and bring the latter into clearer alignment with a lifestyle TV project.

22. Audience demographic data retrieved via a private data purchase from AGB Nielsen Taiwan, September 2013.

23. See Master Hsieh's homepage, accessed November 25, 2015, http://www.masterhsieh.url.tw.

24. In Hinduism, its inherent cosmology as well as more intellectual forms of Brahminical knowledge leave no place for ghost or spirit entities, whereas these "folk" forms of supernatural forces are a central presence in some traditional folk religions in East Asia that also have modern institutionalized forms, including Shintoism and Daoism.

25. Southern Chinese Minnan and Hakka ethnicities are Han Chinese groups who occupied Taiwan prior to the influx of northern "mainlander" Chinese with the KMT in the 1940s. Although numerically dominant by a wide margin, Minnan (and Hakka) ethnicities were marginalized for many decades by the political and cultural hegemony of the KMT administration. The cultural life of these southern peoples, including gender roles within the family, is distinct in important respects from the northern Chinese cultures of the "mainlanders."

26. See also Tzu Chi's global website, accessed November 25, 2015, http://tw.tzuchi.org/en/index.php.

27. The descriptions are based on Fran Martin's visit to the facility in 2010.

28. Interview with Ms. B., 2010.

29. Interview with Ms. B., 2010.

30. Interview with Ms. B., 2010. In our wider television audience research in Taiwan, it was common for younger viewers to mention a middle-aged mother or elderly grandmother who would monopolize the family apartment's main TV set each evening with her passion for Da Ai dramas.

31. Interview with Ms. B., 2010.

32. Other religious channels also feature life advice programs. For example, *lohas: Lehuo Zai Renjian* (Lifestyles of health and sustainability among the people), BLTV's sixty-minute weekday morning show, is a secularized talk show that features a thirty-something female host (A Jiao) in conversation with a daily expert offering health or psychologized child-rearing advice.

33. Audience demographic data retrieved via a private data purchase from AGBNielsen Taiwan, September 2013.

34. Audience demographic data retrieved via a private data purchase from AGBNielsen Taiwan, September 2013.

35. Indeed, in another episode Li Ali explicitly updates the traditional Confucian feminine ideal of obedience to father, husband, and son (*san cong*); Li reinterprets this as "respectful care for parents; loving care for husband; educative care for children." *San Dai zhi Jian*, March 24, 2013.

SEVEN. **Risky Romance**

1. As in all former forty-two British colonies, Section 377 of the Indian Penal Code introduced in 1861 by the British government criminalized homosexuality. After a two-decade-long move by activist groups to repeal the section, the Delhi High Court legalized homosexual intercourse in 2009. However, the Supreme Court subsequently overturned the decision in 2013, once again criminalizing homosexuality.

2. Interview with programming executive Zulfia Waris, Channel V, Mumbai, India, November 20, 2010.

EIGHT. **A Self to Believe In**

1. See CCTV, "Program Introduction to *Pretty Trendy*" (in Chinese), accessed November 25, 2015, http://news.cntv.cn/special/gss/20110212/107142.shtml.

2. See CCTV, index of past episodes of *Pretty Trendy* (in Chinese), accessed November 25, 2015, http://cctv.cntv.cn/lm/goushishang/fangtan/index.shtml.

3. See CCTV's online shopping mall, accessed November 25, 2015, http://cctvmall.com/.

4. See CNTV's introduction to *Pretty Trendy* (in Chinese), accessed November 25, 2015, http://big5.cntv.cn/gate/big5/news.cntv.cn/special/gss/20110212/107142.shtml.

5. For a more detailed critical examination of the qingshounü in popular Taiwanese television, see Martin 2016b, in which a slightly different version of this section also appears.

6. A 2011 study shows that 64 percent of housework domestic responsibilities are undertaken by women, and just 3 percent by their spouses; the remaining percentage is undertaken largely by the women's parents (DGBAS 2013, 9).

7. Parts of this section appeared in an earlier form in Martin and Lewis 2012 and Martin 2013. Information on *Queen*'s production and ratings, and TVBS's view of the program, is from Fran Martin's interview with Mimi Wang, former deputy director of programming at TVBS (incorporating TVBS-G), Taipei, Taiwan, March 7, 2011.

8. Interview with Mimi Wang.

9. Consider, for example, JET cable channel's *Nüren Yao You Qian* (Women want to be wealthy), a talk show advising middle-aged women on how to save and invest money in order to reach the "dream" of personal wealth; or free-to-air CTS's *Woman Ai Lüxing* (Women love to travel), a travel show targeting middle-class, solo female travelers. See Martin 2013.

10. *Meiren Wo Zui Da* is made by Hubei Satellite, produced by a former producer of *Queen* (Li Sihui), and features several "experts" familiar from the Taiwanese show; *Wo Shi Da Meiren* is made by Hunan Satellite and produced by *Queen*'s original producer, Wen Huaizhi; and *Xin Nüren Wo Zui Da*, recently retitled *Ai Ni Ai Meili*, is made by Shanghai TV's Channel Young via licensed format trade.

11. Amber Lim's interview with "Sally" (pseudonym), MediaCorp, Singapore, February 21, 2013. The copies are *Nüren Julebu* (Girls' night) and *in Nühuang* (Closet affair).

12. Interview with Mimi Wang.

13. Notwithstanding significant viewership in the target audience across income levels, *Queen*'s audience is somewhat skewed toward viewers with higher than average income (clustering between NT$60,000 and NT$80,000 per month in mid-2011, while the average income as of September 2011 was just over NT$43,000). Interview with Mimi Wang; additional information on audience demographics courtesy of AGB Nielsen Taiwan, private data purchase. See also DGBAS 2011.

14. Interview with Mimi Wang.

15. See note 6 this chapter.

16. For a detailed discussion, see Martin 2016b.

17. Lan's adoptive family was collectively interviewed, along with Lan herself, on an episode of the variety show *Kangxi Laile* (Here comes Mr. Big) on October 17, 2012. Thanks to Petrus Liu for alerting us to this episode.

WORKS CITED

Abu-Lughod, Janet. 1989. *Before European Hegemony: The World System A.D. 1250–1350*. Oxford: Oxford University Press.
Abu-Lughod, Lila. 2008. *Dramas of Nationhood: The Politics of Television in Egypt*. Chicago: University of Chicago Press.
Amin, Ash. 2002. "Spatialities of Globalisation." *Environment and Planning A* 34, no. 3: 385–99.
Anagnost, Ann. 2004. "The Corporeal Politics of Quality (*Suzhi*)." *Public Culture* 16, no. 2: 89–108.
Anderson, Benedict. 1983. *Imagined Communities: Reflections on the Origin and Spread of Nationalism*. London: Verso.
Anderson, Stewart, and Melissa Chakars, eds. 2014. *Modernization, Nation-Building, and Television History*. London: Routledge.
Appadurai, Arjun. 1988. "How to Make a National Cuisine: Cookbooks in Contemporary India." *Comparative Studies in Society and History* 30, no. 1: 3–24.
Appadurai, Arjun. 1996. *Modernity at Large*. Minneapolis: University of Minnesota Press.
Asthana, Sanjay. 2008. "Religion and Secularism as Embedded Imaginaries: A Study of Indian Television Narratives." *Critical Studies in Media Communication* 25, no. 3: 304–23.
Athique, Adrian M. 2010. "The Crossover Audience: Mediated Multiculturalism and the Indian Film." In *Bollywood in Australia: Transnationalism and Cultural Production*, ed. Andrew Hassam and Makarand Paranjape, 23–44. Crawley: University of Western Australia Publishing.
Attwood, Feona. 2005. "Inside Out: Men on the 'Home Front.'" *Journal of Consumer Culture* 5, no. 1: 87–107.
Bahar, Mehri. 2009. "Television, Religious Objects and Secularism." *Asian Journal of Social Science* 37, no. 2: 232–41.
Bai, Ruoyun. 2015. "'Clean up the Screen': Regulating Television Entertainment in the 2000s." In *Chinese Television in the Twenty-First Century: Entertaining the Nation*, ed. Ruoyun Bai and Geng Song, 69–86. London: Routledge.

Bai, Ruoyun, and Geng Song. 2015. Introduction to *Chinese Television in the Twenty-First Century: Entertaining the Nation*, ed. Ruoyun Bai and Geng Song, 1–14. London: Routledge.

Bajaj, Vikas. 2007. "In India, the Golden Age of Television Is Now." *New York Times*, February 11.

Bakken, Børge. 2000. *The Exemplary Society: Human Improvement, Social Control, and the Dangers of Modernity in China*. Oxford: Oxford University Press.

Bal, Hartosh Singh. 2013. "The Return of the Ramayana." *New York Times*, April 9.

Barmé, Geremie R. 1999. *In the Red: On Contemporary Chinese Culture*. New York: Columbia University Press.

Bauman, Zygmunt. 2000. *Liquid Modernity*. Cambridge: Polity.

Baviskar, Amita, and Raka Ray, eds. 2011. *Elite and Everyman: The Cultural Politics of the Indian Middle Class*. New Delhi: Routledge.

Beck, Ulrich. 1992. *Risk Society: Towards a New Modernity*. Thousand Oaks, CA: Sage.

Beck, Ulrich. 1994. "The Reinvention of Politics: Towards a Theory of Reflexive Modernization." In *Reflexive Modernization: Politics, Tradition and Aesthetics in the Modern Social Order*, ed. Ulrich Beck, Anthony Giddens, and Scott Lash, 1–55. Cambridge: Polity.

Beck, Ulrich. 2010. *A God of One's Own: Religion's Capacity for Peace and Potential for Violence*. Cambridge: Polity.

Beck, Ulrich, and Elisabeth Beck-Gernsheim. 2002. *Individualization: Institutionalized Individualism and Its Social and Political Consequences*. London: Sage.

Beck, Ulrich, Anthony Giddens, and Scott Lash. 1994. *Reflexive Modernization: Politics, Tradition and Aesthetics in the Modern Social Order*. Oxford: Blackwell.

Beck, Ulrick, and Edgar Grande. 2010. "Varieties of Second Modernity: The Cosmopolitan Turn in Social and Political Theory and Research." *British Journal of Sociology* 61, no. 3: 409–33.

Bell, David, and Joanne Hollows, eds. 2005. *Ordinary Lifestyles: Popular Media, Consumption and Taste*. Maidenhead, UK: Open University Press.

Berman, Marshall. 1982. *All That Is Solid Melts into Air: The Experience of Modernity*. New York: Simon and Schuster.

Bignell, Jonathan. 2005. *Big Brother: Reality TV in the Twenty-First Century*. Basingstoke, UK: Palgrave Macmillan.

Bonner, Frances. 2003. *Ordinary Television: Analyzing Popular TV*. London: Sage.

Bonner, Frances. 2005. "Whose Lifestyle Is It Anyway?" In *Ordinary Lifestyles: Popular Media, Consumption and Taste*, ed. David Bell and Joanne Hollows, 35–46. Maidenhead, UK: Open University Press.

Bourdieu, Pierre. 1984. *Distinction: A Social Critique of the Judgement of Taste*. Translated by Richard Nice. Cambridge, MA: Harvard University Press.

Brosius, Christiane. 2010. *India's Middle Class: New Forms of Urban Leisure, Consumption and Prosperity*. New Delhi: Routledge.

Brunsdon, Charlotte. 2003. "Lifestyling Britain: The 8–9 Slot on British Television." *International Journal of Cultural Studies* 6, no. 1: 5–23.

Callahan, William A. 2013. *China Dreams: 20 Visions of the Future.* New York: Oxford University Press.

Campbell, Colin. 2005. "The Craft Consumer: Culture, Craft and Consumption in a Postmodern Society." *Journal of Consumer Culture* 5, no. 1: 23–42.

Care World. 2013. http://www.careworldtv.com/about-us/channel-profile/. Acccessed March 2, 2013.

Cartier, Carolyn. 2001. *Globalizing South China.* Oxford: Blackwell.

Cartier, Carolyn. 2002. "Origins and Evolution of a Geographical Idea: The 'Macro-region' in China." *Modern China* 28, no. 1: 79–143.

Cartier, Carolyn. 2013a. "Class, Consumption and the Economic Restructuring of Consumer Space." In *Middle Class China: Identity and Behaviour*, ed. Minglu Chen and David S. G. Goodman, 34–53. Cheltenham, UK: Edward Elgar.

Cartier, Carolyn. 2013b. "Uneven Development and the Time/Space Economy." In *Unequal China: Political Economy and the Cultural Politics of Inequality*, ed. Wanning Sun and Yingjie Guo, 77–90. New York: Routledge.

Cartier, Michel. 1995. "Nuclear Versus Quasi-Stem Families: The New Chinese Family Model." *Journal of Family History* 20, no. 3: 307–27.

Chadha, Kalyani, and Anandam Kavoori. 2012. "Mapping India's Television Landscape: Constitutive Dimensions and Emerging Issues." *South Asian History and Culture* 3, no. 4: 591–602.

Chakrabarty, Dipesh. 2007. *Provincializing Europe: Postcolonial Thought and Historical Difference.* Princeton, NJ: Princeton University Press.

Chakraborty, Chandrima. 2007. "The Hindu Ascetic as Fitness Instructor: Reviving Faith in Yoga." *International Journal of the History of Sport* 24, no. 9: 1172–86.

Chandrashekhar, C. P., and Jayati Ghosh. 2002. *The Market That Failed: A Decade of Neoliberal Economic Reforms in India.* New Delhi: Leftword.

Chang, Kyung-Sup. 2010. "The Second Modern Condition? Compressed Modernity as Internalized Reflexive Cosmopolitization." *British Journal of Sociology* 61, no. 3: 444–64.

Chang, Kyung-Sup, and Min-Young Song. 2010. "The Stranded Individualizer under Compressed Modernity: South Korean Women in Individualization without Individualism." *British Journal of Sociology* 61, no. 3: 539–64.

Chang, Tsan-Kuo. 2002. *China's Window on the World: TV News, Social Knowledge, and International Spectacles.* Cresskill, NJ: Hampton.

Chatterjee, Partha. 1986. *Nationalist Thought and the Colonial World: A Derivative Discourse.* Minneapolis: University of Minnesota Press.

Chatterjee, Partha. 1993. *The Nation and Its Fragments: Colonial and Postcolonial Histories.* Princeton, NJ: Princeton University Press.

Chatterjee, Partha. 2008. "Democracy and Economic Transformation in India." *Economic and Political Weekly* 43, no. 16: 53–62.

Chen, Kuan-hsing, and Sechin Y. S. Chien. 2009. "Knowledge Production in the Era of Neo-Liberal Globalization: Reflections on the Changing Academic Conditions in Taiwan." *Inter-Asia Cultural Studies* 10, no. 2: 206–28.

Chen, Minglu. 2008. "Entrepreneurial Women: Personal Wealth, Local Politics and Tradition." In *The New Rich in China: Future Rulers, Present Lives*, ed. David S. G. Goodman, 112–25. New York: Routledge.

Chen, Minglu, and David S. G. Goodman. 2013a. "Introduction: Middle Class China—Discourse, Structure and Practice." In *Middle Class China: Identity and Behaviour*, ed. Minglu Chen and David S. G. Goodman, 1–11. Cheltenham, UK: Edward Elgar.

Chen, Minglu, and David S. G. Goodman, eds. 2013b. *Middle Class China: Identity and Behaviour*. Cheltenham, UK: Edward Edgar.

Chen, Mo 陈漠. 2011. "2010中国电视红皮书" [2010 Chinese television red paper]. 新周刊 [*New weekly*] 343: 45–48.

Chen, Ping-Hung. 2002. "Who Owns Cable Television? Media Ownership Concentration in Taiwan." *Journal of Media Economics* 15, no. 1: 41–55.

Chen, Shaohua, and Martin Ravallion. 2004. "How Have the World's Poorest Fared since the Early 1980s?" *World Bank Research Observer* 19: 141–69.

Chen, Xi. 2010. "Changing Bottom Line: Broadcasting Regulation in China." In *Toward Better Governance in China: An Unconventional Pathway of Political Reform*, ed. Baogang Guo and Denise Hickey, 147–61. Lanham, MD: Lexington Books.

Chen, Yi-Ling, and William Derhsing Li. 2012. "Neoliberalism, the Developmental State, and Housing Policy in Taiwan." In *Locating Neoliberalism in Asia: Neoliberalizing Spaces in Developmental States*, ed. Bae-Gyoon Park, Richard Child Hill, and Asato Saito, 196–224. Chincester, UK: Wiley-Blackwell.

Chen Yu-hua. 2009. "A Cohort Analysis of the Transition to First Marriage among Taiwanese," *Population and Society* 5.1: 25–44.

Chibber, Vivek. 2003. *Locked in Place: State-Building and Late Industrialization in India*. Princeton, NJ: Princeton University Press.

China Post. 2010. "Taiwan Records Drop in Marriage Rate for '09." *China Post*, June 28. http://www.chinapost.com.tw/taiwan/national/national-news/2010/06/28/262440/Taiwan-records.htm.

China Times. 2011. *China Times*, September 4. http://showbiz.chinatimes.com.

Chua, Beng Huat. 2012. *Structure, Audience and Soft Power in East Asian Pop Culture*. Hong Kong: Hong Kong University Press.

Chua, Beng Huat. 2016. "Consumption in Asia: After the New Rich Generation." In *Lifestyle Media in Asia: Consumption, Aspiration and Identity*, ed. Fran Martin and Tania Lewis. London: Routledge.

CIA. 2013. *CIA World Factbook*. https://www.cia.gov/library/publications/the-world-factbook/fields/2172.html.

Clark, Lynne Schofield. 2007. "Introduction: Identity, Belonging, and the Emergence of Religious Lifestyle Branding." In *Religion, Media, and the Marketplace*, ed. Lynn Schofield Clark, 1–33. New Brunswick, NJ: Rutgers University Press.

Cook, Sarah, and Xiao-yuan Dong. 2011. "Harsh Choices: Chinese Women's Paid Work and Unpaid Care Responsibilities under Economic Reform." *Development and Change* 42, no. 2: 947–65.

Copeman, Jacob, and Aya Ikegame, eds. 2012. *The Guru in South Asia: New Interdisciplinary Perspectives*. London: Routledge.

Corbridge, Stuart, and John Harriss. 2000. *Reinventing India: Liberalization, Hindu Nationalism, and Popular Democracy*. Hoboken, NJ: Wiley.

Couldry, Nick. 2002. "Playing for Celebrity: *Big Brother* as Ritual Event." *Television and New Media* 3, no. 3: 283–93.

Couldry, Nick. 2010. *Why Voice Matters: Culture and Politics after Neoliberalism*. London: Sage.

Couldry, Nick. 2012. *Media, Society, World: Social Theory and Digital Media Practice*. Cambridge: Polity.

Croll, Elisabeth. 1995. *Changing Identities of Chinese Women: Rhetoric, Experience and Self-Perception in Twentieth-Century China*. Hong Kong: Hong Kong University Press.

Cruikshank, Barbara. 1996. "Revolution Within: Self-government and Self-esteem." In *Foucault and Political Reason: Liberalism, Neo-liberalism and Rationalities of Government*, ed. Andrew Barry, Thomas Osborne, and Nicholas Rose, 231–52. Chicago: University of Chicago Press.

Davis, Deborah S. 2014. "On the Limits of Personal Autonomy: PRC Law and the Institutions of Marriage." In *Wives, Husbands, and Lovers: Marriage and Sexuality in Hong Kong, Taiwan, and Urban China*, ed. Deborah S. Davis and Sara L. Friedman, 41–61. Stanford, CA: Stanford University Press.

Derné, Steve. 2008. *Globalization on the Ground: Media and the Transformation of Culture, Class, and Gender in India*. Thousand Oaks, CA: Sage.

Deshpande, Satish. 2004. *Contemporary India: A Sociological View*. New Delhi: Penguin Books.

Ding, Xiaojie 顶晓洁. 2013. "IPCN: 左手电视，右手网络" [IPCN: Television on the left hand, Internet on the right hand]. 新周刊 [*New weekly*] 391: 68–70.

Directorate General of Budget Accounting and Statistics (DGBAS). 2010. "Women and Men in R.O.C. (Taiwan): Facts and Figures."

Directorate General of Budget Accounting and Statistics (DGBAS). 2011. "Earnings and Productivity: Statistical Analysis Monthly Report." November 20.

Directorate General of Budget Accounting and Statistics (DGBAS). 2012. "Women and Men in R.O.C. (Taiwan): Facts and Figures."

Directorate-General of Budget Accounting and Statistics (DGBAS). 2013. "Women and Men in R.O.C. (Taiwan): Facts and Figures."

Dirlik, Arif. 2012. "The Idea of a 'Chinese Model': A Critical Discussion." *China Information* 26, no. 3: 277–302.

Discovery Communications. 2013. "Discovery Communications Reports Full Year and Fourth Quarter 2012 Results." February 14. Accessed March 5, 2013. https://corporate.discovery.com/discovery-newsroom/discovery-communications-reports-full-year-and-fourth-quarter-2012-results/.

Doane, Mary Ann. 1999. "Film and the Masquerade: Theorising the Female Spectator." In *Feminist Film Theory: A Reader*, ed. Sue Thornham, 131–45. New York: New York University Press.

Donald, Stephanie Hemelryk, and Yi Zheng. 2009. "A Taste of Class: Manuals for Becoming Woman." *positions* 17, no. 3: 489–521.

Donner, Henrikke. 2008. *Domestic Goddesses: Maternity, Globalization and Middle-Class Identity in Contemporary India*. Aldershot, UK: Ashgate.

Du Gay, Paul, Stuart Hall, Linda Janes, Hugh Mackay, and Keith Negus. 1997. *Doing Cultural Studies: The Story of the Sony Walkman*. London: Sage.

Dussel, Enrique. 2002. "World-System and 'Trans'-Modernity." *Nepantla: Views from South* 3, no. 2: 221–44.

Economic Times. 2008. "Govt Issue Notification Amending Cable TV Networks Rules, 1994." March 18. http://articles.economictimes.indiatimes.com/2008-03-18/news/27708703_1_tobacco-products-products-and-other-intoxicants-advertising-of-liquor-companies.

Eisenstadt, Shmuel Noah. 2000. "Multiple Modernities." *Daedalus* 129, no. 1: 1–29.

Ellis, John. 2000. *Seeing Things: Television in the Age of Uncertainty*. London: I.B. Tauris.

Executive Yuan. 2013. "The Republic of China Yearbook 2013." http://www.ey.gov.tw/en/cp.aspx?n=BE8DFC05912B9563.

Fang, Fang 方芳. 2011. "国内相亲节目运作内幕揭秘：电视红娘二十年" [The secret of how China's dating shows operate: Twenty years of match-making on television]. June 6. http://yule.sohu.com/20110606/n309401136.shtml.

Farquhar, Judith, and Qicheng Zhang. 2012. *Ten Thousand Things: Nurturing Life in Contemporary Beijing*. New York: Zone Books.

Farris, Catherine S. P. 2004. "Women's Liberation under 'East Asian Modernity' in China and Taiwan: Historical, Cultural, and Comparative Perspectives." In *Women in the New Taiwan: Gender Roles and Gender Consciousness in a Changing Society*, ed. Anru Lee Farris and Murray Rubinstein, 325–76. Armonk, NY: M. E. Sharpe.

Felski, Rita. 1999/2000. "The Invention of Everyday Life." *New Formations* 39: 15–31.

Ferjani, Riadh. 2010. "Religion and Television in the Arab World: Towards a Communication Studies Approach." *Middle East Journal of Culture and Communication* 3, no. 1: 82–100.

Fernandes, Leela. 2006. *India's New Middle Class: Democratic Politics in an Era of Economic Reform*. Minneapolis: University of Minnesota Press.

FICCI-KPMG. 2014. "The Stage Is Set: FICCI-KPMG Indian Media and Entertainment Industry Report." https://www.kpmg.com/IN/en/Topics/FICCI-Frames/Documents/FICCI-Frames-2014-The-stage-is-set-Report-2014.pdf.

Flew, Terry, and Silvio Waisbord. 2015. "The Ongoing Significance of National Media Systems in the Context of Media Globalization." *Media Culture and Society* (April 28). doi: 10.1177/0163443714566903.

Fong, Vanessa. 2007. "Morality, Cosmopolitanism, or Academic Attainment: Discourse on Quality and Urban Chinese-Only-Children's Claims to Ideal Personhood." *City and Society* 19, no. 1: 86–113.

Foucault, Michel. 1977. *Discipline and Punish: The Birth of the Prison*. London: Penguin.

Foucault, Michel. 1979. *The History of Sexuality*. Vol. 1, *The Will to Knowledge*. London: Allen Lane.

Fürsich, Elfriede. 2003. "Between Credibility and Commodification: Nonfiction Entertainment as a Global Media Genre." *International Journal of Cultural Studies* 6, no. 2: 131–53.

Gao, Ziming 高子茗. 2011. "浅析《购时尚》栏目成功原因" [A brief analysis of the reasons behind *Pretty Trendy*'s success]. 金田 [*Jin Tian*] 287: 198.

Gaonkar, Dilip Parameshwar. 2001. "On Alternative Modernities." In *Alternative Modernities*, ed. Dilip Parameshwar Gaonkar, 1–23. Durham, NC: Duke University Press.

Gauthier, Francois, and Magali Uhl. 2012. "Digital Shapings of Religion in a Globalised World: The Vatican Online and Amr Khaled's TV-Preaching." *Australian Journal of Communication* 39, no. 1: 53–70.

Gerow, Aaron. 2010. *Visions of Japanese Modernity: Articulations of Cinema, Nation, and Spectatorship, 1895–1925*. Berkeley: University of California Press.

Ghosh, Palash. 2012. "As China Urbanizes, India Remains Overwhelmingly Rural." *International Business Times*, January 20. http://www.ibtimes.com/china-urbanizes-india-remains-overwhelmingly-rural-213795.

Giddens, Anthony. 1991. *Modernity and Self-Identity: Self and Society in the Late Modern Age*. Cambridge: Polity.

Giddens, Anthony. 1992. *The Transformation of Intimacy: Sexuality, Love, and Eroticism in Modern Societies*. Stanford, CA: Stanford University Press.

Government Information Office (GIO). 2009. *Republic of China Yearbook*. Taipei: Government Information Office.

Government Information Office (GIO). 2013. "Mass Media." In *Republic of China Yearbook*. Taipei: Government Information Office.

Goodman, David S. G., ed. 2008. *The New Rich in China: Future Rulers, Present Lives*. London: Routledge.

Goodman, David S. G. 2013. "Conclusion: What's Wrong with Inequality, Power, Culture and Opportunity." In *Unequal China: The Political Economy and Cultural Politics of Inequality*, ed. Wanning Sun and Yingjie Guo, 200–208. New York: Routledge.

Gooptu, Nandini. 2013. Introduction to *Enterprise Culture in Neoliberal India*, ed. Nandini Gooptu, 1–24. London: Routledge.

Greenhalgh, Susan. 1994. "De-Orientalizing the Chinese Family Firm." *American Ethnologist* 21, no. 4: 746–75.

Greenhalgh, Susan. 2005. "Globalization and Population Governance in China." In *Global Assemblages: Technology, Politics, and Ethics as Anthropological Problems*, ed. Aihwa Ong and Stephen J. Collier, 354–72. Malden, MA: Blackwell.

Guenzi, Caterina. 2012. "The Allotted Share: Managing Fortune in Astrological Counseling in Contemporary India." *Social Analysis* 56, no. 2: 39–55.

Guha, Ranajit. 1997. *Dominance without Hegemony: History and Power in Colonial India*. Cambridge, MA: Harvard University Press.

Guo, Xin 郭欣. 2011. "我国生活类电视节目类型研究" [A study of the various genres of life-themed television programs in China]. Master's thesis, Northeast Normal University.

Guo, Zhenzhi. 2007. "Television Regulation and China's Entry into the WTO." In *Internationalization of the Chinese TV Sector*, ed. Manfred Kops and Stefan Ollig, 41–54. Berlin: Lit Verlag.

Gupta, Akhil, and Aradhana Sharma. 2006. "Globalization and Postcolonial States." *Current Anthropology* 47, no. 2: 277–307.

Gurtoo, Himani Chandna. 2012. "Spiritual Small Screen." *Hindustan Times*, September 23. http://www.hindustantimes.com/business-news/spiritual-small-screen/article1-923489.aspx.

Hansen, Thomas Blom. 1999. *The Saffron Wave: Democracy and Hindu Nationalism in Modern India*. Princeton, NJ: Princeton University Press.

Harindranath, Ramaswami. 2013. "The Cultural Politics of Metropolitan and Vernacular Lifestyles in India." *Media International Australia, Incorporating Culture and Policy* 147: 147–56.

Hartley, John. 1999. *Uses of Television*. London: Routledge.

Harvey, David. 2005. *A Brief History of Neoliberalism*. Oxford: Oxford University Press.

Hearn, Alison. 2009. "Insecure: Narratives and Economies of the Branded Self in Transformation Television." In *TV Transformations: Revealing the Makeover Show*, ed. Tania Lewis, 55–63. London: Routledge.

Heller, Dana A., ed. 2007. *Makeover Television: Realities Remodelled*. London: I. B. Tauris.

Hershatter, Gail. 2007. *Women in China's Long Twentieth Century*. Berkeley: University of California Press.

Hindu. 2014. "Court Refuses to Ban Astrology-Based TV Shows." *Hindu*, December 14. http://www.thehindu.com/news/national/court-refuses-to-ban-astrologybased-tv-shows/article6690738.ece.

Hoffman, Lisa. 2006. "Autonomous Choices and Patriotic Professionalism: On Governmentality in Late-Socialist China." *Economy and Society* 35, no. 4: 550–70.

Hoffman, Lisa. 2010. *Patriotic Professionalism in Urban China*. Philadelphia: Temple University Press.

Holden, Todd Joseph Miles, and Hakan Ergül. 2006. "Japan's Televisual Discourses: Infotainment, Intimacy, and the Construction of a Collective *uchi*." In *Medi@sia: Global Media/tion In and Out of Context*, ed. Todd Joseph Miles Holden and Timothy J. Scrase, 105–27. London: Routledge.

Hollows, Joanne. 2003. "Feeling like a Domestic Goddess: Postfeminism and Cooking." *European Journal of Cultural Studies* 6, no. 2: 179–202.

Hong, Qizhen 洪琪真. 2012. "紀實娛樂頻道的國際化策略分析" [The International Strategy of Real-World Entertainment Channel]. Master's thesis, National Chengchi University, Taiwan, Businesss Management Studies.

Hong, Yu. 2010. "The Politics of a Socialist Harmonious Society in the Aftermath of China's Neoliberal Development." *Chinese Journal of Communication* 3, no. 3: 311–28.

Hong Fincher, Leta. 2014. *Leftover Women: The Resurgence of Gender Inequality in China*. London: Zed Books.

Hoover, Stewart M. 2006. *Religion in the Media Age*. New York: Routledge.

Hoover, Stewart M., and Jin Kyu Park. 2005. "The Anthropology of Religious Meaning Making in the Digital Age." In *Media Anthropology*, ed. Eric Rothenbuhler and Mihai Coman, 247–59 London: Sage.

Hsiao, Hsin-Huang Michael. 2010. "Placing China's Middle Class in the Asia-Pacific Context." In *China's Emerging Middle Class: Beyond Economic Transformation*, ed. Cheng Li, 245–63. Washington, DC: Brookings Institution Press.

Hsiao, Hsin-Huang Michael. 2014. "Characterizing the Middle Classes in Taiwan, Hong Kong, Macao and Urban China." In *Chinese Middle Classes: Taiwan, Hong Kong, Macao and China*, ed. Hsin-Huang Michael Hsiao, 3–13. New York: Routledge.

Hsiung, Ping-Chun. 1996. *Living Rooms as Factories: Class, Gender, and the Satellite Factory System in Taiwan*. Philadelphia: Temple University Press.

Hu, Yang, and Jacqueline Scott. 2014. "Family and Gender Values in China: Generational, Geographic, and Gender Differences." *Journal of Family Issues* (April 7). doi: 10.1177/0192513X14528710.

Hua, Wen. 2013. *Buying Beauty: Cosmetic Surgery in China*. Hong Kong: Hong Kong University Press.

Huang, C. Julia. 2008. "Gendered Charisma in the Buddhist Tzu Chi (Ciji) Movement." *Nova Religio-Journal of Alternative and Emergent Religions* 12, no. 2: 29–47.

Huang, C. Julia. 2009. *Charisma and Compassion: Cheng Yen and the Buddhist Tzu Chi Movement*. Cambridge, MA: Harvard University Press.

Huang, Junjie 黃俊杰. 2013. "视频瓦解电视" [Video is eroding television]. 新周刊 [*New Weekly*] 391: 26–28.

Illouz, Eva. 1997. *Consuming the Romantic Utopia: Love and the Cultural Contradictions of Capitalism*. Berkeley: University of California Press.

Illouz, Eva. 2012. *Why Love Hurts: A Sociological Explanation*. Cambridge: Polity.

India Brand Equity Foundation. 2003. "India's New Opportunity—2020." http://www.ibef.org/pages/14328.

India Today. 2014. "Censor Board Snips Sleazy Shows on TV." *India Today*, August 1. http://indiatoday.intoday.in/story/censor-board-snips-sleazy-shows-on-tv/1/375042.html.

Institute of Media and Communications Policy. 2013. "Media Data Base: Discovery Communications." Accessed March 5, 2013. http://www.mediadb.eu/en/data-base/international-media-corporations/discovery-communications.html.

International Monetary Fund. 2013. "World Economic Outlook [WEO] 2013." Accessed January 13, 2014. http://www.imf.org/external/pubs/ft/weo/2013/01/weodata/download.aspx.

Iwabuchi, Koichi. 2002. *Recentering Globalization: Popular Culture and Japanese Transnationalism*. Durham, NC: Duke University Press.

Iwabuchi, Koichi, ed. 2004. *Feeling Asian Modernities: Transnational Consumption of Japanese TV Dramas*. Hong Kong: Hong Kong University Press.

Jacka, Tamara. 2006. *Rural Women in Urban China: Gender, Migration, and Social Change*. Armonk, NY: M. E. Sharpe.

Jackson, Peter. 2009. "Markets, Media and Magic: Thailand's Monarch as a 'Virtual Deity.'" *Inter-Asia Cultural Studies* 10, no. 3: 361–80.

Jain, Bhavika. 2010. "62% of Mumbai Lives in Slums: Census." *Hindustan Times*, October 17. http://www.hindustantimes.com/mumbai/62-of-mumbai-lives-in-slums-census/story-I3bUsll9w5f6ePEfuXJEbM.html.

Jeffrey, Robin. 2002. "Communications and Capitalism in India, 1750–2010." *South Asia: Journal of South Asian Studies* 25: 61–75.

Jenkins, Richard. 2000. "Disenchantment, Enchantment and Re-Enchantment: Max Weber at the Millennium." *Max Weber Studies* 1: 11–32.

Jensen, Robert, and Emily Oster. 2009. "The Power of TV: Cable Television and Women's Status in India." *Quarterly Journal of Economics* 124: 1057–94.

Jones, Gavin W. 2007. "Delayed Marriage and Very Low Fertility in Pacific Asia." *Population and Development Review* 33, no. 3: 453–78.

Kaiman, Jonathan. 2014. "China Gets Richer But More Unequal." *Guardian*, July 28. http://www.theguardian.com/world/2014/jul/28/china-more-unequal-richer.

Kang, Myung-koo. 2004. "East Asian Modernities and the Formation of Media and Cultural Studies." In *The SAGE Handbook of Media Studies*, ed. John D. H. Downing, Denis McQuail, Philip Schlesinger, and Ellen Wartella, 271–88. Thousand Oaks, CA: Sage.

Kapur, Jyotsna. 2009. "An 'Arranged Love' Marriage: India's Neoliberal Turn and the Bollywood Wedding Culture Industry." *Communication, Culture and Critique* 2, no. 2: 221–33.

Karlström, Mikael. 2004. "Modernity and Its Aspirants: Moral Community and Developmental Eutopianism in Buganda." *Current Anthropology* 45, no. 5: 596–619.

Kasbekar, Asha. 2006. *Pop Culture India! Media, Arts, and Lifestyle*. Santa Barbara, CA: ABC-CLIO.

Kaufmann, Vincent, Manfred Max Bergman, and Dominique Joye. 2004. "Motility: Mobility as Capital." *International Journal of Urban and Regional Research* 28, no. 4: 745–56.

Kaul, Mahima. 2013. "Saradha Group Scandal Exposes Ties between India's Media, Politicians." Uncut: Free Speech on the Frontline, May 8. http://uncut.indexoncensorship.org/2013/05/financial-scandal-exposes-ties-between-indias-media-politicians/.

Kavka, Misha. 2004. "The Queering of Reality TV." *Feminist Media Studies* 4, no. 2: 220–22.

Kavka, Misha. 2006. "Changing Properties: The Makeover Show Crosses the Atlantic." In *The Great American Makeover: Television, History, Nation*, ed. Dana Heller, 211–29. New York: Palgrave Macmillan.

Keane, Michael. 2002. "As a Hundred Television Formats Bloom, a Thousand Television Stations Contend." *Journal of Contemporary China* 11, no. 30: 5–16.

Keane, Michael. 2004a. "Asia: New Growth Areas." In *Television across Asia: TV Industries, Programme Formats and Globalisation*, ed. Michael Keane and Albert Moran, 9–20. London: Routledge.

Keane, Michael. 2004b. "It's All in a Game: Television Formats in the People's Republic of China." In *Rogue Flows: Trans-Asian Cultural Traffic*, ed. Koichi Iwabuchi, Stephen Muecke, and Mandy Thomas, 61–62. Hong Kong: Hong Kong University Press.

Keane, Michael. 2015. *The Chinese Television Industry*. London: BFI/Palgrave Macmillan.

Keane, Michael, Anthony Y. H. Fung, and Albert Moran. 2007. *New Television, Globalisation, and the East Asian Cultural Imagination*. Hong Kong: Hong Kong University Press.

Keane, Michael, and Albert Moran, eds. 2003. *Television across Asia: Formats, Television Industries and Globalization*. London: Routledge Curzon.

Kelsky, Karen. 2001. *Women on the Verge: Japanese Women, Western Dreams*. Durham, NC: Duke University Press.

Kim, Youna. 2011. *Transnational Migration, Media and Identity of Asian Women: Diasporic Daughters*. New York: Routledge.

Kipnis, Andrew. 2006. "*Suzhi*: A Keyword Approach." *China Quarterly* 186: 295–313.

Kleinman, Arthur, Yunxiang Yan, Jing Jun, Sing Lee, Everett Zhang, Pan Tianshu, Wu Fei, and Guo Jinhua. 2011. *Deep China: The Moral Life of a Person*. Berkeley: University of California Press.

Knauft, Bruce M. 2002. "Critically Modern: An Introduction." In *Critically Modern: Alternatives, Alterities, Anthropologies*, ed. Bruce M. Knauft, 1–54. Bloomington: Indiana University Press.

Kohli, Atul. 2006. "Politics of Economic Growth in India, 1980–2005: Part I: The 1980s." *Economic and Political Weekly* 41, no. 13: 1251–59.

Kohli-Khandekar, Vanita. 2014. "Getting into Rural India." *Mid-Day*, July 25. http://www.mid-day.com/articles/getting-into-rural-india/15476186.

Kong, Tat Yang. 2005. "Labour and Neo-Liberal Globalization in South Korea and Taiwan." *Modern Asian Studies* 39, no. 1: 155–88.

Kotwal, Ashok, Ramaswami Bharat, and Wadhwa Wilima. 2011. "Economic Liberalization and Indian Economic Growth: What's the Evidence?" *Journal of Economic Literature* 49, no. 4: 1152–99.

Kraidy, Marwan. 2007. *Hybridity, or the Cultural Logic of Globalization*. India: Pearson Education.

Kraidy, Marwan. 2008. "Reality TV and Multiple Modernities in the Arab World: A Theoretical Exploration." *Middle East Journal of Culture and Communication* 1, no. 1: 49–59.

Kraidy, Marwan, and Katherine Sender, eds. 2011. *The Politics of Reality Television: Global Perspectives*. London: Routledge.

Kuang, Chung-Hsiang. 2011. "The Three-Pronged Approach to Reforming Taiwan's Media under Neoliberalism." *Capitalism Nature Socialism* 22, no. 2: 72–87.

Kumar, Shanti. 2014. "Media Industries in India: An Emerging Regional Framework." *Media Industries* 1, no. 2. http://www.mediaindustriesjournal.org/index.php/mij/article/view/46/91.

Lakha, Salim. 1999. "The State, Globalisation and Indian Middle Class Identity." In *Culture and Privilege in Capitalist Asia*, ed. Michael Pinches, 252–74. London: Routledge.

Larkin, Brian. 1997. "Indian Films and Nigerian Lovers: Media and the Creation of Parallel Modernities." *Africa: Journal of the International African Institute* 67, no. 3: 406–40.

Lee, Anru. 2004. *In the Name of Harmony and Prosperity: Labor and Gender Politics in Taiwan's Economic Restructuring*. Albany: State University of New York Press.

Lee, Ching Kwan. 2014. "A Chinese Developmental State: Miracle or Mirage?" In *The End of the Developmental State?*, ed. Michelle Williams, 230–76. New York: Routledge.

Lee, Ching Kwan, and Mark Selden. 2007. "China's Durable Inequality: Legacies of Revolution and Pitfalls of Reform." *Asia-Pacific Journal: Japan Focus*. http://japanfocus.org/-Mark-Selden/2329.

Lee, Leo Ou-Fan. 1999. *Shanghai Modern: The Flowering of a New Urban Culture in China, 1930–1945*. Cambridge, MA: Harvard University Press.

Lefebvre, Henri. [1971] 2002. *Everyday Life in the Modern World*. London: Continuum.

Leng, Zhihong, and Yuqi Xu 冷智宏,许玉琪. 2003. 《电视生活服务类节目：定位、形态与包装》，中国广播电视出版社 [Shenghuo-themed television programs: Definitions, forms, and packaging]. Beijing: China Broadcasting and Television Publishing.

Lewis, Tania. 2007. "'He Needs to Face His Fears with These Five Queers!': *Queer Eye for the Straight Guy*, Makeover TV and the Lifestyle Expert." *Television and New Media* 8, no. 4: 285–311.

Lewis, Tania. 2008. *Smart Living: Lifestyle Media and Popular Expertise*. New York: Peter Lang.

Lewis, Tania, ed. 2009. *TV Transformations: Revealing the Makeover Show*. London: Routledge.

Lewis, Tania. 2011a. "Making over Culture? Lifestyle Television and Contemporary Pedagogies of Selfhood in Singapore." *Communication, Politics and Culture* 44, no. 1: 21–32.

Lewis, Tania. 2011b. "'You've Put Yourselves on a Plate': The Labours of Selfhood on *MasterChef Australia*." In *Real Class: Ordinary People and Reality Television across National Spaces*, ed. Beverley Skeggs and Helen Wood, 104–16. London: Palgrave Macmillan.

Lewis, Tania. 2014. "Lifestyle Media." In *The Cultural Intermediaries Reader*, ed. Jennifer Smith Maguire and Julian Matthews, 134–44. London: Sage.

Lewis, Tania, Fran Martin, and Wanning Sun. 2012. "Lifestyling Asia? Shaping Modernity and Selfhood on Life Advice Programming." *International Journal of Cultural Studies* 15, no. 6: 537–66.

Li, Chunling. 2013. "Sociopolitical Attitudes of the Middle Class and the Implications for Political Transition." In *Middle Class China: Identity and Behaviour*, ed. Minglu Chen and David S. G. Goodman, 12–33. Cheltenham, UK: Edward Elgar.

Li, Chunling. 2014. "A Profile of the Middle Classes in Today's China." In *Chinese Middle Classes: Taiwan, Hong Kong, Macao and China*, ed. Hsin-Huang Michael Hsiao, 78–94. New York: Routledge.

Liao, Pei-Ru. 2012. "The Mediating Role of Mediatised Religious Content: An Example of Buddhist Institutional Use of Prime-Time Dramas." *Australian Journal of Communication* 39, no. 1: 37–51.

Liechty, Mark. 2003. *Suitably Modern: Making Middle-Class Culture in a New Consumer Society*. Princeton, NJ: Princeton University Press.

Lin, Chun. 2015. "The Language of Class in China." *Socialist Register* 51: 24–53.

Lin, Shih De, Shih De Shu, and Joseph Chan, eds. 2010. "Tzu Chi: Inspiring Great Love around the World." http://tw.tzuchi.org/en/html/intro/.

Lin, Yu-han 林妤函. 2011. "《女性當家? 談話性節目《今晚誰當家》中的大老婆意識與當代儒家式的「家庭」展演"》" [Woman as family head? Head-wife consciousness and the performance of contemporary Confucian-style "Family" in the talk show *Who's Family Head Tonight*]. Master's thesis, National Taiwan Normal University, Taiwan.

Litzinger, Ralph. 2008. "Afterword: Thinking Outside the Leninist Corporate Box." In *Privatizing China: Socialism from Afar*, ed. Li Zhang and Aihwa Ong, 230–36. Ithaca, NY: Cornell University Press.

Liu, Yu-Li, and Yi-Hsiang Chen. 2003. "Cloning, Adaptation, Import and Originality: Taiwan in the Global Television Format Business." In *Television across Asia: TV Industries, Programme Formats and Globalisation*, ed. Michael Keane and Albert Moran, 54–73. London: Routledge.

Lobato, Ramon. 2012. *Shadow Economies of Cinema: Mapping Informal Film Distribution*. London: Palgrave Macmillan for the British Film Institute.

Lu, Hwei-syin. 1998. "Gender and Buddhism in Contemporary Taiwan: A Case Study of Tzu Chi Foundation." *Proceedings of the National Science Council, Part C: Humanities and Social Sciences* 8, no. 4: 539–50.

Luhmann, Niklas. 1998. *Love as Passion: The Codification of Intimacy*. Stanford, CA: Stanford University Press.

Lull, James. 1992. *China Turned On: Television, Reform, and Resistance*. London: Routledge.

Lury, Celia. 1996. *Consumer Culture*. Cambridge: Polity.

Lutgendorf, Philip. 1997. "All in the (Raghu) Family: A Video Epic in Cultural Context." In *Media and the Transformation of Religions in South Asia*, ed. Lawrence Babb and Susan Wadley, 217–53. Philadelphia: University of Pennsylvania Press.

Lynes, Russell. 1954. *The Tastemakers*. New York: Grosset and Dunlap.

Ma, Eric. 2012. *Desiring Hong Kong, Consuming South China: Transborder Cultural Politics 1970–2010*. Hong Kong: Hong Kong University Press.

Madsen, Richard. 2007. *Democracy's Dharma: Religious Renaissance and Political Development in Taiwan*. Berkeley: University of California Press.

Madsen, Richard. 2008. "Religious Renaissance and Taiwan's Modern Middle Classes." In *Chinese Religiosities: Afflictions of Modernity and State Formation*, ed. Mayfair Mei-hui Yang, 295–322. Berkeley: University of California Press.

Marston, Sallie, and Neil Smith. 2001. "States, Scales and Households: Limits to Scale Thinking; A Response to Brenner." *Progress in Human Geography* 25, no. 4: 615–19.

Martelli, Stefano, and Gianna Cappello. 2005. "Religion in the Television-Mediated Public Sphere: Transformations and Paradoxes." *International Review of Sociology* 15, no. 2: 243–57.

Martin, Fran. 2010. *Backward Glances: Contemporary Chinese Cultures and the Female Homoerotic Imaginary*. Durham, NC: Duke University Press.

Martin, Fran. 2013. "'A Tangle of People Messing around Together': Taiwanese Variety Television and the Mediation of Women's Affective Labour." *Cultural Studies* 27, no. 2: 207–24.

Martin, Fran. 2016a. "Differential (Im)mobilities: Imaginative Transnationalism in Taiwanese Women's Travel TV." In *Lifestyle Media in Asia: Consumption, Aspiration and Identity*, ed. Fran Martin and Tania Lewis. London: Routledge.

Martin, Fran. 2016b. "From Sparrow to Phoenix: Imagining Gender Transformation through Taiwanese Women's Variety TV." *positions: asia critique* 24, no. 2: 369–401.

Martin, Fran, and Larissa Heinrich, eds. 2006. *Embodied Modernities: Corporeality, Representation, and Chinese Cultures*. Honolulu: University of Hawai'i Press.

Martin, Fran, and Tania Lewis. 2012. "Lifestyling Women: Emergent Femininities on Singapore and Taiwan Television." In *The Precarious Self: Women and the Media in Asia*, ed. Youna Kim, 53–76. Basingstoke, UK: Palgrave Macmillan.

Martin, Fran, and Tania Lewis, eds. 2016. *Lifestyle Media in Asia: Consumption, Aspiration and Identity*. London: Routledge.

Mazzarella, William. 2003. *Shoveling Smoke: Advertising and Globalization in Contemporary India*. Durham, NC: Duke University Press.

Mazzarella, William. 2012. "'Reality Must Improve': The Perversity of Expertise and the Belatedness of Indian Development Television." *Global Media and Communication* 8: 215–41.

McCarthy, Anna. 2001. *Ambient Television: Visual Culture and Public Space*. Durham, NC: Duke University Press.

McCracken, Ellen. 1993. *Decoding Women's Magazines*. Basingstoke, UK: Macmillan.

McCracken, Grant David. 2005. *Culture and Consumption II: Markets, Meaning, and Brand Management*. Bloomington: Indiana University Press.

McMillin, Divya C. 2001. "Localizing the Global: Television and Hybrid Programming in India." *International Journal of Cultural Studies* 4: 45–68.

Mehta, Nalin. 2008. *Television in India: Satellites, Politics and Cultural Change*. London: Routledge.

Meng, Dan 孟丹. 2013. "购时尚 节目形态分析" [An analysis of *Pretty Trendy*'s program style]. 新闻传播 [News and Broadcasting] 2: 63.

Miller, Daniel. 2009. *The Comfort of Things*. Cambridge: Polity.

Miller, Toby. 2007. *Cultural Citizenship: Cosmopolitanism, Consumerism, and Television in a Neoliberal Age*. Philadelphia: Temple University Press.

Ministry of Home Affairs. 2001. "Census Data Online." Government of India. http://censusindia.gov.in/2011-common/censusdataonline.html.

Moores, Shaun. 2012. *Media, Place and Mobility*. Basingstoke: Palgrave Macmillan.

Moorti, Sujata. 2004. "Fashioning a Cosmopolitan Tamil Identity: Game Shows, Commodities and Cultural Identity." *Media, Culture and Society* 26: 549–67.

Moran, Albert. 1998. *Copycat Television: Globalisation, Program Formats and Cultural Identity*. Luton, UK: University of Luton Press.

Morley, David. 2000. *Home Territories: Media, Mobility and Identity*. London: Routledge.

Morley, David. 2009. "For a Materialist, Non Media-Centric Media Studies." *Television and New Media* 10, no. 1: 114–16.

Moseley, Rachel. 2000. "Makeover Takeover on British Television." *Screen* 41, no. 3: 299–314.

Mukhopadhyay, Bhaskar. 2006. "Cultural Studies and Politics in India Today." *Theory, Culture and Society* 23, nos. 7–8: 279–92.

Münster, Daniel, and Christian Strümpell. 2014. "The Anthropology of Neoliberal India: An introduction." *Contributions to Indian Sociology* 48, no. 1: 1–16.

Murphy, Patrick D., and Marwan M. Kraidy, eds. 2003. *Global Media Studies: Ethnographic Perspectives*. London: Routledge.

Nanda, Meera. 2011. *The God Market: How Globalization Is Making India More Hindu*. New York: New York University Press.

Naughton, Barry. 2006. *The Chinese Economy: Growth and Transitions*. Cambridge, MA: MIT Press.

Neveling, Patrick. 2014. "Structural Contingencies and Untimely Coincidences in the Making of Neoliberal India: The Kandla Free Trade Zone, 1965–91." *Contributions to Indian Sociology* 48, no. 1: 17–43.

Neves, Joshua. 2015. "The Long Commute: Mobile Television and the Seamless Social." In *Chinese Television in the Twenty-First Century: Entertaining the Nation*, ed. Ruoyun Bai and Geng Song, 51–66. London: Routledge.

Nijman, Jan. 2006. "Mumbai's Mysterious Middle Class." *International Journal of Urban and Regional Research* 30: 758–75.

Noonan, Caitriona. 2011. "'Big Stuff in a Beautiful Way with Interesting People': The Spiritual Discourse in UK Religious Television." *European Journal of Cultural Studies* 14, no. 6: 727–46.

Oakes, Tim, and Louisa Schein. 2006. Introduction to *Translocal China: Linkages, Identities, and the Reimagining of Space*, ed. Tim Oakes and Louisa Schein, 1–35. London: Routledge.

Oakes, Timothy. 1998. *Tourism and Modernity in China*. London: Routledge.

Oakes, Timothy. 1999. "Selling Guizhou: Cultural Development in an Era of Marketization." In *The Political Economy of China's Provinces*, ed. Hans Hendrishke and Chongyi Feng, 31–67. London: Routledge.

Oba, Goro, and Sylvia M. Chan-Olmstead. 2005. "The Development of Cable Television in East Asian Countries: A Comparative Analysis of Determinants." *Gazette: The International Journal for Communication Studies* 67, no. 3: 211–37.

Ohm, Britta. 2011. "The Secularism of the State and the Secularism of Consumption: 'Honesty,' 'Treason' and the Dynamics of Religious Visibility on Television in India." *European Journal of Cultural Studies* 14, no. 6: 664–84.

O'Neill, Mark. 2010. *Tzu Chi: Serving with Compassion*. Singapore: John Wiley.

Ong, Aihwa. 1999. *Flexible Citizenship: The Cultural Logics of Transnationality*. Durham, NC: Duke University Press.

Ong, Aihwa. 2007. "Neoliberalism as a Mobile Technology." *Transactions of the Institute of British Geographers* 32, no. 1: 3–8.

Ong, Aihwa. 2008. "Self-fashioning Shanghainese: Dancing across Spheres of Value." In *Privatizing China: Socialism from Afar*, ed. Li Zhang and Aihwa Ong, 182–96. Ithaca, NY: Cornell University Press.

Ong, Aihwa, and Donald M. Nonini, eds. 1997. *Ungrounded Empires: The Cultural Politics of Modern Chinese Transnationalism*. New York: Routledge.

Oren, Tasha, and Sharon Shahaf, eds. 2012. *Global Television Formats: Understanding Television across Borders*. New York: Routledge.

Ouellette, Laurie, and James Hay. 2008. *Better Living through Reality TV: Television and Post-Welfare Citizenship*. Oxford: Blackwell.

Palmer, Gareth. 2004. "'The New You': Class and Transformation in Lifestyle Television." In *Understanding Reality Television*, ed. Su Holmes and Deborah Jermyn, 173–90. London: Routledge.

Palmer, Gareth. 2008. *Exposing Lifestyle Television: The Big Reveal*. Aldershot, UK: Ashgate.

Park, Bae-Gyoon, Richard Child Hill, and Asato Saito, eds. 2012. *Locating Neoliberalism in Asia: Neoliberalizing Spaces in Developmental States*. Chichester, UK: Wiley-Blackwell.

Pazderic, Nickola. 2013. "Smile Chaoyang: Education and Culture in Neoliberal Taiwan." In *Global Futures in East Asia: Youth, Nation, and the New Economy in Uncertain Times*, ed. Ann Anagost, Andrea Arai, and Hai Ren, 127–49. Stanford, CA: Stanford University Press.

Peng, Huanping 彭焕平, and Lianli Hu 胡连利. 2009. "繁荣图景的背后： 电视生活服务类的困境与突围" [Behind the spectacle of prosperity: The dilemma and solutions for shenghuo-themed television programs]. 中国电视 [*China Television*] 4: 54–57.

Pernia, Elena, San Pascual, Maria Rosel, and Dong Hwan Kwon. 2006. "Religion in the Box: Viewership of Religious Television Programs in the Philippines." *Journal of Communication and Religion* 29, no. 2: 484–510.

Pertierra, Ana Cristina, and Graeme Turner. 2013. *Locating Television: Zones of Consumption*. London: Routledge.

Petersen, Alan. 1997. "Risk, Governance and the New Public Health." In *Foucault, Health and Medicine*, ed. Alan R. Petersen and Robin Bunton, 189–206. London: Routledge.

Philips, Deborah. 2005. "Transformation Scenes: The Television Interior Makeover." *International Journal of Cultural Studies* 8, no. 2: 213–29.

Powell, Helen, and Sylvie Prasad. 2010. "'As Seen On TV': The Celebrity Expert: How Taste Is Shaped by Lifestyle Media." *Cultural Politics* 6, no. 1: 111–24.

Prakash, Gyan. 1999. *Another Reason: Science and the Imagination of Modern India*. Princeton, NJ: Princeton University Press.

Qiu, Ruixian 邱瑞贤. 2010. "'神医'层出凸显科普困局 电视被指传播伪科学" ['Guru doctors' appear like mushrooms, pointing to the predicament of science education; Television is accused of spreading pseudo-science], 中国新闻网 [China News Web]. Accessed November 25, 2015. http://www.chinanews.com/jk/news/2010/06-18/2349291.shtml.

Raja, John Samuel. 2014. "Actually, the Nuclear Family Is on the Decline in India." *Quartz India*, July 1. http://qz.com/228405/india-is-urbanizing-rapidly-but-the-nuclear-family-is-actually-shrinking/.

Rajagopal, Arvind. 2001. *Politics after Television: Hindu Nationalism and the Reshaping of the Public in India*. Cambridge: Cambridge University Press.

Ramasubramanian, Srividya, and Parul Jain. 2009. "Gender Stereotypes and Normative Heterosexuality in Matrimonial Ads from Globalizing India." *Asian Journal of Communication* 19: 253–69.

Ray, Manas, and Elizabeth Jacka. 1996. "Indian Television: An Emerging Regional Force." In *New Patterns in Global Television: Peripheral Vision*, ed. John Sinclair, Elizabeth Jacka, and Stuart Cunningham, 83–100. Oxford: Oxford University Press.

Redden, Guy. 2002. "The New Agents: Personal Transfiguration and Radical Privatization in New Age Self-Help." *Journal of Consumer Culture* 2, no. 1: 33–52.

Redden, Guy. 2007. "Makeover Morality and Consumer Culture." In *Reading Makeover Television: Realties Remodeled*, ed. Dana A. Heller, 150–64. London: I. B. Tauris.

Redden, Guy. 2008. "Economy and Reflexivity in Makeover Television." *Continuum: Journal of Media and Cultural Studies* 22, no. 4: 485–94.

Redden, Guy. 2011. "Religion, Cultural Studies and New Age Sacralization of Everyday Life." *European Journal of Cultural Studies* 14, no. 6: 649–63.

Ren, Hai. 2010. *Neoliberalism and Culture in Hong Kong: The Countdown of Time*. London: Routledge.

Ren, Hai. 2013. *The Middle Class in Neoliberal China: Governing Risk, Life-Building, and Themed Spaces*. London: Routledge.

Richards, Michael, and David French. 2000. "Globalisation, Television and Asia." In *Television in Contemporary Asia*, ed. David French and Michael Richards, 13–27. London: Sage.

Risk, Ahmad, and Carolyn Petersen. 2002. "Health Information on the Internet: Quality Issues and International Initiatives." *JAMA* 287, no. 20: 2713–15.

Ritzer, George. 2005. *Enchanting a Disenchanted World: Continuity and Change in the Cathedrals of Consumption*. 3rd ed. London: Pine Forge Press.

Robbins, Joel. 2002. "God Is Nothing but Talk: Modernity, Language and Prayer in a Papua New Guinea Society." *American Anthropologist* 103, no. 4: 901–12.

Robison, Richard, and David S. G. Goodman. 1996. "The New Rich in Asia: Economic Development, Social Status and Political Consciousness." In *The New Rich in Asia: Mobile Phones, McDonald's and Middle-Class Revolution*, ed. Richard Robison and David S. G. Goodman, 1–18. London: Routledge.

Rodrik, Dani, and Arvind Subramanian. 2004. "From 'Hindu Growth' to Productivity Surge: The Mystery of the Indian Growth Transition." *IMF Staff Papers* 52, no. 2: 193–228.

Rofel, Lisa. 1999. *Other Modernities: Gendered Yearnings in China after Socialism*. Berkeley: University of California Press.

Rofel, Lisa. 2007. *Desiring China: Experiments in Neoliberalism, Sexuality, and Public Culture*. Durham, NC: Duke University Press.

Roof, Wade Clark. 1993. *A Generation of Seekers: The Spiritual Journeys of the Baby Boom Generation*. San Francisco: HarperSanFrancisco.

Roof, Wade Clark. 2001. *Spiritual Marketplace: Baby Boomers and the Remaking of American Religion*. Princeton, NJ: Princeton University Press.

Rose, Nikolas. 1989. *Governing the Soul: The Shaping of the Private Self*. London: Routledge.

Rose, Nikolas 1996. *Inventing Our Selves: Psychology, Power, and Personhood*. Cambridge: Cambridge University Press.

Roy, Abhijit. 2008. "Bringing up TV: Popular Culture and the Developmental Modern in India." *South Asian Popular Culture* 6: 29–43.

Roy, Abhijit. 2012. "A Reflexive Turn in Television Studies? Conjectures from South Asia." *South Asian History and Culture* 3, no. 4: 636–48.

Schmidt, Volker H. 2006. "Multiple Modernities or Varieties of Modernity?" *Current Sociology* 54, no. 1: 77–97.

Schwarcz, Vera. 1986. *The Chinese Enlightenment: Intellectuals and the Legacy of the May Fourth Movement of 1919*. Berkeley: University of California Press.

Sen, Biswarup, and Abhijit Roy. 2014. Introduction to *Channeling Cultures: Television Studies from India*, ed. Biswarup Sen and Abhijit Roy, 1–16. New Delhi: Oxford University Press.

Shambaugh, David. 2013. *China Goes Global: The Partial Power*. New York: Oxford University Press.

Shen, Huiping 沈慧萍. 2009. "透析上海电生活视服务类节目" [A probing analysis of the service-oriented television programs on Shanghai TV]. 新闻爱好者 [*Journalism Enthusiasts*] 11: 180–81.

Sherman, Yael D. 2008. "Fashioning Femininity: Clothing the Body and the Self in *What Not to Wear*." In *Exposing Lifestyle Television: The Big Reveal*, ed. Gareth Palmer, 49–63. Aldershot, UK: Ashgate.

Shih, Chih-yu. 2003. *Negotiating Ethnicity in China: Citizenship as a Response to the State*. London: Routledge.

Shih, Shu-mei. 2001. *The Lure of the Modern: Writing Modernism in Semicolonial China, 1917–1937*. Berkeley: University of California Press.

Shirk, Susan. 2007. *China: Fragile Superpower*. Oxford: Oxford University Press.

Shivakumar, Girija. 2013. "India Is Set to Become the Youngest Country by 2020." *Hindu*, April 17. http://www.thehindu.com/news/national/india-is-set-to-become-the-youngest-country-by-2020/article4624347.ece.

Shome, Raka. 2012. "Asian Modernities: Culture, Politics and Media." *Global Media and Communication* 8, no. 3: 199–214.

Shrinivasan, Rukmini. 2012. "200 Million Indians Have No TV, Phone or Radio." *Times of India*, March 14. http://timesofindia.indiatimes.com/india/200-million-Indians-have-no-tv-phone-or-radio/articleshow/12253614.cms.

Shukla, Rajesh. 2010. *How India Earns, Spends and Saves: Unmasking the Real India*. New Delhi: Sage.

Shumway, David R. 2003. *Modern Love: Romance, Intimacy, and the Marriage Crisis*. New York: New York University Press.

Silverstone, Roger. 1994. *Television and Everyday Life*. London: Routledge.

Sinclair, John, Elizabeth Jacka, and Stuart Cunningham, eds. 1996. *New Patterns in Global Television: Peripheral Vision*. Oxford: Oxford University Press.

Skeggs, Beverley. 2005. "The Making of Class and Gender through Visualizing Moral Subject Formation." *Sociology* 39, no. 5: 965–82.

Skeggs, Beverley, and Helen Wood. 2009. "The Labour of Transformation and Circuits of Value 'around' Reality Television." In *TV Transformations: Revealing the Makeover Show*, ed. Tania Lewis, 119–32. London: Routledge.

Skeggs, Beverley, and Helen Wood. 2012. *Reality Television: Performance, Audience and Value*. London: Routledge.

Srinivas, Tulasi. 2010. *Winged Faith: Rethinking Globalization and Religious Pluralism through the Sathya Sai Movement*. New York: Columbia University Press.

Stockmann, Daniela. 2013. *Media Commercialization and Authoritarian Rule in China*. Cambridge: Cambridge University Press.

Strange, Niki. 1998. "Perform, Educate, Entertain: Ingredients of the Cookery Programme Genre." In *The Television Studies Book*, ed. David Lusted and Christine Geraghty, 301–12. London: Arnold.

Su, Herng 蘇蘅, and Shu-Wen Cheng 鄭淑文. 2009. "紀實娛乐節目之全球在地化历程—以探索頻道在台灣為例" [Glocalization of nonfiction entertainment media: Programming strategies of Discovery Communication Inc. in Taiwan]. 廣播與電視 [*Journal of Radio and Television Studies*] 30 (June): 1–28.

Subijanto, Rianne. 2011. "The Visibility of a Pious Public." *Inter-Asia Cultural Studies* 12, no. 2: 240–53.

Sun, Wanning. 2002. "Discourse of Poverty: Weakness, Potential and Provincial Identity in Anhui." In *Rethinking China's Provinces*, ed. John Fitzgerald, 153–78. London: Routledge.

Sun, Wanning. 2005. "Anhui Baomu in Shanghai: Gender, Class and a Sense of Place." In *Locating China: Space, Place and Popular Culture*, ed. Jing Wang, 171–89. London: Routledge.

Sun, Wanning. 2007. "Dancing with Chains: Significant Moments on Chinese Television." *International Journal of Cultural Studies* 10, no. 2: 187–204.

Sun, Wanning. 2009. *Maid in China: Media, Morality, and the Cultural Politics of Boundaries.* London: Routledge.

Sun, Wanning. 2010. "Narrating Translocality: Dagong Poetry and the Subaltern Imagination." *Mobilities* 5, no. 3: 291–309.

Sun, Wanning. 2012. "Localizing Chinese Media: A Geographic Turn in Media and Communication Research." In *Mapping Media in China: Region, Province, Locality,* ed. Wanning Sun and Jenny Chio, 13–27. London: Routledge.

Sun, Wanning. 2013. "Scaling Lifestyle in China: The Emergence of Local Television Cultures and the Cultural Economy of Place-Making." *Media International Australia Incorporating Culture and Policy* 147, no. 1: 62–72.

Sun, Wanning. 2014. "Teaching People to Live: Shenghuo Television in China." In *Chinese Television in the Twenty-First Century: Entertaining the Nation,* ed. Ruoyun Bai and Geng Song, 17–32. London: Routledge.

Sun, Wanning, and Jenny Chio. 2012. Introduction to *Mapping Media in China: Region, Province, Locality,* ed. Wanning Sun and Jenny Chio, 3–12. London: Routledge.

Sun, Wanning, and Yingjie Guo, eds. 2013. *Unequal China: The Political Economy and Cultural Politics of Inequality.* New York: Routledge.

Sun, Wanning, and Yuezhi Zhao. 2009. "Television Culture with 'Chinese Characteristics': The Politics of Compassion and Education." In *Television Studies after TV: Understanding Television in the Post-Broadcast Era,* ed. Graeme Turner and Jinna Tay, 96–104. London: Routledge.

Sun, Xiaofan 孙晓凡. 2012. "生活方式类真人秀节目的中国化解析" [An Analysis of the China-fication of Lifestyle Reality TV Genre Programs]. Master's thesis, Harbin Normal University, China.

Sundaram, Ravi. 2010. *Pirate Modernity: Delhi's Media Urbanism.* London: Taylor and Francis.

Taipei Media Agencies Association. 2013. 2013 年台灣媒體白皮書。 [*Media Book 2013*]. Industry report. http://www.maataipei.org/upload/1368779201.pdf Taipei.

Talwar, Ruchika. 2013. "Telly Me the Future." *Indian Express,* May 12.

Television Audience Measurement (TAM). 2011. "TAM Annual Universe Update." http://www.tamindia.com/webview.php?web=ref_pdf/Overview_Universe_update_2011.pdf.

Television Audience Measurement (TAM) India. 2014. "TAM Annual Universe Update." http://www.tamindia.com/webview.php?web=ref_pdf/Overview_Universe_Update-2014.pdf.

Thomas, Amos Owen. 2005. *Imagi-nations and Borderless Television: Media, Culture and Politics across Asia.* Thousand Oaks, CA: Sage.

Thomas, Michael K., and Wan-Lin Yang. 2013. "Neoliberalism, Globalization, and Creative Educational Destruction in Taiwan." *Educational Technology Research and Development* 61, no. 1: 107–29.

Thornton, Arland, and Hui-sheng Lin. 1994. *Social Change and the Family in Taiwan.* Chicago: University of Chicago Press.

Times of India. 2011. "India's Income Inequality Has Doubled in 20 Years," December 7. http://timesofindia.indiatimes.com/india/Indias-income-inequality-has-doubled-in-20-years/articleshow/11012855.cms.

Times of India. 2013. "TAM abused position on TV ratings: CCI." May 4. http://timesofindia.indiatimes.com/business/india-business/TAM-abused-position-on-TV-ratings-CCI/articleshow/19875869.cms.

Titzmann, Fritzi-Marie. 2011. "Medialisation and Social Change—The Indian Online Matrimonial Market as a New Field of Research." In *Social Dynamics 2.0: Researching Change in Times of Media Convergence; Case Studies from the Middle East and Asia*, ed. Nadja-Christina Schneider and Bettina Gräf, 49–66. Berlin: Frank and Timme.

TLC Asia. 2013. "Fun Taiwan Challenge." Accessed March 6, 2013. http://www.tlcasia.com/tv-shows/funtaiwanchallenge.

Tsai, Ming-Chang. 2001. "Dependency, the State and Class in the Neoliberal Transition of Taiwan." *Third World Quarterly* 22, no. 3: 359–79.

Tsai, Ming-Chang, Gang-Hua Fan, Hsin-Huang Michael Hsiao, and Hong-Zen Wang. 2014. "Profiling the Middle Class in Taiwan Today." In *Chinese Middle Classes: Taiwan, Hong Kong, Macao and China*, ed. Hsin-Huang Michael Hsiao, 17–35. London: Routledge.

Turner, Graeme. 2009a. *Ordinary People and the Media: The Demotic Turn*. London: Sage.

Turner, Graeme. 2009b. "Television and the Nation: Does This Matter Anymore?" In *Television Studies after TV: Understanding Television in the Post-Broadcast Era*, ed. Graeme Turner and Jinna Tay, 54–64. London: Routledge.

Turner, Graeme, and Jinna Tay. 2009. *Television Studies after TV: Understanding Television in the Post-Broadcast Era*. London: Routledge.

Urry, John. 2002. *The Tourist Gaze*. London: Sage.

Urry, John. 2007. *Mobilities*. Cambridge: Polity.

Urry, John, and Jonas Larsen. 2011. *The Tourist Gaze 3.0*. London: Sage.

Vairon, Lionel. 2013. *China Threat? The Challenges, Myths, and Realities of China's Rise*. New York: CN Times Books.

Varman, Rohit, and Ram Manohar Vikas. 2007. "Rising Markets and Failing Health: An Inquiry into Subaltern Health Care Consumption under Neoliberalism." *Journal of Macromarketing* 27, no. 2: 162–72. doi: 10.1177/0276146707301333.

Waisbord, Silvio. 2004. "MCTV: Understanding the Global Popularity of Television Formats." *Television and New Media* 5, no. 4: 359–83.

Wang, Chia-Huang. 2012. "Moving toward Neoliberalization? The Restructuring of the Developmental State and Spatial Planning in Taiwan." In *Locating Neoliberalism in Asia*, ed. Bae-Gyoon Park, Richard Child Hill, and Asato Saito, 167–95. Chichester, UK: Wiley-Blackwell.

Wang, Hong 王泓. 2012. "健康类节目的经营与发展--以北京电视台《养生堂》栏目为例" [The operation and development of health-related television programs: The case study of Beijing TV's Yangsheng Tang]. 现代传播 [*Modern Communication*] 192, no. 7: 163–64.

Wang, Jing. 2005. Introduction to *Locating China: Space, Place and Popular Culture*, ed. Jing Wang, 1–30. London: Routledge.

Wang, Lanzhu 王兰柱, ed. 2012. 中国电视收视年鉴 [*China TV Rating Yearbook*]. Beijing: Zhongguo Zhuanmei Daxue Chubanshe.

Wang, Weimin 王唯铭. 1996. "穿劣质制拖鞋满街跑的女人" [Women running around in the street wearing shoddily made sandals]. 上海青年报生活周刊 [*Life Weekly of Shanghai Youth Daily*], July 27.

Wang, Yalan 王雅蘭. 2010. 老總請吃飯大戶藍心湄不習慣 [Honoured Guest Lan Xinmei Unused to Dinner Invitations from Mr President], *Yahoo News*. Accessed January 15 2011. tw.news.yahoo.com/article/url/d/a/101218/2/2j7tg.html.

Warrier, Maya. 2003. "Processes of Secularization in Contemporary India: Guru Faith in the Mata Amritanandamayi Mission." *Modern Asian Studies* 37, no. 1: 213–53.

Warrier, Maya. 2004. *Hindu Selves in a Modern World: Guru Faith in the Mata Amritanandamayi Mission*. New York: Routledge.

Weber, Brenda R. 2009. *Makeover TV: Selfhood, Citizenship, and Celebrity*. Durham, NC: Duke University Press.

Weber, Max. [1919] 1946. "Science as a Vocation." In *From Max Weber: Essays in Sociology*, ed. H. H. Gerth and C. Wright Mills, 129–56. New York: Oxford University Press.

Weber, Max. [1922] 1963. *The Sociology of Religion*. Boston: Beacon Press.

Weller, Robert P. 1999. *Alternate Civilities: Democracy and Culture in China and Taiwan*. Oxford: Westview Press.

Wen, Huike. 2013. *Television and the Modernization Ideal in 1980s China: Dazzling the Eyes*. Lanham, MD: Lexington Books.

White, James D. 2005. *Global Media: The Television Revolution in Asia*. New York: Routledge.

Wittrock, Björn. 2000. "Modernity: One, None or Many? European Origins and Modernity as a Global Condition." *Daedalus* 129, no. 1: 31–60.

Wood, Helen, and Beverley Skeggs. 2004. "Notes on Ethical Scenarios of Self on British Reality TV." *Feminist Media Studies* 4, no. 2: 205–8.

Wood, Helen, Beverley Skeggs, and Nancy Thumim. 2008. "It's Just Sad: Mediated Intimacy and the Emotional Labour of Reality Television Viewing." In *Feminism, Domesticity and Popular Culture*, ed. Stacy Gillis and Joanne Hollows, 135–50. New York: Routledge.

Wu, Fan 吴凡. 2010. "2009年全国综艺娱乐节目收视分析" ["An analysis of ratings for general entertainment programs on Chinese television in 2009"]. In 中国电视收视年鉴 [*China TV Rating Yearbook*], ed. Wang Lanzhu, 115–30. Beijing: Zhongguo Zhuanmei Daxue Chubanshe.

Wu, Jing. 2012. "Post-socialist Articulation of Gender Positions: Contested Public Sphere of Reality Dating Shows." In *Women and the Media in Asia: The Precarious Self*, ed. Youna Kim, 220–36. Houndsmills, UK: Palgrave Macmillan.

Xinhuanet. 2011. "各界热议广电总局'限娱令': 莫为娱乐遗忘道德" ["Discussions on SARFT's 'ban on entertainment': Don't forget morality in pursuit of entertainment"]. *Xinhuanet*, October 28. http://news.xinhuanet.com/ent/2011-10/28/c_122208016.htm.

Xu, Fei 徐非. 1996. "'穿'文宣扬了什么?'" ["What does the article on 'clothing' promote?"]. 新安晚报 [*Xi'an Evening Post*], August 7.

Xu, Janice Hua. 2007. "Brand-New Lifestyle: Consumer-Oriented Programmes on Chinese Television." *Media, Culture and Society* 29, no. 3: 363–76.

Xu, Junqian. 2011. "Chanel Finds a Fashionable Home on Channel Young." *China Daily*, February 28. http://www.chinadaily.com.cn/bizchina/2011-02/28/content_12088348.htm.

Yan, Hairong. 2008. *New Masters, New Servants: Migration, Development, and Women Workers in China*. Durham, NC: Duke University Press.

Yan, Yunxiang. 2009. *The Individualization of Chinese Society*. Oxford: Berg.

Yan, Yunxiang. 2010. "The Chinese Path to Individualization." *British Journal of Sociology* 61, no. 3: 490–513.

Yang, Fang-chih Irene. 2002. "Variety Shows: Exploring the Genre of the 'Most Local Show' in Taiwan." *Dong Hwa Journal of Humanistic Studies* 4: 295–330.

Yang, Frang-chih Irene. 2008. "The Gentrification of 'Korean drama' in Taiwan." *China Information* 22, no. 2: 277–304.

Yang, Fang-chih Irene. 2016. "*Empresses in the Palace* and the Project of 'Neoliberalization through China' in Taiwan." In *Lifestyle Media in Asia: Consumption, Aspiration and Identity*, ed. Fran Martin and Tania Lewis. London: Routledge.

Yang, Jie. 2014. "The Happiness of the Marginalized: Affect, Counseling, and Self-Reflexivity in China." In *The Political Economy of Affect and Emotion in East Asia*, ed. Jie Yang, 45–61. London: Routledge.

Yang, Mayfair Mei-hui. 2004. "Goddess across the Taiwan Strait: Matrifocal Ritual Space, Nation-State, and Satellite Television Footprints." *Public Culture* 16, no. 2: 209–38.

Yi, Chin-chun, and Ju-ping Lin. 2009. "Types of Relations between Adult Children and Elderly Parents in Taiwan: Mechanisms Accounting for Various Relational Types." *Journal of Comparative Family Studies* 40, no. 2: 305–24.

Yu, Wei-Hsin, and Kuo-Hsien Su. 2009. "On One's Own: Self-Employment Activity in Taiwan." In *The Reemergence of Self-Employment: A Comparative Study of Self-Employment Dynamics and Social Inequality*, ed. Richard Arum and Walter Müller, 388–425. Princeton, NJ: Princeton University Press.

Zha, Jianying. 1995. *China Pop: How Soap Operas, Tabloids and Bestsellers Are Transforming a Culture*. New York: New Press.

Zhang, Jun, and Peidong Sun. 2014. "When Are You Going to Get Married? Parental Matchmaking and Middle-Class Women in Contemporary Urban China." In *Wives, Husbands, and Lovers: Marriage and Sexuality in Hong Kong, Taiwan, and Urban China*, ed. Deborah S. Davis and Sara L. Friedman, 118–44. Stanford, CA: Stanford University Press.

Zhang, Li, and Aihwa Ong. 2008. "Introduction: Privatizing China: Powers of the Self, Socialism from Afar." In *Privatizing China: Powers of the Self, Socialism from Afar*, ed. Li Zhang and Aihwa Ong, 1–19. Ithaca, NY: Cornell University Press.

Zhang, Xiaoling, and Zhenzhi Guo. 2012. "Hegemony and Counter-Hegemony: The Politics of Dialects in TV Programs in China." *Chinese Journal of Communication* 5, no. 3: 300–315.

Zhao, Wuzhou 赵五洲. 2012. "解读《购时尚》的策划思维" [Deconstructing *Pretty Trendy*'s planning and thinking]. 华章 [*Huazhang*] 36: 303.

Zhao, Yuezhi. 1998. *Media, Market, and Democracy in China: Between the Party Line and the Bottom Line*. Urbana: University of Illinois Press.

Zhao, Yuezhi. 2008a. *Communication in China: Political Economy, Power, and Conflict*. Lanham, MD: Rowman and Littlefield.

Zhao, Yuezhi. 2008b. "Neo-liberal Strategies, Socialist Legacies: Communication and State Transformation in China." In *Global Communications: Towards a Transcultural Political Economy*, ed. Paula Chakravarty and Yuezhi Zhao, 23–50. Lanham, MD: Rowman and Littlefield.

Zhao, Yuezhi, and Zhenzhi Guo. 2005. "Television in China: History, Political Economy, and Ideology." In *A Companion to Television*, ed. Janet Wasko, 521–39. Malden, MA: Blackwell.

Zhou, Yuanzhi. 2012. "Capitalizing China's Media Industry: The Installation of Capitalist Production in the Chinese TV and Film Sectors." PhD diss., University of Illinois at Urbana-Champaign.

Zhu, Ying. 2012. *Two Billion Eyes: The Story of China Central Television*. New York: New Press.

Zhu, Ying, and Chris Berry, eds. 2009. *TV China*. Bloomington: Indiana University Press.

Zhu, Ying, Michael Keane, and Ruoyun Bai. 2008. *TV Drama in China*. Hong Kong: Hong Kong University Press.

INDEX

Aastha TV, 168–69, 175–76
advice on life/lifestyle. *See* lifestyle television
aging viewers. *See* senior viewers
Alva, Niret, 43, 82, 83
Amin, Ash, 22, 84, 104–5, 269
Anand, Ambika, 134, 137
Andy (VJ Andy), 149, 201–3, 204, 209
Anhui Province: comparison with Shanghai, 53–55; perceptions of, 54–55, 68
Appadurai, Arjun, 100, 102, 107
Arora, Bharat, 134
Art Beat, 131
Asian tiger economies, 3, 9, 13. *See also* Singapore; Taiwan
astrologers, 162–65
Astronomics, 164
Astro Uncle, 164–65, 194
At Your Service, 32
audience studies, 20, 268

Bachchan, Amitabh, 90
Baike Quan Shuo (Encyclopedia), 31
Balaji, Akul, 94
Balinghou Juchang (The Post-80 Theater), 214–16, 220–21
Band Baajaa Bride, 134–38
Bao Xiaoqun, 33, 56–58, 63, 64
baraeti bangumi. *See* Japanese variety shows
BBC, 30
BBTV (Bengbu Television), 34, 55–56, 103; audience, 69, 72; content and programming, 69–75, 80; health shows, 144–47; intermediary between citizen and local government, 77–81; lifestyle programs, 71, 75–79, 80; local nature, 68–75; pedagogical orientation, 70, 72–77, 80, 144. *See also* specific programs: *Let Me Help You*; *Zero Distance to Health*
Beauty Rescue Team, 148, 152
Beck, Ulrich, 162–63, 193, 194–95, 199, 256
Beijing, comparison with Shanghai, 56–57
Beijing TV, 32; *Yangsheng House*, 34, 73, 74
Bengbu, 68; television channels available, 68–69. *See also* BBTV (Bengbu Television)
Bergman, Manfred Max, 107–8, 125
Between Generations, 187–93
Bharatiya Janata Party (Indian People's Party), 159–60
Bhihane Bhihane, 138–39
Bhojpuri language programs, 138–39
Bigg Boss (*Big Brother*), 47, 90, 94
The Biggest Loser, 5, 20; in China (*Chaoji Jianfei Wang*), 30
Boddhi Among the People, 186
Bollywood culture and aesthetics: transnational reach of, 7
Bonner, Frances, 31
Bourdain, Anthony, 48, 109
Bourdieu, Pierre, 114, 127, 136
Buddhism: Da Ai TV, 184, 185–95, 264; in Taiwan, 176–77, 183–85

cable television, 43; India, 45, 47; Taiwan, 36–38, 39, 42–43
Care World, 142
CCTV (China Central TV), 28, 223; genres, 29–30, 35; life advice programs, 32, 35, 223–24; pedagogical style, 148, 223–24, 236–37; "throat and tongue" of Chinese party-state, 35, 261. See also *Pretty Trendy*
celebrity chefs, 109, 127. See also experts
Chadha, Kalyani, 93
Chandra, Vikram, 132, 133
Channel V, 48, 201, 203, 210
Channel Young, 32–33, 34, 55–56, 79–81, 214; audience, 58–59, 125, 237; business strategy, 58–59, 80; *daren* and authority figures, 148–56; high-rating shows, 148; *New Queen*, 30, 149–51; pedagogical aim and notion of "good taste," 58–59, 63–68; popular programs and desire for "good value," 59–63, 64; style and tone contrasted with CCTV, 237
Chaoji Jianfei Wang (The biggest loser), 30
Chawla, Puneet, 165–66
Cheng Yen, 183, 185, 186, 187, 195, 264
Chiang Ching-kuo, 14
Chiang family, 35
Chiang Kai-shek, 13
China: authoritarianism, 154–55, 156, 207–8, 260–61; cultural and social changes, 11–12, 128, 224–25, 261; economic reforms and growth, 10–12, 263; government from afar, 78, 79; inequality, 10–11, 53–54, 128–29; influence of Taiwanese television culture, 9; internal migration to cities, 53–55; metropolitan versus rural places, 53–55; neoliberalism, 11, 79, 128, 259–61; post-socialism and feminine identity, 224–27; socialist visions of modernity, 10, 11. See also lifestyle television: in China; television industry: in China
China Central TV. See CCTV (China Central TV)
"China Model" approach to politics and economics, 11
Chinese Communist Party, 10
Chinese Nationalist Party, 13, 35
Chinese television. See lifestyle television: in China; television industry: in China

Chinese Television System, Taiwan. See CTS (Chinese Television System, Taiwan)
Christianity in Taiwan, 176–77
Colours channel, 46, 49
consumer citizenship, 63, 67–68, 132, 142–43, 194–95, 256–60, 268
cookery shows, 10, 48, 94, 96, 98–103, 109–10, 131, 140–41
cosmetic surgery, 222–23, 226–27
cosmopolitanism: methodological, 256–57; negotiated, 270–71
CTS (Chinese Television System, Taiwan), 35, 36; Culture and Education, 40
CTV (Taiwan), 35, 273n5
cultural difference and diversity accessed through food/travel television, 98–103
cultural differences between city and rural viewers: China, 70–71, 73–74, 77; India, 95–96
cultural globalization: impact and socio-economic divisions, 17, 129; televisual mediascapes, 107; tensions, 125
cultural intermediaries, 63–64, 70–71, 72, 80, 127, 128, 135–36, 154–55, 221, 236. See also experts
cultural patterns, emergent, 253
Custom Made for Vir Sanghvi, 132, 133

Da Ai TV, 184, 185–95, 264
Daoism, Taiwan, 176–77
Dare2Date, 201–3, 204, 208, 220
daren, 148–56
Dasheng shuo chulai (Say it out loud), 217–19, 221
Date My Folks, 209–10, 211, 212, 220
dating shows, 23–24, 28; Chinese, 205–9, 220; Indian, 199–204, 209–12, 220. See also *If You Are the One*; love, marriage, and family
Democratic Progressive Party (Taiwan), 35
Derné, Steve, 17, 259
Discovery Communications Inc, 107, 108–9; Asia-specific content, 116–19; Travel and Living Channel, 109. See also *Fun Taiwan*; TLC India; TLC Taiwan
Doane, Mary Ann, 222
Dongneng Yixiang, 117, 119, 120
Donner, Henrikke, 262

Doordarshan, 43, 44, 45, 83, 85–88, 160, 274n15
Dussel, Enrique, 6

East Asian Middle Class Project, 11
economic equality/inequality. *See* equality/inequality
economic performance (GDP): China, 10; India, 16; Taiwan, 13, 14
elderly viewers. *See* senior viewers
Emotional Atyachaar, 201
Endemol, 30
equality/inequality, 267–68; China, 10–11, 53–54, 128–29, 265; India, 16–18, 90–92, 129, 134, 265; Taiwan, 14–15
Euro-American content and formats: in China, 222–23, 237, 252; escapist, 109–10; in Taiwan, 42, 106–9, 247–48, 252; and viewer internationalist identity, 111–13, 124–25. *See also* TLC India; TLC Taiwan
experts, 126–29, 155–56, 194; Chinese television, 144–56, 227, 236; Indian television, 128, 129–43, 156, 175
Extreme Makeover, 107, 210, 222

family. *See* love, marriage, and family
Farquhar, Judith, 154
Fashionable Granny, 64–65
fashion shows, 64–68
Fei Cheng Wu Rao. *See If You Are the One*
feminine identity, 24, 252–53; China, 222–27, 263–64; India, 92, 262; Taiwan, 238–39, 243, 244, 249–52, 262–63; young-mature woman (*qingshounü*), 24, 238, 243, 248–50, 262–63. *See also* women
feng shui, 178, 277n21
Fengshui! You guanxi (Feng shui matters), 178–83, 186, 194
Feng Taiwan. *See Fun Taiwan*
Fernandes, Leela, 18, 88, 266
The Flavor of India, 100
food television. *See* cookery shows
fortune-tellers, 162–63. *See also* astrologers; spiritual lifestyle programming
FremantleMedia, 30, 92
Freudian theory, 225–26
FTV (Fashion TV, India), 46

FTV (Taiwan), 35, 36, 39
Fun Taiwan (Feng Taiwan), 116–24, 270; compared with other local travelogues, 119–21; hybridity and audience reaction, 121–24; other formats, 117, 121; style, 118–20, 121
Fürsich, Elfriede, 108
futurologists. *See* astrologers; fortune-tellers

Gadget Guru, 131–32
Gandhi, Amrita, 133
Gandhi, Indira, 16, 43, 86, 160
Gandhi, Rajiv, 16
Gang-Tai (Hong Kong-and-Taiwan) media, 9
Gangwani, Rita, 175
Gao Bo, 227
gender status, 149, 196, 202, 204. *See also* feminine identity; women
geomancy: *I Ching*, 277n21; vaastu, 165–66. *See also* feng shui
Giddens, Anthony, 5
"good taste," influence and pedagogical aims, 63–68
"good value," perceptions of, 58–63
Gooptu, Nandini, 17, 174–75
Gou Shishang. *See Pretty Trendy*
government, local: television as intermediary between citizen and local government, 77–81
government regulation. *See* state involvement in/control of television
Grande, Edgar, 256
grassroots, staying close to, 59, 70–71, 77, 79–80
Gupta, Akhil, 16
gurus, lifestyle. *See* experts

Hakka people, 183, 278n25
Han Song, 69
Hao Xiaoxi (Good TV) Christian channel, 277n20
Harindranath, Ramaswami, 96
health advice, 72–75, 141–47
"Health Hotline," 144, 145
Highway on My Plate, 94, 100, 101, 270
Hindi programs, 86–91, 92, 93, 94
Hinduism, 159–60, 278n24; Vedic astrologers, 164–65, 276n5

Hindu nationalism, 86–87, 276n3
Hindutva, 276n3
Hinglish programming, 49, 93, 131
homosexuality, 150, 202; criminalization of, 278n1
Hong Kong commercial media, 9
host-personalities. *See* experts
Hsiao, Hsin-huang Michael, 11
Hsieh, Janet, 117, 118, 120–24
Hsieh Yuanjin, 178, 179
Hua, Wen, 226–27, 229
Hua Yang, 66–67, 68
human quality (*suzhi*). *See suzhi* (human quality)
Hum Log (We people), 86
Hunan TV, 28, 31, 69
Hu Yingzhen, 178

I Ching (Book of Changes), 277n21
Idol (Indian version), 43, 83, 91
If You Are the One, 6, 28, 69, 104, 205–9, 220; commodification of "search for love," 255; compared to Chinese life advice formats, 216–17; format and style, 205–7; popularity and revenue, 205; provincial copy-cat versions, 205; state intervention, 207, 220, 266
Illouz, Eva, 196, 197, 198
India: colonial period, 15; cultural and socioeconomic diversity, 83–84, 92–93, 129, 259–60; health sector, 142; inequality, 16–18, 90–92, 129, 134; neoliberalism, 16–17, 258–59; population, 49; post-independence economic development, 16–18, 259. *See also* lifestyle television: in India; television industry: in India
Indian cookbooks, 100, 102
Indian Idol, 43, 83, 91
Indian television. *See* lifestyle television: in India; television industry: in India
individualization of social relations, 193, 198–99, 212, 220–21, 261–64; Chinese dating shows, 205–9; Chinese relationship advice shows, 212–21; Indian dating entertainment shows, 199–204; Indian dating shows involving parents, 209–12
industry studies, 20
inequality. *See* equality/inequality
Internet, 26; connections in India, 49; online content alternative to broadcast television, 49, 69, 129, 227, 243; online dating, 203

Jamie at Home, 107, 109
Japanese variety shows, 41, 243
Jaya TV, 96–97
Jiangsu TV, 28, 69, 205
Jiankang Ling Juli (Zero distance to health), 69, 70, 72–75, 144–47
jie di qi (staying close to the grassroots), 59, 70–71, 77, 79–80
Jin Ri Yinxiang (Today's impression), 59, 60–61
Joye, Dominique, 107–8, 125
Junior MasterChef (India), 48
Just for Women, 174

Kannada programs, 94, 95–96
Kapoor, Sanjeev, 48, 98
Karnataka, India, 93–95
Kaufmann, Vincent, 107–8, 125
Kaun Banega Crorepati, 88–91, 94
Kavoori, Anandam, 93
Kelsky, Karen, 107, 111
Khana Khazana, 98
Kim, Youna, 107
Knauft, Bruce M., 8
Koachar, Sundeep, 164
Kumar, Shanti, 104
Kumar, Shiv, 138
Kuomintang (KMT; Chinese Nationalist Party), 13, 35

Lakhsman, Rajiv, 92, 138
language: British accents on Indian TV, 131, 133; local dialects on television, 26, 71–72, 93–95; official state languages of India, 93; and TV regionalism in India, 93–98, 103–5
Lan Xinmei (Pauline Lan), 237, 242, 243, 249–52, 253
Lee, Ching Kwan, 11
Let Me Help You, 75–79
life advice television. *See* lifestyle television
Life Channel (BBTV): lifestyle programs, 75–79, 80; locality-specific programming, 71–72
Life Channel (SHTV). *See* Channel Young

308 / INDEX

Life's a Beach, 46
lifestyle consumers, and the self-governing citizen, 5
lifestyle experts. *See* experts
lifestyle television, 254–57, 267–71; definition, 18; localization of content, 26; provincializing neoliberalism, 257–60; research methods, 18–21; transnationality, 7, 20, 94–97, 243–44; use by states, 260–61. *See also* experts
—in China, 30–34, 154, 237; characteristics, 34–35, 261; *daren* and experts, 144–56, 227, 236; health advice, 143–47; "lifestyle television" genre not widely recognized, 31, 38; localization of content, 26, 30–31, 68–75, 80–81; popular programs and desire for "good value," 59–63; programming, 32; regional programming style versus SMG style, 147–54; target audiences, 31, 32–34, 35; typical programs, 31–34. *See also* BBTV (Bengbu Television); Channel Young; dating shows; love, marriage, and family; television industry: in China; women's advice shows; *and names of specific shows*: *If You Are the One*; *Pretty Trendy*
—in India, 88; advisors, aspirational, 130–38, 156; advisors, everyday, 138–43, 156; advisors, spiritual/mystical, 162–76; and aspirational consumer culture, 88, 92, 130–34, 270; channels, 48, 130, 162; disconnect between lifestyles and "imagined worlds" of television, 90–92, 270; experts, 128, 129–43, 175; key characteristics, 49–50; localization, 26, 48–49; reality shows, 47–48, 49, 90–91; regionalization, 50, 94–98, 103–5, 138–39, 269; target audiences, 48–50; well-known genre, 47. *See also* dating shows; NDTV Good Times; spiritual lifestyle programming in India; television industry in India
—in Taiwan: characteristics, 42–43, 270; concept of, 38–40, 42; content embedded in variety shows, 40–43; gender representation, 239; "glocalization," 116–17, 122–24; influence in China, 9, 20; scattered content, 38–39, 42. *See also* spiritual lifestyle programming in Taiwan; television industry in Taiwan; women's advice shows;

and specific shows and channels: *Fun Taiwan*; TLC Taiwan; *Queen*
—types of shows. *See* dating shows; reality shows; spiritual lifestyle programming; women's advice shows
Life without Wife, 48
Li Jingbai, 118
Li Peizhen, 178
Live Vaastu, 165–66, 194
Li Zhang, 260
local dialects on television, 26, 71–72, 93–95
local government: television as intermediary between citizen and local government, 77–81
localization of content, 26; China, 26, 30–31, 68–75, 80–81; India, 26, 48–49; Taiwan, 116–17, 122–24. *See also* regionalization of television
love, marriage, and family, 197–99, 208–9, 219–21; arranged marriages, 198, 262; Chinese dating-game shows, 205–9; Chinese life advice shows, 212–21; Indian dating entertainment shows, 199–204, 262; Indian dating shows involving parents, 209–12, 220; Indian wedding reality shows, 135–38; online dating/matrimonial markets, 203, 204, 212; in Taiwan, 238–39. *See also* dating shows; feminine identity
Love Kiya to Darna Kiya (Why fear when you love), 210–12, 220
Love Lockup, 201
LoveNet, 203–4, 220
Lu, Hwei-Syin, 183
Lüxing Yingyuan Tuan (Travel relief team), 120

Ma, Eric, 8, 9
Madsen, Richard, 184
magic. *See* supernatural belief systems
Mahabharata, 161
Mahi, Manju, 131
Mahua TV, 138–39, 144–45
Makni, Rajiv, 132, 133
Man vs. Wild, 100, 141
marriage. *See* love, marriage, and family
Martin, Fran, 225
MasterChef India, 3, 20, 48, 94, 141
Mazzarella, William, 85, 88

media consumption: significant markets, 33–34
Meng Fei, 205
Menon, Sunita, 276n6
Menz, 173–74
methodological cosmopolitanism, 256–57
metrosexuality, 109, 150–51, 152
middle class in China, 11–12, 156, 197, 260, 264–67; lifestyle marketed in aspirational terms, 58–59, 67–68; in Shanghai, 53, 55, 57, 58; stabilizing/destabilizing influence, 12, 259, 266–67
middle class in India, 17–18, 86–87, 134, 156, 197, 259–60, 264–67; consumer-based aspirationalism, 88, 92, 130–34, 167, 265–66; expenditure on spiritual pursuits, 161; focus of reality television, 90, 92; and rise of lifestyle experts, 128; risk management, 198–99
middle class in Taiwan, 14–15
Minnan people, 183, 278n25
Minute to Win, 95
mobile devices, 33–34
mobile phone services, 26, 49
modernities, 4, 6–7; compressed modernity, 13, 116, 271; Euro-American definitions of modernity, 6; plural nature of, 6–8, 271; satellite modernity, 9; telemodernities concept, 7–8
moral education, 128, 185–86, 207–8, 216, 259–60
Mother-in-Law Eyes Her Son-in-Law, 212–14, 220–21
motility: appropriation of idea, 108; defined, 107–8; and TLC Taiwan programming, 22–23, 107–8, 111–13, 124–25
MTV, 48, 131
MTV Roadies, 92, 95, 138
Mukherjee, Sabyasachi, 134, 136, 137
Mukhopadhyay, Bhaskar, 161
multiple modernities. *See* modernities
Mummy No. 1, 95–96
mythological shows. *See* spiritual lifestyle programming

Naidu, Balaraj, 95
National Geographic, 39
NDTV Good Times, 46, 48, 49, 94; aspirational lifestyle genres and shows, 130–38; content, 130–31; cosmopolitanism, 131; everyday advice shows, 138–43; reality formats, 134–38
negotiated cosmopolitanism, 270–71
Nehru, Jawaharlal, 15
neoliberalism: associated ideologies, 14, 257–60; China, 11, 79, 128, 259–61; India, 16–17, 258–59; and self-responsibility, 5, 258; Taiwan, 13–14
Neveling, Patrick, 17
New Delhi Television. *See* NDTV Good Times
New Queen, 30, 149–51
No Reservations, 48, 109
Nüren Wo Zui Da. *See* Queen

Ohm, Britta, 160
Ong, Aihwa, 216, 260
online content, 33–34, 49, 69, 129, 227, 243
online dating/matrimonial markets, 203, 204, 212

Peng Jie Liao Shi (Sister Peng's chitchat), 71
People's Republic of China. *See* China
Perfect Couple, 201
Perfect Shrimati, 139, 140
personal relationships. *See* love, marriage, and family
Pertierra, Ana Cristina, 3–4
place, scale of. *See* scale of place (China)
Popular Food, 59–60
The Post-80 Theater, 214–16, 220–21
posttraditional society, 5, 6, 257
Pragya TV, 162, 170, 172–76, 195
Pretty Trendy, 32; audience, 237, 240; fashion and selfhood, 223, 229–33; format and content, 227–29; models of femininity, 252–53; pedagogical style, 223–24, 236–37, 252–53, 261; policing normative feminine life stages, 223–24, 233–36
problem-solving power of the media, 77–81. *See also Let Me Help You*
Public Television Service (Taiwan), 36

qingshounü (young-mature woman) concept, 24, 238, 243, 248–50, 262–63
Qing Xuedong, 69, 70
Qing Yin, 230

Queen: audience, 237, 243, 244; copies of, 243, 253; format and content, 224, 237, 240–46; models of femininity, 248–53; pedagogical style, 224, 247, 252

Queer Eye for the Straight Guy, 20, 107, 202, 203; copies of, 148, 152, 237; and metrosexuality, 109, 150–51; popularity of and interpretations of in Taiwan, 109. See also *Beauty Rescue Team*

Radio and Television Law (Taiwan), 40
Ramayana, 160, 161–62
Ramdev, Baba, 168–70, 171, 172, 176, 195
reality shows: China, makeover format in city versus country, 70; India, 47–48, 49, 88, 90–91, 94–97, 134–38; regionalization, 94–97. See also dating shows; women's advice shows
regionalization of television: China, 50, 147–54; India, 50, 94–98, 103–5, 138–39, 269. See also localization of content
regulation of television. See state involvement in/control of television
religion, 162–63, 193, 195; India, 157–59; Taiwan, 176–77. See also spiritual lifestyle programming
Renjian Puti (Boddhi among the people), 186
Renqi Meishi (Popular food), 59–60
Republic of China. See Taiwan
risk and vulnerability, 198–99
Road Rules (Indian version). See *MTV Roadies*
Rofel, Lisa, 225, 226
Rose, Nikolas, 5
Roy, Abhijit, 85, 86
Royal Reservations, 133

San Dai zhi Jian (Between generations), 187–93
"sandal scandal," China, 52–53, 55
Sanghvi, Vir, 132, 133
San Lih Taiwan, 36, 273n5
Sanskar, 168
Satellite Instructional Television Experiment (India), 43
Say It Out Loud, 217–19, 221
scale of place (China), 22, 53, 54, 55, 70, 71–72, 80–81, 103–4, 268–70

secularism, in India, 159–60
self-governing citizen, cultural dominance of, 5, 257–58
self-help and lifestyle experts. See experts
selfhood: fashion and, 223, 229–33; privatization of, 225–26. See also feminine identity
self-responsibility, 78–79, 155–56, 257–58, 259, 260; and health shows, 74–75; and life advice TV shows, 207–8, 216–17
Sen, Nilendu, 82, 103
senior viewers (target audience), 31, 32, 35, 73–74
Shanghai: citizen consumption practice, 61–63, 67–68; comparison with Anhui, 53–55; comparison with Beijing, 56–57; history and "classy past," 64–66; leader in fashion and taste, 52, 53, 56–57, 64–67; socioeconomic stratification, 57–58, 68
Shanghai Media Group, 32, 33, 143; regional programming style versus SMG style, 147–54. See also Channel Young
Shanghai Youth Daily, 52–53
Sharma, Alok, 95–96, 99
Sharma, Aradhana, 16
shenghuo television, 31–34, 38. See also lifestyle television: in China
Shijie Di Yi Deng (World's number one), 119
Shimao Waipo (Fashionable granny), 64–65
Shi Shang Wan Jia (Super taste), 119, 120, 121
Shumway, David, 197–98
Sidhu, Navjot, 173–74
Singapore, 243; popularity of *Queen*, 243–44, 250–51; sociodemographic developments, 238–39; tiger economy, 13; women's variety-talk shows genre, 223, 224, 237, 243
Singh, Arati, 131, 134
Sinha, Pawan, 164
Sister Peng's Chitchat, 71
social conflict: class-related, 207–8, 266; reduction and mediation of, 216–21
social equality/inequality. See equality/inequality
social identities: changes in China, 11–12
social media, 49, 76, 227. See also Weibo; YouTube
social stability and the middle class, 259, 266–67

socioeconomic stratification. *See* equality/inequality
Sony Entertainment Television, 45, 49
South Indian Sun network, 45
spatial ontologies, 84, 85, 103–5
spatial ontology, alternative framing of, 104–5
spiritual lifestyle programming:
— in India, 23, 160, 193–95, 264; advice on fate and fortune, 162–68, 194; channels, 162, 168, 170; money-making aspects, 169–70, 276n4; popularity, 162; religious programming, 158–62, 168–76
— in Taiwan, 158; Buddhist Da Ai TV, 184, 185–95, 264; channels and programs, 177–78; feng shui advice shows, 178–83, 194
spiritual television, 23, 87
Splitsvilla, 200
Star India, 46
Star Plus, 48, 49
Star TV, 25, 45
State Administration of Radio, Film and Television (China), 29, 207, 232–34
state involvement in/control of television: China, 27, 28, 29, 35, 78, 104, 207–8, 259–61; India, 43, 45–46, 85, 86; Taiwan, 35, 37, 40, 42
Sun TV network, 45, 46, 96–97
Sun Xiaofan, 233
Sun Yingying, 245–46
Sun Yunyun, 245–46
"super consumers," 132, 156
supernatural belief systems, 23, 177, 178–83, 193. *See also* spiritual lifestyle programming
Super Taste, 119, 120, 121
suzhi (human quality), 12, 154, 208, 217, 259
Swaymwar, 200

Taiwan, 9; cultural and social changes, 14–15; economic restructuring and growth, 13–14; Hakka people, 183, 278n25; linguistic pluralism, 14; Minnan people, 183, 278n25; models of femininity, 238–39; neoliberalism, 13, 14; statist regime, 13
Taiwanese television. *See* lifestyle television: in Taiwan; television industry: in Taiwan
talk-show format, 31, 178, 186
Tamil channels and programs, 96–98

TAM Media Research, 44, 162
Tay, Jinna, 26
technologies for delivering and accessing television, 26
telemodernities concept, 7–8
television industries development in Asia, 25–26, 50–51
television industry:
— in China: audience and market penetration, 27, 28, 33–34, 86, 129; content, 27, 28, 29–34; contrasted with India's, 104–5; experts' role in "exemplary society," 154–55; private-sector investment, 29, 30; regionalization, 50, 147–54; scale of place, 22, 53, 54, 55, 70, 71–72, 80–81, 103–4, 268–70; spatial politics, 268–70; state involvement/control, 27, 28, 29, 35, 78, 104, 207–8, 259–61; structure and channels, 27–29, 30, 33, 55, 128; television as intermediary between citizen and local government, 77–81. *See also* BBTV (Bengbu Television); CCTV (China Central TV); lifestyle television: in China
— in India: audience and market penetration, 43–45, 47, 48–49, 92, 129; Bhojpuri language programs, 138–39; commercialization, 43–45, 160; content, 43, 46–47; contrasted with China's, 104–5; food television, 98–103; Hindi programs, 86–91, 92, 93, 94; Hinglish programs, 49, 93, 131; history, 43, 85–88, 160; Kannada programs, 94, 95–96; ratings system, 44, 92; regionalization of language and programming, 50, 93–98, 103–5, 138–39, 269; spatial politics, 269–70; state involvement/control, 43, 45–46, 85, 86; structure and channels, 43–46, 82–83, 86–87, 93; Tamil channels and programs, 96–98. *See also* Doordarshan; lifestyle television: in India
— in Taiwan, 35, 40, 253; audience and market penetration, 36, 39, 42–43; commercialization, 35–36, 37, 42; content, 36–38, 39, 40; "education and entertainment" demarcation, 37, 40, 42; homogenous programming, 39; market share, 36, 39, 273n5; politicization, 37; state involvement/control, 35, 37, 40, 42; structure and channels, 35–37; transnational reach in Sinophone Asia, 9, 20, 24, 41, 42, 243–44,

312 / INDEX

250–51; variety show ubiquity, 40–42. See also lifestyle television: in Taiwan

Tian Wei, 75

tiger economy nations, 3, 9, 13. See also Singapore; Taiwan

Tiwari, Noopur, 131, 133

TLC India, 48

TLC Taiwan, 48; audience demographic, 109, 114–15; content, 39, 106–7, 109, 270; "glocalization," 116–17, 122–24; impacts, 22–23, 107–8; issues of class, 113–16; market share, 39; and motility, 22–23, 107–8, 111–13, 124–25; popular programs, 109–10; presentation of fantasy Euro-American life, 109–11, 113–14; viewer descriptions of, 109–10; viewer internationalist identity, 22–23, 111–13, 122–25; viewer reidentification with local lifeways, 116, 125. See also *Fun Taiwan*

Today's Impression, 59, 60–61

transnationality, 26; of lifestyle television, 7, 20, 94–97, 106–7, 122–24, 131, 243–44; reach of Taiwan television programs, 41, 42, 243–44, 250–51; reach Taiwan television programs, 24

Travel and Living Channel. *See* TLC India; TLC Taiwan

Travel Relief Team, 120

travel shows: India, 48, 100–103, 131; Taiwan, 117–21; television and imaginative travel, 107–8. *See also Fun Taiwan*; TLC India; TLC Taiwan

Travel XP, 48

TTV (Taiwan), 35, 273n5

Tu Lei, 217–19

Turner, Graeme, 3–4, 26

Tzu Chi Buddhist organization, Taiwan, 177, 183–85, 195, 264; Da Ai TV, 184, 185–95, 264

vaastu, 165–66

variety shows: copying and adaptation, 41, 42; Japanese, 41; life advice content, 41–42; popularity in Asia, 40–41; in Taiwan, 40–42; typical elements, 42

Vedic astrologers, 164–65

Viacom, 46

video online. *See* online content

VJ Andy, 149, 201–3, 204, 209

Wang Shuzhen, 60–61

Wang Weimin, 52–53, 58

Waris, Zulfia, 203

Warrier, Maya, 193

Washington Consensus approach to politics and economics, 11

Weber, Brenda, 222, 223

Weber, Max, 157, 193

wedding-format reality shows, 135–38. See also dating shows

The Week the Women Went, 48

Weibo, 33, 227

Wei Nin Fuwu (At your service), 32

Wei Xin channel (WXTV), 277n21

Weller, Robert P., 177

We People (*Hum Log*), 86

White, James D., 26

Who Wants to Be a Millionaire, Hindi version, 88–91

Why Fear When You Love, 210–12, 220

Wife Bina Life (Life without wife), 48

women: business ventures and familial roles (Taiwan), 190–93; eroticization and commodification of feminine beauty, 226–27; feminine identity (China), 24, 222–27, 263–64; feminine identity (India), 92, 262; feminine identity (Taiwan), 24, 238–39, 243, 244, 248–52, 262–63; life-stage-appropriate style and behavior (China), 233–36; non-familial middle-aged femininity, 249–52; *qingshounü* (young-mature woman) concept, 24, 238, 243, 248–50, 262–63; role and gendered risks (China), 224–25, 263–64; selfhood (China), 223, 229–33, 237; in Tzu Chi Buddhist organization, 183

women's advice shows, 24, 222–24; Chinese makeover show case study (*Pretty Trendy*), 223–24, 227–37; Taiwan fashion and beauty talk-show case study (*Queen*), 224, 239–52. *See also* feminine identity

WXTV (Wei Xin Christian channel), 277n21

X Dang'an (X files) (fashion show), 66–67, 125

Xiao Yu, 76, 144, 145

Xiao Zhen, 178

Xin'an Evening Post, 52–53

Xin Nüren Wo Zui Da (New Queen), 30, 149–51
Xin Shang Hunli, 152–54
Xu Fei, 52–53

Yan, Yunxiang, 62, 67, 263
Yan Fu, 120
Yang, Fang-chih Irene, 114–15
Yangsheng Tang (Yangsheng house), 34, 73, 74
Yan Jun, 120
yoga, 170, 171, 172, 176, 195
young-mature woman concept (*qingshounü*), 24, 238, 243, 248–50, 262–63
young professional audiences, 35, 38, 39, 50; female, 32, 34; urban, 31, 32, 33, 35; viewers of TLC Taiwan, 107–16, 120–25; youth channels and market in India, 48, 49. *See also* Channel Young

You Shi Wo Bang Nin (Let me help you), 75–79
YouTube, 26, 49, 171

Zaika India Ka (The flavor of India), 100
Zee Kannada, 95–96
Zee TV, 45, 49, 131
Zero Distance to Health, 69, 70, 72–75, 144–47
Zhang, Qicheng, 154
Zhang Jing, 227
Zhangmuniang Kan Nüxu (Mother-in-law eyes her son-in-law), 212–14, 220–21
Zhejiang TV, 28
Zhongguo Hao Shengyin (The voice of China), 28
Zhou, Kevin, 150–51
zongyi jiemu. See variety shows

www.ingramcontent.com/pod-product-compliance
Lightning Source LLC
Chambersburg PA
CBHW070751230426
43665CB00017B/2329